Republican Portugal

A Political History

1910–1926

Published 1978
The University of Wisconsin Press
Box 1379, Madison, Wisconsin 53701

The University of Wisconsin Press, Ltd.
70 Great Russell Street, London

First printing
Printed in the United States of America

For LC CIP information see the colophon
ISBN 0-299-07450-1

For Katie

Contents

Maps

Illustrations

Tables

Preface

The purpose of this study is to provide a concise yet full treatment of Portugal's first attempt at democracy, the First Republic, 1910–26. When I began to teach the history of modern Portugal and to attempt to relate it to the history of Western Europe and to the past of Portuguese-speaking Africa, I found that no adequate, introductory treatment of the First Republic existed in any language. In this study I have attempted to combine narrative with interpretation and I have drawn upon a variety of unpublished and published materials in Portugal, Britain, and the United States.

It has not been my intention to write an exhaustive history of this brief but highly significant era. Such a work will be feasible, perhaps, only after the Portuguese official records in various ministries are made available to researchers. While I have taken care to present a narrative survey of this sixteen-year period, I have not sought to cover in detail all historical fields. Rather, I have emphasized a strangely neglected area in modern Portuguese history: political history, which comprises both political parties and the role of the military in politics. Recent foreign and Portuguese scholarship on the First Republic has emphasized the social and economic at the expense of the political. I am attempting here to redress the imbalance.

One further point about the design of this study should be made: I have placed the First Republic firmly within the context of Portuguese history since 1807. In so doing I have discussed the course of modern Portuguese history since the coming of liberalism and constitutional monarchy in the early nineteenth century, and I have provided a brief introduction to the sequel of the First Republic, the Dictatorship, 1926–74.

On 25 April 1974 the importance of the role of the military in Portuguese politics again emerged: in a swiftly executed military coup an organization of young Portuguese officers overthrew a dictatorship that had lasted forty-eight years. Portugal has now given birth to a "Second Republic," a new, democratic, highly politicized, controversial, and sometimes tense, political experiment, in some ways comparable to the First Republic. The pre-1926 republic warrants serious study, I believe, by all those who are concerned with building a new Portuguese democracy.

Since beginning this book in 1969, I have acquired many friendly debts on two continents. I am grateful to the University of New Hampshire for a sabbatical leave for research and for Central University Research Fund grants in 1974 and 1976 in order to prepare the manuscript. To my colleagues in the Department of History and to Professor Robert C. Gilmore, in particular, who bore the inconvenience of a chairman who took an early sabbatical, I am grateful. I must thank Jan Snow and Catherine Bergstrom for excellent typing. I am indebted to Professor Stanley Payne, University of Wisconsin, Madison, and Professor Francis A. Dutra, University of California, Santa Barbara, for their critical readings of the manuscript and to the editors at the University of Wisconsin Press for the excellence of their editing work.

Many Portuguese friends and acquaintances were helpful. I would like to thank those whom I interviewed (see Bibliography), as well as Dr. Joel Serrão, Dr. Raúl Rego, Sr. David Ferreira, Dr. A. H. de Oliveira Marques, and Commander A. Teixeira da Mota.

I am grateful to Professor Richard Robinson, University of Birmingham, for sharing sources on Portuguese integralism.

I am indebted also to the Calouste Gulbenkian Foundation, Lisbon, which helped support my research while I lived in Lisbon, 1972–73. Sra. Dra. Maria Clara Farinha, of International Service, has my gratitude for her very positive attitude. I am grateful to the United States government which in June 1969 awarded me a Fulbright-Hays Faculty Research Grant for travel and research in London and Lisbon, 1969–70, when I began this study in earnest.

To my wife, Katherine Wells Wheeler, I will always be most grateful. Without her encouragement this complex project could not have been completed. Any errors in this work, of course, remain my responsibility.

Durham, New Hampshire
January 1977   D. L. W.

Republican Portugal

A Political History

1910–1926

1 / An Introduction to Modern Portuguese History

> . . . a people who accomplished what we did has the
> moral duty to continue existing.
>
> Attributed to Miguel Torga, 3 April 1976
> (*Expresso*, 29 October 1976)

The Nation That Refused to Die

"Long Live the Republic!" shouted a few deputies as they left the halls of the First Republic's Congress. The date was 31 May 1926. Portugal's first experiment with a modern democracy was ending. A bloodless military coup was in progress and young soldiers were in the streets of Lisbon. Western Europe's most unstable parliamentary regime was finally collapsing. One superlative was giving birth to another: Europe's most unruly parliamentary system was midwife to Europe's longest surviving authoritarian system.

The historical puzzle that is Portugal's long past demands an attempt at explanation. Portugal is a nation that refused to die, yet her existence is constantly questioned. Some writers claim that the Portuguese are a people of paradox, that they have a penchant for self-effacement which is disarmingly combined with self-aggrandizement. The Portuguese nationality is one of Europe's oldest, and yet her leaders and thinkers again and again have despaired. In many nations independence and existence are taken for granted. Through the centuries in Portugal they have not been. Why does little Portugal exist at all? How can a country less than one-fifth the size of Spain* remain independent and free of her much larger and more powerful neighbor in the Iberian peninsula?

Other questions arise. What was this First Republic? Why did it fall? Is there any resemblance between this unusual political phenomenon and patterns among the Portuguese today? Is the Second Republic (25

---

* Portugal has an area of 35,430 square miles, including the Azores and Madeira Islands; Spain, including the Balearic and Canary islands, covers 196,607 square miles.

3

April 1974–) following a path similar to that of its ill-fated predecessor? Just how much of a burden is Portugal's heavy past? Even today, some Portuguese thinkers hesitate to reject the old Portuguese peasant saying, "When the evil is within a people, even the strength of soap cannot wash it away!"* Portuguese were disillusioned in 1926. Some are disillusioned fifty years later.

This national anxiety that will not go away has a complex history. It surfaced first in the sixteenth century or perhaps earlier. A sense of national crisis is a unique part of the Portuguese consciousness, indeed of the very nationality itself. This sense of crisis was a problem in the late nineteenth century and reached a new intensity in 1926. Nor has it gone away. Today some Portuguese thinkers are again concerned about the future of a people who have refused to be beaten by adversity or absorbed by their larger neighbor. In the 1970s a sense of despair, a national inferiority complex, a lack of pride, a dearth of confidence, a collective identity crisis have reemerged. Some of Portugal's finest minds are asking the old questions in a new crisis. National anxiety is playing its continuing role in Portuguese politics. A profound sense of déjà vu regarding a familiar malaise is clearly expressed in a recent article by António Quadros in a major Portuguese newspaper.

> In the identity crisis, in the ignorant nonsense of the Fatherland rejected, in the vile and suicidal self-vilification of which many now seem to partake, there is a crisis of nationality which is more dangerous for Portuguese survival than our economic problem, the totalitarian threat, or the temptations of *golpismo*.† It is the spiritual corruption which comes from within. It is the mental poison of which Fernando Pessoa speaks.‡ It is the national suicide whose antidote urgently requires preparation.[1]

Lest the reader also despair after this, the historian may provide counsel: historical perspective is required. To understand how the forty-eight-year dictatorship gave rise to the new Portugal of the 1970s, one must analyze the prologue to the dictatorship—the First Republic. In fact Portugal's past is replete with prologues. In examining her history, therefore, one must begin at the beginning, at the start of a nationality that, given the choice on several occasions over eight centuries, has refused to die.

* The original words of the proverb are: "Quando o mal é de nação . . . nem a poder de sabão!"

† *Golpismo* is a tendency to military coups; for full definition see Glossary.

‡ In this same article, the poet Fernando Pessoa is quoted as writing: "A nation which habitually thinks poorly of itself will end up by deserving the self-image which it first formed. Mentally, it poisons itself."

Portugal to 1820

In the middle of the twelfth century, Portugal first became independent of Castile and Leon. Castile and, later, a unified Spain, were a constant threat to the small country's independence. Although Portugal and Castile were linked by history, kinship, economics, language, and ethnic features, and thus similarities between the Iberian nations appeared to outnumber the differences, Portugal chose to go her own way. She expanded from her tiny foothold in western Iberia to build the first great European seaborne empire. Anticipating Spanish expansion by nearly a century, the small nation pioneered European explorations, discoveries, and colonization in Africa, Asia, and the Americas. During what the Portuguese call the "Marvelous Century," roughly 1415–1515, Portugal was a world power. In the middle of the sixteenth century a severe crisis gripped the country. Her hold on her overseas, largely coastal, empire deteriorated. At home, Castilianization deepened. In 1578 young King Sebastião, an impetuous imperialist, was killed with much of his army in the battle of Alácer Quibir in Morocco. The result was a fatally weakened country. In 1580 Spain under King Philip II invaded and annexed Portugal; Spanish rule continued until 1640, when a revolution restored the nation's precarious independence. Not until 1668, in a treaty with Spain, did Portugal win some assurance that the Spanish threat would abate. Still, the "Spanish menace," as expressed in literature, history, politics, and even sermons in church, has profoundly influenced the history of Portugal.

Lisbon dominated the official life of Portugal, while the rural masses remained largely unaffected by political changes. In the provinces, where agriculture greatly declined during the centuries following the Era of the Discoveries, peasants continued to live in their traditional society consisting of ancient customs, patriarchal habits, and communitarian activity. Indeed, rural Portugal remained a passive backdrop to coastal Lisbon.[2] Although Évora, Coimbra, and Oporto enjoyed prominence during the premodern era, Lisbon was usually the dominant beneficiary of what new ideas, developments, and imports arrived at Lusitanian shores. Even before the crisis of the nineteenth century, tensions were evident between Lisbon and the rest of the country.

Homogeneity of society and lack of differentiation among the ruling groups characterized premodern as well as modern history. Although there are distinct regional and provincial differences between Minho and Algarve, tiny Portugal did not have the severe cleavages and centrifugal forces found in neighboring Spain. In Portugal, with the exception of Lisbon, and in some cases, Oporto, no separatist regional movements—such as those in the Basque provinces and Catalonia in Spain—developed. The few non-Europeans who came to the metropole from Africa, Asia, and America were eventually absorbed, and Portugal remained a largely homogeneous, Caucasian society, even while tolerating miscegenation and some cultural pluralism in her multiracial colonies.[3]

After 1668 Portugal increasingly turned to Western Europe, particularly to France and even England, for new ideas and skills. This was part of a gradual de-Iberianization, as Portugal consolidated her cultural as well as her political independence in a reaction against Spain. In Portuguese society fear of Spanish invasion continued to be the ultimate argument against any opponent, any time. The deepening of the roots of Portuguese nationalism produced hostile reactions to Spain and to things and persons Spanish. As a contemporary Portuguese historian describes the post-1668 status of Portuguese independence, this "independence had always been defined as a challenge to Castile and a determination not to be confused with that country."[4]

By this time, Portuguese society was composed of two basic elements, those who participated in the gradual Europeanization process, the "political nation," and the rural masses, the majority of the people, who remained largely unchanged in the provinces, apolitical and passive. Even in the question of Portugal's relationship with Spain, this fundamental cleavage persisted into the modern era. In the Revolution of 1640, the apolitical masses had been mainly anti-Spanish, while the upper classes in Lisbon, though divided, had tended to side with Spain in her control of Portugal. The politically minded, including some commercial groups, had, according to one historian, "betrayed" the masses by being pro-Spanish.

Portugal's independence remained in doubt throughout the seventeenth and eighteenth centuries, and into the nineteenth century. She sought to preserve her freedom by means of her foreign and colonial policies. The Anglo-Portuguese Alliance, dating from the fourteenth century,[5] and an extensive empire in Africa, Asia, and America were intended to compensate for her small portion of Iberia.

Historical Explanations of Portugal's Decline

The reasons for Portugal's decline as a world power which began in the sixteenth century have concerned Portuguese thinkers in the succeeding four centuries. Various explanations for this decline have been given. During the seventeenth and eighteenth centuries, concepts of decadence and degeneration[6] were emphasized, ideas which have been discussed in the post-1820 era as well. The explanations in this era often postulate that the Portuguese people possessed a distinct national character, some of whose traits were inimical to modern progress and national revival. The national-character explanation became common and reappeared in the nineteenth and twentieth centuries as new European ideas of sociology, anthropology, and race filtered into the educated groups. A few earlier thinkers, such as the seventeenth-century writer Severim da Faria, explained the decline by social and economic factors such as emigration to the colonies and the "laziness" of the upper classes.

In the nineteenth century Portugal underwent catastrophic crises: the French invasions in 1807-11; a liberal revolution, 1820-23; the loss of her major colony, Brazil, in 1822; and civil wars between absolutist and constitutional monarchists over the form of government the country should have. Following this devastating era, during what the Portuguese call the Regeneration Era, 1851-71, Portugal enjoyed the wisdom of some of her greatest writers, men formed in the romantic, European traditions. Of these, the most deservedly celebrated was the historian Alexandre Herculano (1810-77), whose researches and writings revolutionized ancient and medieval Portuguese history. Although his famous *História de Portugal* did not treat history beyond the thirteenth century, Herculano wrote on contemporary problems. He postulated that the decay of agriculture was a major factor in the decline of Portugal in the sixteenth century; like his friend, the writer-statesman Joaquim Pedro Oliveira Martins (1854-94), Herculano was for a long time a convinced "little Portugal" man and was skeptical of the advisability of developing colonies.

Oliveira Martins had his own explanations for the decline of Portugal. Although he was a brilliant and colorful writer, he was more of a synthesizer and a popularizer of the past than an original historian. His historical theories reflected contemporary pseudoscientific racism and amateur physical anthropology, which he freely applied both to Portuguese and to African history. Oliveira Martins explained Portugal's decline in the sixteenth century by pointing to the land division in southern Portugal, where the *latifundia* developed. These large estates, owned by few men, deprived the peasants of land and work. Many Portuguese, therefore, emigrated to the overseas colonies.[7] The noted historian extended his analysis to the era in which he lived; Portugal was behind the rest of Europe because of her stagnating agriculture. He deplored emigration, which in his day was largely to Brazil, as a hindrance to economic development. He suggested that Portugal "colonize" the lands in the central and south provinces, which had a sparse population due to heavy emigration.[8] Oliveira Martins, known to some as "the glorious singer of national miseries,"[9] offered the original proposition that Portugal should be her own best colony by resettling thousands of emigrants from Brazil on Portuguese land.[10]

In order to explain Portugal's decline, the Republican writer Basílio Teles (1856–1921) had a complex racial theory which bears a resemblance to the national-character analysis of the Spanish medievalist Claudio Sanchez Albornoz, who in discussing Spanish history ascribed great importance to the Arab invasion and conquest of Iberia. Teles's explanation was based on the supposed incompatibility of two groups; the people of north Portugal, whom he called "Arian," and the people of the south, nomadic "Semites," who originated in the Islamic invasions of the eighth and ninth centuries. The people of the north, from provinces of the Beiras, Douro, Minho, and Trás-os-Montes, represented the rural, rude masses, strong in localisms and municipal autonomy, warlike, and agricultural. To Teles, those of the south were the group which dominated Portugal after the end of the fourteenth century and brought the nation into crisis through policies of centralism, absolutism, commercialism, and the disastrous overseas expansion policy directed from Lisbon. "Southern man," mainly Semitic, thus mastered all of Portugal and caused the decline in the sixteenth century. Clearly, Teles, who was also a brilliant student of rural poverty and agriculture, admired the peasant, whom he epitomized as "northern man" in his interesting if simplistic theory.[11]

Since the establishment of the First Portuguese Republic in 1910, historians of later generations have sought new explanations for the country's sixteenth-century decline and continuing weakness. Perhaps the most original and celebrated of the older historians was António Sérgio (1883–1969), known chiefly as a critic, educational pioneer, and essayist. Sérgio's advanced ideas in education and politics were roughly comparable to those of the progressive wing of the "Generation of 1898" in Spain. As a thinker, he was probably influenced more by contemporary English, American, French, and German writers, than he was by Spaniards, though he was attuned to some of the ideas of Miguel de Unamuno. Like Ortega y Gasset, who was influenced by his study of Nietzsche, Sérgio was an advocate of a strong elite to educate the Portuguese masses.

Sérgio attempted to explain what he termed decadence, or decline, not by national character, but by the "structure of society" or social and economic factors during the sixteenth century and later.[12] He laid the blame for a rigid hierarchical society on the monarchs, who used the wealth from the colonies to concentrate and centralize their own.

Sérgio further attributed the decline to the failure to develop a strong rural nobility or gentry which could sustain a viable agriculture, or an independent middle class capable of carrying on commerce and trade. Centralization of royal power led to the dominance of an expansion policy ("política do transporte," as he described it), which exported people, capital, and skills to the colonies leaving Portugal weakened and decadent. To this unwise expansion policy, Sérgio placed in juxtaposition a "politica de fixação," a policy of home settlement and development which was never fully implemented either in the sixteenth century or later. Overseas expansion ruined Portugal, he suggested, as agriculture stagnated, and what wealth returned from colonial exploitation was soon spent on importing wheat or on frivolous luxuries. As the empire diminished and the youth of the nation was drained away, members of the upper class benefitted from the colonial wealth while the masses remained in the Middle Ages. More will be said about Sérgio's ideas in a later section of this chapter.

After World War II, Portuguese historiography moved further away from national-character explanations with the work of Vitorino Magalhães Godinho, trained in social and economic history in France.[13] As he analyzed the motivation for the Portuguese discoveries, Godinho saw the decline as the result of a series of economic factors such as price fluctuation and social factors which included lack of skilled manpower after 1550, heavy emigration, lack of a strong independent middle class, extreme centralization of power and initiative in the state, and rigid class structures.

If not an actual student of Godinho's, the younger historian A. H. Oliveira Marques has largely followed the master's socioeconomic explanation of the decline. Beginning his scholarly career as a medievalist, Oliveira Marques was concerned with social and economic structures in post-1550 Portugal and did not favor political, anthropological, or psychological explanations of the decline and crises. By implication, he attacked studies by C. R. Boxer on administrative conflict, confusion, and corruption in Portugal and her colonial empire,[14] and he deemphasized the role of national traits by stating flatly that there was no evidence that the Portuguese were more corrupt or more personally divided than other Europeans in their homelands and empires. Going even further, this historian describes those who focused on such matters as "historian-moralists," or "moralist-politicians."[15] This verbal assault is perhaps the result of a chauvinistic reaction to foreign criticism of Portuguese colonialism as well as hostility to the nineteenth-century tradition of Portuguese pessimism and a common tendency of amateur historians to ascribe the decline of Portugal to a distinct national character which, allegedly, spawned fatal personal quarrels.

In the past few decades other historians of Portugal's decline have emphasized economic causes. The Brazilian sociologist Gilberto Freyre,[16] in a brilliant but rambling and erratic essay saw the origin of decline in the victory of commercial interests over the agricultural. Freyre's theory resembles Sérgio's concept of two antagonistic policies: the policy of developing an autonomous, productive home economy versus that of exploiting and transporting wealth. The Portuguese essayist-poet Miguel Torga (1907–) sees the cause of the decline in the triumph of Lisbon's commercial-colonial interests over the agricultural base in the provinces. Adding a psychological factor that he calls "moral anemia," Torga asserts that the provinces did not willingly follow the leaders in Lisbon into overseas expansion, and that to this day their antagonism is expressed in custom and feelings. In accord with various other writers before him, Torga, born a northerner and a staunch champion of the city of Oporto, sees in the "Old Man of Restelo" (*O Velho do Restelo*), in Luís de Camões' famous epic poem *Os Lusíadas* (1572), the literary embodiment of the provincial, agricultural opposition to overseas expansion. As did the "Old Man of Restelo" in his famous discourse on the eve of Vasco da Gama's departure for India, Torga ascribes decline and decay at home to this expansion.[17]

The most favored current explanations of the decline emphasize socioeconomic factors based on precise quantitative research by scholars like Magalhães Godinho. Nevertheless, the following factors cannot be dismissed lightly: the importance of Lisbon in the expansion and development of Portugal; the cleavage between rural provincial interests and the coastal, commercial middle-class interests; or, put in another way, between two Portugals, the rural and the urban, the apolitical and the political; finally the relationship with Spain which, especially in the educated elite, fomented fear, hostility, and conflict.

Analyses of Portugal's Crises of the Nineteenth and Twentieth Centuries

A historical discussion of post-1820 Portugal has begun with a treatment of the sixteenth-century decline. That discussion is relevant to an analysis of the modern era for a number of reasons. Portuguese thinkers, yesterday and today, have a profound sense of historical tradition, which projects their analyses into the remote past. A number of the historians of the contemporary crisis regard the decline, which began with the sixteenth-century crisis, as a semi-permanent state for Portugal. Such a discussion is useful, also, for a negative reason: in the mid-1920s, influential conservatives, in analyzing the failure of the republic, emphasized a simplistic analogy between the sixteenth-century crisis and that of the 1920s. Living in 1925-26, these writers believed that as in 1580, Portugal was about to lose her independence. This likelihood was commonly given as a reason for supporting a dictatorship, which, its partisans claimed, would never allow what happened to Portugal in 1580 to occur in 1926.[18] Such tendentious claims and false analogies, often clothed in hysterical alarmism, represented some of the more common arguments of the Right.

The events of 1807-51 profoundly altered the destiny of Portugal. The foundations of the absolutist monarchy were shattered, leaving Portugal with constitutional monarchy. The economic loss of Brazil in 1822 was severe. The political and social conflicts of these years encouraged a series of experiments with various forms of representative government, parliamentary systems, and eventually, military and civil dictatorship. In 1926, after almost sixteen years of existence, the republic gave way to a military junta and army command, causing many observers to remark that Portugal was not suited to democracy and parliamentary government. This opinion soon became the subject of much political and historical debate among stalwarts of the Left, Center, and Right.

With the establishment of the "New State," directed largely by the premier, Dr. António de Oliveira Salazar (1889-1970), the historical debate reached a new stage. The government and its largely rightist supporters espoused an interpretation of Portuguese history, 1820-1926, which was based on a Traditionalist school of writers. Opposing this interpretation, as they opposed the Dictatorship, was a group of writers who may be described collectively as the Modernist school. In general, the historiography of post-1820 Portugal is divided along these lines.

The Traditionalists have emphasized concepts of a national character which they claim is unique to the Portuguese or among what they describe as "Latins" in general, and have attempted to explain both liberalism and subsequent developments in terms of value judgments about culture and a conspiracy theory. The leading Traditionalist writers of the twentieth century have been Integralists such as António Sardinha (1888-1925), the major theoretician of Integralismo Lusitano during 1914-26, and João Ameal (1900-),[19] an Integralist of a younger generation, active in journalism and amateur historiography. If Sardinha and Ameal are contemporary standard-bearers of the Traditionalist school, they are indebted to the ideas of earlier writers: French rightists in the Action Française group 1890–1930 and Portuguese nationalists such as Jacinto Cândido, whose 1909 book, *A Doutrina Nacionalista,* represented an early program for a conservative rightist government which called for considerable administrative decentralization and a corporate representative system where political parties, such as those of the Constitutional Monarchy, 1820–1910, would have no place.[20]

The Traditionalist school explains the decline of Portugal and the apparent failure of liberalism and democracy to be planted firmly in Portugal after 1820 by stating that imported European ideas and customs had corrupted the Portuguese. Rejecting the ideas of the French Revolution and of the nineteenth-century European liberal tradition, Traditionalists called for a restoration of traditional institutions such as the monarchy as it was before 1820, the Church, the army, and the family. "Demo-liberalism," they claimed, was unsuited to the Portuguese character and past. Individualism and popular sovereignty should be replaced by authority, hierarchy, and tradition. Some writers claimed that the undermining of the monarchy was the result of conspiracies by Portuguese Freemasons, whose ideas and secret plots were subversive. The Traditionalists' major program, essentially that of the Integralists, prescribed for post-1926 Portugal: hereditary monarchy, decentralized administration where there would be considerable autonomy at the municipal, district, and provincial levels, and corporatism. Characteristic of the Traditionalist school is their approach to Portuguese history, which is at once mystical, messianic, and semi-religious. Although the Traditionalists decry individualism, their history is replete with the concept that "great men" perhaps more than institutions, ideas, and customs made Portugal great in the past.

It is not surprising that the Traditionalist interpretation dominated official propaganda, school texts, and general history books of the New State after 1933. Even in neighboring Spain, the few recent historical studies on Portugal have been infused with a Traditionalist view of the First Republic's history.[21] When a Spanish historian such as Pabón did not cover Portugal in adequate detail in a volume dealing with both countries, a Portuguese Traditionalist like Caetano Beirão was selected to present Portuguese history.[22]

More than the Modernists, the Traditionalists have tended to stress the factor of national character, however they might differ about precisely defining it. Leading Integralist writers, perhaps the ideological vanguard of the Traditionalists, have viewed Portuguese national character as a major reason why European liberalism was unsuitable in Portugal and the Republican institutions failed. An outstanding literary critic and contemporary of Salazar's, Fidelino de Figueiredo (1889–1967), attributed the failure of the First Republic largely to what he cryptically described in 1926 as "a psychic decadence."[23]

Nor was the national-character explanation confined to thinkers and theoretical Traditionalists. Dr. Salazar himself, perhaps the supreme man of action of Traditionalism during 1928–68, used the argument in an article he wrote for a foreign audience in 1963.[24] Salazar claimed that parliamentary government and wide personal freedoms were un-suited to what he defined as "the Portuguese character" since, despite their virtues, his people were too individualistic and emotional or "generous of soul" for democracy. The Portuguese, he suggested, was "profoundly Catholic, when he is religious, at the same time the Por-tuguese is anticlerical; studious and conscientious he does not respect, on principle, the Master-Professor; highly competent when a profes-sional, he finds it difficult to adapt himself to communal work."[25]

The Modernist school explained the failures of liberalism and the First Republic by an emphasis not upon national character but upon political, economic, and social factors and conditions. António Sérgio was probably the outstanding theoretician of the Modernists. Sérgio stressed a rational, humanist approach to the Portuguese past, and sug-gested that Portuguese failures were not caused by an excess of Euro-peanization but by a lack of it.[26] In an article in 1924 Sérgio elaborated further on this idea that Portugal failed to transplant liberalism because of not going far enough in breaking with the past: *"The great mistake of the Portuguese was not that they broke with tradition, but the very contrary, that they broke with tradition only in its superficial aspects. . . .* In other words, the weakness [sic] of [nineteenth-century] liberalism (like those of absolutism) were not the cause, but the consequence of the basic [political] vices from which the motherland sickens . . . "[27]

The Portuguese imported some of the forms, or the shells, of parliamentary government and democracy, but the essence was lacking, since the masses were largely apathetic and ignorant and since the educated groups were unruly, factionalized, and not oriented to work-ing for the civic good. Authority was not the prescription for carrying out needed reforms. Sérgio stressed the need for a massive, public-education program which would reform the "mentality" of the Por-tuguese, who, if educated correctly, would respond favorably. A true republic was not established in 1910, he claimed, since the educational and economic systems were not profoundly reformed. Sérgio felt that if the republic had addressed itself to basic reforms of the general economy, including agriculture and industry, and had tackled the specific problems related to property holding, credit, welfare, and education, Portugal would have been on her way to stability and some prosperity by 1926. As it was, an "oligarchy" gained control of the state, and the people received few benefits.

A friend and contemporary of Sérgio's, Raúl Proença (1884–1942), also emphasized a slow, public-education process as a prescription for reform. It was faulty civic education, he said, not national character, that was to blame for the disasters of the Republican experience. Like Sérgio, Proença believed that the First Republic was bankrupt politically because of a failure to address key problems in the economy and education. Although some leaders of the opposition to the post-1926 dictatorship, like Torga,[28] mentioned psychological factors, national character did not play a major part in their analysis of the troubles which followed the coming of liberalism to Portugal.

After World War II, younger generations of Modernists attempted to explain Portuguese history. In a series of books and articles, Carlos Ferrão, a journalist and amateur historian, became a self-styled defender of the positive aspects of the First Republic.[29] Ferrão's style was polemical and his arguments not well documented, but his work suggested the outlines of a wing of the Modernist school. He claimed that much of the truth about what happened during the republic was obscured by the New State propaganda and censorship or by a program of "mystification"; that the republic was undermined by its enemies on the Right, including monarchists and Integralists, who subverted and overthrew it. In some respects, Ferrão's modified conspiracy theory is a liberal parallel to the Freemason conspiracy theories of Traditionalists.

The professional historian Oliveira Marques represents a more scientific, rationalist branch of the Modernist school. Dismissing national character as an explanation of the recent past, just as he rejected it as an explanation of the decline, this historian emphasizes instead political, social, and economic factors. He explains the failure of the First Republic as the inability of parliament to function effectively, excessive politicization, poor party discipline, the absence of an opposition party to offer an alternative to the strong Democratic party, violence as a method of transferring power, lack of strong authority, and the undermining of the regime by plots from the Right. His explanation draws in part upon the analysis of Portuguese constitutions by the former premier, Dr. Marcello Caetano (1906–).[30]

Other Modernists also stress political and economic causes. Leading oppositionists who belong to what remains of the old Portuguese Republican party point to what they feel was a tragic mistake early in the history of the First Republic: the division and factionalization of the once united Republican party during 1911-12.[31] Others see the republic undermined by tragic legacies from the Constitutional Monarchy, such as corruption, subversive monarchists and their allies, and local bossism (*caciquismo*).

The professional historians among the Modernists have tended to be partisans of social and economic history, and while they give lip service to political factors such as excessive factionalism, they have not delved into the politics of the era in any great depth.[32] There are several reasons for this trend: First, disillusionment with the Republican experiment has caused a reaction against involvement in politics or political analysis. Second, and perhaps most important, the New State attempted a de-politicization process in Portugal and penalized or limited participation in partisan politics and in discussions or analyses of recent political history. Writing histories of the republic was discouraged, especially during the years 1928-68, when the country was under the sway of Dr. Salazar. After a long era of state censorship, educated individuals learned to protect themselves by that most subtle and insidious form of "previous censorship": self-censorship.

Even fifty years later, the history of the First Republic remains a controversial topic in Portugal. Next to the events of 1974, the First Republic was perhaps the seminal and most highly concentrated political experience of the country over the past two centuries. For Portuguese who lived under the First Republic, it has been difficult to discuss the period openly. Although various historical studies of the Republican experience have been published since 1968 by a group of young historians headed by Oliveira Marques, and a host of facts have been uncovered, no general systematic analysis of consistent political patterns during the last century has been produced. Even the work of Oliveira Marques is highly controversial. His works on the republic were attacked by partisans of the Right and the Traditionalist school,[33] and, before the collapse of the Dictatorship in 1974, Oliveira Marques faced a conflict with the censors in publishing the second volume of his general history of Portugal, the volume dealing with post-1920 history. Some of the Left in Portugal, who analyse the republic in terms of class conflict, have also attacked his work.[34]

Foreign historians and writers have been influenced by New State propaganda and by the excessive discrediting of the First Republic. In giving superficial analyses of the Republican experience they have purposely or unwittingly reinforced Traditionalist and New State arguments.[35] These historians and journalists often agree on a common theme: that the post-1910 trouble was fundamentally financial, that political instability was simply a result of heavy debt and frequent devaluations.[36] A logical corollary is that somehow Portuguese politics was only sound and fury, unrelated to the problems confronting the nation, and either too tragic or unimportant to study seriously. Alien to this analysis is the idea that Portuguese politics was partly concerned with legitimate conflicts of opinion and ideology. The works of the more conservative foreign historians harmonized well with the Dictatorship's post–1926 program of deliberate de-politicization, when political parties were abolished and the parliament was subordinated to an absolutist executive.[37]

With the collapse of the New State and the emergence of a more democratic system, the Second Republic (1974–), freedom of discussion has increased. The controversy over Portugal's modern history continues unabated in journals, newspapers, meetings, books, and in election campaigning. The discussion focuses on the current political situation and explanations of the modern past. Why did the First Republic collapse? Was a major cause a psychological flaw rooted in the past, or only contemporary conditions? If Portugal went that way yesterday, which way will Portugal go tomorrow?

Four Major Tensions in Modern Portuguese Society

Professor Richard Herr has introduced for modern Spanish history a conceptual analysis which identifies "tensions" in society to explain political instability in the nineteenth and twentieth centuries.[38] Herr examines three such tensions: (1) Ideological tension, between the clericals and the anticlericals; between the parliamentarists and the authoritarians; and between the liberals and the conservatives. The clerical issue, suggests Herr, obscured the fact that ideologies were sometimes used to defend vested interests and privileged groups. (2) Tension caused by an unequal division of land in central and southern Spain, where a great deal of land was held by few owners and many Spaniards were landless. (3) Geographical tension between the rural and the urban, between the rural, central plateau and the urban, better-watered periphery, which included the Basque provinces, Catalonia, and sometimes Galicia, Asturias, Navarre, and Valencia. Herr attributes much of the instability of post-1820 Spanish politics to contemporary conditions, not to national character. He claims that a major problem which led to the defeat of progressive policies during the twentieth century in Spain was the "alienation of the common people of rural Spain from the urban groups holding progressive doctrines."[39]

Herr's analysis appears to have considerable application to Portugal, which in some ways is a variant of the Spanish case. Nevertheless, as suggested in discussions above, the Portuguese experienced tensions special to themselves and to their conditions. In the following discussion, I will attempt briefly to adapt Herr's suggestive concept of tensions to Portugal.

There are at least four major tensions which have influenced the course of politics in modern Portugal. These may be identified as personalism; political and ideological factionalism (*partidarismo*); an imbalanced land division between north and south; and geographical-administrative tensions between the provinces and Lisbon.

Personalism

Personalism is not included in Herr's scheme, but is supported in the Portuguese case by massive evidence from many Portuguese sources. Almost without exception, authorities on Portuguese political history, as early as the sixteenth-century decline, ascribe great importance to the personal factor. The Portuguese word for this, *personalismo* (see Glossary) is often defined as "personalism," or a "vice of egotism."[40] Although this trait is not necessarily peculiar to the Portuguese or to any other people, it is indisputable that the personal element has played a great role in Portuguese politics. Related to this tension and reinforcing it are the behavior patterns of individual leaders whether king, queen, prince, regent, president, premier, mayor, governor, administrator, local cacique, or simply the head of a family. The personal factor in politics was reinforced by the small size of the population and the restricted area of the home country. Furthermore because of Portuguese traditions of respect for age and masculinity as well as a preoccupation with individual honor and shame, there has long been a tendency to interpret history as the acts of a handful of "great men."

Even *sebastianismo,* an atavistic yet messianic form of popular nationalism that emerged in different forms long after persons claiming to be King Sebastian had ceased to appear, was always a personalist creed for both credulous masses and some educated groups.[41] It was a hope for national revival founded on the belief that a person, a personal hero, a great man would make all the difference. For some, twentieth-century Sebastians were Major Sidónio Pais, or Dr. Salazar, or General António de Spínola, or General Ramalho Eanes.

Also reinforcing personalism were strong local and regional traditions. There were few educated persons to lead a small country with a poor educational base. In these circumstances, men counted for more than institutions.

One consequence of tension is conflict. Personalism played its role in political party, parliamentary, and government instability. Because personal relations between leaders, personalities, personal likes and dislikes, and personal ambitions were important in Portuguese politics and government, personal conflicts formed a part of many political situations. In the First Republic, then, personalism had a role which cannot be dismissed.

Political and Ideological Factionalism

As in Spain, in Portugal there was a struggle between those who espoused liberal, parliamentary government and those who desired an authoritarian, hierarchical government; between the clericals and the anticlericals; between Republicans and monarchists. During the First Republic, as well as during the Constitutional Monarchy, numerous political parties underwent rapid fragmentation. The conflict between parties was sometimes ideological, but it could also be personal, and therefore the first and second tensions overlap. Differences of opinion could also be based on differing experiences, real or imagined conflicts, a struggle for public office and its spoils, or vested interests of an economic or social nature. An important aspect of the politics of the republic was the instability of political parties. Also, extraordinarily intense politicization of many groups and classes played a role in fomenting conflict and instability.

In Portugal political and ideological factionalism was influenced by traditional fears among the educated groups. Fears, which at times bordered on mania especially among the Right, were: Spanish invasion and dominance; the loss of the African colonies; and the loss of independence of Portugal itself. In a small country with a small educated class, such fears were self-fulfilling. Nationalism intensified during political crises and did so in part because of the narrow perspectives of a small educated group. As I have suggested in an earlier work, the educated class, anxious for national revival, frequently relied on policies of colonialism, authoritarianism, and nationalism.[42]

Land Division

In north and south Portugal there were serious problems concerning the rural poor and the land and property division. In northern Portugal, small, uneconomical plots with overcrowded conditions were common. In southern Portugal, especially in the Alentejo province, were the latifundia, large estates owned by upper- and middle-class landlords and worked by a largely landless peasantry. Rural poverty and few economic opportunities for the lower classes—a tradition of unsuccessful agriculture—created great problems for successive governments whether under the monarchy, the First Republic, the New State or the Second Republic. In the past, then, emigration has been heavy from these rural areas to Europe and the Americas.

Geographical-Administrative Tension

A fourth and final tension derived from the Lisbon-provincial cleavage—the dominance of Lisbon in most spheres of activity, and the comparative impotence and dependence of the provinces. Compared to the countryside, Lisbon has long been oversized, overdeveloped, and overpowerful. In a special sense, Lisbon possesses a geographical-regional individuality. The place of Lisbon in Portugal parallels that of the commercialized and industrialized periphery of Spain in the Catalan and Basque provinces. Lisbon was a major force in the overseas expansion, and, in the modern age, the crucial politics and government activity were centered there. Lisbon's society could represent, in terms of Unamuno's analysis of Spain, the historical section or political society, while the provinces represented the intrahistorical, or apolitical, with the masses of common people in rural areas forming a silent Iberian majority. The population of the rural provinces did not experience the same First Republic as did the people of Lisbon. In some ways, too, Lisbon epitomized in Portugal Robert Redfield's concept of "great tradition of the reflective few," and the provinces represented the "little tradition of the largely unreflective many."[43]

Conflicts between Lisbon, the capital, virtually omnipotent, and the provinces are brilliantly described in Miguel Torga's work. He suggests there has long been a "lack of harmony between the conscience of the country and of the capital. . . ." This key tension was expressed in various political and bureaucratic and economic debates: between those who wanted an economic policy to favor commerce and those for rural agriculture; between those who supported strong authority at the capital and those who supported local and provincial autonomy.

The Lisbon-country tension has not diminished with time. Even in relatively recent days, a peasant saying from Beira province summed up one common expression of the tension: "O país não é o Terreiro do Paço" ("The country is not the [Lisbon] Commerce Square").[44] It is significant, too, that for military movements to gain control over Portugal in the modern age, they have had to first control Lisbon. The 1910 Revolution, which resulted in the fall of the monarchy, was initiated in the Lisbon area and spread to the provinces. And the 1926 coup which overthrew the First Republic was organized by a military movement directed deliberately against the political predominance of Lisbon, by then a city with a reputation of strong Republican resistance to the Right. The political ascendancy of Lisbon was again clear in the Revolution of 25 April 1974.

These four tensions are comprehensive but by no means exclusive. Nor is this conceptualization meant to preclude differing analyses which might provide insight into Portuguese political history. The selection was made at the risk of some oversimplification, and in order to introduce and to clarify key factors and trends which will be discussed at some length later. They may provide a background to this study of the First Portuguese Republic, Portugal's first major political experiment, which helped make her at once one of the most political and apolitical of countries in the twentieth century.

2 / A Monarchy without Monarchists

I remember a kind and false Lisbon with *progressista* and *regenerador* politicians in high hats discussing matters in the *Arcada;* a smiling Lisbon, with the point of the handkerchief coming out of the coat pocket. . . . The great man of the time was Pinheiro Chagas—the great politician Fontes [Peireira de Melo]. . . . Life was easy. The supreme ambition was to arrange a job with a salary of forty-five *mil-réis* a month.

All this was yesterday—it was buried three thousand years ago. . . . The timid *Lisboeta* was replaced by the *Lisboeta* who fires off shots in the cafés.

Raúl Brandão[1]

A New Monarchy

Between 1820 and 1834 Portugal acquired a constitutional monarchy. Portugal's attempt to establish a stable constitutional monarchy was strongly influenced by ideas from the French Revolution, the Napoleonic invasion of Iberia, a liberal revolution in neighboring Spain, and Portugal's relationship with her ally, England.

The birth of liberalism and constitutionalism in Portugal, however, was troubled by severe problems. In 1807 French troops invaded and devastated sections of the country. The Portuguese royal family, led by Prince Regent João, fled to Rio de Janeiro, Brazil, where they remained until 1821. The French invaders were defeated and expelled with British aid, but Portugal's economic and political condition was gravely weakened.

Portugal's economy did not recover for decades. Industry, which though small had been growing, lay prostrate. Agriculture suffered, and parts of the rural population were uprooted by famine, disease, and war. Portuguese commerce with her vast colony, Brazil, had been adversely affected by the 1810 Anglo-Portuguese Treaty of Commerce and Alliance, whereby Brazilian ports were opened to British trade.[2] In 1822 Brazil, with Pedro, the son of King João VI, at its head, declared itself independent.

Portugal's experience in the campaigns against the French, and under the tutelage of British army officers who virtually ran Portugal during the period 1808-20, was a bitter one. The Portuguese army officers resented being commanded by the British, and the British leader, Marshal William Beresford, was unpopular. In 1817 a small group of officers including General Gomes Freire, a Mason and liberal, attempted to launch a revolution to expel the British and to establish a liberal, constitutional monarchy, but the plot failed. But in August and September 1820, first in Oporto and then in Lisbon, Portuguese army officers staged successful *pronunciamentos* ("uprisings," see Glossary), established a provisional form of government under a junta, and demanded that King João VI return from Brazil and swear allegiance to a constitution.

Until 1851, the Portuguese army played an important role in politics and could be decisive in saving or destroying governments. By 1820 the traditional forces in Portuguese society were in great disarray. The monarch was in Brazil and appeared reluctant to return to Portugal, and some resented his retreat to Brazil in the face of the French invasions. The Church retained some power but lacked leadership, although some priests had supported the liberal revolutions of 1817 and 1820. The nobility was divided and somewhat discredited because a number of aristocrats had not opposed the French invaders and had even collaborated and joined the French armies.

The Portuguese army officers corps, however, under the influence of French revolutionary ideas and English liberalism, was to some extent transformed by the events of the years 1807-20. In Lisbon and Oporto Masonry increased among officers. The tolerance and liberalism of the English officers, exemplified by General Wellington's protest to Portuguese authorities concerning the persecution of political enemies, made an impact. In fact influence of English was crucial in that it produced professional improvement and a process of politicization along liberal lines.[3] As a result, the Portuguese officers corps became more self-confident, independent, and intent upon promoting a self-defined mission. Increasingly, the officer corps viewed itself as a "depository of honor and national interest."[4] The officer corps' desire for change, which was in strong contrast with much of the rest of Portuguese society, struck a spark with certain sections of the upper and middle classes. Their goal would now be to end English dominance, restore Portuguese self-respect and strength, and establish a constitutional monarchy.

King João VI returned from Brazil in 1821, and he swore to uphold a constitution which was drafted in 1822. Modeled in part on the Spanish

Constitution of 1812, the 1822 Constitution was created by a Cortes ("parliament"), consisting mainly of middle-class landowners, merchants, soldiers, and bureaucrats. The document contained ideas which were too advanced for some sectors of Portuguese society: sovereignty was to be in the hands of the nation, not the king, the press would be free, legal and tax privileges would be abolished, and the Inquisition would be ended.

But the day of the liberals had not dawned. The new leaders and ideas were too closely aligned with generally unpopular people and events: the foreign influences which had swept urban society since 1807 and the independence of Brazil in September 1822. Furthermore, the Portuguese masses, living largely in rural, semi-feudal conditions, failed to understand or to appreciate the new ideas. They remained faithful to the traditional Church and monarchy.[5]

In May 1823 the 1822 Constitution was overthrown in a revolution led by antiliberals, and for the next three years King João VI reigned as an absolute monarch. On his death in 1826 his son Pedro in Brazil abdicated the throne in favor of his seven-year-old daughter, Maria. Pedro's brother Miguel, then in Austria, was to return to become regent for eleven years until young Maria reached her majority. Pedro personally wrote a new constitution, later known as the Charter (*Carta*), and expected Miguel to abide by it while regent. Dom Miguel returned to Portugal in 1828 and, pressured by conservatives, restored absolutism and established a conservative and repressive regime. Liberals in the Azores led a revolt against "Miguelism" in 1829, which was followed in 1832–34 by a full-scale civil war. Pedro abdicated his Brazilian throne and returned to Portugal with armed forces to restore his daughter Maria to the throne.[6] In 1834 Pedro's Liberal party triumphed—with British aid—and Miguel went into exile. The 1826 Charter was restored as the nation's constitution. Pedro had saved the throne for his daughter but at the expense of his own life. He died in 1834, leaving Maria, at the age of fifteen, with a legacy of political confusion and economic ruin.[7]

The fate of Pedro, known in Portuguese history as "Dom Pedro IV, the Liberator," marked a sad beginning to the personally tragic history of the Portuguese constitutional monarchs. His daughter, Queen Maria II, worn down by a stormy reign and many pregnancies, died in 1853 at age thirty-four, while giving birth to her eleventh child. Her eldest son, Pedro V, succeeded her on the throne. His reign was also brief and tragic. His wife, a Hohenzollern princess, died in 1859 after only a year of marriage. Young Pedro V died in 1861 at age twenty-four of typhoid fever, which also carried off one of his brothers. Maria II's second son,

Luís, succeeded to the throne and enjoyed a long and reasonably tranquil reign, 1861–89—a period of some stability in government and politics. But his son Carlos, who became king in 1889, had a tragic reign.

The royalty who headed the monarchy in its last years was composed of strong personalities. King Carlos I (1863–1908) and his French wife, Queen Amélia (1865–1951), were a formidable pair. Amélia was a tall, big-boned woman who towered over her short, increasingly obese husband. Born to French royalty, the daughter of the count of Paris, pretender to the French throne, Amélia married Carlos in 1886. Amélia was dogged by tragedy. Although she was noted for her welfare work for victims of tuberculosis, and though she established Lisbon's elegent Coach Museum in 1905, she was unpopular, perhaps because she was French and appeared to dominate her husband. She had three children by Carlos. The oldest, Luís, the crown prince, was assassinated with his father in the streets of Lisbon in 1908. A second son, Manuel, only eighteen, succeeded to the throne. He was expelled and exiled in October 1910 after a Republican revolution, never to return to his throne or his homeland. Manuel was forty-two when he died in England. A third child, a daughter, Ana Maria, was born prematurely and survived only two hours. Queen Amélia followed her son into exile and lived with him until he married in 1913. Then she moved to Versailles, where she remained for most of her long life. She returned to visit Portugal only once, briefly, in 1945, with the permission of the Salazar government. In 1951 she died, a lonely old woman of eighty-six, having observed the destruction of both the Portuguese royal family and the monarchy.[8]

The "System"

> Portugal doesn't need reform, Cohen!
> What Portugal needs is a Spanish invasion!
>
>   Ega, in Eça de Queiroz's novel,
>   The Maias[9]

After 1834, the Portuguese Constitutional Monarchy settled into a Lusitanian version of a liberal monarchy, modeled upon the French and British examples. With minor revisions, the major constitutional instrument was the 1826 Charter, which gave the king considerably more power than did the 1822 Constitution. The Charter was in force from 1842 to 1910, and a leading Portuguese constitutional expert describes it as the "most monarchical" of such constitutions.[10] Under it the king enjoyed considerably more political power than that held by constitutional monarchs elsewhere. The Portuguese king held the *poder moderador* ("moderating power"), by which he could act as a neutral executive, presiding over the other branches of government and resolving disputes among them. His powers were extensive since he could convoke, postpone, or dissolve the Cortes and freely name and dismiss the prime minister and cabinet; he also had powers of amnesty and pardon and, under certain conditions, could legislate by decree.

During most of the life of the Constitutional Monarchy, the major constitutional conflict centered upon the division of powers between the executive (which technically included both the king, as poder moderador, and the cabinet), and the legislative branches (Chamber of Deputies and House of Peers). How much constitutional power the monarch should retain was a major political issue. In general, the political parties that developed opposed any significant increase of royal powers. Yet in the period 1834–51 the monarchs' powers provided necessary stability. During this era the military intervened in politics with generals such as João Carlos Saldanha acting as military dictators (men on horseback). More radical politicians attempted to restore the 1822 Constitution, which lessened royal powers, but the 1826 Charter prevailed.

In 1851 the political system entered an era of relative calm, some economic recovery, and reform. For the time being intervention by the armed forces in politics ceased. Despite the tragic lives of the monarchs in the next decade, able politicians developed a stable party system. In this era of the Regeneration, the Constitutional Monarchy matured. The first Regeneration ministry held office—with few changes—for over five years (April 1851–June 1856), a remarkable record. This government laid the foundations of modern transportation by building the first railroads; it reformed administration and passed some balanced budgets.

Despite some progress by the last third of the century, however, the monarchy did not evolve into a stable, progressive, and well-entrenched constitutional system. Three interlocking crises—a political crisis, a financial crisis, and a moral crisis—worsened and undermined the monarchy as an institution and complicated the practice of government and politics.[11]

Among the causes of the political crisis were: a growing lack of faith and respect for the person of the monarchy and its institutions among both monarchists and Republicans; a wasteful, inefficient administration, which made it difficult to carry out reforms; and political conditions that prevented power from changing hands or governments from changing in response to genuine expressions of public opinion or issues of importance. Parties, elections, parliamentary activity, and public opinion often reflected only the views of small groups of the elite in the two cities (Lisbon and Oporto) and a few towns. Politics and government were dominated by agrarian and financial oligarchs and their clients from the upper class and upper middle class. The capital dominated the system and its resources. A major obstacle to serious reform of administration and government was the refusal of this small oligarchy to allow any changes that might endanger their monopoly of revenues, bureaucratic offices, and prestige.[12]

In this system of "pseudoparlamentarism,"[13] parties were cliques of political and private friends and clients revolving about "great men," such as Regenerador politician Fontes Pereira de Melo, who headed governments during 1871-77 and 1881-86. The chief function of the parties, whether in times of stability or crisis, was to dispense patronage.

The Cortes functioned poorly. Meetings were turbulent and sometimes violent; personalities prevailed over ideas; governments rarely got the opportunity to execute their programs; election results were often disputed; there was heavy absenteeism among deputies; the opposition was rarely "loyal" and employed such tactics as obstructionism, abstention from key votes, unfair criticism, conspiracy, and libelous journalism in their newspapers; the parties lacked cohesion and even programs;[14] if the government in power had a majority in the Chamber of Deputies, it rarely had one also in the House of Peers unless the monarch used his prerogative of "creating" extra peers, who would belong to the majority party (fornada, "batch from oven," see Glossary).

A major mechanism for keeping the machinery of parliamentary government running was dissolving the Cortes, one of the monarch's moderating powers according to the 1826 Charter, which had been denied to the king in the 1822 Constitution. This power of dissolution was apparently borrowed from Article 50 of the French Constitutional Charter of 1814 and from the political theory of the French political thinker Benjamin Constant.[15] Two sets of figures, both incomplete, demonstrate that the monarchs used the dissolution power frequently. According to one estimate, there were forty-three parliamentary elections between 1834 and 1910 and the monarch dissolved the Cortes at least thirty and possibly as many as thirty-four times.[16] Another estimate suggests that there were forty-one legislatures between 1826 and 1900 and that of these only nine completed full terms in office and were not dissolved. During the twenty-eight-year reign of King Luís I (1861-89) alone, parliament was dissolved eleven times and twice in 1870.[17] What did dissolution accomplish? Before the establishment of a reasonably stable two-party system known as *rotativismo* (literally, the "rotational system") by 1871, the king often dismissed the parliament for obstructionism and opposition to reform programs. After 1871, however, the two major political parties rotated in office at fairly regular intervals, and when the king dissolved parliament before the end of its legal term, he was simply setting in motion the parliamentary process for transfer of power. When one party decided to leave office, whatever the reason —a lost vote in parliament, an incident or scandal, tired leadership, or lack of royal confidence in the leadership or program—the king dismissed the premier and nominated a new one from the other major party. This new government was then "granted" dissolution of parliament, elections were held, presided over, and invariably controlled by the newly appointed government. Because elections were rigged, this government was bound to receive a majority in the new parliament.

The artificiality of the system was a serious flaw. The growing centralization in Lisbon of power in government, politics, and administration created a gap between the people and the small circle of leaders. Government manipulation of local and national elections was a common practice. Rural areas had no voice except through a narrow patronage system based on local caciques. Caciquismo flourished. Local bosses "arranged" the local vote in return for such favors as money, exemption from the army, and jobs. Unlike parliamentary monarchy in Britain, where elections produced governments, in Portugal governments produced elections. The function of elections, then, was to ensure the government in power in Lisbon the majority of seats in the Cortes needed to continue in office and to execute legislative programs. In virtually all the parliamentary elections held between 1834 and 1910, with the exception of an election in 1870, the government in office, because it presided over the election, won a majority of seats in at least the Chamber of Deputies.

As the system of government and politics became increasingly discredited, the monarchy was undermined, because the person of the monarch and the institution of monarchy were intimately associated with the "system."[18] The two major parties which emerged as the chief beneficiaries of the rotativist system after 1871 were the Regenerators and Progressists. The Regenerators (Partido Regenerador) supported the 1826 Charter and the programs of economic development in the 1850s and 1860s. As the more royalist and conservative of the two parties, they dominated during the years 1851–56 and 1862–89.[19] The Progressists (Partido Progressista) were slightly more liberal. By 1890, however, the programs and policies of the two rotativist parties were virtually indistinguishable.[20] The heyday of this arrangement of "political musical chairs" was 1871–90, but both before and after that period political leaders spoke of the desirability of a stable, two-party arrangement along the same lines. After 1890, the political crisis worsened; foreign, colonial, and personal issues further weakened the system and the monarchy.

The financial plight of Portugal was at once separate from and part of the political crisis. A great deal of time and energy in government and politics were expended in discussing it and attempting to solve it. The disasters of 1807–34—an invasion, civil strife that developed into civil war, the loss of Brazil—greatly depleted Portugal's finances. Although some recovery occurred in 1851–56, succeeding decades produced almost constant budget deficits. By 1890 Portugal had a foreign debt that totaled over £140 million. In 1892 the Portuguese government was forced to declare bankruptcy. In 1902, with foreign creditors pressuring the government to act, Portugal again declared bankruptcy, and interest payments were reduced by an agreement with major creditors. By late 1905 the total debt, both external and internal, was over £187 million, and annual deficits ran to over £1 million. Such financial problems provided political opponents with handy ammunition to attack governments in power.[21] Some intellectuals considered the financial problem a danger to Portugal's independence. Portugal was once more "the sick man of the West," an epithet historian Oliveira Martins had used to describe it in the 1820s.[22]

As the financial situation worsened, it became a leading issue in politics. Financial weakness disillusioned many thinkers, and a growing pessimism among writers fed upon this crisis. The novelist Eça de Queiroz (1845–1900) could not resist commentary on the topic, and his satirical and cynical statements only glossed over an increasingly profound pessimism felt among the educated elite about Portugal's future. In his novel of 1880, *The Maias,* Eça de Queiroz has a character named Cohen discussing finance with a certain Carlos: "Loans in Portugal nowadays constitute one of the sources of revenue, as regular, as indispensable, as well known as taxation. . . . Bankruptcy is inevitable—like the answer to a sum!"[23]

If the financial crisis was serious, the moral crisis was probably worse. Even taking into account the exaggeration of the deep pessimism found in the writings of Oliveira Martins, Eça de Queiroz,[24] and others of the so-called "Generation of 1870," that graduated from Coimbra, Portugal's only university, it remains true that a widespread sense of crisis, frustration, and fear pervaded elite circles. This crisis was manifested in several ways: a desire among the Europeanized elite to see Portugal and the Portuguese restored to a portion of the greatness and

power enjoyed during the Era of the Discoveries, 1415-1550. This
desire was sometimes expressed in the term *ressurgimento*. In part it
was a search for fresh ideas and new leadership. Some turned to the
past to revive medieval heroes, while others sought reform in new
heroes with such modern ideologies as socialism, democracy, and anarchism. Many found their models in contemporary French society with
such political stalwarts as Léon Gambetta, or later, the socialist leader
Jean Jaurès.

Imbued with a sense of decadence, the more sensitive educated elite
felt trapped by Portugal's impotence. Increasingly disillusioned,
especially after the 1890 crisis, some Portuguese leaders sought escape
in suicide or in drug addiction. In his 1908 visit to Portugal the Spanish
writer-philosopher Miguel de Unamuno described the Portuguese as a
"suicidal people" bent on self-destruction out of frustration with their
plight.[25]

Suicide[26] and drug addiction were not the only routes of escape from
the financial disasters of the government and the stifling atmosphere of
political Lisbon. Self-expression, escape—and fortunes—could be had
in the Portuguese colonies in Africa or in spacious Brazil. Eça de
Queiroz's interesting character Gonçalo Mendes Ramires, in *The Illustrious House of Ramires,* sought to "escape" (from a stifling Portugal) to Africa. He symbolized several generations of Portuguese who
took this way out.[27] The list included Mousinho de Albuquerque, the
"hero of Africa," and a number of famous Republican politicians such
as António José de Almeida, once a physician on São Tomé in West
Africa.[28] From Brazil came other positive assistance for an ailing Portugal: revenue in the form of immigrants' remittances, and capital investment in Portuguese utilities, housing, and public buildings and
bridges helped prevent a complete financial collapse during the years
1850-1910. Revenue and trade from the African colonies, too, aided
both the soul and body of the Portuguese elite and the system. Especially prior to 1910, colonial revenue and trade made possible part of
the financing of basic industrial and commercial development in and
near Lisbon and Oporto.[29]

Analysis of the political, financial, and moral crises leads to the conclusion that the political system's functioning was at the heart of the
problem. The system was locked into a vicious circle from which
monarchists and Republicans sought release.[30] While Republicans, who
became significant in the system only after 1880, placed most of the
blame for the system's evils on the Church and the monarchy, many
groups of various political beliefs agreed that the parliamentary
political system infused with a Portuguese form of liberalism was the
major evil.[31] Many simplistic solutions were suggested: the defeat of in-

dividual politicians; expulsion of the king; replacing the monarchy with a republic;[32] a large foreign loan. The character in Eça de Queiroz's novel was perhaps not altogether facetious in suggesting "a Spanish invasion."[33]

An Ignored Remedy?

One set of suggested remedies came from the pen of a monarchist, a moderate civil servant–diplomat who had served Portugal abroad. In his book *Considerations of the Political Present and Future of Portugal,* D. G. Nogueira Soares analyzed the flaws in Portuguese liberalism.[34] It is significant that, writing in the early 1880s—well before the time when historians usually suggest the political system was in its final stages of decadence—he already considered the monarchy and the political system to be gravely damaged.[35]

To this Traditionalist thinker, the major evil in Portugal lay in the ignorance, apathy, and indifference of the masses (illiteracy was between 80 and 90 percent in his day), and in the activity of ambitious monarchist politicians, whose deeds tore down the Constitutional Monarchy. Personal attacks on the king's reputation were increasing along with factionalism. The press, consisting largely of daily and weekly newspapers in Lisbon and Oporto, reflected personal and partisan interests, and libelous and slanderous articles were rarely prosecuted in the courts of law. Administrators rigged elections. Under these conditions, no broadly based informed public opinion was possible.

Nogueira Soares made a number of serious suggestions for reform of government and politics in 1883: (1) Professionalize the civil service, remove it from partisan politics and extensive patronage, and punish in the courts of law the abuses of the civil service by political forces. (2) Draft a new reformed press law to defend the public against the press, "the most pernicious school of perversion and political demoralization,"[36] by prosecuting accused liars, libelers, and slanderers. (3) Disband the corrupt two-party system of rotativismo, and replace it with two large coalitions of liberals and conservatives with national bases broad enough to win honest elections. (4) Make new electoral laws to prohibit government interference in elections and to prevent rigging of elections; punish all officials such as civil governors, county administrators, and parish officials who attempted to corrupt elections. (5) Enforce new tax laws to enable the state to receive the revenue lost through the oligarchy's failure to pay taxes.[37]

This idealistic reformer wished to borrow useful political ideas from England, France, Spain, and Italy, but he was essentially a Traditionalist who admired the practices of pre-1850 Portugal as part of a golden age of honesty and justice. His harking back to what he termed, "the old and honored Portugal," to bring a ressurgimento to an ailing nation whose ancestors "first and furthest spread the faith and Christian civilization,"[38] betrayed his naiveté as well as his fundamental honesty. He urged his countrymen to adopt a system whereby the rule of law, not the rule of men, prevailed.

Few of Nogueira Soares's ideas of reform were seriously considered, much less adopted in law or in practice. His important book, however, marks the maturation of the political crisis.

Public attitudes toward politics and politicians represented one more manifestation of the total crisis. The conduct of government and politics became the subject of a general cynicism, public jokes, ridicule, and satire in cafés and in newspapers, journals, and books. Political satire was only one part of the broad canvas of Eça de Queiroz's satirization of the follies of the Portuguese middle classes, but it was a vital part.[39] In the apogee of the age of realism in the Portuguese novel, writers, essayists, and political cartoonists in the newspapers created new caricatures and new words to describe politicians and political activities. A deep and growing cynicism about politics was not obscured by the wit. The cartoonist Rafael Bordalo Pinheiro created the caricature of the Portuguese rural peasant (*Zé Povinho,* see Glossary), simple, honest, ignorant, and somewhat credulous.[40]

Then there was the vain, windy, and incompetent politician (*Conselheiro Acácio*).[41] His more vicious and powerful political counterpart, the important politician and oligarch without any scruples, was *Conde do Abranho.*[42] There were many words which ridiculed the superficial, cheap culture of the emerging middle classes, the *sebentismo,* and their hankering after easy office jobs in the civil-service patronage system (*empregomania, pedintismo, tubaronismo*). A whole set of words emphasized stereotypes of the pettiness of politicians and politics.

In 1889, as discredited pseudoparliamentarism eroded confidence in the monarchy, King Luís I died. He was succeeded by his son, Carlos I. This temperamental but shrewd monarch—once noted for his bullfighting ability—was well aware of the crisis. He noted in his personal diary in 1901 after closely observing the naval officer corps—one of the more exclusive of elite groups—that most naval officers were no longer monarchists, although they performed their duties well.[43] As Carlos was later quoted as saying, Portugal was becoming "a monarchy without monarchists."[44]

3 / Republicanization

> My Lord, I do not know what a Republic is, but it could
> not help but be a holy thing. Never even in Church have I
> felt such a fit of chills. I lost my head then, just like all
> the others . . . we all shouted together: *Viva, viva, viva a*
> *República!*
>
> Rebel soldier to judge in 1891 trial
> of Republican rebels in 30 January
> 1891 Oporto revolt.[1]

In the 1880s few considered the Republican party a major threat to the
monarchy. Nogueira Soares, in his thorough political survey, did not
take the Republicans very seriously.[2]

The Portuguese Republican party, Partido Republicano Português
(PRP), claimed that it offered a real alternative to the Constitutional
Monarchy. It suggested that Republican ideals, methods, and goals
would provide the necessary reforms for the national ressurgimento
which was desired by many Portuguese. What were the origins, beliefs,
and character of this Republican party? What was the process of the
republicanization of Portugal after the 1890 crisis, and the course of
politics during the reigns of the last two monarchs, 1889–1910? The
republicanization of Portugal was much more thorough, rapid, and intensive than in Spain. The Portuguese Republican experience was an interesting case of powerful propaganda influencing public opinion
through the press and oratory rather than by votes in elections and a
show of military strength. If the Republicans claimed that they offered
a true alternative to the monarchy, historians must ask what substance
there was to this claim.

The Republicans

Who were the Republicans? There is evidence to support Serrão's
judgment that republicanism was a vehicle of the urban petty bourgeoisie and the rural middle bourgeoisie in their struggle against the entrenched upper middle class, or *alta burguesia,* who dominated the
oligarchy of the Constitutional Monarchy, 1870–1910.[3] This must be

qualified, however, since some Republican party membership and general support came from other groups, including some rural peasants, and, initially, urban lower-class workers in the two cities and larger towns. Republicanism even found some support from the upper class—large landowners Bernardino Machado and José Relvas were major Republican leaders.[4] A few Republican leaders who reached high office, too, were the sons of monied peasants who aspired to the middle class. The majority of the Republican leaders, numbering perhaps a hundred, came from the lower middle class in the cities, born in the 1860s and 1870s (with some from earlier generations in the 1840s and 1850s). Few held high political office before 1910, but a number were experienced in politics. Many were lawyers from the university at Coimbra, or doctors, pharmacists, engineers, teachers, or journalists. Some were soldiers. The largely middle-class Republicans were usually graduates of or students in major city high schools in Lisbon and Oporto. Not all Republican leaders were born in Portugal. Some major figures such as Bernardino Machado, Miguel Bombarda and João Chagas were Brazilian-born, and the latter had Amerindian ancestry as well as Portuguese.[5]

The Republicans' intellectual style was heavily middle class and urban with a strong dose of French influence. Much admired was the French Third Republic, whose system many Portuguese Republicans wished to transplant to their country. There was a hardly concealed cultural mimicry and a good deal of intellectual superficiality. The Republican leadership which came into its own in the first decade of the twentieth century nevertheless contained many of the best educated persons in the country. Some, like Afonso Costa in law, Sidónio Pais in mathematics, Bernardino Machado in education and anthropology, and Miguel Bombarda in psychiatry, and later Egas Moniz in neurosurgery, were not only brilliant students in their generations at the university but were successful teachers and internationally known in their fields as pioneers and advanced practitioners.[6]

Republican ideology was indebted to the French positivist Comte and the socialist Proudhon.[7] In published Republican programs of 1876 and 1891, their ideology was democratic but also nationalistic. From an earlier Republican penchant for Iberian federalism and a more radical socialism, the ideology after 1891 featured municipal autonomy, political and economic democracy, universal male suffrage, direct elections for legislative assemblies, a national militia instead of a professional army, secularization of education, and the separation of Church and State.[8] In their analysis of the ills of Portugal, the Republicans placed great blame on the Catholic church and on the monarchy. Most striking about their ideology after 1890 is its inclusiveness and "vagueness,"[9] which attracted a variety of supporters. Its nonradical economic programs would not necessarily frighten capitalists, although socialist tendencies were always present. In its plea for a decentralization of administration the party allowed considerable freedom for free enterprise.

The party's ideas owed something also to Spanish Republican ideas and to the examples of recent Republican victories. Portuguese Republicans were encouraged by the establishment of the Third Republic in France (1870) and the Brazilian Republic (1889). French revolutionary traditions held a pervasive attraction for numbers of Portuguese Republicans and the 1789 Revolution was considered an inspiration and model. The manner in which the Republican party developed, including its organization and ideology, allowed it to avoid a narrow partisan appearance. By the turn of the century it had become not merely one more opposition party, but one which could attract followers from a variety of other groups as a "party of attraction and assimilation."[10]

The party included within its membership, and as its allies, other groups: secret societies and groups of socialists and anarcho-syndicalists who temporarily supported republicanism as a means of achieving change and ending the monarchy. A significant number of Republican leaders were members of Masonic orders in the cities and larger towns, and some were members of the secret society Carbonária. The Portuguese Carbonária secretly recruited revolutionary Republicans and played a role in organizing military conspiracies after 1907. Although it was technically under the control of the Directorate of the Republican party and was often led by Masons, the Carbonária, as a hard-core activist organ, became virtually a state within a state. It served as a small, secret "popular front," arranging at least the temporary cooperation and collaboration of a disparate group of anarchists, socialists, and radical Republicans. Its rituals were unusual and its discipline rigid, but its ideology was inclusive enough to allow a range of opinion, with anarchist tendencies, which agreed upon the common goal of overthrowing the monarchy. The Carbonária had some millenarian features which appealed to the messianic tendencies of those followers who may have viewed participation as a kind of substitute for religion.[11]

In 1897 a Carbonária group was established in a working-class sector of Lisbon, Alcântara; it called itself The Workers of the Future.[12] A new version of a republicanized Carbonária was founded in Lisbon in 1907 by Luz de Almeida, eventually the chief of the highest body within the group, the Alta Venda. Political repression during the Franco dictatorship (1906–8) encouraged the growth of such bodies. But it was unlikely that the Carbonária was, as monarchist die-hards later suggested, part of an international conspiracy. By the rules of the Carbonária only Portuguese could join, and initiates were obliged to pledge their lives for "the regeneration of the Portuguese fatherland."[13] Among the more nationalistic leaders of this important subgroup was naval commissary lieutenant António Machado Santos, who became a popular hero of the 1910 Revolution.[14]

If the Carbonária contributed to the success of the revolution, so did the atmosphere of working-class unrest and popular ferment in the cities and major towns, and the willingness of many Portuguese to support the changes. The Carbonária represented only a small part of a much larger movement: the politicization of the urban working class. More and more of a threat to the established system was the evolution of the Republican party into a well-organized mass organization with roots in rural and urban areas. Despite the defects of its leaders, the amorphous nature of its ranks, the oratorical hyperbole and failed promises, the Republican party was, from about 1890 to the end of the First Republic, the largest, best-organized and most electorally effective political party up to that point in Portuguese history. No other party or political group could rival it for size and efficiency. In modern history the only other party which can match it for longevity, efficiency, and grass-roots support—if not for the size of its following—is the Portuguese Communist party (founded in 1921), which survived underground for over forty years during the New State dictatorship.

The Republican party owed its growing support and size to many factors. As a coalition it combined various Republican-like tendencies and sympathies; its dynamic leaders were ceaselessly generating oratory, intensive press campaigns, pamphleteering, public meetings, lectures, and electoral and parliamentary activity. The following list indicates the growth of Republican representation in the monarchy's Cortes. (The sources for this list are given under table 1.)

Election Year	Number of Republican Deputies Seated
1878	1 (Oporto)
1892	3
1906	4 (Lisbon)
1908	7 (4 Lisbon; 2 Setúbal; 1 Aljustrel)
1910	14 (11 from Lisbon alone)

How can Republican successes be explained? The Republicans were very well organized in rural and urban areas, though support was more urban than rural. After 1904 the party underwent a reorganization as its

TABLE 1

Portuguese Republican Party Organization on Eve of 1910 Revolution

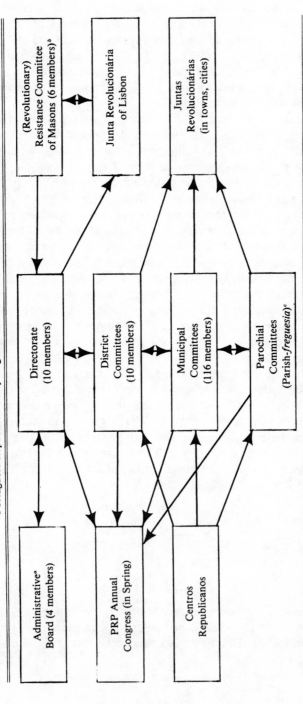

Sources: A. H. de Oliveira Marques, *A Primeira República Portuguesa* (Lisbon, 1972), pp. 130–31; David Ferreira, *História Política da Primeira República Portuguesa (1910–1915)*, 2 vols. (Lisbon, 1973), 2:16–17; Ferreira, "Partido Republicano Português," *DHP*, 3:602; António Maria da Silva, *O Meu Depoimento*, vol. 1, *Da Monarquia a 5 de Outubro de 1910* (Lisbon, 1974), pp. 259–62.

[a] Elected triannually until 1912, biannually afterwards.

[b] Two members nominated to represent Resistance Committee on PRP Directorate June 1910.

[c] Out of total 3,921 parishes in Portugal, 242 had parochial committees.

leadership was linked with *centros republicanos,* which acted as recruitment areas, and *juntas revolucionárias,* or shadow governments to follow a Republican takeover, in nearly every village, town, parish from north to south. These were the local, important organizations at three levels: district, municipal, and parish (see table 1). The PRP had about 370 committees with a total committee membership of perhaps three thousand. After 5 October 1910 in nearly every population settlement in the country, not only did local Republican agents proclaim the republic, seconding Lisbon, but local Republican juntas, appointed before the revolution, immediately assumed power of local government. These juntas then dispensed offices and appointments without any pretense of public election.[15]

Republican victories and representation were insignificant until the elections of 1906 when, despite the attempts of the government in office to manipulate votes for a government sweep,[16] four Republican deputies from Lisbon were elected. Harassed by government authorities, Republicans could not win a majority, but they participated actively, contesting in legal cases the seating of monarchist deputies. Out of a total of over two hundred Cortes seats under the monarchy, the party never won more than fourteen seats (August 1910), and these came mainly from Lisbon, the center of Republican support. After the final election before the Republican revolution, the king adjourned parliament to give attention to court cases concerning election-rigging: over half the seats were challenged by the Republicans.

The Republican party owed much of its success in winning public support, especially in the capital and in Oporto, to its political propaganda and verbal attacks on the monarchy. In Republican history, in fact, the era of 1890–1910 is often known in the Portuguese language as "the era of propaganda," meaning antimonarchical, Republican argumentation.[17] The outpourings of the Republican newspapers, pamphlets, political cartoons, poems, songs, public lectures, and meetings were prodigious. The volume alone was remarkable for a small country with widespread illiteracy (estimated to be 79 percent in 1906), poverty, and relative backwardness compared with most of Western Europe. More remarkable still was the nature of the argumentation which helped to rapidly undermine support for the monarchy and for the monarchist establishment. It must surely rank as one of the most scurrilous, derisive, unfair, yet shrewd and canny public-opinion campaigns in Western political history.

Why was the Republican propaganda—much of it so simplistic—so devastating? Monarchist weaknesses provide one answer: monarchists were increasingly fragmented and demoralized after the 1890 crisis.

Their parties were not as active or as well organized as the PRP, despite the rigging of elections by civil authorities, and they increasingly lost control of the majority of the press and the sympathy of the public.

One gauge of success for the Republican propaganda was the response of the press. Between 1890 and 1910 nearly all the major newspapers of Lisbon and Oporto, including the major daily *O Século* of Lisbon, became either openly Republican, pro-Republican, or neutral but hostile to monarchist politics. Especially after 1895, even in the provincial press, which remained largely conservative, Republican sympathy had greatly increased. Most papers abandoned open support of the major monarchist parties and expressed cynicism and resentment concerning monarchist politics. The Catholic press urged immediate reforms. The growing press tendency to call for political "neutrality" gave the Republicans a clear advantage in their campaign to achieve power.[18]

As republicanism unceasingly emphasized colonialism in Africa and democracy and anticlericalism at home, it appealed greatly to the middle and lower classes in urban areas. The validity of many antimonarchist arguments was less important than their impact upon their audience. In his memoirs Republican politician Francisco Cunha Leal suggests that "the idea of the republic" became a "myth,"[19] a messianic idea which like a panacea appealed to both the illiterate and the partially literate, that is, most of Portugal, which, in 1910, had a population of 5,500,000. Infused with nationalism, Republican appeals were part of a general public feeling for ressurgimento. To many the "republic" was a remedy for a sick country, a fourth-rate power aspiring to a higher station among nations. To those concerned with progress, it was "a leap forward," *O salto em frente,*[20] in an era of general disillusionment.

Urban masses, locked into severe poverty and drudgery, became enthused over the idea of a mythical future republic which would solve all problems. No quantitative evidence from public-opinion surveys exists, but some revealing glimpses of lower-class feelings and attitudes have turned up. Family memoirs tell of a not atypical housemaid in Lisbon, one Rosa Ramos Pereira, who fought as a civilian combatant in the 1910 Revolution. Later she proudly posed for a photograph holding a bayonet and pistol. This modest day maid (*mulher-a-dias*) was a Republican, she claimed, because she sincerely believed that a republic would give her class a voice and that it would result in a "redeemed Portugal."[21] In the novels of Eça de Queiroz, which depicted Portuguese contemporary life, are sympathetic portraits of working-class men who were Republicans. In *The Maias* (1880) there is a fond description of a working-class foreman, "Senhor Vicente," a Republican, who dreamed that Portugal would be "free" once Republicans chartered a ship on which to deport the royal family and the "stupid" politicians.[22] Thus Republicanism represented for a variety of Portuguese a "Republican Sebastianism," which was especially effective in winning support for the party among uneducated masses. It was effective, too, among some sectors of the urban elite who believed that Portugal was in a crisis which might result in the loss of her African colonies, greater degradation among European states, and even a possible loss of independence to Spain. While the dangers facing Portugal were exaggerated by writers and speakers, many underrated the strength of the Republican party and republicanism, and many failed to note the growing importance of the popular idea and myth of a future, wondrous republic.[23]

Republican attacks on the monarchy were not fair but they became increasingly effective, precisely because they were so outrageous. The personalist nature of politics was both a cause and symptom of the style and finesse with which Republicans attacked the person of the monarch and the institutions. In a session in the Chamber of Deputies in the Cortes in November 1906, the newly elected Republican deputy-orator Afonso Costa won the admiration of many Republicans and some monarchists when he attacked King Carlos I on the issue of monetary advances made to the royal house from the government budget. He gave a speech which contained the following passage: "For many fewer crimes than those committed by D. Carlos I, the head of Louis XVI rolled on the scaffold in France!"[24] When Costa refused to retract this statement, the president of the Chamber censured him and had him expelled bodily (by soldiers) from the Chamber for a month.[25] In a public speech of 2 December 1906, the Republican poet Guerra Junqueira referred to the king, who was increasingly obese, as a "pig" who tyrannized a people. Junqueira was arrested, prosecuted, and fined for this public speech in 1907.[26] Finally, a popular journal of cartoons, Os Ridículos, in 1909 depicted the Portuguese Everyman, Zé Povinho, urinating on a tombstone of some monarchist politicians; the tombstone engraving read, "Here Lies the Shame of Portuguese Politics."[27]

A Crisis Atmosphere

The Republicans' militant activity was effective because of the atmosphere of crisis. Especially in the urban areas, the lower classes were increasingly dissatisfied. An idyllic, pastoral view of Portugal in 1910, like that given by monarchist defender Ramalho Ortigão, is largely a

mystification. On the day of the 1910 Revolution, Ortigão wrote, in all
of Portugal, "there was no despotism, there was no oppression, there
was no hunger."[28] On the contrary, living and working conditions
among the urban poor were worsening during the final decade of the
monarchy. Rapid and intensive urbanization of Lisbon and Oporto led
to overcrowding, hunger, and terrible living conditions for the urban
peasant, sometimes recently arrived from the countryside. Between
1890 and 1911, the populations of both Lisbon and Oporto grew by
nearly 50 percent. The economic slump inflicted on the poor rising costs
for food and lodging, and an abnormally high incidence of such diseases as pellagra, gastroenteritis, and tuberculosis.[29] Urban workers'
wages lagged behind rising prices, and the working day was twelve to
fourteen hours. Though rural conditions were perceived as less desperate, the rural peasant (*camponeses*) worked seventeen to eighteen
hours a day, were paid starvation wages, and often had to rely on communitarian practices such as pooling of income, resources, and food
among villagers, as well as from the more kindly patrons and landowners. In July 1910 the writer Raúl Brandão, a keen observer of urban
conditions, suggested that the increasing lower-class agitation in Lisbon
was directly linked to the rising cost of living.[30]

There were other manifestations of the socioeconomic crisis. As was
traditional in Portuguese society, an increase in emigration to Brazil, or
to other countries, was an expression of worsening or uncertain
economic conditions. As shown in the following figures, there was a
significant increase in Portuguese emigration after 1886.[31]

Year	Number of Emigrants
1886	13,998
1887	16,932
1893	30,383
1895	44,746
1905	33,610
1906	38,093
1907	41,950
1908	40,145
1909	38,223
1910	39,515

Strikes and labor disputes increased in the same period and Portuguese workers in the towns became more militant. Strikes were illegal
under the monarchy, and the government called out the police and the
army to repress them. Especially after 1900 clashes between workers,
police, and the Municipal Guard (*Guarda Municipal*), an arm of the
government in Lisbon and Oporto, became common.[32]

The political crisis took a new turn just after King Carlos assumed the throne in late 1889. In January 1890 there was a popular, national outcry against Britain's ultimatum to Portugal concerning the clash of interests in Central Africa. Britain threatened to sever relations with her oldest ally, Portugal, in order to force the weaker nation to withdraw an armed expedition from Nyasaland, Central Africa. Defeated in an attempt to expand colonial sovereignty into that sector, Portugal's government recalled the expedition and resigned. Crowds in the larger towns became hysterical with rage, and there was a wave of vandalism, crime, personal attacks on British citizens, boycotts, public subscription funds for arms, and calls for a declaration of war on Britain. The effect of the crisis was to rally support for the Republicans and weaken the monarchy.[33] But the Ultimatum was only the beginning of a series of financial, colonial, and political disasters for the king. Despite Carlos's intent to execute meaningful reform in Portugal, his efforts were largely undermined by monarchist inefficiency, incompetence, factionalism, and Republican propaganda.

The Ultimatum episode encouraged some Republicans to plan armed conspiracies. Up to 1890–91, most Republicans advocated legal, peaceful means of changing regimes from monarchy to republic. The Oporto 1891 abortive coup was an important precedent and episode. Led by young Oporto journalist João Chagas, some Republicans in that city, against the wishes of most of the Lisbon Directorate of the Republican party, called for a revolution and attempted to organize a military rebellion among Oporto armed forces. Chagas's plot failed, as his group could not win over more than three junior officers and some sergeants and enlisted men. Within hours—after a dramatic proclamation of the republic at city hall and the naming of a provisional government—the Republicans' cause collapsed.

Because the government feared a hostile public reaction to harsh sentences, the rebels were, with the exception of three officers, amnestied by King Carlos after only two years.[34] Since Portuguese law forbade capital punishment,[35] no conspirator was executed.

The pronunciamento tradition was revived among radical Republicans beginning in 1891, and in other plots in 1895, 1896, 1901, 1906, 1908, and two in the summer of 1910, Republicans attempted and failed to foment rebellion among army and navy units, primarily in Lisbon and Oporto.[36] The monarchy's security system, especially the Guarda Municipal and the army, thwarted these plots. It was clear from the history of such attempts by 1910 that the Republicans could overthrow the monarchy only if they won over most of the units in the capital, and that they could not do this unless they republicanized more of the officer corps, or at least neutralized a good portion of it. The ranks were increasingly Republican, especially among naval units, but respect for authority was such that only Republican officers could add the victory touch.

The political crisis became more obvious after 1890 as the monarchy's rotativist system began to disintegrate. Among monarchist politicians personal and factious disputes burgeoned. New opposition parties arose which challenged monarchist assumptions, and some rightist groups became neutral on the issue of the regime: monarchy or republic? Some called for reforms which the major monarchist parties could not put into effect because of the unwillingness of the supportive oligarchy to endanger personal revenues, positions, and power. The revival of reformist Catholicism and praetorian monarchism on the Right further complicated the political crisis. A conservative movement composed of elite intellectuals, soldiers, nobles and churchmen rejected both republicanism and liberal monarchism. It included the famous monarchist Major Mousinho de Albuquerque, who proposed a new dynamic militarist monarchy which would sweep out Republicans by repression and reform. He advocated an increased role in politics for the officer corps of the army and navy and called for a military dictatorship, presided over by a strong King Carlos.[37] There was also a new conservative Catholic party, the Partido Nacionalista, founded and headed by Jacinto Cândido da Silva in 1901, which advocated decentralization of administration, a balanced budget, no more loans, and a strong Catholic role. It was neutral on the issue of monarchy or republic and later claimed that it was never truly a monarchist party. Finally, there was a private Catholic group, Centro Académico de Democracia Cristã (CADC), originally a Coimbra University student group, which advocated a revitalized Catholicism and reform of politics and government.[38] Many of the arguments of these largely Traditionalist thinkers were founded on their belief that Portugal's contemporary weakness was based primarily upon social disintegration, moral laxity, and the breakdown of Portuguese tradition before excessive Europeanization. These groups were especially concerned about developing and keeping Portugal's African colonies as part of a program of national revival and a return to the lost glory of the Era of the Discoveries.

The monarchy, too, participated in the colonial revival of the post-Ultimatum years. The king was aware that the Republicans exploited any colonial setbacks by blaming them on the monarchy. Yet the king carefully supported colonial efforts through his work with the Society of Geography of Lisbon, founded in 1875. The Portuguese officer corps was also strongly linked with colonial activity in Africa since the Angola and Mozambique campaigns to conquer claimed territory provided welcome training, promotions, income, and personal glory.[39]

After the splintering of the major monarchist parties in 1901, the political crisis reached a new stage. Former minister Cândido da Silva and some friends split from the Regenerators to form his Nationalists that year. João Franco and his political friends also broke away and formed a new party, the Liberal Regenerators. In 1905 the Progressists suffered the defection of Deputy João de Alpoim, who formed the Dissident Progressists.[40] It soon became impossible to form noncoalition cabinets that could win a majority of Cortes seats. The parties increasingly pressured King Carlos to dissolve the Cortes in order to give them electoral opportunities. Carlos reasserted his royal prerogatives by refusing to use this power at monarchist request. By 1906 parliament almost did not function because passionate arguments interrupted all business and obstructed legislation.

Dictatorship and Regicide

The political dilemma facing Carlos was agonizing. As the Republican writer João Falcão wrote earlier, in 1891: "There is only one remedy, and this remedy must come from the revolution. Either revolution made by the king or the revolution made by the people."[41] Carlos knew that a reassertion of the poder moderador would anger Republicans and that a weakening of royal power would alienate many monarchists. The Constitution gave him considerable power, but he hesitated to use it because of the growing unpopularity of his exercise of royal authority.

In May 1906 King Carlos appointed João Franco as premier. Franco's plans were admirable but the opposition became unmanageable. In early 1907, having promised earlier to work with the Cortes, Franco dismissed it sine die, censored the press, jailed oppositionists and began to put his reforms into law by decree. These reforms at first involved a decentralization of government, a program which stole thunder from the Right and from the Republicans. Franco's administrative dictatorship marked the beginning of the end for the monarchy, since it aroused so much hostility and violence in urban areas.

Franco's dictatorship earned the monarchy and the king great unpopularity among Republicans, won over more monarchists to republicanism, and failed to bring needed reform. The financial crisis, for example, remained serious. Some of the last supporters of the monarchy among the oligarchy were alienated by the unconstitutional acts of both Franco and Carlos during 1907–8.[42] What the public did not know was that Carlos planned a Brazilian trip in May 1908 to garner political support and perhaps funds from the large monarchist community of Portuguese emigrants in Brazil. Carlos began to base his plans for reform on the success of this trip.[43]

The king never took that trip. A Republican plot was discovered by Franco's police on 28 January 1908, and after widespread arrests and jailings of Republican leaders and some monarchists, Franco made the king sign a decree ordering the deportation to the colonies of the political prisoners indicted. A Carbonária plot planned to murder Franco, but when the conspirators could not locate him at his home they sought the king, who was returning from a vacation in the Bragança estates at Vila Viçosa. On the afternoon of 1 February 1908, Carbonária bullets killed both Carlos and his eldest son, the crown prince. The regicide mortally wounded the monarchy, although public sympathy for the royal family was much more widespread than later was popularly believed. At the State funeral thousands of Portuguese peasants mourned and in a confused moment panicked and ran, causing several persons to be trampled to death.[44] Although the two murderers were killed on the spot, other known conspirators disappeared and the murder investigation, mysteriously, was never completed.

Carlos's second son, Manuel II, barely eighteen, ascended a throne more an "orphan than an heir."[45] Franco was dismissed and went into exile in Spain. But despite good intentions, some modern ideas, and his appointment of conciliatory premiers in the remaining two-and-a-half unstable years of the monarchy, Manuel could neither resolve major problems nor save the throne. The loss of the assertive if temperamental King Carlos was decisive, and his young son was both unprepared and poorly advised. The increasingly vociferous opposition considered him a nonentity. Widespread public sympathy for the royal family briefly weakened Republican inroads, but within a year of the tragedy of February 1908, harassed young Manuel, backed up by his unpopular French mother, Queen Amélia, was making little progress in turning back Republican attacks. Manuel's appointment of a renowned French sociologist to study living conditions in Portugal was a promising act, but there was no time to act upon Leon Poinsard's interesting findings.[46]

Conspiracies, 1908–10

The republicanization of Portugal became especially rapid after the regicide. Monarchists grew steadily more demoralized, and, despite the constitutional support for royal power,[47] Manuel's authority was weak. The Carbonária and republicanism won over numbers of soldiers and sailors in the ranks of the armed forces. More prominent monarchists joined the Republican party, and plans for reform and counterrevolution became increasingly impossible to execute. A major factor in Republican success was the control of the municipal government of the capital. In the 1908 elections the Republican party won control of the town hall or municipal government—the heart of the political system and the site of the government. Entrenched in Lisbon and its suburbs, the Republicans could control the major transportation nexus. With strong footing in the civil services, too, Republicans had an effective intelligence network. Royalty felt less secure in their palaces. Queen Amélia preferred to avoid using telephones while conferring with ministers since, she feared, even the telephone operator was a Carbonário.[48]

Time was running short for the monarchists. Last-minute plans and plots soon became historical curiosities. In vain King Manuel planned to counter Republican inroads in the working classes by collaborating with the small Socialist party. Teixeira de Sousa, the last monarchist premier, hoped to outflank the Republicans' anticlericalism with advanced anticlerical measures of his own; the day before the revolution began he signed a decree which put severe restrictions upon the Jesuit order.[49] Other monarchists, including the marquis of Soveral, Portugal's minister in London and a close friend of King Edward VII's, favored a military dictatorship. Some advocated requesting official British intervention to save the throne from a Republican takeover. British observers, however, were reluctant to commit themselves to supporting this monarchy, an institution they saw as tainted by the 1908 regicide and by the government's precipitous dismissal of Premier Franco. In August 1910 Republican representatives were unofficially informed during a visit to the Foreign Office that the alliance was between nations not regimes and that British intervention was out of the question.[50]

Even Spanish aid for the shaky throne was contemplated. In a little-publicized visit to Spain in the spring of 1910, a disconsolate, tearful Queen Amélia pleaded with the Spanish premier for armed intervention to save the Braganças.[51]

If the monarchist cause was increasingly desperate, the Republicans were growing impatient to take power. Republican party leadership was divided on the means of overthrowing the monarchy. Some still desired an evolutionary, electoral process. Others wanted a decisive break with the past in a revolutionary coup. The results of the August 1910 general elections gave new ammunition to the revolutionary advocates. Out of a total of over 200 seats in the Cortes, the Republicans won only 14 and it was clear that although Lisbon was mainly Republican, the monarchist cacique system of rigging elections remained intact in the rural provinces. No early Republican victory at the polls was possible.

Other factors favored the conspiracy of the revolutionary group of Republicans. An atmosphere of growing violence, passion, and confusion began to influence Republican plans. Beginning in August a wave of rural agitation and violence and a series of strikes took place in the larger towns and in Lisbon and Oporto. Continuing into October, especially in central and southern Portugal, these strikes threatened to lead to a general social explosion.[52] The monarchist establishment and even moderate Republicans feared that a general working-class uprising was about to occur. Republican leaders began to worry that if labor got out of control, the moderate, middle-class revolution they dreamed of would be endangered. If this occurred, the Republican party's main base in the two cities, the lower middle class, would become alienated.

Student radical republicanism added to the Republicans' anxiety. Republicanism had made important gains among high school and university students. Student membership in organizations of Masons and Carbonária grew rapidly. In some respects students between the ages of fifteen and twenty were the most ardent revolutionaries and formed the vanguard of republicanism in Lisbon, Oporto, and in Coimbra. At Coimbra University, students attacked both the antiquated educational system and the monarchy. Superimposed upon the traditional student romanticism, rowdiness, and antiestablishment pranksterism, was a new fervent republicanism among a significant minority of students. The Republican poet, Guerra Junqueira, undoubtedly with student approval, wrote that in order to bring some light to crusty, old Coimbra, it was first necessary to put the place to the torch.[53]

The final decisive factors that brought about revolutionary action were the pressures from the naval ranks in the Lisbon area and the work of the highly organized Masons and Carbonária.[54] In June 1910 the Masons elected a Committee of Resistance which elected two key representatives to the Directorate of the Republican party and which metamorphosed into the Junta Revolucionária of Lisbon, the group that actually planned the coup of October. This disciplined organization prodded the Directorate to support a coup and to use their large cache of imported arms and the republicanized ranks of army and navy personnel in Lisbon.[55]

Aware of some of the plots, the government prepared to oppose an armed conspiracy in which workers were expected to play a large part. Some observers feared civil war.

The rapid republicanization of certain sectors of Portuguese society was the result of both Republican activism and monarchist failure. A serious part of this failure was the oligarchy's refusal to allow meaningful reform. Evidence of substance to the Republicans' promises was lacking but the acceptance of the idea of a republic extended beyond the urban areas into the countryside. Young Manuel II's brief reign was a parenthesis, a largely defensive last act of the monarchy which began with a shocking regicide. The monarchy's position had become too intimately tied to the bad reputation of monarchist politics and politicians. As one premier wrote to King Manuel in 1908 concerning the inner workings of politics: ". . . each one [monarchist politician] wants to use the king for his own private purposes" (". . . cada um quer o Rei para seu uso").[56]

4 / The Fifth of October

The struggle is over! Now there are no enemies! Today all Portuguese, exchanging fraternal embraces, will collaborate in the work for the regeneration of the Fatherland! There are no more enemies now! There are only brothers!

António Machado Santos[1]

The First Portuguese Republic began with an unusual pronunciamento. On 5 October 1910, a popularly based revolution which concentrated in the Lisbon area resulted in the overthrow of the Portuguese monarchy. After brief fighting, this revolution led to the expulsion of the Bragança dynasty, which had ruled Portugal since 1640. The final Republican conspiracy was laid in meetings in September and early October. The plan was to foment a revolution in Lisbon, the capital and the First Military Region, by causing infiltrated—so-called compromised—army regiments of the garrison to revolt, commandeering the big naval vessels in the harbor, and attacking and defeating the remaining loyal units. The revolutionaries thought they had firm commitments from the First Artillery, Fifth Infantry, Sixteenth Infantry, Second Infantry, Second Lancers, Fifth Caçadores ("chasseurs"), and Second Caçadores to support the republic.[2]

Presumably the day set for the revolution was either in the middle or at the end of October. The government apparently expected it on 13 October, which was the anniversary of the execution of the Spanish radical martyr Francisco Ferrer, a date revered by Republicans.[3] It has been suggested that the appointed day was to be at the end of October.[4] The outbreak of violence on 3 October, therefore, was a surprise not only to monarchists but to many Republicans as well.

The conspiracy did not go according to plan for many unexpected reasons, the first of which was the assassination of a high Republican leader, Dr. Miguel Bombarda, on the afternoon of 3 October, by an insane man who was one of his patients. This sensational news, coupled with rumors that the patient was "a reactionary monarchist," prompted the gathering of unruly crowds of *populares* (the pro-Republican, street people), who throughout the evening of the third

48

threatened violence against anyone or anything that symbolized the monarchy. Among the objects of the crowd's wrath were priests in the streets and the Catholic newspaper *Portugal*. By 8:00 P.M. all government security forces were on alert, and an order had been sent to two vessels anchored in the harbor to depart for the Atlantic islands. Such an order, which put the ships out of reach of the Republicans, had frustrated revolutionary action in the August plot.[5]

The Bombarda assassination precipitated the revolution; the conspirators felt they had to act. The final revolutionary meeting occurred at 8:00 P.M., 3 October on Rua da Esperança (Hope Street). The signal for action was to be cannon fire from naval vessels in the Tagus harbor at 1:00 A.M. (4 October). Scattered firing was heard at this hour, but in distant sections of Lisbon some revolutionaries failed to hear the signal and became disheartened. The military leader of the conspiracy, retired Rear Admiral Cândido dos Reis, believing that the revolution had failed, promptly committed suicide.[6] Even Republican conspirators were taken by surprise by the popular response to news of Bombarda's murder. But, in the meantime, at Alcântara, a working-class section of Lisbon, revolutionary sailors attacked and took the navy barracks. Between 1:00 A.M. and 2:00 A.M., a group of populares, many of whom were members of the Carbonária and Grandella warehouse workers, rushed the barracks of the Sixteenth Infantry Regiment and took them with only light casualties. Led by naval officer Machado Santos (later known as the "Founder of the Republic"), the armed civilians and the pro-Republican soldiers (150 men in the regiment refused to oppose the monarchy) proceeded to attack monarchist positions in the city. Meanwhile at Campolide, just outside Lisbon, the Republican Captain Afonso Pala had aroused most of the First Artillery to revolt. At about the same time, the crews of the cruisers *S. Rafael* and *Adamastor* joined the revolutionaries and later helped to overwhelm the largest naval cruiser nearby, the *D. Carlos,* whose officers had prevented its crew from revolting.[7]

Despite the groundwork of the Carbonária, only two units, the Sixteenth Infantry and First Artillery, actually fulfilled their commitments to revolt. The other compromised units remained neutral or supported the monarchy during most of the fighting.[8]

The fighting was characterized by little movement and maneuver but considerable small-arms fire and shelling. Two columns from the First Artillery marched, one toward Necessidades Palace, where it hoped to capture King Manuel, and the other to Carmo Square in order to attack and subdue the major unit of Guarda Municipal, by reputation the bulwark of the monarchist security forces in both Lisbon and Oporto.

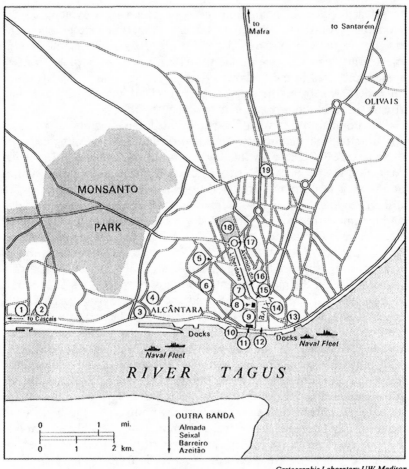

Lisbon, 1910

1 Jerónimos Church	11 Navy arsenal
2 Belém Palace	12 Comércio Square (Paço Square)
3 Navy barracks, Alcântara	13 Santa Apolónia Railway Station
4 Necessidades Palace	14 São Jorge Castle
5 Rato Square	15 Rossio Square
6 São Bento parliament building	16 Restauradores Square
7 Rossio Station	17 Rotunda crossroads (now Marquês
8 Carmo Square (GNR barracks)	de Pombal Square)
9 Câmara Municipal (town hall)	18 Edward VII Park
10 Cais do Sodré Station	19 Bullring at Campo Pequeno

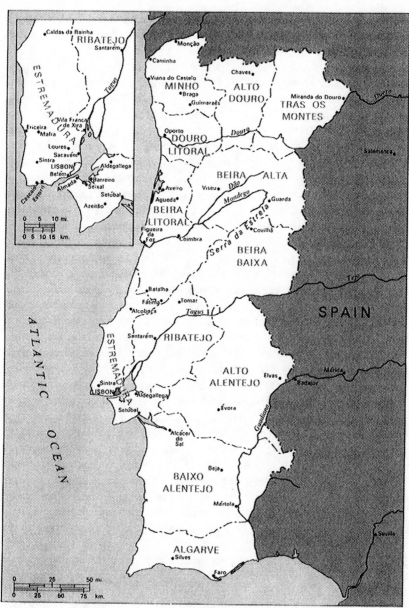

Portugal

Cartographic Laboratory UW-Madison

Having failed to accomplish either mission, both columns ended up at
Rotunda, a large crossroads on a commanding hill at the top of the major Avenida da Liberdade.

Rotunda became a focal point for much of the fighting. The revolutionary nucleus made up of civilians and troops from the two
"republicanized" units numbered no more than 400 to 450 men; they
remained entrenched in this encampment—although later reinforced by
populares—until after 5 October. The monarchists attacked Rotunda
and tried in vain to dislodge the Republicans. The government also
failed to prevent the landing of revolutionary sailors and arms at points
along the main harbor. With the aid of the Carbonária, the Republicans during 4 October cut off nearly all telephone and telegraph communications as well as most train service between Lisbon and the
provinces; railroad tracks outside Lisbon were sabotaged.[9]

Loyal monarchist officers later criticized the actions of the government forces. Henrique Paiva Couceiro, colonial hero, monarchist, and
one of the few officers who fought bravely for the king in 1910, pointed
out that the regime had failed to use loyal cavalry units against the
Republicans and that no concerted attack had been made against the
Rotunda. Manuel Gomes da Costa, another talented and loyal monarchist, then absent from Lisbon on colonial duty in Mozambique,
boasted grandly in his memoirs that he could have destroyed the revolution at the Rotunda with only one loyal regiment.[10]

By the evening of 4 October, the Republican forces at Rotunda and
at the Alcântara naval barracks held fast. At about 11:00 A.M. the two
republicanized vessels had begun to shell the Necessidades Palace, the
living quarters of the king. At 1:00 P.M., King Manuel left the palace
by car for Mafra, a town some twenty miles northwest of Lisbon. Yet
even at this juncture, it appears that the government forces still held the
initiative.[11] The Republican troops were heavily outnumbered and
outgunned; and the Guarda Municipal, if unaggressive, remained loyal.
Moreover, the government had ordered army reinforcements to march
to Lisbon from the area of Santarém, and it was supposed that they
were on their way. Counting monarchist units such as the Guarda
Fiscal, the civil police, and the regular forces of the Lisbon garrison,
the monarchy had over 3,500 troops to fight barely 450 Republicans.[12]
This calculation, however, fails to take into account many armed
people of the streets—the populares—inspired by Republican and Carbonária propaganda. It is clear that lower-class Lisbon by 1910 was
largely pro-Republican and that arms and bombs were available.
Monarchist forces were fully aware of the prevailing mass hostility to
the monarchy. Few monarchists were willing to risk their lives.[13]

It was obvious why so many monarchists refused to support the government openly. Large groups of the lower class, some of them rural peasant types, were roaming the capital's streets. One eyewitness observed a "pseudoregiment" of "barefoot women, little boys and ragged men. All of them carried sticks, pitchforks and rifles at the ready. . . . Some women carried sabers in their belts. All of them sang the hymn of 'Maria da Fonte,' with force and glee. On their faces was stamped 'hope.' "[14] This perceptive witness—a Portuguese actress— later wrote that she was certain that these peasants did not know what a republic was. To her, in the free-for-all, plebeian atmosphere of 5 October, the situation resembled more the traditional celebration of St. Anthony's Day (13 June) than a political revolution.[15]

By the evening of 4 October, then, it was clear that—save by a miracle—the government could not defeat the revolutionaries. Most of the armed forces in Lisbon were, in effect, neutral. Several factors kept them from actively attacking the Republicans. Within every so-called loyal regiment, any offensive military activity was severely restricted by both internal conflicts and external pressures. There were conflicts between monarchist officers, who were still in command, and Republican partisans led by a Carbonária-planted "revolutionary commission" often consisting of Republican sergeants—the backbone of many barracks revolts—and a few junior officers. Field-rank officers attempted to prevent the sergeants and lieutenants from organizing the ranks to fight for the republic. Officers had all they could do to hold the potential rebels in check, much less take the offensive against the revolutionaries. A case in point is the ineffectiveness of the Fifth Infantry Regiment assigned on 4 October the mission of patrolling the streets at the lower end of Rossio Square. A "revolutionary commission" of seventeen corporals, twenty sergeants, and sixteen junior officers tried in vain to get enlisted men from this regiment to join the revolutionaries at Rotunda. Monarchist units prevented this by blocking their way out of the square.[16] Nevertheless, this regiment played no effective role in defending the monarchy. A recent study suggests that the neutrality of most of the army, leading to defeat and surrender, might be termed *retraimento* ("abstention").

Neutralization of monarchist forces in Lisbon was further caused by external pressures from the lower classes of Lisbon. The populares, who not only harassed the troops but also threw bombs and fired their rifles and pistols, played a vital role in that they tied down monarchist forces. Some units, such as the Fifth Caçadores, surrendered, not to official Republican leaders, but "to the people."[17]

By early morning on the fifth, the monarchist reinforcements from

Santarém had not arrived in Lisbon, the Rotunda was still in Republican hands, and the monarchist forces in positions in the major downtown squares of Rossio and Restauradores were largely inactive. King Manuel and his family, having left Lisbon, were at Mafra awaiting news of the Lisbon fighting. At 2:00 P.M. the king learned that the republic had been proclaimed and that his troops had surrendered. At about 4:00 P.M. he and his family embarked on the royal yacht at Ericeira, a seacoast village near Mafra. Convinced at first that he could proceed to Oporto, where he hoped to find loyalist armed forces, Manuel was soon persuaded that his cause was hopeless. He boarded a British vessel at Gibraltar for exile in England.[18]

The final act in the drama at Lisbon ended in a peculiar misunderstanding. Following the account in the Barcelos history, Livermore suggests that this event was a decisive one,[19] but much evidence refutes this. The German chargé d'affaires, early on the fifth, requested that commanders in Lisbon declare a truce in order to allow foreign residents safely to leave the scene of the fighting. When a white flag was raised from the government headquarters at Almada Palace to signify the onset of the truce, the revolutionary forces, both military and populares, interpreted the gesture to mean that the monarchists were surrendering. Fraternization between troops of both sides followed, and Machado Santos led his forces into the government headquarters exactly one minute before the truce was to begin officially at 8:45 A.M. The government commanders surrendered. On first examination, the surrender appears to have been gratuitous, if not the result of a clever ruse. Contemporary accounts, however, pay little attention to this incident, since the major monarchist units were in the process of surrendering *before* the truce went into effect, and monarchist demoralization was widespread after the king left Lisbon. An hour-by-hour report of the fighting submitted to London by the British minister fails even to mention the incident, which might best be regarded as an odd postscript to the Republican victory.[20]

From the balcony of the Lisbon *câmara municipal* ("city hall") at 9:00 A.M., the republic was proclaimed and a provisional government appointed. The fighting had lasted only thirty-one hours. For all the shooting and bomb throwing, casualties were fairly light. The most reliable casualty estimates, which included the several days of sporadic shooting following the fall of the monarchy, suggest that there were at the very least 65 dead and 728 wounded.[21] A study of the casualty lists reveals that many more urban civilians than military personnel were killed and wounded; of the 65 listed as killed by 8 October, 43 were civilians, mainly populares; and only 22 were soldiers. Of the soldiers killed, only a handful were officers.

What occurred outside Lisbon? Studies of contemporary newspapers suggest that, although little fighting occurred beyond the suburbs of Lisbon, enthusiasm for the revolution was widespread. Between 5 October and 7 October, towns all over the country followed Lisbon in proclaiming the republic. Leaders at Oporto declared the republic at noon on 6 October. In fact the earliest proclamation of the republic was not in Lisbon, but across the Tagus on the Outra Banda, in the town of Aldegallega at dawn on 4 October. The towns of Almada, Barreiro, Seixal, and Loures (northeast of Lisbon) followed during the day. In these largely working-class towns, police and army forces remained neutral; when sounds of firing in Lisbon were heard, populares took over and declared the republic, anticipating even the fervent republicanism of the capital. Crowds in these towns celebrated wildly, marching by the town halls singing the Republican revolutionary hymn, "A Portuguesa," as well as the "Marseillaise."[22]

In the Lisbon suburbs, the activity of the Carbonária among the working classes produced more antimonarchist violence than occurred in many provincial towns. In Olivais, Belém, Cascais, and other towns, populares wrested control of the streets from the intimidated police and other security forces and in some cases attacked army units. By sealing Lisbon off from the north and west, these conspirators helped to assure the success of the Lisbon revolution. The army units of the Third Artillery and Sixth Caçadores, ordered by the government on the fourth from camps near Santarém, made only modest efforts to reach Lisbon. The Sixth Caçadores never reached Lisbon, and the Third Artillery got there at 9:00 A.M. on the fifth, after the republic had been proclaimed. This unit began firing and caused some casualties, but when its commander realized the revolution had been victorious, he adhered to the new regime.[23]

In most of Portugal, outside Lisbon, army units remained neutral or at any rate inactive until official news of the result of the fighting in Lisbon had been received. This neutrality was a crucial factor. Most senior, field-grade officers were not willing to commit themselves or their troops to active combat; many feared for their lives and some "disappeared" during the days of 4–6 October or remained in barracks. There is evidence of some conflict within individual units, however. In a few cases officers opposed aggressive Republican sergeants and enlisted men until official word of the republic came from Lisbon. In Oporto, on the evening of 4 October for example, some Republican sergeants of the Eighteenth Infantry (in part implicated in the previous 1891 abortive coup) led a section of the regiment to "declare" for the republic; they were promptly arrested and confined to barracks by monarchist officers until definite news arrived on the sixth.[24]

A few officers leaning toward the monarchy clashed with revolutionary groups. In Oporto, General Pimentel Pinto, a former minister of war under the monarchy, was rumored to have plotted a counter-revolution and was "arrested" by populares who were directed by a "committee"; he was held under suspicion until news and orders from Lisbon arrived. At Funchal, in the Madeira Islands, the refusal of the commander of the Twenty-seventh Infantry Regiment to raise the Republican banner led to a barracks revolt on 9 October; the ranks fraternized with townspeople and a junior officer raised the controversial flag.[25]

In the provinces, the pattern of popular acceptance of the Lisbon revolution was almost ritualistic. In many towns, news of the assassination of Dr. Bombarda and the subsequent Lisbon struggles brought large crowds into the streets waiting for further developments. Army units, with the exception of the Guarda Municipal, which in Oporto patrolled major streets, remained in or near their barracks to hear news of the outcome.[26] Pressure from lower-class elements on some army units was often intense, if usually bloodless. The cheers and singing of crowds in the streets presaged the news of Republican victory from Lisbon. Popular exclamations first hailed the republic; these were followed by official commitments to the new government from the top district army commanders. In the final phase of the revolution, crowds of populares cheered the army units for remaining neutral and for adhering to the republic.

Few among the officer corps in provincial army units took aggressive action or initiative. Junior officers tended to be more pro-Republican or neutral than senior officers. Speaking of the Portuguese army as a whole, the last monarchist prime minister later noted that, although the army did not actually fight for the republic, in the main it was Republican.[27] The revolutionary hero of Rotunda, Machado Santos, later wrote that the victory of the republic in 1910 was really "the victory of the people." He asserted that most of the officers in the Lisbon garrison and in the provinces were "completely indifferent to politics."[28]

The attitude of army commanders, then, was crucial to the "victory of the people." Many feared at the time that a bloody civil war would have resulted if a significant portion of the army had been willing to fight the revolutionaries. Since 1870 the Portuguese army had not actively intervened in politics by means of pronunciamentos, as it had during 1822–51. Republican propaganda and discouragement with the monarchy had worked a kind of de-politicization. In 1910 most of the army commanders were not sufficiently promonarchist or anti-Republican to oppose what appeared to be the will of large sections of the urban lower and middle classes.[29]

The 1910 Revolution included significant revolutionary-anarchist outbursts which the bourgeois Republican leadership disavowed and tried to suppress. Anticlericalism was common in Lisbon and Oporto and in surrounding towns. As the Spanish journalist Lorenzo later reported, popular hatred of the Jesuits was one of the outstanding characteristics of the revolution.[30] Several convents were burned in nearby towns. Scientific equipment at the Jesuit college at Campolide was destroyed. Several priests were murdered by populares, including the French Lazarist confessor of Queen Maria Amélia.[31] During the period of 4–7 October, especially, persons wearing priests' or nuns' clothing were in danger of assault in public places.[32] In the towns south of Lisbon, such as Barreiro or Azeitão, armed populares "searched" for priests who might be suspected of "counterrevolutionary" acts. Anticlerical mobs assaulted the offices of such Catholic newspapers as *Portugal* in Lisbon and *A Palavra* in Oporto; as a result, publication of *A Palavra* was forcibly but temporarily suspended on 6–7 October. There was also vandalism in the churches.[33]

Revolutionaries were concerned about Republican symbols. A crowd in Alcobaça demanded that local soldiers wear armbands of the Republican colors of red and green after officers had ordered them removed when the men were in formation. Crowds in nearly every town were anxious to sing both the "Marseillaise" and the Republican hymn, "A Portuguesa," songs which inspired feelings of intense nationalism and a sense of glorious tradition. Some zealots waved French Republican flags, as well as those of the Portuguese republic. Crowds of students and populares destroyed royal symbols such as royal portraits and busts and crown symbols on buildings. In some places, royal busts of King Carlos or King Manuel were ostentatiously replaced by portraits of anticlerical dictator-tyrant, the marquês de Pombal (in office, 1750–77).[34]

There were also anarchistic activities, especially in and near Lisbon. These included the burning of town records at Almada and Barreiro and the searching of passengers on trains from Oporto to Lisbon and on the Sud-Express. The frequent and almost ritualistic use of bombs, some of them designed by the Portuguese anarchist José Nunes,[35] was evident in urban areas.

Populares in Lisbon and Oporto, and in a few towns of the Outra

Banda, made violent attempts to release all prisoners from municipal jails. In Almada and Olivais some prisoners were freed in this manner.[36] The most serious incidents took place in Oporto 5–7 October, where crowds tried to release prisoners at six city jails. At the main city jail at least two died and nearly twenty were wounded on 6 October, after the Guarda Municipal fired on prisoners to end an attempted jail break. Apparently these were the only fatalities in Oporto during the 1910 Revolution.[37]

Accompanying the revolution was an increase in crime and vandalism in Lisbon and Oporto. In towns outside Lisbon, populares assaulted posts of the Guarda Municipal and the Guarda Fiscal, burned buildings, and destroyed telephones. There was damage and thievery in barracks as well as in downtown stores in Lisbon during 5, 6 October; authorities noted that criminals became bolder and that daylight robberies increased. Some populares, however, became guards for banks.[38]

The Provisional Government of the republic deplored most of these activities. Official decrees were published in the major newspapers warning "the people" in the streets to respect the persons and property of all citizens.[39] The new government, appointed by the Republican leadership and not elected by popular vote, feared a social revolution, feared for its reputation abroad, and hoped to calm the lower-class elements. Statements by Republican leaders warning the people of dangerous consequences of anarchy and crime are clothed in rhetorical, even utopian language, typical of much Republican propaganda. The Republican newspaper O Mundo stated shortly after the revolution that the republic's establishment opened "an era of peace, of prosperity and of justice."[40] Most striking was the mystical language of one of the revolutionary heroes himself, Machado Santos, who, in his "Order of the Day No. 1," especially praised the sailors and the people (here he did not mention the army!). Significantly, he urged a kind of euphoric, millennial unity: "Now there are no enemies! There are only brothers!"[41]

After a cabinet meeting of the Provisional Government on the evening of 7 October, decrees were issued proclaiming: a general amnesty for political prisoners convicted under the monarchy, separation of Church and State, abolition of press-censorship laws, application of the anticlerical laws of Pombal and others to religious associations (including the banishment of the Jesuits), the dissolution of the Guarda Municipal and its replacement by the Guarda Nacional Republicana, and replacement of the monarchist police by a new "civil police."[42] These decisions soon became the objects of bitter controversy.

The 1910 Revolution did not usher in the millennium or a social revolution.[43] The men who took power on 5 October were largely middle-class intellectuals and professional men, some of whom were ambitious for public office. In most towns in Portugal, the câmara municipal was taken over by a preappointed group of local Republicans, essentially lower middle-class men. Few Carbonária leaders held upper-echelon jobs, and even fewer workers achieved public office. While the grand master of that mysterious organization, Luz de Almeida, had said before the revolution that the Carbonária program was "the complete and radical remodeling of Portuguese society,"[44] and, although anticlericalism was at times extreme, few institutional changes occurred at first, beyond the expulsion of the Bragança dynasty. The professed program of the new regime, as promised in interviews with the *Times* (London), and the *New York Times,* was a moderate, in part traditional one, which, despite decades of Republican fulminations against the Anglo-Portuguese Alliance, emphasized an alliance with England.[45] It also featured a balanced budget and autonomy but not independence for the colonies. The financial community reacted mildly to the revolution. While some Portuguese stocks dipped in value temporarily, no panic or sellout took place in the stock exchanges of London, New York, and Paris. By 7–8 October stockmarket prices were virtually the same as before the upheaval, and investors were assured by the Provisional Government that they would honor their obligations. To insure further tranquility, the Provisional Government ordered taverns closed and bread shops opened. In short, there would be a bourgeois republic.[46]

After the proclamation of the republic, some violence continued in Lisbon; shooting occurred in or near religious buildings such as the Quelhas Convent, where revolutionary populares suspected or imagined that priests or nuns were hiding and firing on the people. The government, however, maintained a semblance of law and order, since the major security forces and the army obeyed the new regime; and since populares voluntarily patrolled the streets and guarded key installations. The transition had been facilitated by the government order of 5 October that all officers of the army and navy who had not "participated" in the revolutionary movement present themselves and swear an oath of loyalty to the republic. Many officers did so, though a number refused to take the oath. Some officers, such as Paiva Couceiro, later resigned.[47]

The Portuguese Revolution of 1910 succeeded largely because of popular support in the larger towns and two cities of Portugal. The

NA LUA DE MEL...

Até que emfim... casados!...

"On the honeymoon . . . 'At last . . . married!'" Zé Povinho contemplates his bride, Lady Republic, on the wedding night. (Cartoon in *Os Ridículos,* Lisbon, 12 October 1910.)

"republic" for many groups was a kind of Republican Sebastianism,[48] expressed by the demands of the lower classes for improvement in social and economic conditions, and by the demands of the emerging lower-middle classes for an end to the monopoly of privileges held by the entrenched oligarchy. Whatever the form of the before 5 October protests and agitation—whether Jacobin republicanism reminiscent of France in 1789, or a vague anarchism and socialism derived from France, Italy, and Spain, or the simple desire of the urban proletariat for better wages and living conditions—the revolution was held to be "a leap forward."[49]

The revolution witnessed the defection of large numbers of monarchists. In the streets of Lisbon a monarchist Spanish journalist who observed events could find "no monarchists."[50] This initial support was conditioned, in part, by fear of lower-class violence. Yet enthusiasm for the new republic was widespread. Even most of the right-wing conservative press welcomed the republic.[51] The Nationalist leader, former monarchist minister Jacinto Cândido da Silva, had urged his partisans just before the revolution to join the right wing of the Republican party.[52] An editorial in a former monarchist daily stated that "those who did not enthusiastically proclaim the republic, accepted it without reluctance, as a necessity, as a fatal consequence of the state to which things had come."[53]

The 1910 Revolution was not an orthodox army pronunciamento. Instead, it was the work of an armed conspiracy of Republican civilians, a handful of republicanized naval and army officers, and large numbers of noncommissioned officers and enlisted men of both services. The leadership and direction was mainly by civilians and not by professional military officers. The initiative was not with the officer corps, since they largely deserted, withdrew, or abstained from action beginning 3 October. The revolution, therefore, was much less military than it was civilian and popular. In later years, this would have serious, unfortunate repercussions among army and navy professional officers, some of whom were in Africa at the time of the revolution.[54]

But the Portuguese Revolution of 1910 was more than a case of a few Republican conspirators taking advantage of the weakness of the monarchy's defenders and riding to power on a popular outcry against the murder of the leading Republican politician Bombarda. The revolution was also a popular response to a historic Portuguese crisis. Supported initially by much of the urban lower class and led by lower middle-class Republicans, the revolution represented an attack on a discredited past and a popular surge toward a more hopeful future.[55]

If later, under different circumstances, witnesses and observers with the wisdom of hindsight judged this revolution to be "premature,"[56] this was not clear on 5 October. The republic was untested and the euphoria in the capital was delirious. On the morning after, in a slightly more sober place, readers of the *New York Times* read a prescient editorial on the event. It stated that the Constitutional Monarchy had been a

sad failure, but it seems to have failed precisely because of the lack of conditions necessary to an orderly and efficient republic. . . . The new republic, from the moment of its stormy birth, will be assailed by great difficulties, which may well arouse the sympathy, the pity, of all friends of the principle they are undertaking to apply.[57]

5 / Young Republic: First Steps

October 1910—January 1913

> The Portuguese Republic has before it a great mission to carry out—to create a new Fatherland, to build a modern people.
>
> Alves da Veiga[1]

> The Portuguese Republic needs peace and harmony; it requires, for its full consolidation, order in the streets and in people's minds. . . .
>
> Alfredo Pimenta[2]

The Decline of Benevolent Expectancy

In the weeks following the Fifth of October, Portuguese citizens began to reappraise what "the republic" might be. When the euphoria drifted away and the messianic rhetoric died, the reality of Portugal's situation was jolting. Republicans' laughter turned to tears. The legacy of the Bragança monarchy was deadly. Portugal's population of some 5,800,000 was composed mainly of poor, ignorant peasants. The general illiteracy rate, which was estimated at between 78 and 79 percent, may have been an underestimate.[3] Numbers of those classified as literate were functionally illiterate, and some of the remainder rarely comprehended what they read. Poverty was severe. The country inherited a large deficit in the trade balance, a large foreign debt of over £41,490,000 and an internal debt of about £120,120,346.[4] Most of the Portuguese economy was agrarian; some 57 percent of the work force was engaged in agriculture and barely 20 percent was in industrial pursuits.[5] For such a small country a significant proportion of the work force (5.5 percent) was engaged in the liberal professions, domestic service, and the civil and military bureaucracy.[6] With slow industrialization and a backward agrarian economy, Portugal was well behind even underdeveloped Spain.

Nor was the backwardness evenly distributed. The highest literacy rates, wages, politicization, and republicanism concentrated in the two cities, Lisbon and Oporto, and in a handful of other towns in central-south Portugal. The greatest illiteracy, 67 to 85 percent, was to be found in rural, north Portugal in the areas of Braga, Bragança, and Vila Real, where monarchism was strongest and republicanism weakest. Northern monarchism was further encouraged by heavy emigration from this region and by close relations with the Portuguese monarchist community in Brazil, which regularly sent back money and repatriates, and maintained close familial relationships.[7] Despite the growing organization of the Republican party in rural and urban Portugal, the fact remained that when the republic was declared, the largest single organization in the country was not that of the Republicans, but that of a lay Catholic religious body, the Apostolado da Oração, an arm of the Jesuits, which in 1908 claimed about one million Portuguese members.[8]

The Portugal Republicans inherited from the monarchy was a country with different groups and classes that held divergent conceptions of what a "republic" would be. At first enthusiasm for the new regime obscured these different "republics," though they were evident in the Lisbon streets on 5 October, where the contrast between the raw, barefooted peasants armed with pitchforks and the formally dressed middle-class riflemen was startling and almost comical.

The new regime faced many formidable tasks. It would have to unite various Republican groups and reconcile their divergent views. It would have to defeat its monarchist enemies, who would reappear after a few months of inactivity. It would have to find and preserve wise and honest leadership that would remain steady under great pressures. Finally, it would have to control and moderate the excesses of its supporters and friends. With the legacies from the monarchy, and the great new problems to be faced, the republic probably had little chance of success, but at first contemporary opinion was sanguine. In the urban areas great hopes were immediately placed in the new regime. Members of the diplomatic community in Lisbon were almost uniformly enthusiastic and positive. Argentina was the first foreign nation to recognize the Portuguese republic, and on 22 October Brazil recognized the regime.

The European powers were more circumspect. The American minister did not regret the passing of the monarchy and informed his colleagues that the United States would conduct business with the republic, but would withhold official recognition until the first elections brought forth a constituent assembly. In the meantime, the United States regarded the republic with, in the words of the American minister in Madrid, "benevolent expectancy."[9] Led by Britain, the European powers withheld recognition and argued that they would wait until the republic elected a constituent assembly and approved a constitution. The United States recognized the Portuguese republic on 11 May 1911, France on 25 August, and Spain, Britain, Germany, and Austria waited until 11 September 1911.[10]

Symbols were an immediate concern of many Republicans, who used them not only to disassociate the present and future republic from a monarchist past, but also to embody promise for the future. The blue and white monarchist flag was replaced by the Republican flag of red and green. The monarchist national anthem, the "Hino da Carta" ("Hymn of the Charter"), was replaced by the stirring, romantic 1890 composition "A Portuguesa," the Republican hymn of outrage against the British Ultimatum and an invocation of the past greatness of the nation. In a law published on 22 May 1911 the old coinage, the real was replaced by the new Republican escudo.[11] A spelling reform in 1911 simplified spelling and freed Portuguese orthography from certain foreign influences including Frenchified accenting and spelling of some words. Other symbolic changes included naming streets and buildings for Republican heroes. The names of the mourned Republican "martyrs" of the revolution, Miguel Bombarda and Cañdido dos Reis, figured prominently, especially following their massive public funeral.

The Republic and the Working Classes, 1910–12

The October Revolution occurred in the midst of unprecedented labor unrest in central and southern Portugal. Especially in the Lisbon and Oporto areas, the working classes had played a key role in creating the antimonarchist, hostile atmosphere which so intimidated the last defenders of the monarchy. The Provisional Government's law legalizing strikes (the Decree of 6 December 1910, introduced by Minister Manuel Brito Camacho), which had been illegal under the monarchy, did not satisfy a significant portion of the workers, who had expected that the republic would bring immediate improvements in wages and living conditions. Some of the armed, barefoot workers who had guarded Lisbon banks in early October now were striking in protest against the status quo. Indifference and even hostility replaced the workers' initial enthusiasm for the republic.

The labor question was a difficult one for Provisional Government. While the main support for republicanism came from the middle classes in the towns, groups of workers had aided in the overthrow of the monarchy, and the government was aware of the importance of working-class support. Although the working-class movement was only in its infancy in Portugal, organizing was intense, and, as in Spain, the largest, most powerful and radical working-class organizations were anarcho-syndicalist. The Provisional Government—and later governments—soon found that it was impotent to change the lot of workers, that it could do little to arbitrate disputes between labor and management, and that in enforcing the law on public order and security when strikes or lockouts occurred, the government was blamed for heavy-handed repression by troops, police, and unofficial vigilante groups.

Whereas the working classes had expected the republic to bring them higher pay, better hours, lower prices, especially for staples such as codfish and bread, and cheaper rents, in fact the opposite occurred. Prices rose, wages remained the same (and hours increased after the elimination of the religious holidays), and rents also rose. Labor discontent increased. Workers began to strike, but their strikes met resistance from management and an unfavorable response from the government, which was under pressure from management groups. The year 1911 was a bad one for workers since there was increasing unemployment as well as price rises and strikebreaking by management and the government. Workers' organizations were disbanded by local administrators and the protests of the workers usually were to no avail.[12] Strikebreakers rendered strikes less effective; they were aided by the Guarda Nacional Republicana (GNR), the army, and Republican vigilante groups such as the so-called Battalions of Volunteers, who brutally repressed workers in the series of labor clashes in 1910–12. By the spring and summer of 1911, whatever the long-range impact of labor hostility to the Republican governments, there was indeed a state of "latent war between the working classes and the more pure (radical) urban Republicans."[13] One response of some workers' groups was vandalism and sabotage of property, acts which further troubled labor relations.[14]

Radical working-class organizations soon attacked the government as bourgeois and oppressive. Within weeks of the revolution, the Oporto Committee of Syndicalist Propaganda issued a militant program which, in effect, declared war on the new Provisional Government in Lisbon. Conditions for workers had not improved, and, they alleged, the change of political regime mattered little. Their program asserted that "the cause of all these evils is in the very economic makeup of capitalist society. It is in the principle that establishes the right of the capitalist to possess all the natural and social wealth, which should be the patrimony of all the community."[15]

The Republican government now confronted a much more massive wave of strikes than had occurred under the monarchy. In the year 1911 alone, there were 162 strikes, a record number. The workers' high expectations of Republican reforms intensified disappointments; though a fair portion of the 1911 strikes were settled to the workers' advantage, later strike settlements on the whole were less favorable.[16] Urban workers, especially in the Lisbon area and to some extent in Oporto, were the best organized and were backed by a press which attacked the Provisional Government as repressive and undemocratic. The anarcho-syndicalist groups espoused a creed which called for workers' owner-ship of factories, and they advocated general strikes to paralyze capitalist society. Although the anarcho-syndicalists in Portugal never gained the prominence of their Spanish counterparts in the 1930s, they were a formidable leftist foe for Republican governments and caused considerable embarrassment.

Rural strikes, concentrated in the Alentejo area, reached a peak dur-ing 1911-12. Increased wages headed the list of workers' demands in the rural provinces as in the towns, but there were a few attempts to ex-propriate land and divide up the great estates in the south. A 1911 general strike in Alentejo, organized by outside labor organizers, pro-vided rural workers with some redress of grievances.[17] Provincial labor movements, however, had little chance of success, since the government cooperated with the landowners in dissolving the unions and in jailing agitators.

The Republican government could do little in rural areas in the face of the traditional intransigence and conservatism of the landowning classes. In the early years of the republic, the government attempted to improve the lot of unemployed laborers in Alentejo by allocating laborers to different landowners during difficult times; but this scheme met severe opposition from landowners and was discontinued. This episode clarifies a basic dilemma of the Republican regime: most of the blame for the workers' lot could be laid at the door of the landowning and industrialist groups who later came to support the extreme Right; thus a poorly developed sense of justice on the part of the conservative classes[18] lay behind the grievances of the Left, and the government could not effectively pressure these groups to make concessions to labor.

Emigration, especially from the rural north, vastly increased during the years 1911-12. Official statistics suggest that the emigration was largely to Brazil; the following official figures do not reflect the con-siderable clandestine emigration that occurred:[19]

Year	Number of Emigrants
1910	39,502
1911	59,652
1912	88,920
1913	77,633
1914	25,722

While the increased emigration during the first years republic can be partly explained by poor living conditions, uncertainty and instability under the new regime, unemployment, and government repression of labor movements, such an extraordinary increase requires additional analysis. The army's plan to set up a new national militia in 1911 called for greater conscription of the lower classes than had been required under the monarchy. Evidence from military records in 1911 suggests that the rural population resented the recruitment and that desertion rates increased accordingly in the north.[20] This attitude was not surprising in view of the low pay, poor conditions, and bad reputation of the army in the provinces. When anticonscription feelings were combined with monarchist activity in Minho and Trás-os-Montes provinces during 1911–12, increased emigration was natural.

Unemployment and steeply rising prices in 1911 also explain the exodus of workers.[21] Another explanation was unsupervised emigrant labor recruitment by agents, especially in the north. A Lisbon newspaper complained about this recruitment and proposed that the government improve rural conditions by reducing taxes.[22] Although the historian Oliveira Martins was correct in his claim that Portuguese emigration was "the barometer of national life,"[23] such emigration in the early years of the republic must be viewed in perspective. Heavy emigration from much of southern Europe was common in the years preceding World War I. In Spain, through which some Portuguese emigrants passed on their exodus, emigration also reached an all-time peak in the year 1912.[24]

Provisional Government and the Church

High on the agenda of the Republican leaders was a new policy toward the Catholic church. The Provisional Government instituted a severely anticlerical policy which became the subject of great and continuing controversy. Traditionalists have attacked the policy as wrong and ultimately fatal to the First Republic; Modernists have defended it as essential for the survival of the new government and for the modernization of Portugal.[25]

The Republican leaders had certain anticlerical models in mind: they borrowed from the legislation of Pombal and the Constitutional Liberals of the 1830s, and from the anticlerical policy of France's Third Republic during the years 1900–1906, in particular. But even using such models, and even accepting the Republican arguments that the Church deserved much blame for Portugal's backwardness, the Portuguese anticlerical policy was unnecessarily harsh. The Provisional Government's

Church policy only temporarily weakened the Church, but, more important, alienated potential political support and polarized a portion of Portuguese society that might have been willing to support the republic in a number of other policies. Furthermore, this policy angered the representatives of those European and American powers that had nationals engaged in religious work in Portugal or her colonial territories. The Church issue became a cause célèbre that contributed substantially to the republic's unfavorable foreign press.

In power with no parliament as a watchdog, the Provisional Government was a virtual dictatorship. On 8 October 1910, the anticlerical onslaught began with decrees published by the new minister of justice, Afonso Costa. The Jesuits were expelled and all religious orders were to be dissolved, whether foreign or national. The property of the orders became State property.

After October there followed a deluge of legislation which decreed a thoroughgoing secularization of life: at Coimbra University religious oaths were abolished; the Coimbra Theology School was closed; the Chair in Ecclesiastical Law was extinguished; the religious orders were to end religious instruction in private and normal schools; the State assumed responsibility for public education; all religious holidays were to be abolished (Sunday would remain a day of rest); the armed forces would have no more religious services, and the Chaplains' Corps was abolished; all religious organizations would be replaced by civil commissions under government control. On 3 November divorce was made legal,[26] and in decrees known as "family laws," marriage was made "a purely civil contract" and women and illegitimate children acquired more rights. Public religious worship underwent restrictions: the government owned the churches, and worship was not permitted at certain times. Priests and nuns were forbidden to wear their habits in public.

The Provisional Government's anticlerical legislation from October 1910 until April 1911 was the most extraordinary and severe anticlerical action taken by a government in Europe up to that time; perhaps later only in Russia in 1917 or in Spain in 1931 was such fanatical anticlericalism equaled or surpassed. The Provisional Government's program was exceedingly personal, arbitrary, and legalistic. Undoubtedly the attack on the Church was popular with sections of the urban lower and middle classes. Even larger groups in the towns and country, however, opposed it and soon became alienated from the republic on this issue. In view of the internal and external reactions to the government's action, the program was a major error. By mid-1911 what had been intended as religious reform had become religious persecution. It took the republic years to settle the questions and disputes which resulted from the anticlerical laws.

On 20 April 1911 the Provisional Government published its "Law of Separation," which separated Church and State. The law was to take effect on 1 July, and there is evidence that the government expected bitter opposition and prepared to defend itself. The Ministry of War issued orders to military units,[27] especially in the northern provinces, to expect a possible monarchist-inspired armed rising associated with the forthcoming May elections for the Constituent National Assembly. The Law of Separation set off another series of protests, but no monarchist coup. The conspirators were only beginning to plan for such an act.

Justice Minister Afonso Costa became the personal symbol of the republic's anticlericalism. The more radical press idolized Costa, portraying him as a new Pombal arrogantly expelling the Jesuits; radical Republicans adopted Pombal as a historical hero who represented their brand of freedom: the strong man able to attack the Church, like the popular bullfighter, proud and arrogant, gaining the applause of eager crowds. Speaking at Braga, the city of Portuguese bishops, Costa forecast an end to Catholicism in several generations. Significantly, he stated that religion was the "major cause" of Portugal's backwardness. Church leaders soon reacted strongly, protesting in pastoral letters to the faithful during 1910–11. Costa reacted with the willful arrogance,

Afonso Costa as minister of justice, Provisional Government. (By Correia Dias, from Braz Burity [Joaquim Madureira], *A Forja da Lei* [Coimbra, 1915], p. 375.)

the *tesura,* that radical Republicans admired: he expelled for two years numbers of churchmen who protested: the patriarch of Lisbon, the archbishop of Guarda, the bishop of Oporto (the Africanist missionary, António Barroso), the bishop of Beja, and others. To offended Catholics these exiled leaders became martyrs.

The clerical issue gave ready weapons to the opponents of the Republican regime. Dissatisfied monarchists who wished to restore the monarchy used the issue to win over adherents. Groups of young people, previously only nominally Catholic and pro-Republican, changed their opinions on the Church issue. Church persecution, so open, so severe, shocked them. The anticlerical storm nudged them into a new religiosity. Especially revealing is the experience of the Integralist leader António Sardinha (1888–1925), later the leading theoretician of Portuguese fascism. Once the Catholic religion became the subject of outright persecution, whatever its previous role in society had been, it grew in popularity. People returned to religion with a vengeance. Before 1911 Sardinha had been a Republican, discouraged with the corruption of the monarchy. His mother apparently influenced his shift both to monarchism and Catholicism when she confided to her son, "Now that they [the government] want to destroy religion it is necessary to go to church."[28]

The Church issue damaged the young republic's reputation abroad. Foreign diplomats in Portugal became highly critical of the anticlerical campaign. Ironically, it was Anglo-Saxon Protestant diplomats, primarily the British, who found themselves defending the rights of Catholics in Portugal. The Law of Separation also affected the foreign Catholic religious orders. English Catholic orders, long exempt from Portuguese anticlerical measures, now in 1911 were involved in a bitter dispute with the Portuguese government over ownership of property and their rights.

In Anglo-Portuguese relations the Church issue also made its impact. The diplomatic recognition of the republic by Britain was delayed by the anticlerical disputes and the first constitutional government was toppled in part because of the issue. British representatives criticized what they termed "the vexatious formalities and restraints" of the Provisional Government's Church laws, as they affected English and Irish Catholic churches, convents, and seminaries in Portugal and Madeira.[29] After the Law of Separation was published in April 1911, the British minister in Lisbon "insisted" that British religious institutions be exempt from the law's provisions. Conflict reached the point where the British minister, Arthur Hardinge, threatened that if Portugal did not comply Britain would deny official recognition of the republic. Because of this pressure and growing internal opposition to the anticlericalism, the government was forced to compromise. In late August 1911, the government promised not to apply the full force of the law on "the foreign churches served by ministers of foreign nationality." After the constitution was approved and a president of the republic elected, Britain and other major European powers recognized the Portuguese republic on 11 September 1911.[30]

Even with fairly sympathetic audiences, the young republic's reputation was besmirched by the anticlerical measures. Positive accomplishments of the republic were forgotten in condemnations of the official attack on the Church. The press in England, France, Spain, and Germany was largely unfavorable to the young republic; the bizarre Church issue exacerbated foreign criticism and made the Portuguese representatives abroad sensitive to foreign hostility on the issue. Portuguese diplomats, especially in the key capitals of London, Paris, Madrid, Berlin, and Rio de Janeiro, made efforts to improve the republic's image by developing good relations with the foreign press and issuing Lisbon's "official" versions of events in Portugal.[31]

Despite government efforts, the clerical issue remained embarrassing. Even the diplomats from secular, democratic states could not defend the Church persecution. The British minister in Lisbon at the time of the Separation Law, Sir Francis Villiers, predecessor of Hardinge, described the law as "an arbitrary and inquisitorial measure, whose general provisions are wholly incompatible with its opening declarations in regard to freedom of religion and liberty of conscience."[32] The British reported to London in confidential dispatches that the laws of 1910–11 went beyond the campaign promises of the Republicans while in opposition to the monarchy. Indeed, these acts did more than disestablish the Church, for they had now subjected the institution, in effect, to "a slavery to the civil power,"[33] an act which alienated even Catholic-hating Protestants and friends of the republic.

The Provisional Government's anticlerical program, and especially its Law of Separation, became the hottest political issue of the early years of the republic. One's attitude to the Republican attack on the Church, and to the man most responsible for the legislation and its enforcement, Afonso Costa, determined one's political path and party. The Church issue helped to make possible the calling to power by President Arriaga of weak, moderate Republican coalitions from September 1911 until January 1913.[34] Finally, the Church question caused a serious division in Republican ranks at a time when unity was crucial. The parties that

arose to oppose the Democrats based their programs on a more
moderate, conciliatory Church policy.

The Provisional Government and the 1911 Constitution

Many of the same pressures that had determined the government's
approach to labor and to the Church were brought to bear as the
leaders of the republic turned to the questions of what kind of government and constitution to devise. Republican radicalism, usually referred
to as Jacobinism, was brewing in the streets of Lisbon and Oporto.
Numerous groups of unofficial militants acted as self-appointed or
secretly sanctioned vigilantes; their intervention in public affairs caused
great resentment in the officer corps, in the bureaucracy, and in the
Church. The names of these groups were as bizarre as the acts of their
members: the Carbonária, the Battalions of Volunteers, the Social
Vigilance Group.[35] In some cases, these radical vigilante groups were
encouraged by irresponsible elements in the Lisbon press.

The pressures were many. Besides radical pressures from militants
who threatened from the Left—especially an anarchist Left—
Republican leaders, within weeks of the revolution, heard rumors of
monarchist conspiracies, many of them connected to the name of Captain Henrique Paiva Couceiro, who demanded a national plebiscite to
allow the nation to choose between monarchy and republic. During the
crucial days of June and July 1911, the constitution-makers were in
part influenced by fears of monarchist plots.

The deputies to the Constituent National Assembly were aware of the
failures of the Constitutional Monarchy's political system. Urban
popular opinion called for an end to the possibility of dictatorial acts
by any future government. Naturally many deputies were opposed to
granting significant constitutional powers to the executive branch.
Delegates to the Assembly also opposed granting powers which might
limit the prerogatives of the legislative branch. Even the British minister
in Lisbon agreed with the majority of the Portuguese constitution-
makers on the choice of a parliamentary rather than a presidential
system, since, he believed, Portugal then lacked leaders of sufficient
stature to exercise wisely the great powers granted, say, to a president
of the United States. There was a general belief that the granting of
such powers might lead to the abuses and dictatorships that were common in Latin American republics.[36]

The two great issues debated by the Constituent National Assembly
were: Presidentialism or parliamentarism, and whether the Congress
should have one or two legislative chambers. The executive which

emerged from the new 1911 Constitution was subordinate, at least on paper, to the Congress. Several factors had influenced the 200-odd deputies to the National Assembly to choose a parliamentary system. First was the nature of the deputies themselves, who were elected on 28 May 1911 from a list prepared largely by the Directorate of the Portuguese Republican party (PRP): of the 226, nearly one-fourth (47) were armed forces' officers, and there were lawyers (24), medical doctors (48), and civil servants (25). Other groups were not as well represented.[37] They were largely middle-class men (no women were elected) who had learned their republicanism young, and who were active in journalism and teaching. The Constituent Assembly, and also, in effect, the first Republican Congress (1911–15) were mainly representative of the Europeanized, more modern, urban sectors of the country.

These deputies have been depicted as wholly inexperienced in government, but close analysis suggests that this is an oversimplification.[38] Under the monarchy's governments, three of the Republican deputies had held cabinet posts, seventeen had been parliamentary deputies, and a total of forty-two, or just under one-fourth, had administrative experience at a variety of posts from local to national levels. In politics the group was by no means inexperienced, for a majority had been involved since high school days in Republican party activity, and in university student politics, both traditional springboards to national politics in Lisbon.

By contemporary Portuguese standards, they were a well-educated group, an elite with rather homogeneous backgrounds. Fully four-fifths of them had at least university-level degrees from universities, seminaries, or advanced military schools. The common experience of student politics at the University of Coimbra bound together a significant number of them; out of 226 deputies some 88 had attended or graduated from that university. A good number of that 88 had participated in the famous Coimbra strike of 1907 and had been involved in subsequent Republican conspiracies. Early Republican parliamentary politics appeared to be, in some respects, an extension of Coimbra student politics. Most of the university graduates had attended school between the two great crises of that generation: the 1890 English Ultimatum and the 1970 Coimbra strike during the João Franco dictatorship. The deputies who made up the first representative body of the young republic were eminently suited to the establishment of a Republican bureaucracy, military and civil. Although they claimed to represent all of Portugal, they were far removed from the rural majority of field and village.

Though there was a wide range in the age (the oldest was seventy-two and the youngest twenty-two), most deputies to the Constituent National Assembly were in their thirties and forties. But in 1910–11 their leaders were no longer very young. The average age of the members of the Provisional Government was fifty-two, with Afonso Costa, the youngest at thirty-nine, to emerge as the charismatic leader of the hour. The top, prestigious posts went to older men: Teófilo Braga, the president, was sixty-seven; and the elected president of the Constituent National Assembly, Anselmo Braamcamp Freire, was sixty-one.

A choice of parliamentary republic for a regime was favored, too, by the historical traditions of the Republican party, which stressed a strong legislature and a weak executive. The lessons of the João Franco dictatorship, 1907–8, made it appear that a strong executive would not be tolerated. Immediate popular pressures opposed any limitation on legislative power. The Lisbon press almost unanimously argued for a parliamentary republic and attacked presidentialism; even the moderate daily *O Século,* which in the summer of 1911 was by no means a mouthpiece of the radical section of the Republican party, resented any whiff of presidentialism.[39]

Popular antagonism to the idea of giving many powers to the executive was especially clear in the debate on the presidential power of dissolving the parliament. Certain moderate deputies had supported an amendment to the original draft constitution which would have given the chief of state, the president of the republic, the power to dissolve parliament before the end of its term and to call new elections. Hostility

Anselmo Braamcamp Freire, president of the Constituent National Assembly, 1911. (By Correia Dias, from Braz Burity [Joaquim Madureira], *A Forja da Lei* [Coimbra, 1915], p. 18.)

to this idea was expressed in street demonstrations and riots that intimidated deputies. On 2 August 1911, during the debate on the amendment, a mob of urban militants, the Grupo de Vigilância Social, attempted to invade the parliamentary chambers. The National Republican Guard was ordered to disperse them, and a riot followed. There were injuries and arrests.[40] The militants demanded a constitution which would abolish the office of president and a parliament with only one, popularly elected chamber, in short a Jacobin program.

Cogent arguments were put forward for giving the president the power to dissolve parliament. Alexandre Braga argued for a limited presidentialist republic wherein the president's power would "balance"

QUE A NOSSA DIVISA SEJA...

ORDEM E TRABALHO!...

"Let our motto be . . . Order and Work!" Political cartoonist satirizes scene of riot in republic's Constituent National Assembly, summer, 1911. The First Republic's official motto was "Order and Work." (*Os Ridículos,* Lisbon, 29 July 1911.)

the legislative powers and help Portugal appear civilized to the European nations that had not yet recognized the republic. Boos from the galleries and the deputies met Braga's suggestion. Deputy João de Menezes felt that the presidential power of dissolution would "make parliament responsible," by the threat of retiring its mandate.[41] Dr. Egas Moniz, soon to become a member of Almeida's Evolutionist party and later a Nobel Prize winner in neurology, argued that dissolution with "restrictions" (a vote of both chambers would pass on the president's act of dissolution) was essential for the republic. With prophetic foresight, Moniz supported his argument with a hypothetical situation, ironically one which occurred with tragic frequency in later years. Suppose, Moniz suggested, that a parliament is elected which refuses to vote through essential measures; though the governments may fall, the parliament remains during its term. If the president could not dissolve the parliament in such a situation, then the logical result would be an illegal means of dispersing the elected body: a golpe de estado, a coup. Moniz's speech, like Braga's, was loudly protested by many members.[42]

A majority of deputies in the debate associated the power of dissolution with tyranny and abuse of power. Examples of overuse of the power under the Constitutional Monarchy were continually cited. Powerful Republican orators such as José de Castro and Barbosa de Magalhães aroused emotions in the chamber.[43] Some deputies suggested foreign models in constitution-making; the constitutions of the Brazilian Republic, Switzerland, and France played a role. Although the constitution of the Third French Republic included the presidential power of dissolution upon the approval of the senate, many Portuguese

Dr. Egas Moniz in the Constituent National Assembly, July 1911. (By Correia Dias, from Braz Burity [Joaquim Madureira], *A Forja da Lei* [Coimbra, 1915], p. 212.)

deputies felt that such a provision would endanger legislative powers and privileges. Radical deputies raised the specter of revolutionary violence if such a presidentialist measure was put into the constitution.

On 8 August 1911 the dissolution amendment was defeated; popular hostility had played a key role in its defeat.[44] Portugal was to have a parliamentary republic, a *república parlamentar,* words which political punsters could not resist playing with. A contemporary joke described the new regime as also *uma república para lamentar* ("a republic to lament"). After weeks of lengthy debates and haggling, the deputies approved the Republican constitution during an evening session on 18 August.

The Constitution featured a president of the republic, who was the chief of state, elected by the legislative chambers or Congress for four years. The president's key power was to nominate and to dismiss the cabinet of ministers. But the legislative power was clearly to be paramount: the Congress was composed of a Chamber of Deputies and a Senate. Deputies were elected for terms of three years, senators for six. The document stated that "Sovereignty resides essentially in the nation"[45] and a long list of "individual rights and guarantees" (thirty-eight) was placed prominently early in the Constitution. The Constitution could be revised in five years, or in 1916, if revisions were approved by a two-thirds vote of a joint session of Congress. After ten years revisions would require only a simple majority vote.

In a final section, the 1911 Constitution called for the election of the president of the republic three days after the approval of the Constitution, by secret ballot in the Constituent National Assembly. The Senate

Sketch satirizing debate on salaries for parliamentary deputies. (By Correia Dias, from Braz Burity [Joaquim Madureira], *A Forja da Lei* [Coimbra, 1915], p. 660.)

would be elected from among the members of the Assembly who were thirty years and older; there would be 71 senators and the remainder of the deputies would form the first Chamber of Deputies in the first Republican Congress, or roughly, 140 deputies. The number actually fluctuated between 135 and 160 members. The 1926 Chamber of Deputies, for example, was composed of at least 159 members.[46]

The 1911 Constitution faithfully reflected political tensions. A draft constitution composed by a small committee and presented to the Constituent National Assembly on 3 July had featured more power for the president (the adverb "freely" was included in the power to "name and to dismiss" the cabinet ministers), making the office resemble that of a United States president: he could "make use of the armed forces," though he could not assume their command, propose the budget, administer state finances, and take responsibility for the "internal and external security" of the State.[47] Significantly, the Assembly deleted these powers from the final draft; the powers of the president were not only reduced but vague. It was not clear in the text, for example, just how the president would name and dismiss cabinet members, or whether they had to be members of Congress.

The draft constitution of 3 July also contained provisions for a legislature consisting of two bodies, a national council, elected at large in the nation, and a municipal council, to be elected by town councilmen or aldermen, but the deputies voted for a centralized legislative body that would not take municipal or local bodies into account. Thus the Assembly rejected the municipal autonomy plank, a traditional promise of the historic Portuguese Republican party.

The 1911 Constitution featured a powerful centralized legislative body and a weak executive; it clearly rejected presidentialism and municipalism. The reasons for this choice went beyond popular pressures from the press, street demonstrations, and threats from the radical Republican factions. The majority of Assembly delegates owed their May 1911 election victories to a combination of election-rigging by the PRP Directorate, abstention by numbers of independent and liberal monarchists, and a restricted suffrage which eliminated large numbers of illiterate voters (the Electoral Law of 1911). Fear of monarchist counteraction in the elections had prompted the delay in holding them (eight months after the October Revolution); moreover, the Republican leaders, as some later admitted,[48] distrusted the provincial (potential) electorate, and arranged the list of candidates in order to assure a complete PRP victory. Only a few independents managed to win elections, and they were considered "safe" Republicans. The Republican leadership during the Constituent National Assembly decided not to risk

another election for a first Congress, and, hence, they included in the
1911 Constitution provisions to "make" the first Congress, literally,
out of the membership of the Assembly. The arbitrary and dictatorial
actions of the Republican leadership, of course, were of a piece with the
nature of the Provisional Government, which had come to power
through an armed insurrection and remained in power, without an election, for eleven months, passing laws and decrees without benefit of
parliament.

The Constitution of 1911, therefore, was an instrument born of a
highly politicized environment and shaped by the power monopoly held
by the Republican government. Although the legislative branch, on
paper, appeared to hold the most power, how the government would
work out in practice was uncertain. The majority of Republicans who
made the Constitution, as well as the members of the Provisional
Government, were highly conscious that Europe was watching their
experiment—the third republic in a generally monarchist European
system. They were also aware that the poor record of the Constitutional
Monarchy set certain political precedents, and that the country lacked a
large cadre of tested leaders or a mass of educated citizens. Although
later critics such as António Sérgio could well assert that the leaders of
1910–11 had been "carried away on a wave that they did not understand,"[49] that they had been raised to power half-crazed with enthusiasm, the record of the debates of the Constituent National
Assembly demonstrates clearly that a number of deputies were well informed about foreign constitutional precedents and were aware of Portugal's weaknesses. As was suggested above, many feared that Portugal
might follow the unstable path of discredited Latin American republics.
Some of the more moderate leaders, like Manuel de Arriaga, the first
president of the republic, wanted to give more power to the executive
but feared that Portuguese constitutional traditions and character
precluded taking this path.[50] Even the Republican press, like the
mainstream O Século, argued that Portugal was not yet "Europeanized" enough, that if a presidentialist system were installed, personal
vanities would lead to tyranny.[51]

Still, the Constitution that emerged was a rather conservative document. On paper the governmental system resembled a conglomeration
of Republican systems in France, Brazil, and Switzerland. To informed
observers such as the British resident diplomatic corps, the parliamentary form selected appeared rational and logical. Indeed, in terms of
theory, the 1911 Constitution seemed to suit Portugal. Just how the
Constitution would work in practice was a question that no one could
answer. Some Assembly deputies were skeptical. The prophetic doubts

of at least one deputy, João de Menezes, who had failed to get sufficient support to pass the dissolution amendment, were expressed elo-
quently in a speech which was soon forgotten:

> Perhaps I am uttering a heresy, but I am less concerned about a constitution
> than [I am] about an administrative reform and an electoral law. What I want
> is a republic that will not be under the rule of a class of politicians. . . .
> Without a large administrative reform, without an honest electoral law, or the
> independence of public functionaries, the Parliamentary Republic, like the
> Constitutional Monarchy, will be a lie.[52]

Politicians, Parties, and Politics:
The Republican Party Splits, 1911-12

The Provisional Government held power from 5 October 1910 to 1
September 1911, when it was replaced by the first constitutional
ministry or government, the João Chagas cabinet, appointed by the
new president of the republic, Manuel de Arriaga. The members of the
Provisional Government reaped the whirlwind; they became victims of
their own radical propaganda. If they were partly responsible for the
explosion of politicization, for the bitter polarization of opinions and
ideas that surged up after October, they were also subject to irresistible
pressures. The level of public violence increased, only poorly controlled
by the newly created public security force, the Guarda Nacional Republicana (GNR), which was obliged to become more of an urban
praetorian guard to protect government than a rural police force.
Masses of urban militants agitated on the fringes of official institutions
and demanded jobs and compensation. Out of this group came clusters
of roving militant vigilantes, either officially or unofficially enlisted to
protect "the revolution," and to act as spies, soldiers, police, or
bullyboys. Some, but not all, of these groups were recruited by the Carbonária; the more militant groups which made themselves a nuisance in
the activities of labor, the Church, the bureaucracy and the armed
forces, came to be known collectively as "white ants" (formiga
branca). Some of them were employed by the political appointees of the
Republican governments,[53] and others were not, but their activities,
whatever the intentions, alienated the supporters of the republic, and
fed the cause of the monarchist and Catholic opposition.

The moderates, whether monarchist or Republican, had only a slim
chance to prevail while extremists were so active. In the spring of 1911,
monarchists actively began to plan armed consiracy. A major turning
point came when Captain Paiva Couceiro, former governor-general of

Angola, wrote a letter on 18 March 1911 to the Provisional Government urging a national plebiscite to have the electorate decide between a monarchy and republic. Significantly, Paiva Couceiro supported the idea of such a plebiscite by invoking familiar national dangers: possible loss of the colonial patrimony, and even Spanish or German intervention and loss of independence, not to mention a possible civil war. When his proposal was ignored, other monarchists followed him to exile in Galicia, where they posed a continual threat of invasion.[54]

Republican radicals, in turn, were driven further into extremism by monarchist plots and conspiracy. Costa was backed by considerable Republican opinion, when, in his speech of 16 October 1911 in Congress, he urged a "policy of intransigence" with the enemies of the republic.[55]

The record of the Provisional Government became one of the major political issues of the first seven years of the republic. What assets the Provisional Government possessed in its stability and term of eleven months in office, and some of its more progressive legislation in areas of education, tenants' rights, military affairs and agrarian reform, were lost because of the arbitrary and oppressive acts of some ministers and because of some acts of the white ants. These acts, made by a regime which supposedly professed respect for democracy, justice, and fair play, suggested that Republican politics would, like monarchist politics, revolve about the problem of authority and opposition. An example of this arose in the results of the government's prosecution of João Franco, former monarchist premier under King Carlos. The Court of Appeal dismissed the prosecution's case for Franco's alleged crimes while in office, 1906–8. The court disclaimed the right to judge Franco's acts since it found no evidence either that the acts were criminal or that the court had jurisdiction. Costa was not prepared to sustain this loss of political face, so the government fired one judge and exiled to a Goan court the remaining four. There was little public reaction to this act, and the British minister's comment to London was partially justified, yet reflected a patronizing and oversimplistic approach to Portuguese politics. The diplomat suggested that few Portuguese disapproved of the affair since, he claimed, they were long "accustomed to high-handed ways."[56] In fact, this arbitrary act was one more reflection of the extreme radical pressure exerted on the Provisional Government and of Costa's effort to maintain an image of strong authority.

During 1910–11, there was a heavy flow of Portuguese capital out of the country. Numbers of prominent monarchists emigrated. Even Republicans such as the intellectuals Raúl Brandão and Guerra Junqueira grew disillusioned, and as early as December 1911 they felt that if the people were allowed to vote in a freely conducted national plebiscite, such as was suggested by the frustrated Paiva Couceiro, the monarchy might have been voted back in.[57]

Legacies of the Provisional Government's acts were crucial. Not all elements of the coalitionlike Republican party agreed with the major policies of the Provisional Government. The acts and reputation of the controversial but popular minister of justice led to a split in the PRP. An early provocation of a split came over the election by the Constituent Assembly of the president of the republic. The candidate of the radical Republican deputies led by Costa was Bernardino Machado.

Bernardino Machado, October 1911. (By Correia Dias, from Braz Burity [Joaquim Madureira], *A Forja da Lei* [Coimbra, 1915], p. 255.)

The more moderate and conservative Republican deputies, the so-called bloc, opposed Costa's more anticlerical acts and they feared his control of a future government. In a vote taken on 21 August, the bloc managed to defeat Machado, and to elect their candidate, the reluctant but venerable old Republican Manuel de Arriaga (1840–1917), aged seventy-one. Arriaga was not a staunch party man and was a philosophical Republican who had considerable prestige because of his age and experience as a Republican deputy under the monarchy. He led no party faction, yet he was naturally indebted to the moderate deputies under Brito Camacho and António José de Almeida who had elected him.[58]

The split widened further at the PRP congress in late October 1911 where some moderates including Brito Camacho (Almeida did not even

Election of Manuel de Arriaga as first president of the republic, August 1911. (By Correia Dias, from Braz Burity [Joaquim Madureira], *A Forja da Lei* [Coimbra, 1915], p. 683.

attend) were hooted down and left in disgust. The moderates then organized the União Nacional Republicana (UNR), with a directorate consisting of Camacho, Almeida, and Aresta Branco, and headquarters in the offices of Camacho's Lisbon newspaper, *A Lucta* ("the struggle").[59] Formed in early November 1911, the UNR was a coalition of the personal followings of several moderate leaders whose purpose was to get through parliament a program which would revise the more radical acts of the Provisional Government, bring more tolerance and calm to "the Portuguese family," and support moderate cabinets in power. The UNR, like most political parties of the period, had its own newspaper which espoused its editor's opinions and the party program. By late November, it was clear from the *A Lucta* editorials that the UNR leadership was attracting former monarchists as party members, and was calling for a broader suffrage, or electoral law, which would allow their candidates a better chance to oppose the PRP in future elections. Even as early as November 1911, the question of electoral reform and the political machine of the PRP had become an issue.[60]

The PRP came to be known generally as the Democratic party. It had the reputation of being a homogeneous, all Jacobin organization. This was an oversimplification. It contained, too, a large group of lower middle-class Republicans and numbers of former monarchists who had joined the party in the months after the revolution; its program was not especially radical, but it continued to defend the record of the Provisional Government and lacked fresh ideas.[61]

The composition of the Republican party reflected the composition of the government administration at all levels. In the weeks and months following the 1910 Revolution, large numbers of monarchists became *adhesivos* ("instant Republicans"). Whether by conviction, pragmatism, or simple fear, these new Republicans had converted and many of them were in the civil service, foreign service, police, and armed forces. In the first nine months of the republic, for example, only five ministers in the top diplomatic posts were Republicans, and most of the diplomatic corps remained monarchist. In the government administration at the parish, municipal levels, the Republicans did not have the manpower to fill all posts. Therefore, large numbers of monarchists either remained in their positions or became "new Republicans" and were appointed to fill vacancies. Both conservative and liberal commentators agree that most of the monarchist converts to instant republicanism were those less idealistic monarchists with poor qualifications who had held second-rate posts, and that the number included, ironically, some of the more demagogic types.[62] In the fall of 1911, as Afonso Costa emerged as leader of the Democrats, the radical Republican rump, he was faced with reconciling the more radical demands of the urban Republicans with the conservatism of the rural clientele made up largely of former monarchists, and very few historic Republicans. The political machine and policy of the Democrats naturally reflected this grass-roots membership and the political contradictions found therein. As a shrewd Republican observer saw it:

The PRP and its most representative figure [Afonso Costa] were forced to realize a conservative program, in order to keep its provincial clientele, and in order not to lose the goodwill of the urban masses, who were quite explosive, [the Republicans] had to employ a language of radical truculence. And the policy of Portuguese democracy could never again free itself from this hypocritical duality.[63]

The Republican party, too, was weakened when former stalwarts refused to participate and withdrew from politics, disgusted with the course of Republican government and politics. By late 1911, such figures included Basílio Teles, who had been offered a Provisional Government post and had refused, the poet Guerra Junqueira, and Sampaio Bruno and Machado Santos, all historic Republicans now alienated. They had withdrawn from support of the Republican party under Costa, and had deplored both the takeover of key posts by the most radical members of the Democratic party and the substance of the Provisional Government's legislation.[64]

The remaining political machine, radical after the departure of the moderates, was reasonably efficient, well organized down to the local level, even in the provinces, and soon replaced the political patronage system of the monarchist caciques with its own cacique system which included former monarchists. The PRP during 1911 and 1912 further organized its electoral monopoly in the towns and rural areas, even though in parliament it did not yet control a clear majority of deputies.

The UNR developed a split in February 1912, and two Republican splinter parties emerged from it. Personalism in the form of personal ambition for office of the two UNR chiefs, Almeida and Camacho, was generally responsible for the split, but the immediate cause was disagreement over the UNR program as drafted by Camacho. What was left of the UNR became Camacho's party of followers and political friends, renamed the União Republicana, known as the Unionists, and Almeida's party was the PRE, the Partido Republicano Evolucionista or Evolutionists. A look at the PRE's first program, as published in the party's newspaper, *A República,* suggests the motives behind the early fragmentation of the PRP and the split in the offshoot UNR.[65] The program first called for a reestablishment of "order," a word which would be used often during the span of the republic and later in the New State. The PRE wanted an "impartial" application of justice, and to appease the religious conscience of the country. This program was remarkably similar to that of the Camacho group, but it was slightly more liberal, since it paid some homage to the idea of continuing the fight against "clerical dominance."

Brito Camacho, 1911. (By Correia Dias, from Braz Burity [Joaquim Madureira], *A Forja da Lei* [Coimbra, 1915], p. 55.)

By early 1912 the tripartite Republican split was out in the open. Personalism was one factor, but differences of opinion regarding the record of the Provisional Government were also significant. As Brito Camacho shrewdly observed, the split in the PRP was natural and probably inevitable, even without personal disagreements, since public opinion was divided. However, the fact that two moderate, small, Republican parties and not one united party now opposed the PRP was important. Personal ambition continued to lead to splits, coalitions of groups and parties failed to stay together, and the PRP remained the only political party with a mass following, a functioning political machine, and a reasonably democratic internal decision-making system. Early attempts by moderates to form a broad, conservative Center and Right Republican party foundered upon the politics of personalism and differences of opinion.

There was another factor, too, which encouraged the emergence of an unstable multiparty system during 1911–12: volatile, urban political journalism. Despite a small readership, Portugal had a large number of daily and weekly papers, which, especially after 1906, became increasingly political and espoused the ideas of parties and persons. Much of the political journalism was of a low level, containing slander, libel, and banality. Only a few Republican daily papers, such as Lisbon's *O Século* (Republican, independent-moderate after 1915), *Diário de Notícias* (Republican) and Oporto's *Primeiro de Janeiro* (Republican), provided informative reportage.

Why was political journalism, in general, not helpful in informing the public? According to contemporary commentators, journalists were often poorly educated, many of them lacked economic independence, and their readership was ignorant and credulous. There may be a parallel between the journalism of early twentieth-century Portugal and that of early eighteenth-century England, when most writers in order to make a living had to parrot their patrons' opinions and depend on the largesse of "great men," patrons, and godfathers. But another cogent reason for poor journalism was the intense politicization of urban society after 1900.

The emergence of an informed and critical public would take time and an improved educational system. In the meantime, every politician with even modest monetary backing could start his own personal newspaper and with it found his own party. Editorial staffs of these "combative" personal sheets were invariably composed of the political friends, relatives, and dependents of the founder-patron-politician.[66] Some politicians believed that they could not enter politics without their own paper. Thus general conditions encouraged the relatively free operation of a personalist, combative, political journalism. While there were some restrictions on press freedom after the 1912 press laws and wartime censorship, 1914–18, the press remained essentially free. There were few legal penalties applied for slander and libel, and the cost of contracting out newspaper printing to general printers was small. Editors, who did not fear prosecution for misrepresentation of the truth, slander, or libel, had to face the private ire of political opponents in the form of challenges to duels. The parties supported this press, and even if a newspaper spoke for only a small group around one political figure, as was the case with Machado Santos's appropriately titled *O Intransigente*,[67] it had serious repercussions among a comparatively small literate and semiliterate urban populace. In such journalism there was little to distinguish between personal argument and genuine issues. The motivation was the scramble for office, a written expression of a traditional empregomania. Thus, political journalism was both a cause and symptom of the unstable Portuguese multiparty system, dominated by the radical portion of the original Republican party.

Moderate Coalition Governments, September 1911—January 1913

The first constitutional cabinet, nominated on 1 September 1911, was headed by Premier João Chagas, who had returned from Paris, where he had been Portuguese minister to France. Chagas held power only seventy days. Although his government should have been able to lay away credit for defeating the bizarre and semifarcical first monarchist incursion, led by Paiva Couceiro in early October, instead, almost from the beginning of October it was subjected to continual attack from the radical Republicans led by their champion, deputy Afonso Costa. Seconded by the shrill editorials of the radical organ *O Mundo,* the PRP leader attacked Chagas in long speeches on the floor of Congress. Costa asserted that it was neither fair nor democratic that no member of the former Provisional Government had been appointed to the Chagas cabinet, that Chagas was an "outsider," who was in Paris as Portuguese minister and not an elected PRP deputy in Congress. Costa claimed that President Arriaga, in calling Chagas to power without any Republican representation from his portion of the PRP (outside the Almeida-Camacho bloc), and without any members from the Provisional Government of 1910–11, was acting in an unpopular and unconstitutional manner.[68] By mid-October Chagas became the target, too, of such moderate PRP members as Almeida, who in editorials in his personal paper, *A República,* attacked the premier as a man without the ability to hold such a high office.[69] Almeida's abuse was documented by no facts or even accusations; the editorials seemed to be based only on personal dislike or racial prejudice against the Brazilian-born Chagas, who had Amerindian ancestry.

The fall of the short-lived Chagas ministry for seemingly trifling reasons was ominously prophetic. The true cause of the collapse of the Chagas government was the ambition of the radical portion of the Republican party for this highest office. To gain it the radicals had wrested control of the party directorate from the moderates in a vote in the annual party congress in mid-October.[70] Once the new, radical directorate took power in the party, Costa went to the attack in Congress. Chagas soon felt exposed, since the moderate bloc which had nominated him no longer controlled the party. The articulation of political arguments took the form of a façade of largely false legalisms and arbitrary assumptions that obscured the real object of the struggle: power. Costa's arguments about "democracy" and "constitutionality" acted as an attractive cover for attack. Personalism and factionalism prevailed. The fall of Chagas revealed the weakness of President Arriaga, because presumably despite the specious arguments of the radicals, his confidence in Chagas remained intact. His bowing to pressure so early in his term of office was poor precedent for government stability and continuity.

President Arriaga appointed as premier a moderate Republican physician, Dr. Augusto de Vasconcelos, whose cabinet consisted of members of the UNR and a few independents and Democrats. Unionists were dominant. Among those ministers kept on from the Chagas government in this ministry was the Unionist Dr. Sidónio Pais, reserve army major and Coimbra mathematics professor, a man marked for future leadership. The process of choosing premiers—presidents of the Council of Ministers—entailed conferences with party leaders from the parliamentary parties, and the president had not only to select a premier from those acceptable but he had also to secure one who was willing to serve. Refusals by political leaders to accept these invitations became frequent. The reasons were not difficult to find: the terrible pressures of office and fears for their health and their lives. Regular refusals made the president's job very complicated, and often there was a hiatus of at least several days or a week or two between the resignation of one ministry and the finding of a new premier. During the hiatus, effective governance was virtually impossible.

Although Arriaga's appointment of moderate coalition ministries, not dominated by Democrats, was due in part to his personal moderation and apolitical nature, it was also a function of his election as president by bloc votes. The Democrats criticized this president's nominations on the grounds that their party, PRP, had a large number of votes in parliament and therefore should receive the largest number of seats in any cabinet coalition. The Democrats' quest for high office was furthered in November 1911 when numbers of bloc deputies entered the PRP.[71] Even with this increase in Democratic votes, the PRP did not quite have a majority in the Chamber or in the Senate.

President Arriaga worked for a decompression of politics, a moderate policy on the Church. The next question which came to dominate political affairs was the question of the treatment of monarchist prisoners, their trials, jail conditions, and amnesty. This question became, like the Church issue, another source of polarization in Portuguese society.

The Duarte Leite ministry replaced Vasconcelos's government in June 1912, and soon had to face another and more serious monarchist incursion in the north. Bent on overthrowing the republic, Paiva Couceiro and other royalist ex-army officers entered the country in July from Galicia and tested the Republican loyalty of the armed forces. The press and parliament fell into paroxysms of fear and excitement over the question of army loyalty, but the situation produced reasonable Republican unity in the face of monarchists' military conspiracies. There were several reasons why Couceiro's second incursion, like the first, was a failure: The majority of the army officer corps had sworn written and oral support for the republic, and relatively few deserters, mainly enlisted men and few officers, were willing to fight for the monarchy.[72] The conspirators failed to find support in the rural areas when they invaded; the peasants showed no inclination to "rise" and restore the monarchy. Finally, the monarchist invaders lacked arms and had uncoordinated leadership.[73] The monarchist officers who had gone into exile vowing to overthrow the republic were only a fraction of the forty-three officers listed in March 1912 as having resigned or having been dismissed for their political attitudes.[74] Of these forty-three (out of a total of over 1500 in the army officer corps), chiefly lieutenants and captains, at least fifteen were either on the retired or reserve lists. Most of the hard-core monarchists, like the African heroes Captains Paiva Couceiro, Aires de Ornellas, and João de Almeida, had voluntarily resigned their commissions by late 1910 or early 1911, but they did not represent a decisive influence. The officer corps remained, despite fears and doubts, largely unwilling to fight for the monarchy and uncommitted until there were clear signs of monarchist success.

The incursion of July 1912 had more monarchist support in Minho than in Trás-os-Montes. Advance plotting, propaganda, and organizing by priests and other leaders stirred some of the Minhoto population into cheering the monarchist champions as they rode through; there was a local insurrection of the populace at Celorico de Basto, where a Republican *administrador de concelho* was shot dead in the fighting. Discontent in rural Minho over the 1911 army conscription laws was partly to blame; the commander of the Eighth Military Division at Braga considered the new regional recruitment system "premature."[75] The monarchists, though they took part of the town of Valença, could not maintain their foothold, and after suffering heavy casualties for ten days, they were forced to withdraw into Spain. Captain João de Almeida was captured by the Republicans.

The Portuguese monarchists received some aid from local authorities in Galicia, and they were given moral support from the king of Spain himself, Alfonso XII, who was hostile to the republic. Some of the court and higher officials in Spain were willing to aid the Portuguese monarchists to restore the monarchy, but except perhaps for the king, few were willing to consider Spanish military intervention.[76] At a State banquet held in Madrid on 31 December 1910, the king told diplomatic corps representatives from Britain and the United States that Spain in self-defense would soon have to "intervene" in order to "restore order" in Portugal. The monarch inquired what the reaction of the United States would be in the event of a Spanish intervention in Portugal. The American minister replied that the United States would continue to maintain toward the new Portuguese regime an attitude of "benevolent expectancy," but that if Spain intervened, they would exercise "impartial neutrality."[77]

The Portuguese authorities in Lisbon were justifiably concerned about Spanish aid and sympathy for the Portuguese royalist plots in 1911–12. The Portuguese minister made numerous protests at Madrid, and Luso-Spanish relations reached a low in July 1912. The Spanish minister in Lisbon, the marquis of Villalobar, was not only openly hostile to the republic, but allowed Portuguese monarchist army officers to conspire within his very embassy in Lisbon, where apparently he encouraged and aided them.[78] With the failure of the July 1912 incursion and tensions threatening a break in diplomatic relations between the Iberian neighbors, a Brazilian offer broke the deadlock. By a Luso-Spanish convention signed in September 1912[79] a majority of the rank and file monarchist refugees in eastern Spain were to leave Spain for at least three years and were offered refuge and employment in Brazil. Spain deported the monarchist leaders, promised to prosecute those conspirators who came under Spanish law, and signed notes with Lisbon promising no support for future conspiracies against either

Iberian government.[80] The Luso-Spanish convention of 1912, embodied in an exchange of diplomatic notes, effectively halted the immediate monarchist danger. Paiva Couceiro, paladin of activist monarchists, went into exile in London, and many of the Portuguese monarchists were removed from western Spain. Villalobar was transferred from Lisbon only in 1913 after Portuguese protests.

The monarchist plotting and incursions launched from Galicia during 1911-12 had an important impact upon Portuguese politics. Much time and energy were expended on thwarting the conspiracies to overthrow the republic. Parliament, bowing to the exigencies of the monarchist crisis, passed a set of harsh "exception" laws in July 1912 which introduced more stringent press censorship and trial procedures. The government undertook a multitude of trials, arrests, and jailings of real or imagined monarchist plotters; soon many suspects, largely innocent or at least harmless, filled Portuguese jails. The press, parliament, and many urban Republicans grew increasingly alarmed. While a majority of the monarchist population in Portugal was inactive, unwilling to become involved in conspiracies or to take up arms and risk life and limb to restore King Manuel and his discredited establishment, an activist minority stirred up much suspicion, fear, and recrimination.

In parliamentary politics, news and even rumor of monarchist plots and activity outflanked the moderates and favored the radical stands of the PRP and Afonso Costa. Fears of armed insurgency festered in the minds of the more excitable Republican patriots and encouraged further dislike of Spain and Spaniards, a tendency already well established among the Portuguese. Monarchist activity, real or imagined, undermined moderate efforts to establish political consensus, calm, and justice. As the monarchist prisoners grew in number, the question of amnesty became an important issue. Jail conditions and treatment of prisoners as early as 1912 aroused severe criticism from foreign press and observers, and in early 1913 British philanthropists backed a campaign attacking the government's policy.

Alarmism and overreaction concerning monarchist activities pointed up a key Portuguese political problem: although monarchists represented a significant portion of the opposition to government policies, they had no parliamentary representation and no legitimate recourse except through their harassed and besieged press, and their civil rights were in constant jeopardy. Moderate Republicans began to include in their program amnesty for monarchists in order to bring about peace and harmony. Yet there was a more basic issue: the structure of politics did not allow in 1911-13 the legitimate participation of an important segment of society. Until monarchists were able safely to express their opinion, to organize parties, and to enter elections, Portuguese politics would remain oddly schizophrenic.

Like previous premiers, Duarte Leite was worn down by the terrible pressures of office. In early January, ill with nervous prostration, a casualty of the political battles and of the growing power of the PRP parliamentary solidarity, Leite resigned.[81] Reluctantly, President Arriaga fulfilled his duty as chief of state; he nominated a cabinet headed by the PRP leader, Afonso Costa, the chief power in the controversial Provisional Government, who accepted the premiership and the Ministry of Finance. This was the first all-Democratic cabinet and set a significant political precedent in the way power changed hands. Though the 1911 Constitution was vague on the criteria the president of the republic had to employ to choose a ministry, the constant theme of the PRP speeches had now been put into practice; it became customary and expected that if a party held a majority of votes in parliament, the cabinet called to power would reflect that political alignment. Thus the ability of a political party to acquire a majority of deputies and senators would determine its chances for placing its leaders in high national office. In early 1913 the young Portuguese republic entered a new phase of its brief and tormented life.

6 / Democrats' Republic
January 1913—January 1915

> It is not possible to judge the political future of Portugal
> as long as another man, on a par with Affonso Costa,
> does not appear. For now, he is the only one.
>
> João Chagas[1]

The Ultimate Political Man: Afonso Costa

By early 1913, when he was called to head the first government with
an all-Democratic cabinet, Afonso Costa was many things. He was the
idol of the more radical Republican mainstream in the towns and provinces. The most controversial of the Provisional Government ministers
(Justice), Costa was the author of the laws which had polarized the
political nation. More than any other politician in generations, Costa
was "the most beloved and the most hated of Portuguese," especially
during the years 1910–30.[2]

Afonso Costa (1871–1937) was born in the small village of Seia in
Beira Baixa district to middle-class parents. His father was a lawyer and
was prominent in local politics; his mother came from a family of petty
nobility near Viseu. Although his family was not wealthy, Costa
received the best education obtainable in late nineteenth-century
Portugal. Typical of his generation, a generation thrown into politics
by the events of 1890–91, he rapidly became a rising political star whose
every activity drove him further into politics. At age sixteen he entered
the Coimbra University Law Faculty, graduated at twenty-three, and
received his law doctorate at twenty-four. The next year he joined the
Law Faculty, and at age twenty-eight the precocious and energetic
Costa was appointed a full professor, or *catedrático*. His fame as a professor was matched by his reputation as a hard-working lawyer. Entering politics at age nineteen as a student Republican, Costa became active in political journalism, the crucible in which politics for his and
successive generations was fired. In 1900 Costa was elected to parliament as a Republican deputy from Oporto, and he rapidly acquired
renown as a long-winded orator and charismatic debater who, next to
António José de Almeida, was perhaps the most effective opponent of

the monarchy. While in the Provisional Government as minister of justice, Costa became the leading, powerful personality in the government and the champion of the radical wing of the Portuguese Republican party.

The deeds and personality of Afonso Costa have become the subject of a lively debate in Portuguese historical literature. This debate is colored by the very personalismo of which his enemies and critics have accused Costa. His antagonists and their political descendants have leveled at Costa a host of accusations, mainly ill-founded: that he was a dishonest politician, a radical Marxist, an unusually unethical lawyer, an immoral statesman who literally "sold" his countrymen as soldiers to the Allies in the Great War for personal profits,[3] and an anti-Christ who for spite destroyed the Church. Following biased accounts written by Costa's political enemies such as Machado Santos, Almeida,[4] and the newspaper O Século,[5] Spanish historian Pabón went so far as to ascribe much of the political violence and disruption of the First Republic to Afonso Costa alone as "the soul of the disorder."[6] Pabón's unfair and politically deterministic interpretation has been adopted by successive generations of conservative writers, including Integralists and monarchists, who continue to ascribe to Costa much of the blame for the failures of the First Republic.[7] Even the most sympathetic recent writers have not asked fundamental questions about the place of Afonso Costa in the politics of the republic; instead, they have fallen into rather sterile debates about whether or not Costa was a Marxist, and about the wisdom of his policies in the context of the social and class situation of 1910–26.[8]

If Afonso Costa's reputation has been abused and his role exaggerated, his place in Republican history must be carefully assessed. The

Afonso Costa in the Constituent National Assembly, 1911. (By Correia Dias, from Braz Burity [Joaquim Madureira], A Forja da Lei [Coimbra, 1915], p. 457.)

more useful analyses of Costa have placed him in the political context
of his times and have viewed him in the perspective of the pressures
and problems he confronted. Artur Ribeiro Lopes acknowledged that
Costa was pressured by "parliament and the street" and was caught
between labor disorders on the Left, and monarchist plots on the
Right.[9] Perhaps the most realistic yet critical assessment of the
controversial statesman comes from Republican politician Francisco
Cunha Leal, who saw Costa as "a romantic disguised in a dry
intellectualism."[10] According to Cunha Leal, Costa was "a real
conservative" in economic and social policies, manipulating the masses
while being manipulated by friends. Costa's dilemma involved support
and power: in order to please his urban following he was obliged to
employ a language of "radical truculence," and to pursue
anticlericalism; but to keep his provincial clientele, he had to remain
conservative in his policies.

Afonso Costa's record as a politician and statesman during his
thirteen-month term as chief of government, 1913–14, suggest that
Cunha Leal's analysis is essentially accurate. Costa's ideas on reform
were constructive, and, given time and greater political unity, he might
have brought stability to the republic. He attempted a political juggling
act, carefully skirting the amnesty question and perhaps miscalculating
by not introducing it into his program. He was brought down by his
own political and personal stubbornness as much as by President
Arriaga's initiative and by bitter opposition from enemies on the Left
and Right. Costa was a most talented politician and a deft administrator. His personal strength and dislike of losing political face
made him popular with his partisans; such political tesura, such a sense
of personal dignity, however, made him a failure as a conciliator. While
Costa demonstrated inflexibility and probably erred on the side of
political cautiousness in refusing amnesty during his term, it is by no
means certain that an amnesty would have brought political peace. The
conflict aroused by conspiracies against his government and the
republic by elements of the Left and Right was some justification for
his policy.

The First Afonso Costa Government, January 1913—February 1914

The Costa government presented the customary ministerial
declaration, or program, in parliament on 10 January 1913. Making no
mention of amnesty and only a passing reference to the Law of Separation, Costa emphasized a program that would feature a house-cleaning

of the civil service–bureaucracy, presumably one that would please his Democratic following, and a balanced state budget.[11] Clearly, Costa intended to avoid making decisions on issues which might divide his party, and he hoped to run an efficient administration.

The accomplishments of the Costa administration were important. In economy and finance, his government managed to present to parliament in mid-1913 the first balanced budget in years, with a *superavit* ("surplus") of some thousand contos.[12] A Brake Law (*a le-travão*) was also passed, whereby no increases or decreases in expenses could be introduced during the discussion of the general state budget in parliament. Costa's Electoral Law of 3 July 1913 was more controversial. This law required voters to be literate, male and twenty-one or over, thus excluding women from the suffrage. Also excluded were all soldiers and sailors on active duty. All armed-forces personnel, except those on leave, were deprived of eligibility for the Congress, and all military personnel were made ineligible for the civil service.[13] The intent of this law was to undercut potential monarchist or conservative political power in elections and administration and to demilitarize Portuguese politics. One consequence however was to anger and alienate elements of the military leadership.

What credit Costa gained from his financial measures, which also involved a cut in the military budget, he more than lost in labor troubles and violence in the streets. Under Costa's government militant vigilante groups were given fairly free rein; Carbonários clashed with labor groups, usually led by the anarcho-syndicalists. Anticlerical activities continued. On 10 June in Lisbon, militants threw bombs into a procession of Catholics honoring Lisbon's patron saint, Anthony of Padua; several children were killed, and an enraged crowd attacked syndicalist headquarters.

Conspiracies against the government intensified. On 27 April radical syndicalists, angered by the government's sometimes brutal repression of syndicalist strikes and encouraged by independent politician Machado Santos and his political friends, tried to bring off a coup d'etat. The government crushed the plot and jailed many persons. Despite the Luso-Spanish Convention of 1912, some monarchists continued to conspire to overthrow the republic. One monarchist plot was aborted in late July, and a larger, better-organized conspiracy was discovered and crushed on 21 October 1913. The October plot aroused much excitement and controversy and led the government deeper into conflict with the opposition. This plot was in part instigated by the police spy Homero de Lencastre, whose later confessions under oath to a Spanish judge embarrassed the government. Military records reveal,

however, that monarchists were in fact organizing a military pronunciamento using discontented troops in northern Portugal, the region where
their cause found the greatest support.[14] The officer corps remained
loyal and quickly disarmed dissident units near Viana do Castelo. That
the October plot was a genuine monarchist attempt to overthrow Costa
and the republic is amply documented by the extensive reports of
monarchist activity provided by Portuguese consuls in Galicia. The
government, therefore, was prepared, and the attempt was rapidly
crushed with a minimum of bloodshed. It was significant, nevertheless,
that the chief grievance played upon by the monarchist conspirators
was the religious question. In one barracks revolt the rallying cry was
reported as: "Boys, let us defend our religion!"[15]

In Lisbon the monarchist plot fizzled and the only consequence was
the destruction of the bizarre Museum of the Revolution, a radical
Republican institution that housed artifacts of the 1908 regicide in a
former convent. The republic's jails now bulged with prisoners, some
arrested merely on suspicion. Conditions were wretched in some of the
prisons and the government faced intensified protests and pressures to
improve conditions, to free many prisoners, and to legislate a generous
amnesty.

During 1913 the amnesty question linked with the activity of the militant Republican vigilante groups, became a cause célèbre.[16] Pressures
on the Costa regime came from at least three sources: internal
opposition, advice and urging from moderate Republican leaders, and a
foreign press and philanthropic campaign based largely in Britain. The
amnesty question raised the issues of police brutality, human rights,
inhumane jail conditions, and vigilante crimes. The accusations
mounted against the Costa regime contained some truth. During
1910–13 many accusations were leveled at Portugal by foreign powers—
especially Britain—concerning slavery and forced labor in Portuguese
West Africa.[17] But whereas these accusations tended to rally Portuguese
political groups around ideas of national honor and colonial self-
interest, the amnesty question, which concerned prisoners in the
metropole, was especially political and divisive. The Evolutionist,
Unionist, and other opposition parties, allied with the more active
monarchists in Portugal, used this issue to try to defeat the Costa
government and gain power for themselves.[18] Thus the opposition
manufactured and spread exaggerated stories and half-truths to
discredit the Costa government. By mid–1913, these attacks, which
demanded an early and full amnesty, were most useful to monarchists.

To the amnesty demands of the internal opposition were added the
private urgings of moderate Democratic leaders. Most important was

the pleading of Bernardino Machado in his letters from Rio, where he was serving as Portugal's minister to Brazil during 1912-14.[19] Machado's confidential urging reached a crescendo in late 1913. In anxious letters to the Foreign Ministry he urged an amnesty to coincide with the third anniversary of the Fifth of October Revolution, which would involve freeing the allegedly monarchist prisoners from Portuguese jails and deporting them to Brazil. Machado believed somewhat naively that amnesty would solve most of the troubles of the Costa government, since Costa would gain popularity both in Brazil, where the Portuguese colony was largely promonarchist, and in Britain. Machado believed that amnesty would silence the hostile Brazilian press, which was emitting what he described colorfully as "latrine literature," and would consolidate Brazilian support. In long telegrams, too, Machado pleaded with the Foreign Affairs Ministry to use its influence to introduce amnesty, which, he claimed, would tend to "isolate" both the monarchists in Portugal and their monarchist sympathizers in Brazil.[20] Machado's strong advocacy of amnesty had no impact on Costa's policy, but Machado's apparently shrewd formula for consensus probably impressed President Arriaga, who in January 1914 favored Machado as the man to replace Costa.[21]

During 1913 and into early 1914, severe pressures were put on the Costa government by a lurid British press and humanitarian campaign concerned with the political prisoners. Initiated by the critical writing of Aubrey Bell in the London *Morning Post* in 1911-12, the campaign reached a peak with the revelations of the duchess of Bedford in her articles in the *Times* (5 April 1913), and the *Daily Mail* (7 April), based on visits to Portuguese prisons, and with a memorable protest meeting on 22 April in London. At the meeting, even so sympathetic a friend as the African authority Sir Harry Johnston admitted in a speech: "All this is doing vast harm to the position of Portugal among European nations."[22] Widely distributed books and pamphlets demanded an early amnesty. Prominent among these were booklets written by E. M. Tenison (which went into at least five editions) and by Philip Gibbs, the correspondent of the *Daily Chronicle*.[23] Implicit in this British protest, an attack which put into shadow even the British protest over slavery in Portuguese West Africa, were veiled threats of British intervention in Portugal and perhaps a break in Anglo-Portuguese relations.

This British campaign slacked off during 1914, but it brought the Costa government into some disrepute with the British public, and obliged Costa to answer in an officially sponsored pamphlet the statements made by the duchess of Bedford. The British allegations fell upon sensitive ears in Lisbon. Tenison described the political prisoners' situation as a "tyranny which is an insult to humanity and an outrage upon European civilisation."[24] Gibbs's booklet denounced what he claimed was a "reign of terror" by the Carbonária, which he identified as the "secret police" of Afonso Costa's government. The prisons, he asserted, were filled with innocent prisoners arrested on no evidence, and almost all the Portuguese were united against the government. Gibbs concluded his report, which was typical of much of the material in the daily press in Britain in 1913-14, with an appeal to readers to send money to the British Relief Fund, to benefit "destitute families of Portuguese political prisoners."

The reports of Gibbs, Tenison, and the duchess of Bedford revealed injustices and official irresponsibility. Portuguese law decreed that a Portuguese citizen could be imprisoned in solitary confinement for no more than eight days without trial, but Gibbs discovered that some prisoners had been kept in isolation for more than forty days, and some were jailed without trial for fifteen months.[25] Gibbs's observations are confirmed by the reports of other foreign observers of the period, including the writer Bell and diplomat Hardinge,[26] and it is certain that the Costa government and its local administrators of prisons were remiss. But the Costa administration eventually did work to reform prison conditions, and it confronted great pressures hostile to a general amnesty or release of prisoners, pressures which the foreign humanitarians in 1913-14 failed to mention. Monarchist conspirators manipulated the outraged British press. The British protesters unwittingly publicized as facts what was often Portuguese monarchist propaganda. Some of the criticism of the Costa government was based mainly on evidence presented by biased and partisan enemies of the Democrats. Gibbs, for example, accepted uncritically the allegations and exaggerated interpretation of the monarchist lawyer José Soares da Cunha e Costa. Other writers, like the Irish Catholic Francis Mc-Cullagh, consciously attempted to discredit the Republican government with such classic pieces as the article "Portugal: The Nightmare Republic."[27]

Not simply justice and humanitarianism were involved in the problems of prisoners and amnesty. The government leadership sensed Democratic hostility to early and complete amnesty, and was slow to improve the prisons, despite a general consensus that conditions were bad. Prisons, prisoners, courts, and jails were a historic, national Portuguese problem that had been the concern of foreign critics long before 1913 and would surface again in succeeding decades with different regimes. As the issue became complicated with partisan maneuvering, the opposition, including the more irresponsible monarchist conspirators and their allies, spread tales of horror. Ironically, it was the continuation of monarchist armed conspiracy which, during 1912 and 1913—despite the painfully negotiated accord with Spain in late 1912—delayed the passage of an amnesty bill. Once the time for amnesty came, however, few groups could agree on terms of conciliation.

By early 1914, there was no sign that Costa was about to propose an amnesty bill. The British campaign had reached fever pitch in public meetings and sensationalist press reports, and Gibbs's book went into new editions. Other pressures on the government added to its unpopularity: the continued British humanitarian protests concerning labor in Portuguese West Africa,[28] and massive new strikes, including a paralyzing railway strike in northern Portugal. In addition to all of this, a serious deadlock gripped the Congress.

The record of the first Republican Congress, 1911-14, was not a happy one. Daily conduct of affairs in both chambers was hampered by considerable absenteeism and the unruly conduct of deputies and senators—which at times led to noisy arguments, walkouts of groups of deputies, fistfights, and even challenges to duels. Congressional turbulence caused some men to resign their seats.[29] When quorums were present, congressional sessions were long and often unproductive; representatives expended much time and effort in long speeches. By early 1914 most of the legislation promised in the final articles of the 1911 Constitution had not even been drafted, much less approved. Whatever legislation of value had been passed was usually the result of efforts of a strong executive power, such as the Costa government, 1913-14, which did put through a constructive program, including the creation of a new cabinet post, the Ministry of Public Instruction.[30]

A major problem of government had to do with the functioning of Congress. According to Article 52 of the 1911 Constitution, "the ministers must appear in sessions of Congress and always have the right to be heard in defense of their acts."[31] This rule was based in part on traditions inherited from the Constitutional Monarchy and on the supremacy of the legislative power in the minds of the constitution-makers. The executive thus found little time to analyze problems and propose legislative solutions, since it spent an inordinate amount of time in Congress, before both chambers, submitting itself to questioning and discussions. Not only did the cabinet ministers have to appear—there was a special section in the chambers set aside for their seating—but whenever there was a major question from deputies, the premier himself would appear. Under a harmonious system, or one where the opposition was essentially loyal, the appearance of the government in Congress might not have been especially troublesome. In the severely partisan atmosphere in Portugal, however, it was crippling.

Partisan conflicts in Congress grew in intensity during 1911–14. The Democrats achieved an electoral victory at the supplemental elections of November 1913 which enabled them to control a majority of seats (101) in the Chamber of Deputies to 43 for the Evolutionists, and 38 for the Unionists.[32] Though the Democrats could now command most votes in the Chamber, they did not have a majority in the Senate, where the Evolutionists, Unionists, and independents held 47 seats to the 24 of the Democrats. This enabled the opposition to block Democratic projects in the Senate; legislation that passed the Chamber, therefore, was defeated or deadlocked in the Senate.

The increasingly bitter opposition to the Democrats in the Congress was based in part on the widespread conviction among the opposition parties that the PRP had an electoral monopoly that could not be broken and that if public opinion were fairly sampled the Democrats would be defeated. The Democrats were accused of rigging the November 1913 supplementary elections. The PRP won these elections probably because of three natural developments: the PRP political organization was larger, more efficient and more popularly based than the opposition parties; the October 1913 monarchist conspiracies had won the Democrats some voter sympathy; and traditional voting habits favored the PRP. The Portuguese electorate had a history of considerable abstention,[33] and those who did vote tended to be conservative in that many would "vote for the government" (in power), especially since it controlled patronage and the bureaucracy. The Democrats won in the 1913 supplementary elections not by rigging, but by taking advantage of the political situation.

The oppositionist Republican parties were unable to present a united front. During 1911–14 a number of attempts were made to form a single united moderate-conservative Republican party which would effectively oppose the PRP. The bloc and UNR had fragmented in early 1912, as the Unionists and Evolutionists had emerged as two rival parties. In 1913 the impetuous independent Machado Santos, now a mortal enemy of the Democrats, formed a coalition group of opposition parties in order to dispute the November elections. His ephemeral Liga das Oposições ("Oppositions' League") was composed of the parliamentary opposition parties against the PRP and included some Socialists. The Liga was ineffective in its brief life of a few months and disbanded after the elections.[34] A successor coalition of opposition parties, A Conjunção Republicana ("Republican Coalition"), lasted only four months and disintegrated in April 1914 for the reasons that were to undermine all the anti-PRP coalitions during the First Republic: its narrow purpose (to unite only for elections and only against the Democrats), its lack of popular support, personalismo, and basic disagreements as to which party in the group would get its program and leadership accepted by the rest.[35] During 1914 it became clear that the opposition coalitions were not enduring and viable political alternatives to the majority parliamentary party.

Obstruction in the Senate now became the bright hope in the increasingly desperate opposition. The deadlock in the Senate reached a crisis in January 1914. The minister of the colonies in Costa's cabinet had named a new governor of Guiné (Portuguese Guinea), and, instead of waiting for Senate approval of this candidate, had provisionally appointed him on his own authority.[36] The opposition in the Senate claimed that the minister of the colonies had acted illegally and that in order to cover his tracks had published two decrees, which became known as *os gémeos* ("the twins"): one decree dismissing the man named provisionally (apparently he was a political appointee); and the second decree naming the *same* man as "interim" governor! After 19 January the Costa government ministers refused to attend the Senate, even after the issuance of a "note of interpellation," which required the government to go before Congress to answer questions. Costa stated that he would not enter the Senate as long as the opposition leader, Manuel Goulart de Medeiros, was Senate president. On 21 January Senator Alberto Silveira, on a vote of 29 to 5 with a bare quorum, was able to pass a "nonconfidence" motion, which, citing Article 25 of the Constitution, attacked the government for "perverting all parliamentary law," and resolved to inform the president of the republic that the "unconstitutional" Costa cabinet had to be dismissed.[37]

What with labor disputes that resulted in strikes, the failure of the government to act on the amnesty question, and now complete deadlock in the Senate, the prospects of the Costa government of passing further legislation were slim at best. The president of the republic decided to act. He wrote a note on 23 January which called for a cooling-off period in government, *acalmação,* and intimated that the Costa government had to go. Costa submitted his resignation along with that of the government on 25 January 1914, alleging that the president had shown lack of confidence in his government and that the replacement of his government was not constitutional since his party, the majority party in the Congress, desired that Costa continue in power. President Arriaga stated that he desired a nonpartisan government in order to cool off the political situation.[38]

To President Arriaga, and to the moderate Republican press,[39] Bernardino Machado appeared to be the man of the hour. When he arrived at Lisbon on a ship from Rio de Janeiro, he was met by large crowds of well-wishers who hailed him as the leader to solve the republic's political crisis and unify the divided Portuguese family. On 9 February Machado as premier formed a "nonpartisan" government, composed of nonpolitical men, but including three moderate and largely unknown Democrats. Temporarily Machado also took over the key ministries of Interior and Foreign Affairs.[40]

The fall of Costa's government in early 1914 was an important watershed. An all-Democratic cabinet, backed by a majority of votes in the 1913 election, led by the most formidable PRP leader, and backed by his party, despite its real accomplishments, had been unable to remain in power more than thirteen months. It had a majority of votes in Congress, held the lion's share of the electoral machinery, but found itself overwhelmed by a political crisis which only the president of the republic, seemingly, could resolve. That crisis was due as much to the Byzantine tactics of the opposition parties as to the pride and the mistakes of the Costa government and the excesses of the militant vigilante groups, for whom the Democrats were held responsible.

Although there was no textual support in the Constitution, the function of the office of the presidency of the republic was emerging as that of a key arbiter between the parties, even as a moderating power, resembling that of the king in the Constitutional Monarchy. The president lacked the powers and prerogatives to play such a role; he had no party backing, no real control over the armed forces, and he could not dissolve the Congress in case of a deadlock. Yet, in a system where the majority of the Congress still opposed a presidentialist republic, he had, with arguable legality, dismissed a government without the support of a complete congressional vote.

Crippled Coalition Governments, February 1914—December 1914

Who was the new man called to guide the destinies of the young republic? The new man was an old man; Bernardino Machado, born in Brazil in 1851, and aged sixty-two when appointed, was one of the older Republican leaders.[41] A Coimbra professor like Costa, he brought respected age, class (he was independently wealthy and a patriarchal figure with sixteen children), and brains to the office. With his neat white beard, he appeared to ooze political stability, respectability, and moderation. Machado was highly intelligent, a Democrat but not a radical, and a man who was brilliant at diplomacy. His record was extraordinary as foreign minister under the harassed Provisional Government, and as minister to Brazil during 1912–14 he had laid the basis for excellent relations with that South American republic. His strong views on an early and thorough amnesty were the reason he was selected for the post of premier. He had passed them on to the lonely Arriaga, who soon invited him to return to Lisbon. Machado was perhaps the most cultured and polished of the Republican políticos, well traveled, articulate, a Portuguese pioneer in pedagogy and anthropological studies, the holder of Portugal's first University Chair in Anthropology (1886), and creator of Portugal's first ethnological museum (1893). Machado knew personally the European intelligentsia. He was close friends with the Spanish educator and reformer Francisco Giner de Los Rios, and was most impressed with his school, the Institución Libre de Enseñanza.[42]

Machado's flaws were not as apparent as his strengths. He was not as strong a leader as Costa, and was not able to withstand severe pressures. Although he had progressive ideas on the amnesty issue when abroad as a diplomat, once in power he talked and intrigued more than he acted. He was no more Machiavellian than his rivals, but he came under criticism for compromising to such an extent that few were satisfied.[43] Above all, he was ambitious to become president of the republic, an office he felt suited his age, personality, and unofficial status as patriarch of the Republicans.

Machado failed to carry out the difficult assignment Arriaga had given him. An amnesty bill was the paramount point. When his compromise Amnesty Bill passed Congress and was published on 21 February 1914, partisan reaction was not very enthusiastic, although the combined votes of the Democrats and Unionists had secured passage.[44] Monarchists and anarcho-syndicalists opposed the bill, as it did not pardon monarchist leaders, who were to be deported for up to ten years, and it did not pardon workers convicted of violence and sabotage. The militant vigilante groups disliked the Amnesty Bill on general principle, as it might spell an end to their paid employment.

Even in its compromise form, the 1914 Amnesty Bill was a significant accomplishment. Under its provisions between one thousand and two thousand political prisoners were almost immediately released from Portuguese prisons. Only eleven monarchist leaders were deported under Article 2, since most of them were already in exile.[45] The bill initiated a brief period of relief and political decompression. Machado's mission of "peace and reconciliation" appeared to be working. The government relaxed its anticlerical policy and allowed major religious figures to return from exile. The patriarch of Lisbon, António Mendes Belo, returned after two years in exile, and a vast popular attendance marked the celebration of a Te Deum at Lisbon Cathedral.[46] During the religious holidays of spring 1914, church attendance, which was authorized by the government, was heavy. Anticlerical feelings in the Lisbon area ran high, however, and there were public incidents. A Republican public outcry forced Machado to refuse a visa to an ailing Jesuit who requested permission to reenter the country.

Machado found such congressional opposition to a revision of the Law of Separation that he was unable to change the letter of the law and had to settle for altering its interpretation. In carrying out his program, Machado ran into an obstacle that eventually caused his downfall: vigilante activity. The Democratic party controlled the majority of votes in the Congress, and Machado was not a party leader. Afonso Costa was the boss and leading deputy of the PRP. The excesses of the followers of the radical Democrats continued to discredit the government, which many acknowledged as dependent upon the good will of the Democratic party machine. There were complaints in Congress,[47] and in the moderate Republican press,[48] against the acts of the militant vigilante groups, variously called "white" or "black ants," who were giving Portugal a bad image abroad. If the government was aware of these problems, it was ineffective in coping with them. Street violence continued, and the police made few arrests.

The problem of vigilante activity is a complex one which went beyond simple criminal activity or low-level political intimidation. What became known in the First Republic as "the white ants," was not one but a series of organizations of Republican groups, including the Carbonária, often composed of lower-class or lower middle-class urbanites enrolled in local Democratic party organizations. Some appear to have been officially on the payrolls of the civil governments of several districts early in the republic; others were the hirelings of Democratic bosses. Their role is controversial, and until a full-scale history of their activities is written it will remain so. Yet all the forces whose activities worked to discredit the Costa government of 1913–14 and to alienate the officer corps in the army, the militant vigilante groups were perhaps the most decisively important.

The importance of the "white ants" as a political factor diminished during 1914 because of the Machado government policies, the hostility of the general public, and the determination of the Republican leadership to defuse political conflicts and to pursue more lawful methods. Attempts were made to demobilize the vigilante groups, which often acted as unofficial security forces; the Carbonária was partially disbanded.[49] But the government failed to suppress the "white ants," who continued to act as a kind of secret police and spy force which intervened in police and army activity.[50]

After a cabinet shuffle in June 1914, the Machado government, with a mandate from Arriaga, prepared for parliamentary elections. By law, the elections were to be held on 1 November 1914, and on 30 June the first Republican Congress completed its legal term. But the elections, which were to be the first free and open general elections of the Portuguese republic, were forestalled by domestic dissention and World War I.

On 28 June the Austrian Archduke Ferdinand and his wife were assassinated in Serbia.

Portugal's role in World War I was to become the subject of bitter partisan conflicts. At first, however, it appeared that the Machado government, supported by the Democrats, would gain popularity with its war policy. After the outbreak of armed conflict in Europe, Machado called Congress into an extraordinary session on 8 August 1914. He pledged that Portugal would fulfill her obligations to her ally, England. Portugal, therefore, would not remain neutral. Congress voted unanimously to approve Machado's requests for the "necessary powers" "to guarantee order in all the country and to safeguard the national interests. . . ."[51] This grant of war powers to the government was unusually vague and broad. On 23 November in another extraordinary session of Congress, Machado got a bill passed, again unanimously, which gave the government, in effect, carte blanche, for intervening in the war.

In the first few months of the war, the pro-Allies policy of the Democrats, and by implication, the Machado government, was generally well received by moderate Republicans. Fear that Germany menaced the Portuguese African colonies informed some of this support.[52] But several groups opposed too active a pro-Allies policy on the grounds that Portugal, a small, poor nation, should exercise great caution in committing herself when it was uncertain who would win, and some resented England for having exerted so much power over Portugal in the past. Monarchist groups and the Unionist party, with its leader, Brito Camacho, began to express doubts and even opposition to the Machado war policies by December 1914.[53]

The war assumed more serious dimensions when German military units threatened the Portuguese in Mozambique and attacked Portuguese installations in southern Angola. On 18 December 1914 at Naulila, near the border with German Southwest Africa, a German expedition defeated a Portuguese detachment of European and African troops.[54] Naulila and the possibility that the Germans might appropriate the Portuguese African colonies caused considerable excitement in the press. The Portuguese government responded by dispatching army expeditions to reinforce their troops in Angola and Mozambique. By 1915 Portugal was fighting a desultory bush war in tropical Africa against Germany though neither nation had issued a declaration of war. The German threat to Portuguese Africa, by arousing Portuguese fears and intensifying colonial interest and action, greatly influenced the decisions concerning Portugal's role in the war in Europe.

Despite considerable political support for its war policy, the Machado government resigned in December, having failed to arrange for the general elections for Congress because the parties were locked in conflict over which government would preside over these elections and how would they be conducted. Out of this conflict grew the constitutional crisis of January 1915.

The 1915 Elections and the Movement of Swords

A showdown on the general elections was approaching. On 12 December 1914 President Arriaga replaced Machado with a government of Vitor Hugo de Azevedo Coutinho,[55] a Democrat and former president of the Chamber of Deputies. His government was composed of unknown Democrats, except for the crucial post of the Ministry of the Interior, filled now by Alexandre Braga, a radical Democrat with a reputation for ruthlessness. Arriaga had been obliged to call such a government, since the Evolutionists and Unionists lacked the congressional votes to form cabinets alone, and since the Democrats held a clear majority in the Chamber of Deputies. Afonso Costa actually controlled the Azevedo Coutinho government just as he had maneuvered behind the Machado government. Although Arriaga's decision to nominate an all-Democratic cabinet was in accord with the Democrat's predominance in the Congress, and Azevedo Coutinho gave a solemn pledge to preside "impartially" over the 1915 elections, the opposition issued hostile declarations of noncooperation. No question was more important than the elections: the Democrats were determined to remain in control of a majority of votes in Congress, and the opposition parties were equally resolved to throw them out of office.

As of mid-January 1915 political and governmental conditions greatly favored an electoral victory of the Democrats. It appeared that they would win an even greater majority than in 1913 and would also gain, for the first time, a Senate majority, thus undermining the one parliamentary foothold the opposition parties had. The Costa government had consolidated the Democrats' position by means of the 1913 Electoral Law, and the January 1915 Electoral Law, passed by Democratic votes, which again forbade armed-forces personnel to vote and which gave the minorities—those who did not win majority votes in the electoral circles—a reduced representation. In January 1913 Costa had appointed Democrats to the administrative positions that in Portuguese political tradition normally significantly influenced election results: the district civil governors and the administrators of the *concelhos*.[56] With these officials loyal to the party, and with a measure of control over electoral machinery, patronage, and the voters' lists, the 1915 elections appeared to be an easy Democratic victory. To this advantage were added the powers of the Azevedo Coutinho government in presiding over the forthcoming elections. Traditionally, the key ministerial post for domestic electoral influence was Interior, and this was filled by the radical lawyer Alexandre Braga, who came under immediate abuse from the opposition press and parties.[57] There is evidence, too, that the Democrats deliberately defeated Machado in a parliamentary vote in December in order to oust him—since he was likely to compromise in a crisis—and install a new government with ministers like Braga, who might assure electoral victory.[58] In Congress just before adjournment on 11 January, Afonso Costa defended the all-Democratic government presiding over the planned elections by saying that the government had a majority in the Congress, it was "supported by the entire nation," and the PRP, as the strongest party, needed no aid from the government to win. Costa's thesis was that a partisan, not a coalition government was best fitted to conduct elections in the spirit "of complete impartiality."[59]

The opposition parties appeared to have some support in a constitutional "precedent" which President Arriaga tried to introduce. Nearly a year earlier, on 24 February 1914, as the Machado government entered power with a mandate to conduct elections later in the year, President Arriaga had issued to the press an important official statement which later assumed the status of presidential policy. Arriaga deemed it essential that from now on, in order to assure free elections, elections could be presided over only by what he described as "nonpartisan," ("*extra-partidário*") governments.[60] He thus implied that the November 1913 supplemental elections had been rigged. The Evolutionists, Unionists, and independents, led by Machado Santos, seized on this policy statement as a major reason for opposing and obstructing the activity of Democratic-dominated governments during 1914 and early

1915. Cries of illegality and rigging filled the opposition press and speeches in Congress. Leaders like Almeida and Camacho, in their quest for high office, knew that there were only two ways to break legally the electoral grip of the Democrats; one was by parliamentary obstruction, and the other was by allegations in the press and parliament which might discredit Costa and his party. The behavior of the opposition parties reflected the nature of Portuguese politics as well as a general tendency in politics in many nations. To use a variation of Lord Acton's famous phrase: If power corrupts, so does the persistent absence of power. Frustrated by their lack of power, brought up on the practice of intricate maneuvering, the use of legalisms, and a reluctance to lose face, the opposition turned to desperate methods. This in turn triggered desperate responses from the dominant Democrats.

In late 1914 parliamentary obstructionism became an obsessive art. In order to block the legislation of the Machado government in the extraordinary three-day session of 27–30 July 1914, the Evolutionists and Unionists refused to attend Congress, thus halting all official business. In December, as the Democrats were about to nominate new senators to fill vacant seats and thereby gain a majority in that chamber, the Unionists in a body resigned their Chamber of Deputy seats—while retaining their Senate seats—in order to make the approval of the changes by the Chamber of Deputies illegal. Brito Camacho's party organ declared that their motives were to show that the executive had abused the powers of the parliament.[61] Camacho and Almeida, backed up by the impulsive Machado Santos, urged the president to dismiss the Azevedo Coutinho government, since, they alleged, it would not or could not preside impartially over the general elections which were now scheduled for 7 March 1915.

Radical proposals by the rank-and-file Democrats and strong statements by their leaders further alarmed the opposition. In the annual PRP party congress, held in October 1914, Costa declared his program was to abolish the Senate, further restrict the powers of the president of the republic, and eliminate minority representation in parliament. Costa again for public consumption and for the party had employed his language of "radical truculence," but he was forced to compromise. In the January 1915 Electoral Law, the opposition received a guarantee of representation, no matter who won the elections.[62] The opposition supported universal suffrage, which would allow the illiterate and the armed forces to vote. They also demanded that the Azevedo Coutinho government replace the civil governors and administrators of the concelhos with non-PRP bureaucrats. As of 12 January as Congress adjourned until the completion of the scheduled March elections, the oppositions' chances at the polls appeared quite slim, and there was talk that the Evolutionists and Unionists would abstain from the elections.[63]

The political situation suddenly took a dramatic turn: an organized movement of army officers carried out a bloodless golpe de estado that overthrew the Democratic-dominated government and brought into power a military government headed by the senior general of the army, Joaquim Pimenta de Castro. This movement became known as the "Movement of Swords," as the protesting officers ostentatiously surrendered their swords to the president of the republic. The immediate source of the officers' allegedly nonpolitical protest was the transfer of an army officer, Major Craveiro Lopes, from his unit at Figueira da Foz. This transfer, claimed the officers, was blatantly political and was due to pressures from the local formiga branca.

The emergence of the Movement of Swords marked the most serious crisis yet in the life of the young republic.

7 / Wars and Revolutions

January 1915—December 1917

> There was no better occasion to consecrate the flag of the republic than on the battlefields of Europe; but also [there was] no better pretext for the opposition with which to fight the interventionist party with even more passion. . . .
>
> David Magno[1]

The Politicization of the Portuguese Army, 1910–15

> Let us honor the Portuguese army which knew how to maintain its traditions of political independence so well [in the 1910 Revolution].
>
> António Machado Santos[2]

During the first four-and-a-half years of the First Republic, the Portuguese army developed into an active political force. What the navy experienced in the decade before 1910 now happened to the army. Republicanization in the ranks and among the Republican sergeants who had been so important in the 1910 Revolution played a significant role in this process. In 1910 the army officer corps was composed of largely monarchist or neutral officers; only a handful of young junior officers were Republicans. The latter, known as the "Young Turks," attempted further republicanization in all ranks.[3] By January 1915 this politicization had gone so far that pressures emanating from a section of the army officer corps caused a change in government.

The army officer corps was strongly influenced by the convulsions in Portuguese society: the Republicans' revival of the pronunciamento tradition in national politics, 1890–1910; the propaganda and agitation of the Republicans and their Carbonária allies; the influential militarism and praetorian monarchism in the royal court of King Carlos I (1889–1908), and the fame and example of Major Mousinho de Albuquerque, the frustrated man on horseback who committed suicide in 1902. Army officers were also affected by the increasingly violent activities of unions and anarchists and syndicalists to further their causes.

While political parties and their leaders—both Republicans and monarchists—encouraged military insurrections in order to attain public office and to carry out their plans, the officer corps in the first years of the republic remained largely passive. Their passivity, however, could not last long in such an atmosphere of increasing violence and aggressive self-assertion.

On the Fifth of October in Lisbon to the good fortune of the Carbonária and the Portuguese Republican party, the army officers—with rare exceptions—failed to defend the monarchy, preferring to be inactive, or neutral, or to "disappear." After the revolution, civil-military relations deteriorated. Some Republicans considered the army's negative pronunciamento at best an act of weakness and unreliability, at worst, cowardice. Only a few Republican leaders, such as Machado Santos, flattered the army officers and praised what he termed their political "independence" during the fighting. The Republicans organized civilian militia and vigilante groups, such as the Social Vigilance Group,[4] which shook military discipline by invading military posts and barracks, haranguing enlisted men with political oratory, placing the army under their surveillance before, during, and after the abortive monarchist incursions and before attempted coups, 1911–14. The Carbonária on several occasions in 1911 and 1912 decisively intervened in the defense of the Republican regime in military operations in the north and in Lisbon.[5]

During this period public opinion fragmented concerning the reliability of the army. Some Republican stalwarts like Machado Santos defended the officer corps and criticized radical Republican interference in military affairs.[6] Others distrusted the army and believed the statements of critics such as the Spanish journalist Felix Lorenzo, whose 1915 book suggested that many officers had signed the Republican loyalty oath in 1910 only for the sake of expediency ("solo con el mano"),[7] and that the Portuguese army was not to be "trusted."[8] As trouble within the army increased, political parties saw opportunity to recruit support within the officer corps, now beginning to divide along political lines.

The most serious consequence of the republicanization of the ranks and sergeants and the initial passivity of much of the officer corps was widespread insubordination and even mutiny and murder. During the 1910 Revolution there were, of course, prime examples of insubordination, mutiny, and of the murder of some officers by their men. Officers had been gunned down by their men in both the navy—in the fleet anchored in the Tagus—and in Lisbon barracks. After the revolution, as politicization proceeded, the questions of discipline and insubordination grew more controversial. In the navy monarchist officers were purged, and instant promotions gave authority to some individuals unfit or incompetent to operate a fleet. By 1913 most ships in the Portuguese fleet were either docked and inactive or had been damaged in needless, costly accidents; one vessel sank with loss of life. Officers feared the radical sailors on their ships, and some dreaded risking a sea voyage under such conditions of indiscipline and incompetent leadership.[9]

In the army after 1910, indiscipline, insubordination, and acts of mutiny spread. Some soldiers refused to obey commands. The presence near army garrisons of armed vigilantes, including Carbonária, encouraged further insubordination and threatened the safety of officers. Some of this trouble was not undeserved. Enlisted men and sergeants had to cope with wretched conditions, and the Republican revolution gave some hope that their pay, assignments, and work conditions would be improved. Numbers of officers were inefficient and corrupt and set bad examples. Relations between officers and the ranks were put under further pressures once Portugal began to participate in combat operations in her tropical African colonies and later in Europe. Desertions and attempts to avoid military service overseas under dangerous and, in general, very unhealthy conditions became more common. Once Portugal's war policy became a paramount political issue, political parties and groups, both Republican and monarchist, began to pressure armed forces' personnel to commit themselves either to adhering to the policy or to opposing it.[10]

There were now partisan appeals to the army, especially officers, to desert or to refuse to embark for operations against the Germans in Africa or, later, in Europe. It was no coincidence that attempted military coups in October 1914 and in January 1915 both occurred on the very days when army units were about to embark on ships for military service in Angola and Mozambique against German colonial forces.[11] Public excitement and fear among armed-forces personnel burgeoned once the news reached Lisbon that the Germans had attacked Portuguese posts in Angola on 18 December 1914.

The officer corps was threatened with physical violence at the hands of the Carbonária and enlisted men. Some vigilante groups bullied or beat up officers and in 1914 a general was set upon and beaten severely.[12] Conservative army officers, either as monarchists or Unionist-Republicans, banded together, determined to end Democratic interference in military affairs. With the rise of civilian political intervention, the prestige of the officer corps had plummeted. By 1915, indiscipline in the army ranks was such that on the parade grounds during maneuvers some officers carried loaded pistols at the ready.[13]

Responses to insubordination were usually harsh and uneven but rarely effective. Sometimes indiscipline went unpunished; at other times officers put large numbers of soldiers in local civilian jails or had them shipped off to the African colonies either as transported convicts or in expeditions dispatched to fight the Germans.[14]

Intense politicization and discontent among the officer corps was further encouraged by the 1911 army-reform laws passed by the Provisional Government.[15] These laws, in theory, were carrying out the Republican party's pledge to transform the Portuguese army from a monarchist, professional-style army to a citizen-style national militia, fit for a democracy and inspired by the examples of French republican history and by the model of Switzerland's national militia. Army reform was long overdue; military experts since the late nineteenth century had urged that the monarchy begin to carry out important reforms.[16] In addition to providing national defense against the potential Spanish menace, a useful function of the new army would be to act as a national, surrogate school of literacy, patriotism, and technical skills for the masses of illiterate peasants. The ideal of a new citizens' army, a servant of the people rather than a lackey of the state or oppressor, had considerable support among Republicans and some monarchists, both within the armed forces and without.

The 1911 army reforms decreed that all male citizens, not just the poor, would participate in military service. They were designed to end the inequities of army conscription under the monarchy, whereby peasant conscripts suffered wretched training, starvation pay, and inane duty with no educational opportunities, while large numbers of citizens avoided military service through the cacique system. Among other ways of controlling elections, local caciques bought votes in monarchist elections by arranging exemptions from military service.[17]

The new system of universal military conscription was based on the finest ideals but lacked means of support. Following the Swiss pattern, conscription was for all males between the ages of seventeen and forty-five; they would have to serve one year's active duty and fifteen to thirty weeks "permanent volunteer service," each year for the next seven years. During each of those seven years citizens would have to attend at least two weeks of reserve training at special training schools, known somewhat ominously as "repetition schools."[18] In theory, then, all male citizens of the appropriate age who passed health requirements would have to serve in the national militia, regardless of class or influence. If the new system worked, the army would soon acquire large, well-trained reserves backed up by a small, professional, career force. The regular-army cadre would number only 11,699 men, who would serve terms of ten years. The annual recruitment from conscription was to be 30,000 citizen-soldiers. In wartime, if the reserve system had time to function under the reform laws, the army would be able to mobilize 300,000 troops, a much larger number than Portugal had ever mobilized under the monarchy. Reforms called for an elaborate system of army schools for both recruits and reserves.

The 1911 army-reform laws were supplemented by other laws in 1913–14 under Afonso Costa's government, but the reforms were never completed. During the years 1911–14 some repetition schools were established and operated; perhaps as many as 50,000 recruits attended these schools. But the plans of the Provisional Government's War Ministry under Colonel Correia Barreto were too ambitious for a country in Portugal's condition. The implementation of the reform plans required resources which were not at hand: funds for new equipment, schools, and higher pay, as well as numbers of skilled instructors and an efficient organization. Moreover, the idealistic concept of the army as a school of literacy for Portuguese peasants or as a kind of Republican nation-building device did not get sufficient support from the masses. The government failed to make the idea of a national militia attractive and practical.

The controversy over the army-reform laws was complicated by rising resentment on the part of officers concerning their status in society. Their pay had not been raised since 1896, and housing subsidies had remained the same since 1906. While favored civil servants—part of the Democrats' burgeoning electoral machine—received raises, professional soldiers did not.[19] Moreover, the government, despite its promises, did not modernize the army. In 1913 one candid officer described the state of Portuguese national defenses as "disgraceful."[20] Fear of Spain persisted, and the commonly imagined threat appeared to increase once observers compared the strengths of the Spanish and Portuguese armies. While Spain had a peacetime army of 115,432 men and a wartime potential of 500,000, little Portugal had only 11,600 in her regular army, and with the failure of the reform laws most likely she could not possibly attain the strength of 300,000 in a wartime mobilization. Critics found, too, that Portugal spent only 13.1 percent of the budget on the army, whereas Switzerland, Holland, and Belgium spent an average of 25 percent. By 1915, the army-reform laws appeared to be a failure.[21]

Until politicization greatly intensified in 1914–15, most army officers were nominally and passively Republican.[22] Two small activist minorities, monarchists on one side and the Young Turks on the other, attempted to sway the majority to their point of view.[23]

By early 1915 Republican interference in military affairs and the course of government and politics had put severe strains on the fundamental loyalty or neutrality of much of the officer corps, especially in the Lisbon area. The Unionist party, led by Brito Camacho, a reserve major in the Army Medical Corps, successfully recruited party members among the officers in the Lisbon garrisons.[24] Grievances mounted. Civilian interference in military affairs, the Democrats' stated war policy (they now advocated active intervention—even in the European theater), discrimination against army officers in the electoral laws, which excluded regular officers (and policemen) from the vote, and the perceived lowering of military prestige and status since the establishment of the republic alienated the officer corps from the government.

Several incidents precipitated a confrontation. There were physical assaults by Republican ruffians on high-ranking officers in the streets of Lisbon. At a Lisbon theater in November 1914 army officers took offense at some lines in a popular play and demanded that the play be closed.[25] The final spark, which fomented a sensational protest movement among army officers, came when the Ministry of War transferred—on allegedly political grounds—Major Craveiro Lopes, who was the commander of the Twenty-eighth Infantry Regiment stationed at Figueira da Foz. The transfer triggered the republic's most serious political crisis since the 1910 Revolution.[26]

The Movement of Swords and the Pimenta de Castro Regime, 25 January—14 May 1915

The manner in which national power changed hands on 25 January 1915 is worth treating in some detail. A PRP-backed government fell from power because of the president of the republic made a personal decision to bow to pressures from army officers. In effect, there was a bloodless golpe de estado. This was an interesting example, one with profound significance for the future of Republican government and politics, of how in a carefully manipulated crisis political pressure-group tactics replaced the constitutional functioning of government.

The officers involved consisted of: (1) a group of activist monarchist officers from several garrisons who were planning an armed pronunciamento to overthrow the government, to replace it with a military dictatorship, and, perhaps, to restore the monarchy;[27] (2) a somewhat larger group of officers—mainly Republicans—who were protesting the low status and prestige of the army and who were expressing a professional protest to the government; (3) a group of Republican officers from Lisbon and from the Figueira da Foz garrison who—backed by Camacho and the Unionist party, and by dissident independent Machado Santos—wanted to topple the Azevedo Coutinho government and thus enable moderate Republicans to take over.

Once the Ministry of War arrested some of the protesting officers and the Lisbon garrison officers became aroused, the crisis went into full swing.[28] The independent and moderate Republican parties, continually shut out of real power by the electoral dominance of the Democrats, saw the protest movement as a glorious opportunity to score politically. The "Founder of the Republic," Machado Santos, associated himself with the rising chorus of protest by a grand gesture: on 22 January he visited the president at Belém Palace and ostentatiously surrendered his famous "sword of the Rotunda."[29] The government alleged that the officers' movement was largely monarchist and subversive, but Machado Santos's gesture lent the movement respectability. Brito Camacho, too, became a self-styled defender of the army's honor and associated himself with six Lisbon-area officers who had joined the growing protest. Camacho attacked with one hand in blazing editorials in *A Lucta,* and with the other visited President Arriaga as a potential candidate to replace the current government. On 22 January Camacho engineered his own personal "movement of swords" by reporting grandly to the Ministry of War and demanding that he be cleared of "accusations" of treason and disloyalty made against him by *O Mundo,* the Democrats' major newspaper.[30] Camacho's act was supported by numbers of officers who had become Unionist party members and must have looked forward to the political grandstanding that was bound to be produced by a formal court-martial of Camacho. The Unionists hungered for high office and joined and encouraged the protest movement in order to groom a handy political horse.

On constitutional grounds, the situation was confusing. The Congress, already four months past its legal three-year term, had just adjourned. Congressional elections were scheduled for March 1915. But the Democrats held most of the seats—despite their weakness in the Senate—and only great public outcries against the government could sway the president to dismiss Azevedo Coutinho's cabinet. The opposition parties again concentrated on the parliamentary means to power: the forthcoming elections. They had threatened to abstain if the Democrats' government presided over the 1915 elections. Yet once the opportunity arrived to preside over the elections themselves, they did not hesitate to reach for national power.

President Arriaga feared disorder, even civil war, and saw the vigilante forces of the Democrats gathering again to aid the government against the growing protest. At the same time troops were embarking for campaigns against the Germans in Africa,[31] and anti-PRP agitators harangued soldiers in order to prevent or delay the embarkations.[32] Arriaga was overwhelmed by the crescendo of political confusion, but his constitutional role made him, in effect, high power broker, non-political moderator and arbiter above the partisan din. The premier asked President Arriaga to sign a government decree which declared a state of emergency and suspension of constitutional guarantees; with this, Azevedo Coutinho and his PRP supporters could legally crush opposition in the national interest. Arriaga refused to sign the decree. On 23 January Arriaga sent a personal letter to his friend, senior army general Joaquim Pimenta de Castro, aged sixty-eight, inviting him to form a government.[33] The letter coincided with the rebellious army officers' election of a "candidate" representing their interests. The first officer asked, the Chief of Staff General Martins de Carvalho, declined, and then the officers "selected" General Pimenta de Castro, who reluctantly accepted the charge. On 25 January, the Azevedo Coutinho government having resigned, Pimenta de Castro took power and formed a government. Although army partisans later claimed that Pimenta de Castro had no obligations to the officer class that "elected" him,[34] he was considered the army's man.

With the assumption of power by Pimenta de Castro, a military-dominated government replaced a government which had been defeated in the streets and newspapers but not in an election or parliamentary vote. Civil strife had been temporarily avoided, but the Movement of Swords proved to be a costly political precedent. The Democrats railed in their editorials and in private. Afonso Costa was quoted in an interview in Lisbon criticizing the president for his action and disdainfully dismissing the Movement of Swords as illegal and nothing more than a "kind of mini-Saldanhada."[35] But Democrats were startled by the rising collective political consciousness of the officer corps. One motive for the temporary quiescence of the Democratic leaders was their realization that their army policy had been remiss. As the programs Democrats planned later in 1915 demonstrate, a new, more diplomatic army policy emerged as a result of lessons learned in January.[36]

Who was the general called to power by Arriaga? Joaquim Pereira Pimenta de Castro (1846–1918) was the senior general in the army and had been a general under the monarchy. In 1915 he was technically in retirement. He was highly intelligent, honest, hardworking, and courageous, but by the time he was called to power his mental and physical powers were not what they once had been. Despite his reputation as a nonpolitical general, he had taken part in Republican politics.[37] To the more radical Republicans, his record was negative. During the reign of King Carlos, Pimenta de Castro had been among those army officers who had admired Mousinho and who had urged the king to support a strong military dictatorship in order to save the monarchy. In October 1911, as the first constitutional minister of war, under Premier Chagas, Pimenta de Castro had been dismissed in the face of pressures from the Democrats for failing to rush reinforcements to the northern border against the monarchist incursion.

The new government declared that it wished to restore order, and that as a "nonparty" government it would preside impartially over the forthcoming elections. But the chances of so doing were slim in an atmosphere President Arriaga later described as "esta amaldiçoada barafunda política" ("this accursed political confusion").[38] Neither the general's personality nor his vigor was reassuring. The government consisted mainly of naval and army officers. Of these, two were moderate Democrats, three were Unionists, and the remainder were, reputedly, neutral. Some officers had discussed the idea of a "national" government—one not dominated by the Democrats—but few dared suggest restoring the monarchy after the ignominious failure of the incursions and coups of 1911–14. "Order" was a concept, too, which was defined differently by different parties. A party's definition of order might well determine its attitude to the forthcoming elections, when the assumed mastery by the Democrats of the electoral machinery again would be tested.

The Pimenta de Castro government's first major crisis came on 24 February, when its electoral decree was published. The decree revoked the electoral legislation of 1913–15 and granted the right to vote to policemen and to officers and sergeants in the armed forces. June 6 was the date set for congressional elections. Much of the Lisbon press was cool to the new electoral law. The Evolutionists and Democrats opposed it and claimed that it was illegal since it had not been approved in a parliamentary session and was therefore made in *ditadura*.[39]

The Democrats now declared war on the government. The PRP Directorate led by Costa was in control of the municipal government of Lisbon and much of the civil service in the provinces. It ordered party members in the administration to disobey the orders of the Pimenta de Castro "dictatorship." The government countered on 2 March with a decree which attempted to transfer local and district government powers to the civil governors of Lisbon and Oporto, who were appointees of General Pimenta de Castro.

The Congress was scheduled to reassemble 4 March. The crisis widened as the government prevented anxious parliamentary deputies from meeting in the Congress building at São Bento; troops surrounded the buildings and closed the doors. Defying the government, a majority of the members, largely but not exclusively Democrats, met instead in a seventeenth-century palace in the Lisbon suburbs. They declared the acts of the president of the republic and of the government unconstitutional or *fora da lei*. At the same time, the Democrats vowed their determination to topple the government by means of a strike of civil servants, which would bring administrative paralysis. On 6 March the minister of finance, a Democrat, having in vain sought a change of policy, resigned.[40]

The old general was unable to cope with the chaotic situation in the administration. The government did replace some administrators and shift commands among the police, the GNR, and the army; some new appointees, but not all, were monarchists. But the government soon lost the support of the Unionist party and found that the Evolutionists were no longer neutral but hostile. The moderate Republicans became frightened and angry when the Pimenta de Castro government began to give privileges, opportunities, and support to monarchists, including the small rightist group of young men who belonged to Integralismo Lusitano.[41] Pimenta de Castro's policy toward monarchists and monarchist activities doomed his attempts to establish "order."

On 20 April 1915 the government decreed that monarchists could now legally organize political "centers" or parties. Monarchist leaders, including Paiva Couceiro and other incursionists, would receive full amnesty and might return to Portugal to exercise their civil rights. Most of the Republican press attacked these new measures as unnecessary appeasement. Further alarm spread among the Republicans in Lisbon when certain monarchist groups and their increasingly active press now openly organized political parties and advocated an immediate restoration of the monarchy. A final blow to the moderate Republican parties' hopes of political peace came when moderates saw their chances at the 1915 elections would be influenced by monarchist political agitation. On 6 May, both the Unionist organ, *A Lucta,* and the independent Republican *O Século* attacked the government's proposal to have major local polling-place officials appointed by the civil governors and other government appointees. The Republican editorials reminded readers that these acts resembled preludes to familiar monarchist election-rigging before 1910, and they considered this a direct threat to the republic.[42]

Meanwhile, an armed conspiracy planned by the Democrats spread its tentacles. After 4 March, they had secretly formed a Junta Revolucionária, which was led by five noted Republican militants: naval officer-Democrat José de Freitas Ribeiro, already twice a cabinet minister; army officer and lawyer Dr. Álvaro de Castro, former minister in Democrat cabinets; army officer and recently returned governor of Angola José Norton de Matos; António Maria da Silva, Carbonária leader and Democrat-civil servant; and Major Ernesto Sá Cardoso, army officer and Democrat.[43]

The Fourteenth of May 1915 "Revolution"

> The country cannot withstand another shock as profound as that of the 14th of May.
>
> Captain João Correia dos Santos[44]

During the days of 14–18 May 1915 the Pimenta de Castro government, attacked as a dictatorship by the Democrats, was overthrown by an armed insurgency that had been organized by leading elements of the Democratic party. The Fourteenth of May bore strong resemblances to the Fifth of October movement five years earlier in the revived pronunciamento tradition: the meetings of conspiratorial committees or juntas; secret meetings in Lisbon offices, cafés, and barracks; the preparation of "opinion" in the partisan press; the enticement of armed-forces officers to join the movement against the government; and the setting of a date for the "revolution." There was a familiar pattern to the forces which faced one another at first: early in the battle the Democrats had few regular Lisbon army regiments on their side but depended on the navy, marines, and armed civilians; the government was defended by much of Lisbon's artillery, cavalry, GNR regiments, and the police. But once large numbers of civilians obtained arms after the naval arsenal was opened to the insurgents, Pimenta de Castro was in trouble.

The government's commanders were, with few exceptions, unwilling to assert themselves. The energetic attacks of the Democrats and the passivity of much of the Lisbon garrison officer corps were decisive factors in the civil war that engulfed Lisbon for nearly four days, 14–17 May. Except for some struggles in Oporto and Santarém, the provinces waited to see what occurred in the capital; the Democrats, ostensibly campaigning for the June elections, had provided a convenient cover for provincial conspiracies and had recruited support for the coup.[45]

As the fighting raged, the Democrats claimed that they were crushing a real monarchist conspiracy—in the guise of the Pimenta de Castro regime—to overthrow the republic. Moderate Republicans like Brito Camacho tried to assure the public that in the June elections—even with government aid—the monarchists would win perhaps only a half-dozen seats.[46] The fears of the Democrats, however, had some basis in reality: the army general staff had already received information from Portuguese informers in Galicia and in Portugal that monarchist conspiracies were afoot and that the monarchists were split on the issue of whether the coup should come before or after the 6 June elections.

What was at stake in the bloody fighting of May? The Democrats claimed that the republic was in danger,[47] but what they in fact won by 17–18 May, after Pimenta de Castro had surrendered in the GNR head-quarters in the Carmo Monastery, Lisbon, was control of the government administration and hence complete mastery of the electoral machinery for the June contest. The Unionists and Evolutionists, who had finally abstained from direct participation in the armed conspiracy, were deprived of any of the fruits of victory. The Democrats won when a weary and defeated President Arriaga dismissed Pimenta de Castro and called to power a new government under Republican João Chagas, at the suggestion of the triumphant Junta Revolucionária. This junta also named the major new administrative authorities to replace Pimenta de Castro's nominees, thus assuring Costa's party the control of the June elections.[48]

The losses of the Fourteenth of May were more serious than those of the Fifth of October. Total casualties numbered at least 150 dead and perhaps as many as 300, and over 1,000 wounded from fighting in Lisbon, Santarém, and Oporto.[49] Naval bombardment of the capital had resulted in damage to buildings, but more disturbing still were several days of anarchy in Lisbon. On 15 May the ministers of Britain, Spain, and France requested that men-of-war be dispatched to the Lisbon harbor to protect their resident nationals against the dangers, which diplomats described as equalling those of a brief civil war. The state of the Portuguese armed forces was chaotic. Once the government had fallen, Republican vigilantes proceeded to wreck the installations of those newspapers that had backed Pimenta de Castro. The offices of the monarchist papers and those of Machado Santos's O Intransigente were destroyed. More ominously, in the general melee following the fall of the government, some Republicans murdered several policemen and wrecked police stations, private houses, and clubs that were alleged to be sites of support for Pimenta de Castro.[50]

In mid-May 1915 Portugal experienced a brief civil war which was only one terrible symbol of the convulsions gripping politics and society. Especially since the attempted monarchist incursions, coups, and the abortive syndicalist revolution of April 1913, Portuguese urban society was increasingly seared with a new level of public and private violence.

Responding to the government's suppression of a strike in the Alentejo province and to the closing down of the syndicalists' union, União Operária Nacional, Machado Santos and some syndicalist followers had attempted a coup in Lisbon on 27 April 1913. One company of the Fifth Infantry Regiment had rebelled against the government, but armed forced loyal to the government had quickly suppressed the movement and arrested a number of conspirators.[51]

Now there was combat in the streets between Democratic groups and their numerous enemies, including syndicalists and monarchists. In Congress deputies and senators carried pistols; there were fights and duel challenges in the aisles and in the foyer, somewhat wistfully named the Passos Perdidos ("wasted steps"). Large sections of activist high school and university youth—some of them armed with pistols—were now often anti-Republican or anti-Democrat, and monarchist and Catholic activity revived. In February 1915 a youth of fourteen, a member of the rising Catholic Youth Movement, attempted to assassinate Afonso Costa. In March 1915 a Democratic deputy was shot dead outside his home. As João Chagas arrived on the train from Oporto to assume the premiership on 16 May 1915 he was shot three times by Senator João de Freitas and lost his right eye.[52] His assailant was killed on the spot. Political leaders, fearing for their lives, required bodyguards. In July 1915 Afonso Costa suffered a serious concussion when he hurled himself from a moving tram, suspecting—erroneously—that a hidden bomb was about to explode.

This level of political violence in Portuguese society surpassed anything under the Constitutional Monarchy and equalled in intensity the civil strife of the years 1832-51. It was complicated further because large groups of urban civilians possessed firearms and bombs. Every revolution or attempted coup further increased the number of weapons in civilian hands, and the Fourteenth of May was no exception.

With the clear victory of the Democratic party in the general elections of 13 June, the republic reached a new watershed. The constitutional machinery had failed to function during the severe crisis that began in the Senate impasse of January 1914. President Arriaga had attempted in his 24 February 1914 policy statement to impose a legal restraint on

election-rigging. This statement, however, was not in the 1911 Constitution, and the president's powers were vague and not even as strong as
royal power under the monarchy. He was obliged by the law to
nominate governments according to the wishes of the majority congressional party—the Democrats—but opposition tactics decisively swayed
a sincere but ultimately weak old scholar. Arriaga's bowing to pressures
in 1914–15 was only a part of the problem. The opposition, including
radical monarchists, desperately wanted power, and since there was no
legal way to obtain it in parliamentary votes, their choices were limited.
For the opposition, then, the president's decision to dismiss and name
governments as the king had done under the monarchy became the only
legal recourse.

In the confusion President Arriaga, now ailing and disgusted, had
been left behind. On 29 May he tendered his resignation to the enduring
Congress that was still meeting in "extraordinary sessions" nearly a
year beyond its legal term (30 June 1911–30 June 1914). His letter
contained timely insights.[53] He suggested that the bloodshed had been
needless, that Pimenta de Castro's regime was not a dictatorship in the
true sense—implying that previous governments had been in some ways
less moderate and that the congressionally approved laws of August
1914 and January 1915 had given any succeeding governments unusual
war powers. Arriaga recounted how he had tried to get impartial election supervision made a part of Republican custom in his 24 February
1914 statement and that there was no way, with the few constitutional
powers held by the president, to do anything legally to stop the Pimenta
de Castro government on its course of favoring monarchist interests.

The blame for the malfunctioning of the Constitution and for extremist political conduct could be widely shared. Twice the president (in
February 1914 and in January 1915) had bowed to pressure and dismissed legal governments. The opposition was neither loyal nor willing
to compromise. The Democrats, with their control of the civil-service
patronage and electoral machinery increasing, were not about to relin-
quish power. Nor were they willing or able to cleanse their own political
ranks of corruption and incompetence. Costa was the only politician of
real significance among the Republican partisan groups, but by early
1914 he had earned the increasingly violent enmity of not only
Republican moderates and conservatives, but also of monarchists,
anarchists, and the syndicalists, who came to ally with the independent
enfant terrible, Machado Santos.

The key to power remained in Congress, since it elected the president
of the republic. The key to Congress was in the elections. Controlling
the civil service virtually assured electoral victory, as under the

monarchy. The Democrats on 13 June won 106 seats in the chamber and 45 seats in the Senate, their largest margin yet. They continued to control most of the civil service. It was no coincidence that the first demand on the manifesto of the Junta Revolucionária of 18 May 1915 was "the restoration" of *all* civil and military functionaries who were employed before the Pimenta de Castro government,[54] a demand which later was fully executed.

Democrat-dominated Coalition Governments, the War, and the Economy, May 1915—December 1917

The Fourteenth of May did not permanently heal divisions among Republicans. It only temporarily numbed festering conflicts. João Chagas's wounds prevented him from assuming power and Democrat José de Castro took the premiership, backed by Costa's party. The Democrats consolidated their civil-service control by getting Congress to vote that all functionaries "disaffected with the [Republican] regime" would be fired. But the definition of who would fall under such a vague label was never clear, and the Republican daily *O Século,* increasingly moderate and anxious for political peace and reform, fairly remarked that this congressional act would lead to numerous injustices and further conflicts.[55] There could be no political peace, however, until all parties were willing to practice toleration and compromise. Politics dominated government since with such cabinet, civil-service, and executive instability and turnover, no legislation or administration could be completed, or in some cases, even started. This fact further divided Republicans and their enemies since it was perfectly true that government could accomplish little under these hostile conditions and that whoever held power was in part to blame.

In short, even after the bloodshed of May, when there could be no more compelling reason to unite many political groups than to avoid a repetition of the events of January–May 1915, Portugal's political crisis persisted. It was essentially a "crisis of authority," in the words of victimized João Chagas.[56] At every level in politics and government, authority, he believed, was neither understood nor applied. More important as suggested above, it was also a "crisis of restraint and tolerance."

In 1915 the economy once again became a master factor in Portuguese government and politics. Beginning in 1915, even more than in the financial crises during the later Constitutional Monarchy, the Portuguese masses felt the severe impact of a worsening economic crisis. During the first four-and-a-half years of the republic, the economy's problems were not of the same order as they were later, and, as mentioned earlier, in 1913–14 the Costa government had managed to balance the national budget. After mid-1915, however, the Portuguese people became justifiably obsessed with economic crises, which had important political repercussions; since the Democratic party was in power either openly or indirectly in 1915–17, its leaders got much of the blame for the status of the economy. Signs of the problem appeared in a ballooning external and internal debt, severe inflation, increasingly serious depreciation of currency, and large budget deficits.

Although emigration decreased in the years Portugal was committed to war first in Africa and then also in Europe (according to official figures, emigration dropped from 19,314 in 1915 to 11,853 in 1918,[57] the war years brought great misery to the Portuguese masses. The most catastrophic problem—one which people faced every day—was the increased price, poor quality, and insufficient supply of bread. Bread was not only a basic staple in the economy, but, more important, a daily mainstay of the Portuguese diet in every area of the country, rural and urban.

There were many contributing causes to the economic crises which reached a peak in the years 1919–20. The war's impact was, of course, primary, but one of the reasons that the governments during the years 1915–20 were unable to solve major economic problems was because of their short tenure in office. Portugal's foreign trade, which depended to some degree upon shipping cocoa from São Tomé to Europe, was seriously disrupted by the war. Increased military expenses affected the budget, as Portugal sent valuable assistance to the Allies: artillery and ammunition to France during 1914–15 and rifles to South Africa.[58]

The wheat and bread crisis worsened. Wheat production, whether through lack of agrarian reform or inefficient techniques, did not keep up with demand. Portugal was forced to increase wheat importation, which rose from an average annual import of 70,000 tons a year in 1906–11 to 182,122 tons in 1916.[59] Portugal became more dependent upon foreign sources of raw materials, capital, and aid. But with the disruption of shipping by the German navy it became difficult to import sufficient quantities of wheat. Lisbon and Oporto as early as 1915 faced the possibility of famine. At least three major urban disturbances reflected serious popular discontent over the bread question. During the anarchic days of 14–17 May in 1915 in Lisbon, mobs sacked stores searching for food. By 1917 the bread crisis reached a new stage: the wheat shortage was so serious that the government imposed a new law on 10 May requiring that bread contain a new mixture of maize and wheat, which resulted in an inferior quality. On 12 May bakers' stores closed and bread became virtually unobtainable. The government attempted to control the making of bread and its storage. The consequences of this impasse were grave: between 12 May and 22 May sporadic but increasingly serious food riots occurred in the Lisbon area, and the government called out troops and declared a state of martial law.[60] Because of official wartime censorship, the number of casualties was never revealed, but the British minister in Lisbon heard that "at least 200" persons had been killed, not counting many wounded.[61]

The Lisbon bread riots of May 1917 were suppressed, but the bread problem remained. The mass anger and discontent over bread prices and availability was manifest in the revolution of 5–8 December 1917, when the Democrats' government was overthrown in a coup. During the fighting, groups of civilians sacked food shops and appropriated all they could carry off. Observers noted that the hungry mobs were now quite indifferent to the political drama unfolding in Lisbon.

The devastating food and bread riots of 1917 were a phenomenon which had not been experienced in the capital during the Constitutional Monarchy. Afonso Costa, the man who had brought a budget surplus in 1913–14, could not prevail against the economic problems of 1915–17. War expenses mounted as Portugal was obliged to mobilize more troops and equipment than ever before in her history. The expeditions to Angola, Mozambique, and France were expensive and were only partly supported by a British loan of £3,000,000, part of a deal that led Portugal to declare war on Germany in March 1916.[62]

Inextricably linked with the state of the economy was Portugal's war policy. The decision to enter actively in the European war in the spring of 1916 took into account Portugal's tropical African colonies, the Anglo-Portuguese alliance, and the status of government and politics in the struggling republic.

In effect, Portugal was at war with Imperial Germany in tropical Africa beginning in late 1914. Clashes between Portuguese and German armed forces in Angola began in October 1914, and Lisbon dispatched colonial expeditions to Angola and Mozambique. Even after German forces surrendered to the South African army in South West Africa in May 1915—thus ending the German threat in West Central Africa, Portugal remained in a state of belligerency against Germany in East Africa during 1914–16; nearly as many troops were sent to fight in Africa as were later sent to France.[63] Oddly enough, Germany maintained her minister in Lisbon throughout this African conflict (until spring of 1916), and there were a considerable number of German merchant vessels in Lisbon harbor.

The decision to enter the European theater of war against Germany in March 1916 was one of the most controversial and bitterly contested decisions in modern Portuguese history. Many years later the decision remained as disputed as was the religious issue during the first years of the republic. In a speech of 4 October 1971, Premier Marcello Caetano stated that Portugal entered the Great War in Europe simply in order to maintain her rights to her overseas territories.[64] If such a rationale for the 1916 decision provided a nice argument which supported the official defense policy of the New State toward Portuguese Africa in the 1960s and 1970s, it is not sufficient explanation for the decision of 1916.

The immediate cause of the 1916 decision was the British official request in December 1915 that Portugal requisition for Allied use some seventy-six German vessels, with some 240,000 tons, in Lisbon harbor.[65] Portuguese authorities complied with the request, seizing all German vessels in Portuguese harbors on 24 February 1916. On 9 March Germany officially declared war on Portugal. With Portugal's action came the promise from her oldest ally of a loan which would partially compensate Portugal for her material aid to the Allies since September 1914.[66]

The decision of February-March 1916 and Portugal's mounting and dispatching of the Portuguese Expeditionary Corps to fight with the Allies in Flanders during 1917–18 became hotly debated issues. To opponents of the Democrats, they were magnificent opportunities to score politically and perhaps to dislodge the government from power. The Unionists, the independents under Machado Santos, the anarchists and syndicalists, and numbers of monarchists bitterly opposed the decision to enter the European war and to send an army into combat. On these issues there grew up a literature of protest and contention. The major point of the opposition led by Brito Camacho, the Unionist leader, was that while Portugal should give real aid to Britain, Portugal need not enter the European war, or send an army to France, as these moves would be unnecessary, impractical, and even dangerous for a small country with such slim means. Whatever Camacho's views, it is difficult for the historian to determine just how influential his arguments were, and to what extent the Portuguese public was willing to support the government's war policy. A study of the major organs of the Portuguese Republican press reveals that pro-Allied sentiments, at least in urban areas, dominated.

It is also difficult to assess the impact of German undercover activity upon Portuguese politics during the war years. Definitive answers await a detailed study of German unpublished records. What evidence there is now of German interference in Portuguese internal affairs comes largely from undocumented Portuguese allegations, rumors, and British diplomatic records. A study of the British documents and printed Portuguese sources suggests that German agents financed certain monarchist newspapers which produced blatantly pro-German and anti-Allied editorials, especially during 1915–18; they carried out some sabotage of Portuguese war-related industries and installations; they gathered information on the Allies from Portuguese sources; they observed Portuguese defenses and resources; and they furnished financial support to some political groups—possibly monarchist or Integralist—as a way of furthering political instability and even toppling the pro-Allied Democrat-dominated governments.[67]

The accuracy of British diplomatic assertions concerning German subversive activity cannot be evaluated here. What is perhaps equally important, however, is that a number of Portuguese leaders believed that the German menace was a real one.

Aside from the circumstances which drew Portugal into the European theater of the war in 1916, probably the major motive behind the decision by Costa's government had little to do with the future of Portugal's colonies in Africa, or the Anglo-Portuguese alliance, or the cause of the Allies in Europe. The sensitive Costa wished to change Portugal's image in Europe from what he perceived as the legendary "nightmare republic," to the equally legendary idealistic, civilized, and progressive Portuguese republic his political generation had dreamed of and had worked to found. In short, Costa supported the 1916 decision and the dispatch of the costly Corpo Expedicionário Português (CEP) because he wished to reestablish the good name of Portugal before Allied Europe.

The Portuguese republic had received a generally bad press abroad during the years 1911–14 over the issues of forced labor and slavery in Portuguese West Africa and political prisoners and prisons. Portuguese leaders had long felt burdened by their country's position as a poor, third- or fourth-rate power held in low esteem by the nations Portugal respected: particularly Republican France and Britain. The war in Africa was not controversial, as it was merely defensive. But committing Portugal to the European phase of the bloody conflict was quite different. The political opposition easily seized on this as a handy club in Congress. In practical terms the Costa government could defend the policy only by arguing that Portugal would receive much Allied aid and even some profits for the middle class; otherwise, the poor, isolated, mainly illiterate country with a small and unprepared army already committed in Africa could not support such an effort.

Leading Republican liberals, like João Chagas and Afonso Costa, who conceived of Portugal's war policy as a powerful means of improving Portugal's image, were aware of the risks of such a bold policy. As early as 29 December 1914, in an entry in his personal diary, Chagas wrote that his beloved republic could be consolidated "forever" by Portugal's participation in the war, or it could be destroyed.[68]

In analyzing Costa's policy, Portugal's status as a dependent, weak power should also be considered. Portugal had rarely taken the initiative in her diplomacy. She had a reputation of subservience and subordination to Britain and a low rank among "civilized" states. If by a diplomatic master stroke Portugal could not only safeguard her "colonial patrimony"—a major concern of the Portuguese elite—but also contribute to the Allies' cause and clear her "good name," the republic, Costa's government believed, would greatly benefit.

The major reason for the 1916 war policy, then, one which had profound repercussions in the economy and polity in later years, had to do with the Democratic elite's conception of the Portuguese republic and their fondly held hope of creating a modern people, a "New Portugal." Criticism of this policy contained several partisan biases. Some pro-German Portuguese groups attacked Costa as selling out to foreign interests in his pursuit of political power and prestige. One of the more acrimonious attacks came from an unexpected quarter, British resident writer in Portugal Aubrey Bell. Bell wrote of the war policy: "The Democrat party will always be known as the party, which, under cover of the World War, raised itself to power over the dead bodies of its fellow-countrymen."[69] Unmistakable in this attack is a whiff of the rhetoric of the time from the Integralist party, a consistent foe of Costa's war policy. Whatever the idealism behind Costa and the Democrats' decisions, and however misguided were some of the policy's partisan and biased critics, the fact remains that Portugal's war policy was an inviting target for the opposition, a useful issue for manipulation for partisan purposes whatever the cause, and a turning point in the history of the troubled First Republic.

Promise but not fulfillment characterized the government's policy concerning educating the public on intervention in Europe. An excellent illustration is found in the brief war-propaganda campaign of March 1916 to December 1917. In May 1916 leading Republican Magalhães Lima went on a speaking tour in France and Italy to explain Portugal's intervention in the European theater.[70] At home the government attempted to convince the populace of both the wisdom and necessity of active intervention.

Without a great effort, however, chances for success for such a propaganda campaign were not good. Most of the Portuguese press was pro-Allied, it is true, but not necessarily in favor of sending an army to

France.[71] Pro-German monarchist newspapers actively tried to influence opinion against going to war in Europe. But the press aside, the low level of general education of the masses was a mighty obstacle for any literacy-oriented campaign outside Lisbon and Oporto.

Little evidence remains of a real effort by the government to indoctrinate citizens to support the European intervention of 1916-18. The one notable written effort had a mixed history. Having complained in parliament in the spring of 1916 that the government had no propaganda campaign worthy of the name, Democratic deputy and writer Jaime Cortesão, soon to be a volunteer militia officer–physician in France, wrote a brief pamphlet, *Cartilha Do Povo. L° Encontro: Portugal E A Guerra.*[72] The Ministry of War, which may have commissioned Cortesão to write it, bought up some hundred thousand copies for mass circulation. It is not clear just how and to whom this pamphlet was distributed, nor is it known what impact it had.

This document reveals much about the government's attempts at propaganda. The number acquired—a hundred thousand—was in terms of normal publication standards in Portugal quite large. But in terms of educating rural masses or even most of the recruits, it was insufficient. The total number of troops mobilized for the war years, 1914-18, was two hundred thousand men, although only ninety-nine thousand Portuguese actually embarked for the African and European campaigns. The number of literate Portuguese in the country was probably around one million. Although the title of the pamphlet suggests that it was merely the first in a series, there is no evidence that any further pamphlets were produced and distributed.

The content of the pamphlet illustrates the weaknesses and strengths of the ephemeral propaganda efforts.[73] The format adopted was a dialogue between two Portuguese peasants: José Povinho, the father, and a peasant recruit, João Portugal. As an embodiment of peasant Portuguese Everyman Zé Povinho, José Povinho fears that his son will be killed if he joins the army and he is skeptical of the purpose of his son's going on active duty. "Why?" he asks. João Portugal, who represents the government's arguments for conscripting an army and entering the European phase of the Great War, convinces José Povinho that Portugal is entering the European war in order to safeguard her independence by fighting against Germany's imminent enslavement of the smaller nations of Europe. But the major point made in the pamphlet is that if Portugal does not fight, the Central Powers might blockade her ports, and, by preventing foodstuffs from entering, starve the people.

For the sophisticated and well-educated *Lisboeta,* such arguments must have seemed simplistic and full of half-truths. The pamphlet, however, was designed for an audience which was ignorant of the intricate arguments of both *intervencionistas* and *não-intervencionistas*. Further, in addition to its alarmist appeal concerning the food question, the pamphlet contained some rational arguments and honestly reflected the motivations of the Democratic leadership for intervention in the European campaign. If it somewhat unfairly alleged that if Portugal did not intervene England would withdraw from the alliance, leaving Portugal to starve, which would be "the greatest of shames"; it also stated that fighting in Europe would prevent war in Iberia, and that defending the colonial empire would give Portugal "great importance among the other nations."[74] At the end of the piece, Cortesão has José Povinho, now a convinced interventionist, giving his blessing to his son as the young recruit goes off to join the army:

Son, I bless you for what you have said. Never has the sight of you given me such pleasure nor have I felt so happy to be your father. Go where the Fatherland calls you. Now my only regret is not to have the strength to accompany you.[75]

Whatever the reasons for intervention in the war, Portugal paid a high price in the effort. The mobilization was the most massive in her history: over 200,000 men were recruited during the African and European campaigns.[76] Estimates of casualties differ, but the Portuguese Expeditionary Corps (CEP) sent to Europe between January 1917 and November 1918 numbered 65,166 troops, of which at least 7,300 men were lost (dead, wounded, and prisoners of war) at the disastrous battle of Lys (April 1918).[77] In the European theater, 1,935 died in combat and from disease, 5,581 were wounded, and 6,895 were captured by the Germans. Some 34,000 troops were sent from Portugal to serve in Africa. In Portugal's armies in Africa over half of the troops were African soldiers recruited in Angola and Mozambique. At least 1,800 Europeans died, mainly from tropical diseases, and it was claimed that about 23,000 African soldiers died in service.[78] Portugal's wartime navy lost 142 men and two ships in attacks by German U-boats. Several Portuguese towns, too, on the mainland and in the Azores, were shelled by German ships. Portugal's actual imperial losses in the African campaigns, however, were much larger than these figures indicate. At the Versailles Peace Conference in 1919, the Portuguese delegation presented an official report of casualties in the African campaigns against Germany and claimed that Portugal deserved, among other reparation payments, £9,285,714 for "indirect losses to colonies owing to death of 130,000 natives. . . ."[79] This extraordinary figure represented mainly noncombatant Africans, including those conscripted for porterage and labor duties.

Monetary expenses were also high. Indeed, Portugal's grave economic and financial conditions by 1926 were brought on initially by the impact of the war upon the Portuguese economy. The CEP operation cost the government at least £28,000,000.[80] While a final figure on the cost of the war is not available and perhaps, more to the point, not especially meaningful, a reasonable estimate is that Portugal spent at least £60,000,000 and possibly as much as £80,000,000 on war activities in both the African and European campaigns during four years.[81] The debt was still a major cause of the poor reputation of the First Republic at the time of the coup of 28 May 1926. Yet, when one considers the resources available to Portugal during 1914–18, it is obvious that whatever its consequences, the Portuguese effort was remarkable.

In the final analysis, any quantitative attempt to measure Portugal's war effort, or, more important, to assess the war's impact on Portuguese politics, society, and economy, may be only partly successful. From the abundant material available to study the problem—in the contemporary press, memoirs, and political literature, not to mention official archives not yet opened for easy access by scholars—the observer must conclude that participation in World War I had an enormous impact on modern Portuguese history. It is important to know that nearly one hundred thousand Portuguese soldiers fought abroad in Africa and Europe, but it remains more important to learn what effect this had on internal society and why important sectors of society opposed Portugal's participation in the European theater.

The present-day student can observe physical evidence of Portugal's war effort in numerous town squares from Cascais to Lisbon to Oporto. Great War stone monuments list Portuguese deeds—historic reminders that Portuguese participation was not simply a mystification created by one or two partisan governments. Portugal's Unknown Soldiers (one killed in Europe, one in Africa) were buried in the Batalha Abbey, where an impressive tomb near those of the Portuguese kings is perpetually guarded by members of the armed forces.[82]

The Overthrow of the Democrats: The Golpe of 5 December 1917

The political dominance of the Democrats was weakened by the impact of the war and by rising internal opposition. Even moderate Republican newspapers like *O Século* complained that the government's wartime censorship of the press was unfair.[83] The bread problem continued, too; during 1916–17 the average price of bread rose 65 percent.[84]

In the spring of 1917 an all-Democrat Costa cabinet succeeded Almeida's increasingly limp "Sacred Union" coalition (March 1916—April 1917). At the PRP annual congress in 1917 leftist Democrats accused Costa of personalism and reactionary policies.[85] Socialist-oriented Democrats in their newspaper, *Portugal,* urged all left-leaning Democrats to bolt the PRP and to form a "radical-socialist party."[86] Whatever its intentions, the Costa government was ineffective in responding to the food shortages, labor unrest, and police brutality during the food riots.[87] In the November 1917 municipal elections the local support of the PRP appeared to be slipping; while the major party won 92 town governments, the Evolutionists and Unionists between them won 24, the monarchists, 25, and the neutral tickets, 89.[88]

Three legal ways of ousting the Democrats appeared to be all but impossible: an anti-Democrat victory in the June 1918 congressional elections; a constitutional revision which would allow the president to dissolve Congress before the end of its legal term; the dismissal of Costa by the president. The Unionist party launched a campaign to support an early constitutional revision.

Increasing support for a constitutional revision along presidentialist lines was not confined to Unionist circles. The fervent anti-Democratic activities of maverick independent Machado Santos and his call for a new presidentialist constitution were closely linked. In mid-1916 Machado Santos published an important book, *Public Order and the 14th of May,* in which he urged the Portuguese public to adopt his self-styled "national statute." He called for an end to the parliamentary dominance and to the Democrats' government monopoly. The document he drew up emphasized local autonomy, presidentialism, syndicalism, corporativism, and the presidential power to dissolve Congress.[89] Some of his ideas were adopted in both Sidónio Pais's New Republic and Salazar's New State. But at the time Machado Santos published them, they had little effect, so he turned to conspiracy in order to overthrow the government. His 13–14 December 1916 military insurrection ended in failure; the famous naval officer and co-conspirators were imprisoned.[90]

In the minds of many, then, advocacy of the enhancement of presidential power in a constitutional revision was directly associated with attempts to oust the Democrats from power.

By law, revisions of the Constitution could occur only with a two-thirds vote of both houses and only five years after the approval of the Consitution, or after August 1916. In theory, such a consideration of a revision was legal in 1917, but the opposition could never get most PRP deputies or senators to vote for such a revision. By late 1917, however, even moderate Republican opinion, such as found in *O Século,* favored an early constitutional revision which would give the president the power of congressional dissolution; *O Século* viewed this measure as a major reform and even a panacea.[91] To get the Costa government to support it in a PRP-dominated Congress, however, was impossible without illegal pressures from outside.

One other group of Republicans in opposition believed that a large conservative party combining dissident Unionists, Evolutionists, Democrats, and independents might effectively confront the PRP at the polls in 1918. In October 1917 Dr. Egas Moniz, the ex-deputy and prominent physician, formed the Centrist party.[92] Moniz's presidentialist program was essentially only one point: to revise the Constitution to give the president the power of congressional dissolution. Moniz had strongly but unsuccessfully advocated this measure in the 1911 Constituent Assembly. He now called for "peace in the Portuguese family" and hoped that he could mobilize enough support to end the Democrats' hold on parliament. Like many of the small Republican groups, however, the short-lived Centrist party was largely a personal following, a "general staff without an army." Illegal means of unseating Costa's government had more support. It was an ominous but significant commentary on the effectiveness of bringing change through the party system that Camacho's *A Lucta* editorials by mid-1917 mounted a suggestive, threatening slogan, "Dissolution or Revolution," and stated that rule by one party could only result in violent overthrow.[93]

While the Costa government was ineffective in solving major economic problems or in reassuring various classes that they had even the city of Lisbon under firm control in the face of food riots and industrial strikes, the government was aware of a budding armed conspiracy being organized chiefly by Unionist leaders. President Machado was prepared to act only after the conspiracy reached the streets, while Premier Costa was either unconcerned or unaware of the growing danger, since shortly before the conspirators "pronounced" in early December, he and his major advisers went abroad to oversee Portugal's CEP operations.

Who were the conspirators and what were their goals? The chief conspirator was Dr. Sidónio Pais, reserve army major, former Coimbra University professor, a Unionist, and former minister to Berlin, 1912–16. For several months in late 1917, Pais brought to bear his considerable organizational and political talents on a "confused amalgam"[94] of groups who readily supported a conspiracy against the Democrats' government. This varied agglomeration included: elements from the armed-forces officer corps who were either dismissed by the previous governments or were about to embark for war service in France or Africa; disgruntled monarchists and Catholics; large groups of industrial, Lisbon-area workers, many of them in anarcho-syndicalist organizations that had suffered severe repression and persecution under the PRP-dominated governments since early 1913. Among the workers were many who had been involved in the abortive armed conspiracies of 27 April 1913 and 13–14 December 1916, led by Machado Santos.[95] Also included and attracted by Sidónio Pais's many promises of a new, tolerant and humane government were many anti-Democratic individuals from the middle and upper classes, including latifundistas from Alentejo, one of the major bases of the Unionist party under Camacho; army officers anxious to redeem the status and role of the army and anxious to improve officers' status and increase salaries;[96] young army cadets and officer candidates, eager for a taste of combat against a government increasingly under abuse by its enemies and attracted by the charisma of Sidónio Pais.

The conspiracy was organized largely by Unionist Sidónio Pais, but Unionist leader Brito Camacho, although he first consented to the conspirators' use of the party's Lisbon headquarters, which was in the same building as the *A Lucta* offices, later eschewed such an illegal act and withdrew himself. But Pais relied upon Unionist leaders around Camacho and upon the rank and file for organizing contacts, travel to various points, and for finance. Pais raised some 12,000 escudos (12 contos) from Unionist members, and got a good portion of it from one important Alentejo latifundista from the Évora area, António Miguel de Sousa Fernandes,[97] a Unionist long alienated by the Costa government and anxious for a regime which would be more conservative and aware of the interests of his region and of the rural landowning class. To get political commitments Pais made many promises, including promises of political offices. After the coup succeeded, Unionist patron Sousa Fernandes received the post of civil governorship of Lisbon, traditionally one of the top political rewards.[98]

The conspiracy entered its final stages in late November. Pais bribed some of the rank and file of the Lisbon naval garrison, traditionally a pro-Democrat group. As usual, many of the commitments promised beforehand were not honored when the time came for action. Pais managed to lure into the conspiracy mainly young, junior officers, perhaps fifteen to twenty, but from only three or four army units: officers plus four hundred men from the Thirty-third Infantry Regiment of Lisbon, a few officers from the First Artillery and Fifth Chasseurs, some members of the War School staff and their students, and one squadron of the Seventh Cavalry, led by First Lieutenant Theophilo Duarte, a stalwart disciple of Pais's. The military part of the conspiracy was mainly a "revolution of second lieutenants" and cadets, men who remained loyal to Pais, an interesting legacy for politics in coming years, and one which would survive the organizer of the conspiracy.[99]

The armed insurgency went into the streets on the evening of 5 December 1917. The fighting lasted over sixty hours and was the bloodiest and most destructive of the military "revolutions" up to that time. After three days of fighting, which included many bombings and a naval bombardment of central Lisbon, casualties amounted to at least 350 dead and 1,000 wounded.[100] Although they were supported by many armed civilian fighters, including workers from anarcho-syndicalist organizations and government employees in the telephone-telegraph services who worked to isolate Lisbon from outside communications, the uniformed insurgents numbered no more than 1,500 and were heavily outnumbered by GNR, navy, police, and army and navy troops loyal to the Costa government. Pais's conspirators, however, enjoyed several distinct advantages: the premier, Afonso Costa, was absent from the site of conflict; the rebels were supported by more regular, professional army troops than were the government forces; a large part of the regular army was at the time stationed in France or Africa; the government's reinforcements called in from the Santarém and Mafra garrisons never reached Lisbon; most civilians who made their presence known during the fighting in Lisbon were either militantly against the government, and aided the insurgents, or cheered the insurgents from their windows and doors. Government attacks on the entrenched position of the rebels encamped in the strategic Edward VII Park, at Rotunda, were repelled with heavy casualties, despite government superiority in artillery. As usual, once the rebels showed some courage and persistence and the government displayed lack of initiative, the insurgents had won the "wait and see" coup. Pais's insurgents were joined outside Lisbon, where there was little fighting, by another conspirator, Machado Santos, who made a daring escape from his prison in Viseu. With half a dozen fellow officer-prisoners, Machado Santos boldly marched on Coimbra in triumph and seconded the Lisbon rebels' success.[101]

Last-minute maneuvers by President Machado only delayed the complete collapse of the Democrats. Machado sent messages to Sidónio Pais requesting him to cease the fighting if he—the president—dismissed the Costa government. Machado failed to get Pais to agree to the calling to power of an all-Unionist government. On 7 December the government resigned. Pais then asked the beleaguered Machado to resign on 8 December, once the fighting ceased. The insurgents' leadership formed what it called a Junta Revolucionária composed of Dr. Sidónio Pais, Machado Santos, and Unionist Captain Feliciano da Costa. This junta negotiated briefly with President Machado and then decided to fire the senior chief of state, alleging that he had not "intervened in time to avoid the struggle" and that the junta, having won power in the Lisbon streets, was now "the only trustee of National Sovereignty" in Portugal.[102] Costa was arrested in Oporto and jailed; most other major PRP leaders found refuge aboard British vessels in Lisbon harbor; and on the morning of 10 December Machado was held under house arrest as junta troops surrounded his presidential residence at Belém Palace. Soon he was put on a guarded train, the Madrid–Paris Express, and sent into exile.[103]

The 5 December coup was designed, claimed Pais, to expel the Democrats and to "purify" the republic.[104] The Lisbon fighting resulted in the first military defeat in the capital for the Democrats, whose forces had previously triumphed in similar armed conflicts in 1910 and 1915. The ravages of Portugal's controversial war effort, the conflicts among polarized and politicized communities of political belief had led to a very divided Portugal. There is little doubt, however, that like the Republican revolution of 1910, the insurgents and their victory over the Democrats of 5 December 1917—later to be embodied by a charismatic Sidónio Pais—were initially accepted and hailed by large sectors of political Portugal.

For the second time in less than three years—the first was in January 1915—the Unionists had played a key role in a golpe de estado which overthrew a Democrat-dominated government, this time violently. A new republic, coalescing disparate groups of workers, civil servants, soldiers, landowners, intellectuals, and politicians, displaced the Democrats and their supporters. The new government's goal was to move the republic along more conservative paths in foreign and domestic policy.

Angry mobs wrecked the homes and offices of the major Democrat leaders. Also razed were the offices of the Democrats' major daily paper, *O Mundo*,[105] and the headquarters of the party itself. The splintered wheel of political fortune had come full circle.

8 / President Sidónio Pais and the New Republic
1917–18

Arabs believe in persons, not in institutions.
T. E. Lawrence[1]

He was too big a man for such a small country!
Attributed to Colonel Thomas Birch[2]

The New Republic in History

Known variously as "Sidonism," "Decembrism," or the "New Republic," the Sidónio Pais regime marked an interlude in the First Republic: during the year from 7 December 1917, to 14 December 1918, Portugal experienced a form of presidentialism in which parliament was subordinated to executive rule. In modern Portuguese history, Pais's New Republic was more important for what it tried to do, for the young leadership it inspired, for its plans and ideas, and for what the later dictatorship of the New State selected from it, than for what it accomplished. The tragedy of unfulfilled promise was also the tragedy of the extraordinary individual who headed the regime. Sidónio Pais did not live long enough to fulfill his political promise, and his personalism proved both a curse and a triumph. The failure of the New Republic lay partly in the personal nature of its leadership and the absence of other leaders willing to cooperate and take responsibility. Once its personal symbol was gone—the victim of assassination—the system collapsed. This was all the more tragic since it is indisputable that of all the political leaders in the First Republic, Pais was the most popular and attractive. Even more than Afonso Costa, Pais enjoyed a mass public adulation that was a new phenomenon in modern Portuguese politics.

The New Republic anticipated ideas and institutions of the post-1926 New State and it offered a new generation of moderates and

139

conservatives a brief taste of power and political experience. Ten of the ninety deputies of the New State's first National Assembly in 1935 had previous parliamentary experience; half of these had served in Pais's brief parliamentary experiment in 1918.[3] Of eighty-two *procuradores* in Salazar's first Corporative Chamber in 1935, ten had served in the New Republic as deputies, civil servants, or as members of the Senate, which for the first time in Portuguese history had been truly representative of the provinces, economic classes, and occupations.[4] There was a carry-over in leadership as well. A premier in the Military Dictatorship, Colonel Vicente de Freitas, was briefly president of the New Republic's Chamber of Deputies.[5] Leading officers in the abortive pro-nunciamento of 18 April 1925 and in the successful coup of 28 May 1926 had been involved in Pais's 5 December 1917 revolution and had participated at various levels in the New Republic administration. Some of these officers became important in the Military Dictatorship: General João Sinel de Cordes, Pais's chief of staff in the Lisbon garrison; Lieutenant Jorge Botelho Moniz, Pais's aide-de-camp; General Amilcar Mota, an important commander; and Naval Captain Filomeno da Câmara, Pais's appointed governor of Angola.[6] Two members of Pais's cabinets were called to serve after 1926: the physician Dr. Bettancourt Rodrigues, minister in Paris in 1918, and the lawyer Martinho Nobre de Mello, minister of Justice and minister of War.[7]

President Pais sought participation from conservatives and moder-ates who had good reputations in their specialities, but circumstances sometimes obstructed him. Toward the end of his New Republic, he found few persons willing to risk their lives and reputations on the political battlefront. An obscure young economics professor, António de Oliveira Salazar, with doctorate fresh in hand, refused to become minister of finance in August 1918, pleading lack of experience.[8] When young soldiers were available and seasoned administrators were not, Pais recruited his personal aides to perform the most diverse and dif-ficult tasks.[9]

The first two months of the regime offered hope to those eager for a change of government. The Revolutionary Junta began with the pros-pect of support from a varied Republican coalition including dissident Democrats, anxious but still neutral Evolutionists, expectant Unionists, independents, and Centrists. A political consensus that would include groups of monarchists appeared possible. Until mid-February 1918 this coalition remained intact, but the complex political struggle was ap-parent at two levels: on the surface, among those attempting by varying means to reform politics and government under a Republican regime;

and underground, among the groups who conspired to restore the monarchy after gaining decisive power within the Pais regime. Fears that had haunted politics since 1911 again emerged, fomented in part by alarmists and radicals among the ousted Democrats. The New Republic did not succeed in reforming government and politics, nor could it reconcile the volatile groups of warring Republicans and monarchists.

On 15 December 1917, the junta published its proclamation, setting forth programs and goals.[10] The revolutionary government appealed to all "good Republicans and good patriots," making no mention of monarchists. It intended to create conditions in which "parliamentary institutions" could work smoothly and honestly. It attacked alleged corruption and monopoly under the Democrats. The official statement praised the "cause of the Allies" and pledged to continue the war policy. It pledged further to launch a new congress with constituent powers to introduce the principle of parliamentary dissolution as a means to ensure the reform of politics and government. Finally, it promised thrift and stability.

The first New Republic government, formed on 11 December, included three Unionists, two Centrists, and an independent Republican. But the real power to deal with key problems lay in the posts held by the three leading conspirators, the members of the junta: Major Sidónio Pais was premier and held the posts of minister of war and foreign affairs; Machado Santos and Feliciano da Costa were ministers of interior and labor, respectively.[11]

The emergence of Pais as the leading personality and power in the new regime came unexpectedly in January, when the government suppressed a sailors' mutiny on the cruiser *Vasco da Gama*. Pais's decisive action at that time won him the support of the moderate urban populace, and his personal tours of rural districts elicited hysterical acclamation from massive crowds.[12]

Sidónio Pais

Who was Sidónio Pais and what factors influenced his rise to the presidency? Born in Caminha, Minho, in 1872 (he never lost his distinct Minhoto accent), to parents with slim financial resources, Pais worked his way through high school and the University of Coimbra by tutoring. His academic record was outstanding. Taking his doctorate in mathematics, he achieved top honors, which enabled him to become an instructor in calculus at the university.[13] He also won a commission as an officer in the artillery. From membership on the prestigious Coimbra faculty, Pais entered Republican politics. He was a staunch

Republican and a Mason. He joined Manuel Brito Camacho's Unionist party, held minor cabinet posts (minister for development and minister of finance) in 1911–12 and was a Unionist senator.[14] In the summer of 1912 he was appointed minister to Berlin, a post he held until March 1916, when Portugal and Germany officially became belligerents. He returned from his post dejected and saddened by what he had observed in wartime Germany.[15]

The factual record of his career up to his leadership of the 5 December conspiracy only partly describes the personal gifts that electrified the Portuguese public in 1918. The personal aspects overrode the ideological. While Pais remained a Unionist at heart (he apparently read primarily the Unionist organ *A Lucta* while in Berlin),[16] he was not inclined to follow the party line or its head, the forceful Brito Camacho. Rather, he kept an open mind and was flexible. His mathematical gifts enabled him to grasp simultaneously many different ideas. His capacity for hard work, gained in struggling student days, made him a strong conspirator and tireless leader. His personality combined attractive social qualities and strength of character. A contemporary observer described him as "half prince, half *condottiere*,"[17] and a member of his short-lived parliament in 1918 explained his public attractiveness by suggesting that he possessed "spiritual mimetism,"[18] an ability to mimic faithfully several current traits and images. His versatility was extraordinary, but what distinguished him in contemporary Portuguese politics was his readiness to discuss difficult issues openly and to admit in public that he was capable of making mistakes.

Until a serious biographical study is available, we can know little of the process which changed Pais from a Unionist who wanted to continue—with reforms—parliamentary institutions into a determined, revolutionary presidentialist. Some of the sources of his presidentialism are known. First, there was the influence of close friends and colleagues among Unionists, Centrists, and Integralists, among them his minister in Paris, Bettancourt Rodrigues; Egas Moniz, later minister of foreign affairs, who admired Brazilian presidentialism and even the presidential system of the United States; and Martinho Nobre de Mello, an Integralist. There was the influence of Minister Machado Santos, whose 1916 book proposed that under a draft constitution, or national statute, Portugal would elect, by universal suffrage, a president who could dissolve parliament by decree. Pais's experience with a strong executive government in wartime Germany probably had some influence, as did his friendship with the American minister in Lisbon, the former Democratic governor of New Jersey, Colonel Thomas Birch. It is also probable that Pais admired the strong image of leadership projected abroad by Woodrow Wilson.[19]

Presidentialism and Polarization

The laws issued as decrees in the early months of the regime had a double purpose: first, to provide through amnesty, reinstatement, revision of the 1911 Church-separation laws, and other measures, a means to placate large groups of Catholics and monarchists; second, as a consequence of those measures, to win political support and participation from these alienated groups. The laws were controversial and did not entirely win support, but with the exception of the brief dictatorship of Pimenta de Castro, they marked a clear departure from the policies of the first seven years of the republic.

The Church-State relationship was given early priority. The Decree Law of 22 February 1918, signed by Moura Pinto, a Unionist, modified the 1911 Separation Law. Priests were allowed to wear their habits in public, restrictions were eased on the timing, nature, and location of worship services, and on seminaries and priests' pensions. In July the Pais government renewed official relations with the Vatican. These concessions were not large but were politically significant in that they made it possible for the Church to sponsor Catholic acceptance of the Republican regime.[20]

Other laws gave amnesty and pardon to a number of monarchists, including military officers who had deserted or had been separated from the army or navy since 1910. Monarchist officers reentered the officer corp in various garrisons, especially in northern Portugal, while the Lisbon garrison was under the control of monarchist officers such as Sinel de Cordes. The reintegration of monarchist officers in the army, which alarmed Republicans, brought other monarchists back from exile or inactivity.

Tolerance and reconciliation did not extend to the major Republican leaders. Those who had led the government before 5 December 1917 were not allowed to return from exile. The minister at Paris, João Chagas, resigned after the December revolution but was forbidden to return to Portugal until the authorities informed him, the reestablishment of "constitutional normality,"[21] a political condition never attained by the New Republic.

If Pais won the support of some monarchists and Catholics early in his regime, he soon fell out with the only established Republican party that was willing to enter his government in December: the Unionists. Personal disagreements between Pais and Camacho, echoed in *A*

Lucta,[22] were only one facet of the conflict; another factor was the nature of the Unionist party. Few details are known about the party, which at its peak in the early spring of 1918 probably had no more than four thousand or five thousand members. To what extent Camacho's ideas matched those of the membership is not clear, but it is certain that in 1918 the president's prestige and personal appeal—to some Unionists Pais was a "long-awaited messiah,"[23] to others, a grand patron for their causes—undercut Camacho's position within his party. Composed in part of an elite group of friends, patrons, peers, and clients, the party also included upper middle-class and upper-class members from the officer corps, professions, civil service, and diplomatic corps, of which Pais was a member. It also had a base of support in a particular region, the Alentejo, Camacho's birthplace and home, the domain of large landowners who had helped to finance the party and the 5 December coup.[24]

The disagreement between Camacho and his former client and colleague Pais arose from Camacho's ambition for the premiership or a high cabinet post and the constitutional conflict over the structure of the New Republic. The increasingly shrill editorials in *A Lucta* against the Pais government from February to April 1918 provide details concerning the constitutional argument.[25]

Camacho claimed that his party was now the "major organized force of the republic."[26] What lay behind support for the 5 December coup, he suggested, was a growing Republican belief in the need for the president to have the power to dissolve Congress. Pais was initially willing to support this principle, but the real argument concerned the form of the government, which would determine whether the president or Congress would control it. Pais and his close followers now wanted to institute universal franchise for the April general elections. This would broaden the electorate to include illiterates, a move that Camacho and other historic Republican leaders feared. If this occurred, they believed, the republic would move too far to the Right, perhaps toward restoration of the monarchy, and power would shift from the parties and parliament to the president. This was the final breaking point between the Unionists and Pais.

Pais took advice from independents such as Machado Santos, probably from the Centrist Egas Moniz, and Integralists such as Nobre de Mello to restructure the New Republic along presidentialist lines. Public speeches by Egas Moniz in February 1918 outlined the new system. Universal suffrage would fulfill a major goal of the government: "to integrate the nation into the republic."[27] Following the style of the United States, secretaries, not ministers, would form a cabinet. The president would be commander in chief of the armed forces and would be elected for "at least" four years. Congress would consist of two houses: a chamber of deputies with 155 members, and a senate with 77 members. Senators would represent not districts of voters but "corporate" interests—occupations and professions, a feature taken from Machado Santos's proposed national statute of 1916 and the 1903 program of the defunct Nationalist party of Cândido da Silva.[28]

Since the Unionists did not support the government's principles, Pais decided to form an official party, the PNR, Partido Nacional Republicano, which included Moniz's Centrist party, independents, and dissidents from other parties. The Unionists, Evolutionists, and PRP abstained from the elections, and the PNR won a large victory. Seats in this Congress were distributed as follows:[29]

	Chamber of Deputies	Senate
PNR	108	32
Monarchists	37	10
Independents	5	2
Catholics	5	1
Occupations and professions	0	28

Pais was elected president (there was no other candidate) with over 500,000 votes, until then the largest vote in Portuguese history. He made his inaugural speech on 9 May 1918, on the balcony of the Lisbon town hall. Urging his countrymen to help initiate a new, glorious era of peace, reconciliation, and regeneration, he called for support of the Allies in the war. A particular passage makes the speech one of the most conciliatory public addresses ever delivered by a Portuguese leader:

A new era of freedom, of tolerance, of respect for the religious beliefs and the political convictions [of others], has arrived.

Only in such an atmosphere can the nation prosper. The nation requires a stable base which is not possible without a spiritual union of many souls. That union today is a fact. . . . A great national idea popularizes this movement.

The revolution of the Fifth of December has triumphed! The resurgence of our Fatherland is more than a hope, it is a consoling certainty. . . .

I can make mistakes, but merely show me the error and I am prepared to alter it without resentment or vanities, without silly obstinacies, without tyrannical intransigence.

Every Portuguese can count on me as a friend who is prepared to defend his justice. . . .[30]

Despite his capacity for conciliation and his desire to end conflicts, Pais was under continual attack for his government's war policy. Just as deceptive as the myths surrounding the Democrat-dominated government's war policy is the myth concerning the New Republic's war policy. Opponents charged that Pais gave official protection to those who feared going to war; a common conviction was that Pais's government did nothing to reinforce or support the hapless Portuguese army in Flanders.[31] Actually the record of 1917–18 suggests that Pais supported the Allied cause, was genuinely concerned about the welfare of Portugal's forces in Europe and Africa, and that, although his policy was to limit aid to the Allies, his government did provide some reinforcements. Numbers of Pais's supporters in the army did shirk service in the trenches, but others served. The desire to avoid service in France was one of many motives behind the 5 December coup, the greatest being the growing desire to oust the Democrats.[32]

As part of a pro-Allied war policy Pais's government dispatched over a thousand new troops with artillery to France in January 1918;[33] more troops were later sent to Mozambique. The allegation that Pais's regime was entirely to blame for the Portuguese defeat at Lys in April 1918, during the general German offensive, has little substance. The outcome at Lys probably would not have been much different with or without massive prior reinforcement; furthermore, the Costa-Almeida regime's preparation of the expeditionary force had flaws.

The pro-Allied position of Pais was clearly understood by major Allied diplomats, both civil and military, during the final months of the struggle. On 12 November 1918 in the public ceremonies following the Armistice in Lisbon crowds hailed the Allied victory. Pais took part in the ceremonies and was a public mourner for Portugal's war dead. He advocated both the Allied cause and cooperation among Atlantic allies. Under his regime the United States established its first naval base, for antisubmarine activity, in the Azores, at Ponta Delgada, São Miguel Island, in 1917. This was a prelude to United States–Portuguese relations in World War II and the later alliance within NATO. In January 1919, Portugal conferred upon Colonel Birch, the American minister and a close colleague of Woodrow Wilson's, a high Portuguese decoration, the Grand Cross of the Order of Christ, as a reward for Birch's services to Portugal in the war. Admiral H. O. Dunn, commander of the naval base, had been given a medal, the Order of Aviz, in 1918.[34]

How the New Republic Functioned (July–December 1918)

Pais's newly elected Congress first met on 15 July 1918. As a parliamentary institution its record was disastrous. If anything, the chaos during its brief life was worse than those of the previous congresses. With the field open now to monarchists, Catholics, independents, and conservative Republicans, disputation broke out over the issue of what form a new constitution would take: parliamentary or presidentialist.

On 5 August, after two weeks of debate, the government adjourned the chaotic Congress, which had accomplished nothing. Congress was to be, in effect, a new constituent assembly, but the deputies and senators failed to agree on a formula for writing a constitution. Even the presidentialist majority in the dominant PNR feared putting the power of dissolution in the hands of a powerful presidentialist regime, though they would not have opposed doing so in a parliamentary regime.[35]

This brief Congress saw the emergence of a break between the Catholics and monarchists over the issue of restoring the monarchy. The Catholics had now become neutral on this issue, but monarchist deputies continued to insist on treating restoration as a central issue.[36] Pais adjourned Congress until 4 November, since he could not rely on the fragmented body. The Assembly was torn with violent arguments, shouting, and challenges, while in the Senate most senators slept through the sessions.

When in July 1918 Pais observed that Congress had tied itself in knots, he went ahead with the annual budget, made it a presidential budget, and put it into law by simple decree, an arbitrary act which revealed just where power lay in the New Republic and demonstrated that Pais had given up on Congress as a vehicle for instituting change.[37] Even with the system of secretaries, there was a minimum of consultation, and one cabinet member noted that Pais called cabinet meetings only rarely, since the president took action on his own.[38] Congress was recalled into session on 4 November but was forced to adjourn for lack of a quorum. When it did meet again briefly in early December, the only debate was over the crescendo of public violence, and the issue of political prisoners. On 5 December Congress again adjourned for lack of a quorum.[39]

Pais's government now came under bitter attack even from former supporters. Meeting no more than twenty-five times during nearly six months, the frustrated Congress saw the country being run by one man and a few of his closest advisers and secretaries of state in Lisbon. Congress began to form committees to draft a new constitution for the New Republic, a promise made earlier, but the committees took no action, and Pais apparently wished to delay any final constitutional commitment while the war continued and his own official party was so fragmented and unreliable. Not one law or decree issued from this unfortunate body, whereas Pais's offices issued thousands of decrees which were duly instituted and, as was customary, published in the *Diário do Governo*.[40] The main arena of politics was outside São Bento's halls, in the offices of the president and his advisers, and in the increasingly dangerous streets.

The frequent turnovers in Pais's cabinets reflected the status of politics. Most cabinets after the Unionists resigned in March 1918 were makeshift; except for a few talents like Egas Moniz, who was appointed minister to Madrid and later foreign minister, the secretaries of state tended to be inexperienced and ineffective—young army officers and friends of the president.

In a few policy areas, effective administrative action was taken. The government worked to get the Allies to provide Portugal with enough foodstuffs and raw materials to meet minimum needs. Exportation of scarce goods was prohibited and the state tried to guarantee fair distribution of imported goods rather than the system, determined by self-interest, of brutal, unfair, and anarchic hoarding, speculation, and overpricing. A framework was established for controlling, for the first time, external trade and home food supplies in the interests of the war effort. There was a gradual transfer of foreign-trade control to government organs, i.e., the Ministry of Subsistence, under an army lieutenant. The state was to restrict private initiatives with state action in order to prevent the sale of foodstuffs abroad, and to allow importation of needed foods. As compared with previous years, wheat production fared well.[41]

Opposition to the Pais regime grew, especially after the adjournment of the abortive Congress in early August. The wise and prescient Moniz warned Pais in a letter of 9 August 1918 that the regime was in a "precarious position."[42] The PNR lacked backing and substance, and the other parties, both monarchists and Republicans, were organizing conspiracies to overthrow the government. Moniz urged Pais to organize a party concerned with issues, rather than the traditional kind backed by clients and caciquismo. Moniz received no reply from the overcommitted president.

As the street took over from Congress, labor organizations reacted to adverse conditions: effects of the war, low wages, persecution by the government of labor newspapers and associations—by means of arrests, bannings, police searches—and the failure of the New Republic to make good the promises made by Pais at the time of the 5 December coup. The major syndicalist organization, the União Operária Nacional (UON), as early as March had attacked Pais's government for a political breach of promise and passed a motion to the effect that since the

New Republic was no different than "the others that went before," workers must unite and act "outside the action and influence of any political party."[43]

By late summer, all the rival parties and groups, now isolated from Pais's personal *presidentialismo,* began to lay plans for the aftermath of the collapse of the fragile system. It was now considered a distinct possibility that Pais himself might not survive for long, since he was surrounded by a hostile political vortex he could not master. Monarchists, Republicans, and political agnostics began to plot. As a contemporary noted, the "conspiratorial spirit" abounded.[44] In June and July there were abortive plots to kidnap or murder Pais. As supporters like Machado Santos abandoned him, syndicalists organized for revolution and general strikes. Monarchists, alienated by Pais's opposition to restoration of the monarchy, began their plotting.

Conspiratorial activity became as chaotic as government and politics. Groups competed in a struggle to get the confidence of army and navy units who could be enticed into mutiny and insurrection. A serious threat to the Pais regime came in a conspiracy led by the Democrats which "pronounced" on 13–14 October 1918. The conspirators planned that a military insurrection, supported by civilian Democrats, would occur simultaneously in Lisbon, Oporto, Coimbra, Évora, and smaller towns. On 13 October the government declared a state of emergency, and Pais's security forces crushed the uprising easily in Lisbon and Oporto by arresting over a thousand people. But in Coimbra the rebels managed to organize an insurrection in a major local army unit, the Thirty-fifth Infantry Regiment. The commander and most officers fled as the ranks mutinied against the government. The rebels held out for only a day, however, and Pais's government was back in command by 14 October.[45]

The aftermath of the abortive coup brought more tragedy. President Pais's police had a reputation, among even monarchists, for being brutal and "clumsy."[46] Passions were intense after the excitement, and many political prisoners had been produced by the arrests. A massacre of unarmed prisoners on a Lisbon street, the so-called *Leva da Morte,* occurred on 16 October 1918, as 150 prisoners were escorted from one prison to another by 200 trigger-happy police. When a bomb exploded near the procession, the police fired into the helpless prisoners, killing 7, including a Republican notable, the viscount of Ribeira Brava, and wounding 60.[47]

President Pais deplored the brutal treatment of the political prisoners and made personal attempts to intervene. The problem of the handling of political prisoners did not begin nor did it end with the New

Republic, but Pais made special efforts to control the police and to demonstrate concern for the welfare of prisoners, often jailed without charges and held for long periods under wretched conditions. His personal trip to Oporto's Aljube Prison, where he freed some abused prisoners, however, was strongly criticized in the moderate Republican press as being not a humane policy but an abdication of "authority."[48] Political passions appeared to be, indeed, "ungovernable," and Pais's personalist regime and its fragile structures could not cope with the formidable challenges.

As the New Republic drew to its tragic climax in late 1918, one hopeful episode intruded: the end of the war. Pais's controversial war policy had to deal with a deeply divided country. Twenty years later, on the eve of yet another world war, a Portuguese observer offered an accurate observation of one aspect of the national attitude to the earlier war when he stated that "the country did not understand the war."[49] News of the Armistice, however, brought massive crowds into Lisbon's streets. Wild cheering lasted for hours and some participants cried, "Long live Portugal!"[50] If the country did not always comprehend the war, it was glad to celebrate its end.

The Collapse of the New Republic

President Sidónio Pais's New Republic collapsed amidst urban violence and turmoil. The political turmoil—strikes, bombings, coup attempts, and demonstrations—was both a symptom and a cause of a general social crisis, which could be measured to some extent by the amount of crime in the cities and larger towns. Available statistics on crime[51] suggest that there was an important and steady increase in crime and juvenile delinquency during the first eight years of the republic. Whereas in 1890 only between two and three thousand arrests of youths in Lisbon had been made in a year, by 1918 between fifteen and twenty thousand arrests were being made. Police estimated that in Lisbon alone there were twenty thousand "delinquents," few children attended school, and many between the ages of four and seven years were "living" in the streets.

Observers noted that the crime problem became more serious during the war years. As a newspaper article commented just before the Democrats' abortive October coup: "Rare is the person today who dares to undertake even a brief journey or to cross a dark street without going armed. And within one's own home, one lives with the same fear. . . ."[52] Observers attributed the high crime rate to the poverty and misery among the lower urban classes.

Although the New Republic failed as a conservative, coherent regime of "order," its agonies did serve to force the consolidation of important ideas and concomitant trends which bore fruit after 1926. Under Pais's turbulent regime lessons were learned and new questions were asked which laid a foundation built upon later by elements of the Military Dictatorship (1926–33) and by the New State (1933–74). Three general ideas began to mature: First, some members of the intelligentsia became committed to a national, nonpartisan approach to key problems and their solutions. Study-action groups were started in 1917–18 to institute this approach. Second, the army was recognized as a unique and reasonably cohesive institution. A number of observers came to accept the idea that the army—or, to be more specific, its officer corps—could "save the nation" in a nonpartisan manner. Third, an increasingly important conservative group—the Catholic-Integralists— now participating in national and local elections, came to believe that the monarchist restoration was both unlikely and probably irrelevant. After 1916 the Catholic-Integralists fell out with most monarchist groups on the issue of monarchist restoration, and their break with this tradition in 1918 was an important political development.

The League of National Action (A Liga de Acção Nacional) was probably the first of several nonpartisan, nonpolitical study-action groups started in 1917.[53] Founded by Dr. Pedro José da Cunha, rector of Lisbon University, the league insisted that it was "not a party," foreswore any ambition for public office, and suggested that it meant to "inspire and to monitor critically," all governments. Issues, not personalities, were the focus of its activities, and league committees studied key problems. The writer António Sérgio was secretary-general of this short-lived group, which proposed a long-range educational campaign to prepare Portugal for social equality and democracy. Sérgio and other league members later founded the Seara Nova group in 1921, an association whose goals will be discussed later.

A second important idea in gestation was that the army could be a national, stable, institution capable of solving problems. Pais's government encouraged a regeneration of military pride. With a dearth of political supporters in his administration, Pais depended upon army officers. By his personal example in public appearances and by providing amnesty for monarchist officers, Pais drew attention to military virtues and the prestige of the uniform. In public he invariably wore a general's uniform and appeared on horseback. The cult of "Sidónio" began among young officers who early on exalted him as a model soldier and commander in chief.[54] As several garrisons organized juntas militares in Oporto and Lisbon to prepare for the demise of Sidónio

Pais, the origins of praetorianism and military professionalism were well established.

The Catholic-Integralist break with the monarchists was virtually completed between the April 1918 elections and the monarchists' unsuccessful attempt to restore the monarchy in February 1919. The Catholics' brief electoral alliance with the monarchists resulted in only six seats for Catholics and over forty seats for the monarchists. Catholics also resented Pais's apparent neglect of them in favor of monarchists, and many became convinced that the mainstream of monarchists were too partisan and selfish. To the Catholic-Integralists, the restoration was much less important than "law and order" and Catholic rights. A "conservative republic" appealed to them as it did to retired Catholic-Nationalist patriarch Jacinto Cândido da Silva. In a private letter of April 1918 Cândido da Silva emphasized that the form of regime was less important than was establishing the Catholic-Integralist program: "Christian restoration, in the defense of the re-established social order, and that is the basis of the civilization of modern societies."[55] Through such ideas evolved New State ideology.

Toward the end of 1918, it appeared that President Pais had lost control even of his former supporters, now jostling to "rob the revolution" they knew was coming. Law and order, what Pais had pledged to restore to Portugal, was fast eroding. The streets were in turmoil and thousands of political prisoners were in jails. Assaults in the streets by hired bands of *situacionistas* who feared the return of Costa and the Democrats became daily occurrences. Even Machado Santos was disillusioned. In a Senate speech of 3 December 1918, he called the holding of the many political prisoners a national disgrace. He claimed that even the home of the widow of the heroic commander of the German-sunk Portuguese minesweeper, *Augusto de Castilho,* had been recently raided and ransacked by the political police.[56] Less than a week later, in a speech in the Chamber of Deputies, former army officer and currently insurance salesman Cunha Leal stated that the streets were so dangerous that insurance companies refused to insure persons against assault.[57]

Meanwhile, on 5 December 1918 a nineteen-year-old Republican youth, a member of the PRP, attempted to assassinate the president but failed when his pistol misfired three times. It was now common knowledge that Pais was marked for murder. Yet few security precautions were taken and the president's movements were publicized in the Lisbon daily papers. As the military junta in Oporto assumed ominous importance, Pais decided to go in person to Portugal's second city to mollify the discontented officers. About midnight, 14 December 1918, on his risky mission north, President Pais was assassinated in Lisbon's Rossio train station. When Pais first sensed the assassin's presence, he reached for his pistol, but he was felled by two bullets which pierced his chest. When his young military aide desperately flung himself across the body of the fallen president, it was too late. Pais died before he reached the hospital. He was the only president assassinated during the First Republic.

Pais's murder was not the work of "secret societies," as was frequently claimed later,[58] but the deed of a lone individual, one José Júlio da Costa, aged twenty-four. Costa was from a small Alentejo village and had been brought up on radical republicanism by his father. An ardent Democrat who admired Afonso Costa and the Republicans' wartime coalition, the Sacred Union, the young Costa had a secret determination, as he wrote himself, "to kill and to die."[59] His history reveals a life, however brief, totally dedicated to republicanism in the Jacobin tradition. He sought to defend the republic as a soldier in Timor and Angola and was embittered when he was rejected by Portugal's expeditionary army to France and also by French authorities in Lisbon when he attempted to enlist as a foreign volunteer. Literate, self-willed and with intensely rational spurts, the young assassin planned to kill the president in order to restore "freedom" and to destroy "absolutism." He was willing to become a martyr and to die for his "republic." He was fully aware that his deed would probably plunge the country into civil strife. His request to his captors to be killed was not honored, and he was never executed.[60]

The New Republic in Perspective

The Pais regime began as a moderate-conservative coalition response to certain ills of the republic. It ended as an experimental presidentialism, a risky, exposed form of one-man rule. Political Portugal was divided over the war effort and discouraged with the economic crisis, yet was unprepared for monarchist restoration or for full-blown presidentialism. Despite his conciliatory gestures, Pais could not ultimately satisfy a very large portion of Republicans and monarchists and, at the same time, bring peace and unity.

Pais's system was, as one of his last defenders admitted, "a paradox without practical viability."[61] The only functional institution of Decembrism, was the president himself, on whose mortality rode the destiny of his government. Other institutions functioned poorly or not at all. Conspiracy again replaced political participation as the major activity of both friends and foes of the system.

To contemporaries, as well as to later historians, the New Republic's record was mediocre. Except in a few areas such as wheat production, lower emigration, some social-welfare measures and ideas, and fewer strikes, this government failed to respond effectively to key problems: the trade deficit, inflation, food shortages, and the debt.[62] Even in the realm of appointments in the administration, Pais became ever more dependent upon a shrinking circle of army officers.

In the end, Pais was opposed and abandoned by many Republicans, ignored and betrayed by monarchists eager for the return of a king, and opposed by independents like Machado Santos on the labor question. The isolated leader was forced to rule alone in a state of perpetual siege. Sidónio Pais was locked in a deadly race between his mental and physical powers of endurance and relentless pressures. His personalist style of daily governance and his ceremonial visibility, both a habit and a response to crisis, quickly began to consume him physically and to agitate further what was probably an "unstable personality."[63] Chain-smoking, coffee-drinking, with little or no sleep for long periods, the forty-six-year-old Pais by early December was existing largely on his own "nervous energy."[64] In time, even without the assassin's bullets, some sort of physical or mental breakdown—the burden of attempting to reconcile several conflicting republics, and monarchist dreams—would have come.

His sudden and tragic passing readily provided material for legends and cults. A fervent cult of Sidónio grew up, a Sebastianist belief which was poised insecurely between the age of kings and the age of presidents, between hopes and shattered values and illusions. Sidónio Pais became the beloved object of mass worship by ordinary citizens who remembered him. Especially devoted were large numbers of women. The most visible symbol of the cult was in the placing of his picture in many homes.[65] Whatever the legal niceties, Pais became a unique *presidente-rei,* a president-king, in the fine phrase of the poet Fernando Pessoa.[66] To a later prominent New State leader, Pais was the only Republican "national hero" who could be compared favorably with Dr. Salazar.[67]

The consequences of Pais's sudden death, his meteoric passing in the stormy political heavens, were doubly tragic. Both personal and national promise were frustrated. Sidonism's failure went a long way toward convincing post-1926 leaders that both a monarchy and a unitary executive would be too risky and in any case unworkable. In the next months Portugal appeared to be gripped by catastrophe. Close behind the president's dark funeral procession on its way to Portugal's burial place of kings came civil war.

9 / Republic Immobile: The Standstill Polity

> The Republic proclaimed in October of 1910, until now has not resolved the Portuguese difficulties, and the fact that we have not yet found our political equilibrium for the solution of the great national problems, has perturbed the life of the Republic with armed dissensions, violent crises and revolutions without purpose.
>
> Raúl Proença[1]

The Standstill Polity*

Neither the collapse of the New Republic nor Republican victory in a brief civil war in 1919 brought national salvation. A great deal had happened, but though there had been economic and social changes, the political system remained the same. During the first eight years of the republic various forms were tried: parliamentary government, 1910–11, 1911–15, the brief Pimenta de Castro authoritarian regime in 1915, more parliamentarism, 1915–17, and Sidónio Pais's presidentialism, 1917–18. Severe civil disorder, violence, labor strife, and insurrection among the military became increasingly common. Conflicts persisted over questions of the Church, restoration of the monarchy, and participation in World War I. Although some issues lost their original controversial quality, none was finally resolved and new problems arose. What capacity remained for open discussion, compromise, and action was dulled by discontent, grievance, conspiracy, and golpismo.

Instability of the political institutions was a major symptom of the malfunctioning system. Up to the end of 1918 Portugal had fifteen governments, including the dictatorial Provisional Government, and five presidents. The first constitutional president, Arriaga, was virtually forced to resign after the 1915 Revolution, months before his term was up. The third president, Machado, was dismissed by a military junta

---

* In analyzing the political system of France's Third Republic, Stanley Hoffman developed the useful model and synthesis of what he called France's "stalemate society." Stanley Hoffman et al., *In Search of France: The Economy, Society, and Political System in the Twentieth Century* (New York, 1965), pp. 3 ff.

after only two years in office, and Pais, a president elected for the first time by universal male suffrage rather than by Congress, was assassinated after only one year. Congressional instability was equally serious. Of four congresses elected beginning in 1911, including the short-lived Constituent National Assembly, only two served out their full terms (1911 and 1911–15); the other two were summarily disbanded by executive fiat following military coups in 1917 and 1919.

After 1918 instability intensified. By 1920 some twenty-two newspapers and magazines had been assaulted by mobs. There were at least twenty-nine political murders and over 1,500 citizens died in armed combat during disturbances during 1915–19. Governmental instability reached a high point between 30 June 1919 and 2 March 1921, when no fewer than nine governments came and went. By 28 May 1926 and the collapse of the parliamentary republic, Portugal had acquired the record of Europe's most unstable parliamentary regime: forty-five governments during fifteen years and eight months.

Added to post–1919 intensified   instability were economic and financial dislocations without precedent in the country's modern history: new debts from the war, inflation, food shortages, and currency depreciations. There was some improvement in primary education, social welfare, colonial administration, and in the economic position of some sectors of the urban working classes. Urbanization burgeoned and the urban middle class expanded. Republican governments were unable to resolve the historic conflicts and tensions between Lisbon and the country, nor could they significantly alter the traditional landowning patterns and deteriorating agrarian conditions in central and south Portugal.

The last seven years of the republic, 1919–26 saw greater disillusionment with the functioning of the political system. Except for a brief time in 1921, the PRP, the Democrats, dominated elections, held a majority in Congress, and controlled civil administration. The Democrats exhausted their political credit, grew more unpopular among both the middle and lower classes, and yet no viable alternatives appeared. The year 1919 was not the positive turning point it was thought to be, and the constitutional revision of that year which gave the president of the republic the power to dissolve Congress before its term ended did not produce an equilibrium.

The political system became immobile: it was standstill polity. A prisoner of unmanageable tensions, conflicts, and forces, including recurring personalism and factionalism, this standstill polity was not overthrown until 1926. The way this phenomenon functioned can best be envisioned by comparing it to a drowning man in a raging river. The

drowning swimmer survives the rush of water, may temporarily sub-
merge, but manages to surface and keep breathing. By himself he
cannot reach the bank. Nor can bystanders extricate him. He is con-
demned to continual flailing until such time as his forces are spent, the
river's current changes, or bystanders devise a way to rescue him.

The First Republican system, like the drowning man in the river, was
able to survive cycles of tribulation but was never able to emerge from a
governmental and political crisis. It released considerable energies, few
of which lent themselves to consolidating and stabilizing parliamentary
democracy.

The immobility was more than financial and economic. Cycles of
insurrections and counterinsurrections were superimposed upon the
Democrats' electoral dominance and that party's failure to reform.
While the Democrats could survive military uprisings their rule became
more unpopular, unrepresentative, and semiauthoritarian. It would not
"resolve the Portuguese difficulties," as Proença put it, yet short of
revolution no other party could oust it.

A great deal of energy was expended on flailing and little on reaching
the riverbank. Groups mobilized support for a variety of causes. In
1915, 1917, and 1919 thousands volunteered to defeat monarchist insurrections or to fight the Germans in overseas campaigns; thousands of
workers organized and struck to win improvements in hours and wages;
irate businessmen who were determined to avoid taxation managed to
unify against state taxes in 1924–26, and hundreds of officers organized
a movement to shut down the Congress and expel the Democrats. But
these causes did not in themselves bring needed reforms or build the
necessary healthy institutions which could contain the tensions between
authority and freedom.

The standstill polity was neither democratic nor authoritarian. Most
of the post-1919 leaders of PRP-dominated cabinets moved farther and
farther away from the democratic, egalitarian, municipalist, and
representative program Republicans offered in 1891 while in opposition. The franchise was actually restricted under the Democrats.
The republic's policy toward votes for women was conservative.
Although the PRP before 1910 had urged an enfranchisement of
women, after the monarchy fell nothing was done. Despite demands for
a limited franchise for women by the Liberal party in 1919 and by the
Democratic Left party in 1926,[2] no change occurred.

When a few governments attempted to execute the policies of a more
egalitarian, participatory democracy, they faced fervent opposition
from conservative urban and rural groups. During the tenure in office
of only four governments, from 18 December 1923 to 1 July 1925, were

there genuine efforts to put into operation a set of relatively advanced policies which would have gone some way toward fulfilling the PRP's pre-1910 promises. These four governments (see Appendix A) were headed by premiers Álvaro de Castro, recently bolted from the Nationalist party (PRN), to form his own party, the Republican Action Parliamentary Group, Alfredo Gaspar, Democrat (PRP), José Domingues dos Santos, Democratic Left party (PRED), and Vitorino Guimarães, Democrat (PRP). Led by politicians who defied the conservative, mainstream clienteles of the Democrats and the Nationalists, these governments not only discussed fundamental reforms in agriculture, such as nationalization of properties, and free public education at university level, but they also began to put into effect banking, currency, and tax reforms, which were long overdue, and social-welfare programs. When they claimed that they identified with the "exploited against the exploiters," they frightened not only the traditional commercial, agrarian, and financial vested interests, but the conservative core of the civil and military bureaucracy.

This brief attempt to break precedent quickly passed with the fall of these four governments. But considerable political trouble had been stirred up. In eighteen months these well-intended governments of advanced talents, including some thinkers from the Seara Nova group (see chap. 11), did as much to open the way for an authoritarian, rightist regime as did years of military and civil disorder. The brief interlude temporarily united a fragmented Right and helped to create the conditions in which the armed-forces officer-corps movement could organize the overthrow of the parliamentary regime.

Before analyzing the major events of 1919–26 in chapter 11, I shall discuss the role of parties and of the military in politics in the standstill polity. This chapter will deal with parties and the political system, and chapter 10 will examine the armed-forces officer corps: why it became an institution with a key role in politics and how it developed its own political consciousness and will to power.

The Struggle for Power

Why did this system, which could not reconcile freedom and order, which failed to achieve any public consensus on what kind of republic was most desirable, and which did not provide either reasonable stability or lasting reform, survive such a long time in its set pattern of one-party dominance and second-party impotence?

Three important factors explain its persistent immobility: the nature of the struggle for political power, the use of this power; and the nature of the political-party system.

The first factor, the nature of the struggle for power, concerns the manner in which political parties, interest groups, and associations achieved national public office. The revival of the pronunciamento tradition after 1890 by Republican militants, including the Carbonária, insurrectionism or praetorianism among the military, the semicivil war, violent atmosphere of election campaigns and elections, and the political turmoil, both in the street and in Congress were all part of the power struggle. Observers used various images to describe seeking power and holding office during the republic. The process was compared with the traditional Portuguese bullfight,[3] "a herd of bulls in a chinashop,"[4] a "civil war,"[5] or being on a "battlefront."[6] What were some of the causes of this kind of struggle for power? Many could be listed: personal ambition, precedent in political tradition, the example of the style of student politics in the schools and universities, the love of power, personality, emotional character, revenge, and the assertion of self-interest.

Following the example of *exaltado* extraordinary Machado Santos, political dissatisfaction easily led to military conspiracies, or "revolutions." Revolutionary movements, especially after 1918, were launched with the intent to overthrow governments; in some circles such conspiracies assumed a daring respectability. As one contemporary observer noted, street revolutions became, like desertion in some army regiments, simply a "political convenience."[7] Not only individual politicians but also political parties participated in conspiracies to foment insurrection among units of the armed forces in order to oust rivals and to bring into office other groups. By the end of the First Republic the scenario for such conspiratorial activity was almost tedious; it became so familiar by 1926 that one Lisbon newspaper printed a brief "do-it-yourself" treatise on coups which was entitled, "The story of all the revolutions."[8] As the writer of the piece noted, the conspirators, predictably, first organized a *comité revolucionário,* gave arms to civilian groups, arranged for signals to begin the movement at a certain time, and then required the support of at least "three military units," which promised to rebel against the government at the agreed-on time and to back the conspirators' political program. Within each unit, the article claimed, the certainty of political commitment once the "revolution" got into the streets lay in the solemn promises of merely "a sergeant, a corporal, a soldier, or the wife of any of them."[9]

Conspiratorial politics in which the military insurrection and coup became more common than elections or any public consensus on key issues had important consequences. Groups or parties that lost elections turned naturally to military conspiracy to achieve office.[10] Insurrections became broader and bloodier as a larger portion of the citizenry possessed deadly weapons. Even after the 1919 constitutional revision, which will be discussed in detail in chapter 11, the nature of the struggle for power remained largely the same.

Elections were increasingly discredited. Because of their election monopoly based upon an organized election machine and the loyalty of a core of the bureaucracy, the PRP won every election except that of June 1921. Rather than providing the electorate with real choices, most elections served only to consolidate the hold of the party already in power, a tendency which had been institutionalized under the monarchy. Because of their core of loyal bureaucrats in the military, for a long while the PRP could neutralize or co-opt coup attempts. Or, if they lost in the streets, as occurred in 1915, 1917–18, and briefly in 1921, they could organize a comeback by means of a countercoup.

The Use of Political Power

The second major factor causing the standstill polity, the way in which political power was used, was just as crucial as the struggle for power. The major dispenser of political power was the PRP, or Democratic party. Except for brief periods in 1915, 1917–18, and 1921–22, the PRP held a monopoly of electoral power, national office, and patronage. An examination of how the PRP leadership used their power reveals that the major beneficiary was usually a conglomerate of lower-class and lower middle-class citizens in Lisbon, Oporto, and other towns, as well as a few upper middle-class groups who earned high profits during World War I and during the period 1921–26. How the PRP leadership attempted to influence the distribution of rewards, including wealth, status, and jobs, is revealing. Also revealing are the factors that determined whether those who were rewarded—who perceived an improvement in their situations compared to before the world war, or before the republic—supported or failed to support the PRP. A broad coalition of lower-class, lower middle-class and middle-class elements, mainly in central and southern Portugal, supported the Republican party's rise to power in 1910. This coalition began to break down during World War I, especially after 1917, when bankruptcy, inflation, food shortages, and the cost of living worsened. Some lower-class and lower middle-class groups who received jobs, status, and wealth from the party maintained or improved their position. At the same time, the middle and upper ranks of the civil service, the armed services' officer corps, and the merchant-tradesmen became alienated as their position deteriorated.

How power was used and how rewards were distributed is partly documented by a study of wages. It was through jobs in the civil services and armed services that the PRP most directly rewarded its supporters. With every major change in government, for example, in 1913, 1915, 1917, 1919, 1921, and 1922, when the PRP followers either came back into jobs or were dismissed, thousands of jobs changed hands. In May 1919, after the Democrats won a majority of seats in the congressional elections, the PRP again rewarded its lower-class and lower middle-class clientele with civil-service jobs. An exact count of the politically appointed jobs in the civil service will be feasible only when unpublished government records are available. In the city of Lisbon's civil-service positions, at least 17,000 Democrats were placed in jobs in May 1919 following the electoral victory, and *all* their names were duly and tediously published in the official gazette, *Diário do Governo.*[11] Among other consequences of the PRP patronage system of civil-service jobs were a bloated and corrupt bureaucracy which was in part the result of cronyism, pork-barreling, payroll padding, or featherbedding, and a disproportionately large service sector among the employed. A large portion of each annual national budget was expended on bureaucracy. Table 2 indicates the percentages of employees in various economic sectors and suggests that while the employment in the agrarian and industrial sectors diminished, "service," a large part of which was civil and military bureaucracy, increased significantly.

Wage raises for the expanding bureaucracy, part of the political patronage system of the PRP, were manipulated in favor of the lower ranks. After 1914 inflation and currency depreciation seriously reduced the purchasing power of the population living on fixed incomes. The salaried bureaucracy were among the hardest-hit sectors of the population, but within the bureaucracy there was differentiation in the impact of the economic crisis. Both the civil and military bureaucracy suffered, although after World War I the average pay for the military was always

TABLE 2
Percentage Employed in Sectors of Economy, 1890–1930

	1890	1911	1930
Agrarian	61	57	46
Industrial	18.4	21	17
Service	20.6	22	37

Source: Joel Serrão, "Povo," *DHP,* 3:462.

higher than for the civilian functionaries. The upper- and middle-rank civil servants and soldiers, together with pensioners, lawyers, teachers and professors, and the majority of employees in commerce, suffered a severe decline in their standard of living compared to before the war. These groups of "new poor," who saw their purchasing power destroyed as the value of currency plummeted, were much more numerous than the "new rich," the petty bourgeoisie, bankers, businessmen, and industrialists (see table 3).[12]

While the upper- and middle-rank bureaucrats lost most heavily, the lower ranks received higher pay raises and maintained or, in the case of primary-school teachers and the lowest-ranking civil servants and soldiers, actually improved their pre-1914 standard of living. For example, in 1917, middle-ranking civil servants were being paid in value only 61.6 percent of their prewar wages; by 1920–21 this percentage declined to 22 percent of prewar level. Lower-level civil servants fared better, as did lieutenants and sergeants in the army. In 1921 lower-ranking civil servants got in value 76.5 percent of prewar levels, while in 1923 they received 119.1 percent.[13]

By the end of the First Republic, as Dr. Oliveira Marques has pointed out, the purchasing power of the upper and middle ranks of the bureacracy was only half what it had been when the Republicans came to power.[14] This fact had serious political implications. Most PRP-led governments made a policy of favoring the lower ranks with pay raises and depended upon them to vote for the Democrats in elections and to defend them both in routine times and when the spirit of military insurrection was abroad. One-party dominance in parliament and in the streets, then, was intimately tied to the power of patronage, the bu-

TABLE 3
Cost-of-Living Index in Portugal, 1914–25

July 1914	100
July 1915	111.5
July 1916	137.1
July 1917	162.3
July 1918	292.7
July 1919	316.8
July 1920	551.6
July 1921	816.7
July 1922	1,128.0
July 1923	1,719.5
July 1924	2,652.0
March 1925	2,509.1

Source: *Anuário Estatística de Portugal: 1925* (Lisbon, 1926), p. 177.

reaucracy, and the failure of second parties to challenge the one party's monopoly of patronage and elections.

The Democrats' electoral power was dependent upon the support of a largely but not exclusively urban group of government functionaries, what in recent African history has been termed "an administrative bourgeoisie."[15] Even the 1919 change in PRP leadership reflected the shift of emphasis and class support from Afonso Costa, the Coimbra-educated top lawyer as chief, to the post-1919 Democratic chief, the engineer–civil servant António Maria da Silva (1872–1950).[16] Silva was a mining engineer who owed his position in the Republican party to his high post in the Carbonária and his contacts with the civil service as an "interim director of statistics" under the late monarchy and as senior civil servant (administrador) in the (Portuguese State) Telephone, Telegraph, and Postal Services (CTT), a very useful base for power and patronage.

Silva was premier no fewer than six times beginning in 1920, held continuous power once for nearly two years (1922–23) (see Appendix A), and it was his last administration which was overthrown six years later to make way for the Military Dictatorship. Silva's base of support awaits detailed study, but from available evidence it was the lower middle class of the capital and other urban areas, and some lower-class elements who voted PRP consistently election after election and who habitually depended upon government employment. Some of the persons involved in the electoral machine and patronage network were enrolled in the civilian vigilante groups which were important during 1910–14; others had office jobs or were enrolled at least part time in bizarre political gangs in the Lisbon area. Several thousand were included in what was called the revolucionários civis ("civil revolutionaries"). Numbers of them possessed their own arms and were, in effect, regularly up for hire during times of civil strife and power struggles.

Although his statement should be taken with some reservations, General Óscar Carmona, in an interview given in the spring of 1930 to an American writer, provided an interesting description of this PRP "subélite," whose livelihoods commonly depended upon government largesse:

"Revolution," Carmona said, "had become a career like any other. There were certain groups in the city who could provide at any time, for a round sum, any number of resolute scoundrels ready to be armed and sent out against any opponent . . . the Revolucionários Civies [sic]—Lay Revolutionaries—joined themselves to the armed forces . . . whenever there as a coup d'état.

Since then [Revolution of 1910], of course, there has always been a vast number of *Revolucionários Civies* to assert that they had participated in every successful revolt . . . and to claim their recompense. By refusing to recognise them in 1926 I hope that we have now rid ourselves of them. They were a symptom of the political illness which we are trying to cure."[17]

There were severe pressures upon the national leadership to dispense patronage. PRP rank-and-file members, some of whom were former monarchists, pressured members of any government to give them and their relatives and friends jobs and to keep them on the payroll of the state. The job seekers who sought to join the swelling ranks of the aggressive Portuguese administrative bourgeoisie did not have to qualify by merit or by examinations. The first step was to join the Democratic party (PRP) and to become members of the increasingly numerous Republican "centers" (*centros republicanos*). By being members of the dominant PRP, the beneficiary of the patronage system which the Republicans had consolidated during the early years of the republic, 1910–13, would-be civil servants had access to civil-service jobs. A somewhat overdrawn but basically accurate portrait of one aspect of the PRP place seekers comes from a monarchist journalist of note: "The civil revolutionary became a potentate; with his ignorance and violence he installed himself in the public departments, with his lack of discipline in the Army ranks, in the street-life with his boldness which he knew full well would be protected by the public armed forces."[18]

Central to the problem of how political power was used by national leaders and how this use contributed to the failure of parliamentary democracy was the size, wastefulness, and controversial nature of the "immense bureaucracy."[19] The general practice of excessive spending of public monies on patronage and personal gain was known in contemporary literature as *devorismo*. This unusual political-administrative term (see Glossary) was retained as late as 1961 in an edition of a popular dictionary, which defined it as "Exaggerated and unjustified expense. Dissipation of the public treasury for personal gain or in favor of someone else."[20] Observers commonly referred to this practice,[21] which appears to have intensified under the First Republic, as an evil which had ancient roots in Portuguese history. Related to it was *empregomania*.

Corrupt political-patronage practices and a middle-class preference for and dependence upon public offices, of course, were nothing new in Portugal. Under the Constitutional Monarchy, if not earlier, such practices became quite common. Part of the Republican campaign against the corruption of the monarchist politicians concerned those very practices.[22] In some respects, as I have noted, the traditional habits of the monarchy in this respect were transferred to the First Republic and to its own burgeoning administrative bourgeoisie and followers, some of whom participated in the 1910 Revolution. Republican devorismo, however, had some important new features: (1) It appears to have involved a significantly larger number of jobholders and offices than did the same practice under the monarchy. This reflected the pressures of urban growth, spreading literacy, and a more effective mobilization of people. (2) As will be discussed in chapter 10, devorismo influenced the army and navy officer corps and ranks and the expansion of paramilitary units such as the police, GNR, and Fiscal Guard. (3) Besides the regular urban officeholder in government ministries and agencies, the Republicans who benefited from political patronage included a substantial number of armed individuals (whatever they were called: formiga branca, kassais, revolucionários civis, grupos para a defesa da república, etc.).[23] These men, who were to be found in Oporto, Lisbon, and the larger towns, got possession of their arms in a variety of ways: by theft, through service in the armed services during the world war in Africa or Europe, during periods of anarchy and civil strife after 1910—when the civil authorities distributed arms or opened state arsenals to the people, as they did during the revolutions in 1910, 1915, and 1919—or by purchase from stores. In 1922, superficial searches by the authorities in Lisbon failed to unearth numbers of small arms owned by "revolutionaries"; it was estimated officially that at least 12,000 weapons were unaccounted for and in civilian hands.[24] In effect, a large number of people who supported the dominant PRP machine during and between elections were not only armed but sometimes up for hire in return for pay and/or food and provisions.

TABLE 4
Growth of Military and Civil Bureaucracy, 1911–30

	1911	1922	1930
Entire country			
Armed forces	80,317	122,324	124,395
Civil service	57,416	—	105,407
Lisbon district only			
Armed forces	32,781	—	48,005
Civil service	23,700	—	38,228

Sources: Ministério Das Finanças, *Censo da População de Portugal: 1911* (Lisbon, 1916), *Censo da População de Portugal: 1930* (Lisbon, 1934).

The figures in table 4 suggest the dimensions of devorismo in two keys areas where political patronage was dispensed: the armed forces and the corps of public functionaries (civil administration). While it may be argued that the numbers involved are small compared to agriculture, industry, and commerce, the figures suggest that the size of the armed forces in nineteen years increased by over 50 percent and that the civil service nearly doubled in size.

These persons, dependent upon employment by the state, whether as soldiers, sailors, or civil functionaries, a large concentration of whom were in Lisbon and Oporto, made up a significant part of the electorate. They had their representatives in the Congress, some of whom were in the civil service or armed services. Many of them participated in conspiracies and coup attempts during the First Republic and into the Military Dictatorship. In the context of the first third of the century in Portugal, this bureaucratic group's political impact was out of all proportion to its size.

Political Parties

The third major factor that contributed to the standstill polity was the nature of the political-party system. The only viable political party with important local roots was the PRP, the Democrats, who benefited from an electoral machine based on patronage in the bureaucracy. No other political party was able to challenge the PRP; it came to enjoy a monopoly of patronage, electoral power, and the benefits of holding more seats in Congress than other parties.

The party system was only nominally a multiparty system. (For a selected list of the many political organizations that came and went during the First Republic, see Appendix C.) The system resembled a curious combination of a one-party and a multiparty system, since only one party, the PRP, was consistently victorious in elections, and no second or third party ever developed into a potential challenger, with the possible exception of the Liberal party (PRL) which in general elections in June 1921 defeated the PRP and won 48 percent of the seats in Congress. (PRP did hold 33 percent of the seats, however.) Their legally constituted government under Premier Granjo in October 1921 was thrown out of office by a coup d'etat, and Congress dissolved by an intimidated president of the republic. In the January 1922 elections the PRP came back to win an almost customary majority. These events in 1921 represent a very important turning point in the history of the failure of democracy in Portugal. The development of a viable second party—a challenger which could bring to bear pressure to reform, cleanse, and remold the PRP—was short-circuited by a military insurrection, a pliant president of the republic who bowed to the threats of the insurrectionists, and by the failure of conservatives and moderates to unite and cooperate. Without an effective alternative to the PRP there could be no balanced, reasonably stable political system where power could change hands, where governments could peacefully come and go, where significant reforms of the social and economic situation could occur.

There were at least five key reasons why no effective opposition party developed as a counterforce to the PRP. These reasons are, in order of importance: (1) Too much effort was expended in a struggle for political office, the raison d'etre of most so-called parties. (2) Political leaders—while they included some talented and intelligent men—too often lacked courage, and failed to unite and to cooperate for the public good. (3) Pressures from Congress—which resulted in the fall of many governments—hurt the chances of any opposition to form strong alternatives to the PRP power monopoly (4) The expression of public opinion as a balancing factor in the business of government and the practice of politics rarely was effective; illegal practices such as demonstrations, threats, acts of violence, and libelous writing in the press often drowned out a free, full expression of various shades of public opinion. (5) Parties lacked distinct, clear programs, in part because personalities often were substituted for issues and ideas. Each reason will be discussed in turn.

The struggle for public office has already been discussed at length. The pattern remained the same as in the 1840s, when a writer observed that Portuguese politics in his day was essentially wars among public employees,[25] but the struggle in 1919–26 was on a larger and more violent scale, and the stakes were higher. As a way of changing governments, pronunciamentos by relatively small groups of persons became a more common and popular phenomenon than elections or votes in Congress. The armed conspiracy which led to a successful coup, then, became a major means of achieving public office. Election results became less and less meaningful and relevant as an expression of public opinion, or as a democratic exercise.

The political leaders of the second stage of the republic included a wide variety of men: António Maria da Silva—premier on six occasions and leader of the PRP after 1919—was, some believed, "king of the mediocres," with only one kidney and with a pistol in his pocket for protection.[26] But there was also the able Álvaro de Castro (1878–1928), lawyer, colonial governor, army officer, and finance expert, whose record in office was outstanding.[27] As premier from 18 December 1923 until 6 July 1924, Castro enlisted a brain trust of experts in their fields from the Seara Nova group; they included the essayist-educator António Sérgio in the Ministry of Public Education (he resigned after only two months in office), and Mário de Azevedo Gomes, the scholar, in the Agriculture Ministry. Taking the key post of Finances, Premier Castro, by means of strong controls and sales of silver, effectively halted the debasement of the currency. His government fixed the value of the escudo and contributed to its appreciation in the last years of the First Republic.[28]

Castro's brief but effective time in office—nearly seven months, which was longer than the average four-month life of a cabinet—illustrated the political stalemate. For all its genuine accomplishments, Castro's government received a storm of abuse in the turbulent Congress, and his party, Republican Action, never recovered. Castro himself never again took office, which was unfortunate, for he was a shrewd, perspicacious observer of Portuguese politics whose intuitive judgments usually proved to be correct. A study of his writings suggests that he was able to identify both in 1917 and in 1923 three major developments which would lead eventually to the Military Dictatorship: the PRP's persistent monopoly of power and office; the failure of the parties to respond to the needs of the public or to accomplish much in office; and the army's determination to win control of the government, once the parties had bankrupted themselves.[29]

Like so many other political figures, however, Álvaro de Castro was also prone to political messianism when it came to ideas for resolving crises. He believed that only the exiled Afonso Costa could successfully lead a stable government. It was Álvaro Castro in June 1924 who made an arrangement with the PRP Directorate to resign so that the still prestigious Afonso Costa could return to head a government. The president of the republic, and close friend of Costa's, Teixeira Gomes, backed him, also believing that only Costa could wrench politics and government out of immobilism and begin to build a stable system. Costa's long-awaited return, however, never materialized; he refused to form a government, alleging that the opposition—the Nationalists—would not support a "national" government.[30]

Portugal did not lack for talented leaders. But the example of Álvaro de Castro suggests that no matter how remarkable they were, they could not remain long in office, nor could they accomplish much in the atmosphere of political messianism, of semihysteria in the Congress, and of pervasive fear of harm or ridicule from leaders like Costa, who withdrew from public office precisely when they might have helped to break the political stalemate.

The Congress—both the Chamber of Deputies and Senate—did much to breed political instability in its votes of "no confidence," its tumultuous, violent sessions, its failure to deal with essential business. The record of Congress was mediocre at best, in attendance, legislation, and constructive response to executive efforts. A study of the daily sessions from 1911 to 1926 shows that the attendance record of members steadily worsened and that it was common after 1919 to have sessions cancelled for lack of quorums. While congressional committees apparently did some work,[31] their role was insignificant. Congressional votes not only served to cut short the life of incompetent cabinets, they threatened able groups, like the government of Álvaro de Castro, in an alarmist, often hyper-contentious spirit that was commonly a reflection of the struggle for public office.

Public opinion, as an expression of a wide selection of views, rarely had an impact on legislation, the execution of laws, and the decisions on who held power. While there was an extensive daily press in the main towns and two cities, including the dominant capital, and while the press reflected a range of opinion which included Catholic, Communist, Socialist, anarcho-syndicalist, liberal, Fascist, and monarchist, press opinion was divorced from government action. At the end of the republic, however, the rising opposition to the Democrats' control of government was reflected in the press. Between 1919 and 1926, most of the press came to oppose the dominant party's holding of power. By May 1926 only one daily Lisbon paper out of over twenty organs, defended the Democrats' last government. This situation reflected increasing fragmentation of the opposition parties and growing opposition to the Democrats' monopoly of power. Thus public opinion had a rather tardy impact on politics. Even this unusual situation, however, was only a limited example of freedom of the press; the last Republican government, whenever threatened by military insurrections—as it was on at least three major occasions before the successful overthrow of 28 May 1926—heavily censored the Lisbon press in order to prevent the public from learning just how real the threats were.[32]

Major political parties lacked distinctive political programs. In fact, the only truly distinctive and radical programs were those of groups and parties which remained outside of the parliamentary system, which never elected deputies to Congress, and which rarely participated in conventional politics: namely, the Communist party, the Seara Nova group, and the Portuguese Integralists—Integralismo Lusitano.

Despite its strong program during the tenure of the Provisional Government, 1910-11, the PRP lacked any distinctive ideology after 1919 and depended on malleablity to satisfy both rural and urban supporters. As Cunha Leal accurately described the PRP program, it had "few ideological preoccupations" and could, only by a stretch of the imagination, be termed as Left-Center.[33]

But it is the failed oppositions' programs which in their vagueness and generality reveal the nature of the political environment. Although most programs had points which were sensible and necessary reforms— if implemented, and there was basic agreement on the need for what was invariably referred to as order, freedom, and progress, as well as for laws of ministerial responsibility and a reduction of the size of the large bureaucracy, yet opposition-party programs appeared to be carefully designed efforts to appeal to specific grievances of certain groups without differing in an extreme way from the general program of the dominant, mass party—the PRP.

Between 1919 and 1926 two major parties in succession attempted to challenge the dominant PRP: the Liberals (PRL), 1919-23, and the Nationalists (PRN), 1923-26. What was the nature of these frustrated second parties and what was the essence of their programs? The Liberal party (PRL), like most Republican parties, was a coalition, a fusion of the old Evolutionists (PRE), Unionists (UR), Centrists (PC), some independents, and a few Presidentialists (PP). This coalition took form beginning in early September 1919, in order, it hoped, to become "a great Republican party that will establish political equilibrium in Portuguese politics," and to "stabilize the regime" with room "for all opinions."[34] The Liberals' program mentioned all the points which had become standard fare: an independent judiciary, freedom of speech, improved workers' conditions, justice for all, autonomy for the colonies, no strikes in public services, effective labor arbitration machinery, improved public welfare through decentralization, free enterprise for the private sectors, a reform of education. The party program emphasized two of its sixteen points: that it was a "party of order," "without ceasing to be a progressive regime," but that this order would *not* be imposed by "violence." It was an order based on "cooperation and rights." The party proposed a reduction of the size of the civil service and a balancing of the budget. The most controversial section of the program lay in the area of Catholic rights and corporative representation. The Liberals openly proposed a modification of the harsh 1911 Law of Separation, but would not allow Catholic instruction in schools, public or private. They also proposed that the Senate be altered to allow "representation of classes," or a kind of corporative chamber. This represented an early foreshadowing of public support for the corporative concept, an idea which the New State put into practice after 1933.[35]

The Liberal party proved to be a political failure and in 1923 most of what was left of it merged with other Republican factions, including Álvaro de Castro's Reconstituents (PRRN) to form the Nationalist party (PRN). This second post-1919 major Republican opposition party had a program which reflected the increasingly conservative nature of Center and Right Republicans, the rising influence of Catholic rights' supporters, and frustration with the "single party rule" of the PRP. Like the CEDA party under Gil Robles during the Second Spanish Republic, 1933–36, the Nationalists were a "bloc of the Rights," which hoped to incorporate in one party conservative Republicans as well as frustrated monarchists. Its published program in 1923 openly called for "order in the streets, order in spirits, order in the labor movement."[36] Unlike the preceding Liberals, the Nationalists made a more definite appeal to Catholics, who were pressing for a full restoration of pre-1910 rights; they also considered including in their program advocacy of a revision of the Law of Separation to allow Catholic instruction at least in private schools. Republicans like Álvaro de Castro—who later bolted the Nationalists probably on similar issues— adamantly opposed this concession. Castro stated in a debate in the Nationalist party congress of 1923 that such a concession was merely a cover to allow the return of the expelled Catholic orders, a development he believed the Republican masses would oppose.

By 1925 the program of the Nationalists for the November general elections had added the concession Castro had opposed: allowance for Catholic instruction in private schools, a move which appealed to Catholic voters.[37] Like the Liberals, the Nationalists also stressed the necessity for a new Senate structure which would bring in class representation. Significantly, the Nationalists also proposed a further constitutional revision which would have increased the executive power over the parliamentary in the spirit of a government of "order."

Were the programs of the major opposition parties so similar to the PRP program (with the exceptions of the issues of Catholic rights and the proposed Senate with "class representation") because of a fear of offending sensitive voters? Did the parties fear being too explicit before taking power? Or were issues less important then personalities and the manner in which elections were conducted? These questions cannot be answered here. What is apparent, however, is that the opposition parties never provided a clear-cut choice to the electorate.

10 / The Honor of the Army

> [Portuguese deeds in the 1917–18 Flanders campaign show] . . . that the Portuguese race still conserves those qualities of bravery, dedication, altruism and love of country with which, guaranteeing the preservation of their nationality, in many anxious moments and in the past they have made it great and made it triumph.
>
> Lieutenant Colonel Fernando Freiria[1]

> Against the barbarians within and without, the Army is the first condition necessary for peoples who desire to rejuvenate and to fortify themselves by a return to their traditional institutions.
>
> António Sardinha[2]

After 1915 the role of the armed forces in politics became increasingly important. In the 1910 Revolution and in the early years of the republic, initiative for conspiracies and coups was largely civilian, and radical Republican "civilianism" was powerful. In later years initiative began to pass to the military. Also, the Republican governments placed great responsibilities in the hands of the military commanders to defend at home and abroad against a variety of foe.

This chapter will attempt to answer two questions about the standstill polity: why and how did the armed forces, particularly the army officer corps, become politicized, and how was a group of army officers willing and able to organize the 1926 coup which opened the way for a military dictatorship?

Failure of the 1911 Army-Reform Laws

As was noted in chapter 7, a portion of the professional army officer corps resented Republican policies and the political activity of civilian groups in military affairs. The 1911 army-reform laws had established a new militia system based on more extensive male conscription, but this system proved to be ineffective before 1916, when Portugal entered the

European phase of World War I, and was a failure during and after the war. The militia system never worked as it was intended to work. Professional officers resented the militia because they believed it undermined military professionalism. Moreover, in order to make the militia system work, Portugal would have required a level of financial means, mass education, military-cadre support, and public backing which the country did not have.

By 1925, the militia system was thoroughly discredited. As had happened under the monarchy, inequities in conscription became common. Large numbers of citizens never served. Some draftees were rejected because of their poor physical condition, but others used political influence, particularly caciquismo, to arrange exemptions. The burden of the draft fell again largely on the poor. Official statistics for 1925 stated that out of over 85,000 citizens eligible for service, only 55,875 appeared before local draft examination boards; of these only 21,794 entered the ranks. Training periods for draftees were sharply reduced, most of the militia school system was closed down, and hopes of making the army into a surrogate school to teach citizens to read were abandoned. Although the literacy rate of the "average" entering draftee was higher (ca. 49 percent) than the national average (ca. 25–30 percent) in 1925, the general quality of the Portuguese recruit was low and training facilities achieved little improvement.[3]

The Navy

Though its role in politics and in defense later in the First Republic was less important than that of the army, the reputation of the republic's navy was, if anything, more problematic. The navy during the period featured obsolete equipment, poor discipline among personnel, ambitious plans, and neglect.[4]

If the navy was less important in terms of defending Portugal from a possible Spanish invasion or other threats from Europe, it played the crucial role of maintaining a link with the Portuguese colonies. It also provided the republic with five prime ministers and one president of the republic, and had contributed a substantial proportion of the colonial governors in Africa.[5] More than the army, the navy suffered from the ills of the republic; poor finance meant an obsolete fleet which might not be able to defend against even a fourth-rate power, and the politicization of officers and sailors produced poor discipline and bad morale. The increasingly wretched state of the navy aroused fears in members of the Portuguese elite who were concerned with defense of the colonies and feared Spanish aggression.

During the republic the state of the navy, except in the last few years when there were some improvements, grew progressively worse. The Revolution of 1910 had been possible in part because of rebellious sailors and intimidated officers. Insubordination among Lisbon sailors was a serious problem, as were the promotion of poorly prepared officers and the loss of able officers who resigned their commissions. The fleet inherited from the monarchy was small and old, but what there was of it was partially wrecked by 1914 through accidents and incompetent navigation. The accidents which put several ships out of commission in 1912, for example, were caused by inexperienced personnel promoted to command after the revolution.[6] By World War I because of the riotous sailors and some incompetent officers, at least a section of the Lisbon naval establishment was considered not only useless but perhaps more of a menace to Portugal than to potential aggressors.

In March 1916, the navy got hold of better equipment by confiscating German vessels in Lisbon harbor, and the war provided valuable training. But only in 1923 when the Álvaro de Castro government appointed Captain Fernando Pereira da Silva navy minister were prospects of naval reform greatly improved.[7] As the outstanding navy minister of the First Republic, Pereira da Silva remained in office almost continuously for two-and-a-half years (from December 1923 to May 1926), an unusual instance of administrative continuity at the time. In 1924 this officer published a proposal for naval construction which was presented to Congress for action in July 1925. Although not acted upon during the First Republic, this plan for naval rejuvenation became the basis upon which the Dictatorship constructed its plans during the thirties.

Pereira da Silva sadly observed the virtual collapse of the fleet. Its condition was scandalous, especially among those who were conscious of Portugal's reputation as a historic naval power. One particular incident seemed to epitomize its plight. In February 1922 when President of the Republic Almeida made an official visit to Brazil, the government required appropriate oceanic transportation. The president was informed that no warship was fit to make the transatlantic voyage. Instead, President Almeida was obliged to travel on a small steamer, which, once it had reached Brazil, was confiscated by creditors. With no vessel, the chagrined president was forced to book his return passage as a regular first-class passenger on an English vessel.[8]

Minister Pereira da Silva called for ten years of naval construction to increase the fleet from 22,000 tons to 72,000 tons. The Republican parliament did not act on his naval plan, but under his ministry attempts were made to turn the navy into a more professional force. The fleet had remained inactive and crews rarely had sea duty; the Lisbon-based sailors were embroiled in the politics of the capital. In 1925 Pereira da Silva began a program of more sea duty and de-politicization. He initiated extensive cruises to the colonies, and, by establishing a new naval base up the Tagus River at Vila Franca de Xira, he moved a number of sailors well away from Lisbon.[9]

By 1926 professional alarmists urged the government to execute Pereira da Silva's well-recommended naval program. One admiral wrote in the leading military journal that in view of Germany's renewed colonial interests, and indeed, since Spain possessed a navy nearly four times the size of Portugal's, the weakness of the navy endangered Portugal's colonies. National defense, he suggested, had become a "problem of life or death." The admiral warned that without a new navy Portugal itself might fall before either the German or Spanish menace and lose her independence.[10] To this and other armed-forces leaders, the condition of the navy in 1926 was only one more justification for taking the government out of the hands of the politicians.

The Army and World War I, 1915–18

The Movement of Swords in January 1915 showed the Democrats' leadership that a government which neglected or abused its army officer corps did so at its peril. The Democratic party initiated a program which was designed to eliminate military grievances and to satisfy a number of the demands of professional officers made during the January 1915 crisis. Afonso Costa's new, belated but more realistic approach was clearly reflected in his ministerial declaration to Congress, as he took office in December 1915.[11] Second only to the war policy as an ally of England was his government's attention to army interests. Speaking to the army and navy commanders as much as to the members of Congress, Costa promised to complete the 1911 army reforms, to increase the size of the army and to improve its preparation for war, to improve training, and to rejuvenate the fleet. Costa's language and his message were meant to soothe the ruffled feelings of the leaders of the armed forces: he emphasized that the army was "the most genuine expression of the high qualities of the Nation," that politics should be kept out of the army, that lack of discipline and insubordination in the ranks would have to be dealt with, and that he would have a continual concern for military interests. Implicit in his speech was a promise to prevent further incidents involving the formiga branca, and similar civilian interference in army affairs. In short, Afonso Costa attempted to convince military leaders that his administration supported military interests.

The army's experience in World War I, whether in tropical Africa or in Flanders, was a key factor in shaping the relationship between the civil government and the armed forces. At least indirectly, participation in World War I helped prevent a monarchist restoration, but it had other, unforeseen consequences: an increase in the importance of the army's role in society, a new militarism, and an impetus—fed by the war—to put the army at the head of the state and government. If the Democrats' governments believed that the war policy would consolidate public opinion behind the republic and occupy the army, they could not anticipate that it would unsettle the officer corps and provide later pretexts to place the army above the law.

Like the war policy, the preparation of the army for war in Europe generated political controversy. The personalist element again played its role: the task became largely the responsibility of one man, Democratic Minister of War Major José Norton de Matos (1867–1955), an army officer and former governor of Angola (1912–15). To the Democrats, Norton de Matos's effort in training and arming thousands of raw recruits, and shaping the Corp Expedicionário Português, the CEP as it came to be known, was referred to as the "Miracle of Tancos."[12] Tancos was the army engineers' camp which in 1916 was converted to accommodate the mass training required for the CEP. The officers who collaborated with Norton de Matos and who later served in the trenches in France were mainly elite officers, most of them born in the 1870s and 1880s. This group of "Young Turks" included young officers who had helped to overthrow the monarchy. The war effort became associated with the names and ideas of these officers. Many but not all were liberals in politics and became members of parties and later leaders. Before 1917 most of them were members of the PRP, but after the war many joined opposition parties or became nonpolitical. Important officers among them included: Álvaro de Castro (1878–1928), António Ribeiro de Carvalho (1889–19??), Américo Olavo (1882–1927), Augusto Casimiro (1889–1970), Francisco Cunha Leal (1888–1970), Helder Ribeiro (1882–1973), Alfredo Sá Cardoso (1864–1950), Fernando Freiria (1877–1955), and Álvaro Pope (1879–1940).

The Portuguese participation in the Great War made the interventionist administrations especially open to severe criticism. What began as a debate over the war policy extended to the question of fighting conditions and home support for the soldiers in Africa and Europe. An angry Portuguese war literature sprang up which contained many accusations against political leaders. Politicians, some suggested, had not only failed to do much about the generally wretched conditions faced by most soldiers but these *políticos* had betrayed the armed forces merely for the sake of votes, political advantage, and financial speculations.

Though no one disputed that bad conditions existed, the questions of responsibility and accountability became intensely politicized. Portugal had to depend on its allies in Europe for winter clothing, transportation, arms, and even strategic planning. But the Costa government, the one most often criticized, was well aware of adverse conditions, was concerned, and made efforts to improve the situation.[13]

Blaming politicians for the bad state of the Portuguese army overseas in France or Africa became common after 1915. To the charge that Afonso Costa "sold" Portuguese soldiers to the Allies for one pound sterling a head, were added stories which illustrated the allegation that the collective honor of the army had been besmirched in the European campaign, 1917-18. Even as late as 1971 such stories were recorded as fact in supposedly reputable books on military history.[14]

The hate literature on participation in the war rolled off the presses especially during the years 1915-30. Although much of the general literature on war memoirs was amateurish and of no lasting value, there are classics which provide accurate, well-organized accounts of Portuguese participation.

An important body of war literature emphasized positive aspects of Portugal's performance and concluded that the intervention—despite the terrible problems and consequences—was a seminal experience for the Portuguese people and that the government was wise to commit Portugal to the Allies' cause in view of German war guilt and war aims. Among the most persuasive and celebrated of war books was that by the venerable military authority and leading militarist, General José Estevão Morais Sarmento, in his *A Expansão Alemã—Causas determinantes da Guerra de 1914-1918: Suas tentativas e perigos na África Portuguesa.*[15] The work was popular in Portuguese military circles and was translated into French, with a preface by Marshal Lyautey. Morais Sarmento laid the guilt for beginning the war squarely in the German camp. It was significant, too, that his work concentrated on Portuguese Africa, not on the Flemish campaign.

Among the more important war books by liberal intellectuals is the classic memoir, published also in 1919, of the historian-physician Jaime Cortesão: *Memórias da Grande Guerra.* In passages which compare with those of the great European memoirs of the war Cortesão describes the atmosphere of a French insane asylum which served as a

temporary hospital for the Portuguese wounded during the battle of
Lys. He brilliantly paints the scenes in and around the insane asylum
for women at Saint Venaint, where wounded and dying from the raging
battle were brought. As the makeshift hospital-morgue came under artillery fire, those who could evacuated the grim place. Eyewitness Cortesão gives an account of the precipitous retreat:

> On the road we swelled the long cortege of those who were withdrawing:
> shreds of regiments, civilian families with children on their laps, carts with
> household remnants, Chinese workers, and, in morose groups, Portuguese,
> English and Australian soldiers, all in a silent, pressing torrent, devoured by
> the common drama.
> Behind us submerged in the gloom was the palace of the mad, of the
> cadavers, of the martyrs, of the dying; [it was] raised up on the banks of this
> human river, like a gentle monument to affliction.
> We move, like wild animals fear-crazed by fire, from time to time looking
> back with eyes maddened with fear. We move carried along, impelled, dragged
> like inert matter caught in a sorrowful cataract. . . .
> How true?! How terrible?! What hellish nightmare is this?!
> And a terrible desire roots itself within me to gather my last efforts for a
> final rebellion, to throw myself into the road's gutter and wait there till death
> can rescue me.[16]

Of all the effects on Portugal and on the Portuguese which derived
from participation in World War I, even discounting financial dislocations, the most important was the question of "the honor of the
army." The Portuguese performance in trench warfare was at once the
most controversial and painful. It was the first time in over a hundred
years that the Portuguese had engaged a foreign European army. Apart
from the later flippant aspersions cast in official British orders on the
Portuguese as "our noble but nimble allies,"[17] serious questions were
raised about the condition, status, and action of this Portuguese force
of approximately 75,000 troops, of whom some 40,000–50,000 actually
experienced frontline duty. The reputation of the Portuguese army on
the Flanders front was later based on rumor, half-truth, and pseudo-
racist slurs; among some of the Allied forces, the story of the battle of
Lys, 9 April 1918, became a myth, threaded with ethnic jokes about the
Portuguese.

A recent historian of World War I surveys the performance of the
four Portuguese brigades serving with the British at Lys in comparatively kind terms:

Coming on through fog, nine full-strength German divisions attacked. They
drove straight for a sector manned by four Portuguese brigades serving with

the British. It was no contest. The fog wafted away, and the Portuguese saw what was coming in time; these merry men—the most congenial lodgers on the Western Front—threw down their arms and fled. One battalion of British infantry, bicycle-mounted, was rushed to the gap. The retreating Portuguese soldiers out-wrestled them, took the bicycles, and kept going, some making it to Le Havre, where they sat for the rest of the war.[18]

Whatever the views of foreign historians, soldiers, politicians, and diplomats, the most significant factor for Portuguese politics was the Portuguese opinion of themselves. Portuguese literature on the Flanders campaign often features discussions of what happened at Lys and how the honor of the army was stained by the perfidy of the politicians at home, the cowardice of some officers, and the cutting sarcasm of the less sensitive of her Allies' representatives, both official and unofficial. Portuguese who participated in the holocaust of the Western Front were fully introduced into the worst crisis yet experienced in Western civilization. Witnesses like Cortesão saw elements of the CEP destroyed in a matter of minutes. The historian-soldier after the battle of Lys quotes a comrade who referred to Lys as "the Alácer Quibir of the CEP."[19]

If there was despair among some Portuguese veterans, for some others there was also a sense of redemption, self-respect, and admiration for the sacrifices made by a nation not prepared to act as an equal participant. The Portuguese common soldier who survived whole in mind and in body was, according to Cortesão's imaginative analysis, "transformed," and ultimately "saved" by the experience. If to the Allies, later historians, and not a few cynical Portuguese, the common soldier in Flanders—the Zé Povinho of the trenches—appeared grotesque, to those who understood the Portuguese struggle for national self-respect, the foot soldier was patient, all-suffering, and at times heroic. Most criticism was leveled at the officers. Cortesão, himself a militia officer, wrote that "as a general rule, among the officers, the higher the rank, the worse the officer."[20] Why? Was it the tendency of the elite to denigrate themselves, while seeing in the ordinary Portuguese the virtues that leaders believed their ancestors had possessed during the Marvelous Century? Was it the crisis of the Portuguese elite to have lost their nerve and with it their sense of pride? Whatever the answer, the virtues of the regular Portuguese soldier in war—when led by brave and wise officers—were praised by militarists like Mousinho de Albuquerque and antimilitarist liberals like Jaime Cortesão alike. Whatever their political beliefs, veteran officers who survived the war believed that the ordinary Portuguese soldier did not suffer from the decadence, whether real or imagined, of many officers. As Cortesão wrote, "That soldier is still the same one who was at Aljubarrota and on the Seas."[21]

But bravery—even coupled with good luck—was not enough. Nor was an atavistic nationalism. The Portuguese army in Africa and in Europe was poorly prepared and all too often had to fight under hopeless conditions. In the years 1917–18, when Portugal had an expeditionary force in France, the means to train and support it were just not available. As Cortesão admitted later: "In fact we did not have an Army capable of waging modern war."[22] Ironically, a major technical consequence of Portugal's participation in the European campaign, 1917–18, was to increase the size and armament of her army, and this had an impact upon domestic politics.

Technical Effects of Participation in the War

When Portuguese troops returned from Flanders and Africa in late 1918 and early 1919, the military establishment had burgeoned. The army had acquired a nucleus twice the size of the regular force of 1911. Tables 5, 6, and 7 suggest the growth and development of the Por-

TABLE 5
Size of Regular Portuguese Army—Officers and Ranks, 1910–33[a]

1910	12,000
1911	11,690
1914	12,000
1920	23,000
1925	30,000 (approx.)
1926	27,255
1927	34,947
1928	34,236
1929	32,663
1933	12,000

Sources: PRO, F.O., 371/1463, "Portugal Annual Report, 1910," p. 20; *O Século,* 8 Feb. 1913; PRO, F.O. 371/7109, "Portugal, Annual Report, 1920," p. 21; Maj. A. D. Branquinho, "O Orçamento Do Ministério da Guerra," *Revista Militar* 74, no. 5 (May 1922):254; PRO, F.O. 371/13429, "Portugal, Annual Report, 1927," p. 25; *A Noite* (Lisbon), 17 April 1926; *Anuário Estatística de Portugal: 1926, 1927, 1928, 1929* (Lisbon, 1927–30); PRO, F.O. 371/18589, "Portugal, Annual Report, 1933."

[a] It is impossible to estimate the size of the regular army during the period 1916–19, as many Portuguese saw temporary service in the war. Over 110,000 soldiers were in foreign theaters of combat as of Nov. 1918. Data after 1919 include militia officers retained from war service.

tuguese regular military establishment during the parliamentary republic and into the Military Dictatorship.

When officer corps in the postwar era elsewhere were being reduced in size by demobilization, why did Portugal's officer corps remain as large or larger than before the war? The answer lies in the consequences of the war effort and in the politics of patronage and bureaucracy. The size of the corps of regular, professional (career) officers who had been in the army before the war remained relatively constant, between 2,000 and 2,200 officers. The increase in size of the officer corps to around 4,500 officers during most of the period, 1918–26, was due to the incorporation of wartime, supposedly temporary, militia officers into the regular corps. By a decree-law of 23 November 1921, the government legalized what was already a fact: numbers of militia officers who had been recruited and trained for war service were allowed to remain in the regular army, with full pay, if they satisfied fairly simple conditions.[23]

Both in its results and in its political meaning, the 1921 decree-law was controversial. The law was passed by the short-lived coalition Republican government of Carlos Maia Pinto (see Appendix A) and became the object of considerable ire among professional officers.

TABLE 6
Student-Officers Enrolled in Higher Military Schools, 1911–26

1911–12	341
1917	643
1919	165
1921–22	102 (only 16 graduated)
1925–26	220 (only 43 graduated)

Source: *Anuário Estatística de Portugal: 1926* (Lisbon, 1927), p. 112.

TABLE 7
Size of Portuguese Army Officer Corps, 1911–33

1911	2,000
1915	2,600
1917	4,000
1918	4,500
1919	4,500
1925	4,500
1926	4,466
1927	4,569
1933	4,395

Sources: *Almanaque do Exército: 1919–26* (Lisbon, 1920–27); PRO, F.O. 371/13429, "Portugal, Annual Report, 1927," p. 25; PRO, F.O. 371/18589, "Portugal, Annual Report, 1933."

Among certain sectors of the followers of the PRP and among the urban administrative bourgeoisie, however, the law, which favored the retention of several thousand officers who if dropped from the service would have faced difficulties finding jobs, was politically popular. The law opposed the spirit if not the letter of the 1911 army-reform laws, which had been executed with the idea that as soon as units were demobilized militia officers would be given permanent leave or discharged. The 1921 law enabled a large number of militia officers to remain permanently within a special cadre which concentrated in infantry, artillery, and administration, precisely those branches which underwent the greatest wartime expansion.

If there were important political, military, and economic reasons for the retention of militia officers, there was strong professional opposition to it. Professional officers complained that the war-spawned militia officers gained undeserved decorations, pay, and rewards by means of political favoritism. A large group of militia officers enjoyed the pay of regular officers, yet their duties were often undemanding and time-serving in nature. One critic claimed that morale among regular officers dropped when they observed that militia officers, who had few responsibilities, held outside jobs.[24]

A final important effect of Portuguese participation in the European phase of the war was the acquisition of used Allied arms. By the end of the war the Portuguese army had become dependent upon the Allies for arms, since Portugal did not manufacture her own, and since she lacked the means to purchase new arms to replace armament acquired during the João Franco dictatorship (1907–8).[25] Portugal had provided rifles and heavy artillery to the Allies at crucial moments early in the war, and now lacked weaponry herself. In early 1919 the Allies sent substantial shipments of used English and French artillery, rifles, light and heavy machine guns, armored cars, and trucks.[26]

The Increase of Militarism, 1917–19

The new Portuguese militarism which emerged during and after World War I was a revival rather than a novelty. This militarism may be defined as the belief held by a group of military officers that the Portuguese army was not only the most important institution in society but was a vital instrument of national revival. These ideas were rooted in the *fin de siècle* age of colonialism, of the African "Generation of 1895," and were influenced by contemporary French and German militarism. Portuguese militarism was always closely linked to the concepts of decadence and return to a past glorious age. An elite group of officers saw the army as a crucial instrument of revival for a country burdened with a deficient economy and a corrupt political system. The army, then, was viewed not only as an impetus for necessary change, but even as the embodiment of the nation itself. The clearest statement available of this sentiment was found in a 1905 issue of the major professional army journal, later reprinted as conventional wisdom in 1929: "The army [is] the highest essence of the national soul."[27]

Portugal's participation in the war, both in Africa and in France, encouraged a revival of the military ethic—the idea that the military, or specifically, the army, was the most important institution in society. Militarism and military influences had also been encouraged during the regime of Sidónio Pais. During 1917–18, Pais instituted a policy which strengthened the military and paramilitary forces. Above all, Pais attempted to rebuild respect for the military establishment by means of frequent parades, new facilities for the army, and speeches supporting military concepts. As chief of state and head of government performing his duties in public he was a stunning figure in his army officer's uniform. On his sleeves he wore the four stars of a general and chief of staff. If not on horseback in a military parade, he was often seen by the public in a characteristic position of saluting.

The rise of the juntas militares, as was suggested in chapter 8, was more than a sign of professional unrest among conservative officers in the home garrisons of the north.[28] The juntas, whose main strength lay among monarchist officers in garrisons in Oporto and Braga, were organized during the summer of 1918, and were in part the result of Portuguese officers' emulation of similar juntas founded in the Spanish army in 1917.

The Spanish juntas were led mainly by junior and some (company and field-grade) infantry and cavalry officers who were protesting very low pay and political favoritism in promotions.[29] In the background of the grievances of these juntas were the events of the Russian Revolution, and the economic dislocation in Iberia caused by World War I.

The Portuguese officers in the juntas had observed how their Spanish counterparts in June and October 1917 had virtually forced changes of government in Madrid. The Portuguese juntas were determined to organize a defense of army officer corps' prerogatives; more important, monarchist officers, who had only recently been reintegrated into the regular army through the New Republic's new military policy, were conspiring to take action if anything happened to Sidónio Pais.[30]

Calling for the "defense of the military spirit," the juntas wished to maintain Pais's revival of militarism and were ready to support a military dictatorship or even a restoration of the monarchy. Although the militarism encouraged by the New Republic and furthered by the juntas militares in the north lived on among certain circles of officers, a new development appeared with the defeat in February 1919 of the monarchist attempts in Oporto and Lisbon to restore royal power and to overthrow the parliamentary republic. The likelihood of the Portuguese monarchy ever being restored was virtually ended in these conclusive defeats which cost several hundred lives. Veterans from the trenches of Flanders played their part in the defeat of the monarchists; and the army officer corps, at least temporarily, was unified with the aid of such Integralist officers and "Cadets of Sidónio," as Theophilo Duarte, who lent a hand in defeating the monarchists in the north.[31]

When the Republicans emerged triumphant in February 1919, the army again felt the impact of political vengeance: numbers of monarchist officers, brought back under the New Republic, were dismissed. Republican officers, fired under the previous regime, were now reinstated. Ranks of the officer corps swelled as the decree-law of November 1921 maintained the militia.

"Second Army": The Guarda Nacional Republicana, 1919–26

The fortunes of the Guarda Nacional Republicana (GNR), which had been established by the Provisional Government in 1911 as a civil police force, varied depending on the regime in power and the amount of unrest in the country. Whereas Sidónio Pais had reduced its size and armament, moved GNR units into rural areas, and had built up certain army regiments, some later governments swung away from this policy. In 1919 the GNR was strengthened as an urban defender of the state. It became a kind of second army. GNR units were reinforced with army personnel in the key areas of Lisbon, Oporto, and Coimbra. In the larger towns the Guard was now armed with heavy artillery and machine guns and its mission was to guarantee public order, especially in Lisbon, where a large part of the force was to be stationed.[32]

The status, armament, and role of the GNR generated resentments and jealousy in the army. A major grievance, especially during 1919–21, was that the GNR possessed heavy armament which enabled it to intimidate or neutralize army units during civil strife. By 1921 under the Liberals' government the GNR had grown very powerful and elements of it participated in pronunciamentos which overthrew governments in May and October 1921.

When the Democrats assumed power in February 1922, Premier António Maria da Silva weakened the GNR by depriving it of its artillery and heavy machine guns, and by reducing some units in size. Silva's motives were to discourage insurrection in the GNR, to mollify army commanders who resented the power of the GNR, and to weaken the radical elements which had caused public disturbances in 1921. At least on this point some army officers were satisfied: the GNR was no longer a real rival for control of the streets or of the state. Historians who make a detailed study of the GNR, however, will probably not uphold Cunha Leal's thesis that because of Silva's action in 1922 the GNR became a "negligible quantity," thus encouraging an *insurrecionalismo* in the army which bore fruit in 1926.[33] The seeds for such an action were present well before Silva's action in 1922, and the critical political situation in 1926 was a powerful determinant of how armed forces would respond.

Even after Silva had weakened the GNR, bitter resentment remained among some professional officers. Frequent complaints were heard about its growing size and special pay, the intent of which was to encourage army personnel to serve in it. Regular army officers felt that they were hindering their careers by performing GNR duty. They also considered the sort of work assigned to the GNR degrading for officers in the regular army. Then, too, the Guard became one more element in the growing military bureaucracy associated with the Democrats' control of the government. The figures below indicate the strength of the GNR from 1911 to 1929:[34]

Year	Size of GNR
1911	4,991
1919	10,000 (estimate)
1922	11,031
1923	9,627
1924	10,168
1926	11,989
1927	5,688
1928	5,648
1929	5,627

Even taking into account the reduction in the GNR's armament, some professional officers continued to be indignant over its increased size, which by 1926 was nearly 12,000, almost three times its size in 1911, and not much smaller than the total number of men in enlisted ranks in the regular army. The Military Dictatorship's policy toward the GNR reflected some officers' resentments: by 1927 the strength of the GNR was reduced by over half. Yet it remained a force to be reckoned with. In 1928 a British diplomatic report judged the GNR "far more reliable and efficient" than the army.[35]

The GNR did not play the role planned for it in 1911: that of a largely rural police force like Spain's Guarda Civil. Instead, this small second army was a largely urban force, chiefly in Lisbon, Oporto, and Coimbra, a plaything of street and barracks politics. For certain periods, the GNR even assumed the role of a Lisbon Praetorian Guard for the government in office; its controversial status and role, and the political favoritism it received, remained major grievances among professional army officers. Still, whatever the political pressures at work upon this security force, the creation and continued maintenance of the Guard were official Republican responses to an increased level of violence, crime, and unrest in urban society, and to the unreliability of the army as a defender of the government.

Professional Dignity: From Alienation to Action

In a sensational book published in Lisbon in October 1925, the following passage appeared: "The situation of the Portuguese Army, from the point of view of moral considerations or the material, is absolutely wretched. The state of neglect, misery and degradation to which the public force has arrived, would by itself justify a thousand revolutions."[36]

An eager audience, already scandalized by accounts of the September trials of the Eighteenth of April rebels, bought so many copies of the book that it went into a printing of at least 5,000 copies, a rare occurrence whether in 1925 or 1975 in Portugal. The author was one of the rebel officers, Jorge Botelho Moniz, a former "Cadet of Sidónio," an Integralist, and a professional officer at the forefront of the rightist minority of the officer corps. While stating the army's grievances, this irate officer summed up the view of an increasingly large group of younger officers: that the army was the most vital institution in Portugal. This statement expressed the opinion, too, of much of the Right; as Botelho Moniz put it: "[The Army is] . . . the most powerful guarantee of National Sovereignty, internal Peace, and external respect."[37]

Why was there more popular support for such opinions by mid-1925? Why did more Portuguese desire the army to assume a dominant role in society? What enabled the army officer corps to assume such a role?

The answers to these questions are complex. But there are four factors which help to explain the new importance assumed by the army toward the end of the First Republic: a revival of militarism, a new interest in colonialism, a new professionalism among a group of officers, and the growing influence of nationalist and right-wing ideas upon public opinion. These factors must be considered in the context of the growing public disillusionment with the Republican parliamentary regime.

The experience of the officer corps in World War I campaigns in Africa and Europe was of course crucial in developing a new militarism. This experience aroused a new esprit de corps among certain veteran units, and new feelings of hatred toward politicians on whom soldiers traditionally blamed their deficiencies and defeats. It has been suggested how the growth of the army's size, its bloated officer corps, its greater armament—however old or obsolete—and the growth of a military bureaucracy were important parts of this new militarism. The Democratic-dominated governments after 1919 showed by its budget allocations how much it valued the military establishment; while the armed forces spent only 13 percent of the 1911 budget, by 1922–26, over 40 percent of the budget went to the military. The official statistics in table 8 suggest the pattern.

Even when one takes into account postwar inflation and currency depreciation, this massive increase in the military budget in what began as a "civilian" First Republic is startling. To this may be added the growing influence of the military on government leaders. Before the

TABLE 8
Budget of Minister of War, 1911–27
(in escudos)

Date	Regular Expenses	Extraordinary Expenses
1911–12	10,124.717$60.7	124.054$00
1912–13	10,252.158$19.5	122.500$00
1913–14	9,656.470$00	200.000$00
1914–15	10,738.787$00	95.000$00
1915–16	11,722.114$00	2.500$00
1916–17	11,329.775$26	22.500$00
1917–18	11,349.999$36	22.500$00
1918–19	13,658.515$54	207.500$00
1919–20	39,008.846$03	5,219.500$00
1920–21	39,894.673$49	2,008.873$00
1921–22	62,154.320$89	25,516.000$00
1922–23	—	—
1923–24	—	—
1924–25	118,417.495$35	138,381.257$17
1925–26	127,796.592$81	147,805.148$91
1926–27	168,024.841$56	187,739.383$12

Sources: Maj. A. D. Branquinho, "O Orçamento do Ministério da Guerra," *Revista Militar* 74, no. 4 (Apr. 1922): 217; *Anuário Estatística de Portugal: 1926, 1927, 1928* (Lisbon, 1927–29).

Sidónio Pais regime, 1917–18, only about 15 percent of the cabinets were presided over by army and navy officers, but during 1918–26, about 46 percent were headed by military men.[38]

The growing influence of militarism and a new role for the military in government were further encouraged by a new generation of officers. The "Young Lieutenants" were quite different from the aging Young Turks. This new group of adventurous officers, many of them born in the 1890s and early years of the twentieth century, had admired Sidónio Pais and were inspired by the example of Spain's military dictatorship under Primo de Rivera. The Young Lieutenants were largely monarchists, not Republicans, and followed rightist ideas popular elsewhere in Europe. Their ideology was broadly antiliberal and antidemocratic and their life-style was consciously nonconformist and antibourgeois. Duels, adventures of the heart, the daring novelty of aviation, and horsemanship excited them as much as the idea that the armed forces could overthrow the infernal republic and replace it with a regime of force.[39]

Colonialism also led to a new role for the military. Long interconnected, colonialism and militarism were symbiotic. The important colonial campaigns in Portuguese Africa during 1890–1920 had shaped a new elite of army officers, including Major Mousinho de Albuquerque (1855–1902), whose writings and personal legend inspired militarism and colonialism among the Young Lieutenants. Mousinho's solution to rising republicanism's threat to the monarchy was a military dictatorship. This late governor of Mozambique was often quoted in his famous letters to the crown prince, as resenting any attempts by civilians to stain "the honor of the army."[40]

After 1919, there was a revival of interest in the African colonies. Major daily papers in Lisbon, O Século, A Época, and Diário de Notícias, despite the disparity in their political views, began intensive campaigns of publicity and feature articles on the colonies.[41] This interest was both political and economic. As was traditional, some members of the elite feared that Portugal might either lose her colonies to more powerful European colonial rivals, or lose economic control through the machinations of international finance. With regard to both Angola and Mozambique, such fears reached a zenith during the years 1922–28.[42] In 1924 the colonial elite met at the Second National Colonial Congress, sponsored by the Society of Geography of Lisbon, and listened to twenty-nine papers. A major resolution supported by the congress was that Portugal's African colonies were "the most secure guarantee of our economic ressurgimento."[43] The colonial question was a key rallying point for a small elite which was polarized politically on other issues. Some unity in colonial affairs was judged as a positive development in view of excessive political factionalism. During the First Republic, the colonial concept of the indivisibility of Portuguese territorial empire, that Macão, in China, as well as Minho district was "Portugal," became commonly accepted. Thus, Portugal and her colonies were one in a "unitary state."[44] It should be noted that even the Jacobin Republican Mason Magalhães Lima in 1911 was quoted, as president of the União Colonial Portugueza, to the effect that the colonies formed with Portugal, the "Pátria, una, integra e soberana."[45]

A third factor which advanced the idea of the intervention of the military in government and politics was a new military professionalism. After World War I, this professionalism increased. Numbers of officers resented the fact that despite the amount of public monies expended on the military, the army had meager resources. Grievances intensified. For the purpose of analysis a distinction should be made between economic grievances of officers, and those grievances which were noneconomic—military discipline, standards, morale, hierarchy and privileges, and the military's role in society.

The activist officers had valid economic grievances. They had low pay during a period of runaway inflation, when the relative salaries of the GNR, police, and navy were much higher.[46] Furthermore the republic's policy of arranging pay increases discriminated against senior officers. Officers' complaints about low pay became increasingly bitter and shrill after 1916, as economic conditions worsened. Despite pay increases during the years 1918-24, severe inflation, currency devaluation, and other economic ills ate away salary improvements. The policy of most Republican governments was to acquiesce to demands for higher pay for the professional military. During the last Republican government, on 15 May 1926, only two weeks before the officer-led coup overthrew the government, the Silva cabinet ordered a tripling of the pay of officers and sergeants in the army and navy.[47]

The most aggrieved among the officer corps were the middle and higher ranks, from major to general. By 1926, their purchasing power, on an average, was "reduced to half of what it had been in 1910."[48] The governments attempted to equalize pay scales and reduce the inequalities which had been characteristic of the monarchist system. In 1911 the differential in pay between a second sergeant and the full colonel was roughly 10 times; by 1922, after pay adjustments, the differential was reduced to only about 2.27 times. Salary raises for the lower ranks were favored. During 1911-22, for example, noncommissioned officers and junior officers, the groups which were most active in military insurrections, had received pay increases which ranged between 1,200 and 420 percent, while the officers from major to general had received increases which ranged only from 306 to 144 percent (see table 9).

Despite the vociferous complaints of the higher-ranking officers, the historical record suggests that as a group army officers were better off after 1914 than were the civil bureaucrats.[49] For example, in 1925 generals, colonels, lieutenant colonels, majors, and captains all received higher pay than their civil functionary counterparts. Their grievances were based on their earnings relative to other groups and classes and the purchasing power of their pay relative to what it had been during the early years of the republic.

The erosion of the purchasing power of the upper- and middle-rank officers was a serious grievance. To some officers it mattered little that civil servants of equivalent rank were in even tighter straits. They were aware that the Republican governments favored the lower ranks with pay raises and that the purchasing power of the salaries of the lowest ranks in both the armed forces and civil service had not eroded to the same degree. While generals' purchasing power index in 1925 was only 45.9 percent of what it had been in 1914, and purchasing power of the pay of first lieutenants and second lieutenants was 74 percent and 77.2 percent of that of 1914, respectively; significantly, the purchasing

TABLE 9
Increases in Army Pay, 1911–22

Rank	Pay (in escudos)		Percent Increase
	1911	1922	
Generals	2,400$00	5,940$00	147
Colonels	1,320$00	4,500$00	241
Lieutenant colonels	1,044$00	4,080$00	290
Majors	960$00	3,900$00	306
Captains	780$00	3,420$00	338
First lieutenants	600$00	3,120$00	420
Second lieutenants	480$00	2,940$00	512
Senior sergeants	219$00	2,138$00	876
First sergeants	164$00	1,945$50	1,084
Second sergeants	127$75	1,651$25	1,200

Source: Maj. A. D. Branquinho, "O Orçamento do Ministério da Guerra," *Revista Militar* 74, no. 5 (May 1922): 249–55.

Note: The 1977 exchange rate was approximately 2.8 cents (U.S.) to the escudo, or 38 escudos to the U.S. dollar. It is probable that fifty years ago the value of the escudo was three times what it is today in relation to the dollar, in which case an escudo would have been worth close to 7 cents.

power of the pay of the two lowest-ranking groups of civil servants was 89.5 percent and 109.5 percent of what it had been in 1914.[50]

The upper- and middle-ranking officers were now part of a distressed group of "new poor" who resented the relative wealth of the "new rich" of Lisbon.[51] The escudo was reduced to one-fifteenth its value during 1919–25, although there was some improvement during 1925–26.[52] Massive inflation accompanied the devaluation. Table 10 indicates the increase in prices of materials used by the army.

To the economic grievances of officers were added professional grievances relating to discipline, standards, and the military's self-image. Regular officers resented the militia and some complained that 1,900 militia officers were so much dead wood. When the military came to power in 1926 they acted on their grievance, dismissed most of these officers, and abolished the militia system.[53] Complaints, such as Botelho Moniz's published attack that the condition of the army justified "a thousand revolutions," may have been exaggerated but they had their effect in the mid-1920s when a "disaster literature" assailed the republic.

A fourth factor which promoted the rise of a militarist group of officers and their intervention in government and politics was a revival of nationalism. Nationalistic outbursts in Portuguese history had always coincided with scandals, wars, and crises. Post-1917 nationalism was also emotional and was concerned with fears which were not traditional: the Spanish and German menaces to Portugal and her colonies. Private associations, such as the study-action group a Cruzada Nacional D. Nun' Alvares Pereira became more influential in the early 1920s. The hero of fourteenth-century wars against Castile, the medieval knight-monk Nun' Alvares Pereira, the "Holy Constable," was a symbol of revived militarism, Catholicism, and nationalism.

Such nationalistic thinking advanced the idea that the army was now the only "corporation" capable of saving the sinking republic, of initi-

TABLE 10
Increases in Cost of Army Supplies, 1911–22

Item	Percent Increase, 1911–22
Bread ration	800
Mess food	700
Uniforms	1100
Fodder (feed for animals)	1000
Barracks' material for construction	1000

Source: Maj. A. D. Branquinho, "O Orçamento do Ministério da Guerra," *Revista Militar* 74, no. 5 (May 1922): 249–55.

ating profound change. As the tempo of nationalist rhetoric increased, right-wing groups and parties, the Church, some intellectuals, sectors of the upper and middle classes, and the new generations of students encouraged the officer corps to come forward. The army, they believed, could reassume its role as a "school of obedience, of discipline, and of morality."[54] Like a new version of the Church militant or a respected monarchy, the army would instill in a degenerate nation lost virtues of discipline, respect for hierarchy, morality, military spirit, social order, and patriotism.[55] Some even harked back to the militarism of the late nineteenth century, when in a classic military treatise Cristovão Ayres invoked the army's image as "the bulwark of national independence, conqueror and guardian of public freedoms."[56]

By 1925 a minority of officers, perhaps three hundred to five hundred out of twenty-five hundred regular (nonmilitia) officers, mainly lieutenants and captains, with a few senior officers, had reached an internal consensus: only the professional officer corps could "save" Portugal from impending disaster—political, social, and economic. However misguided they may have been, they were energetic and were determined to organize the overthrow of the system, the standstill polity. As militarists, they believed that the honor of the army could be vindicated only by action and violence. They were convinced that Mousinho de Albuquerque's ghost required retribution against the politicians for, as the tragic officer had written of an earlier era: "This kingdom is the work of soldiers."[57] And, as the officer corps took over the state in 1926, so it was again.

11 / In the Kingdom of the Pronunciamento
December 1918—April 1925

> From its first number, *Seara Nova* recognized these fatal errors and vices of our collective life which may well destroy us. But you cannot, should not, and shall not expect that you can remedy them with the illusory elixirs of revolutions. . . . No Government can establish with swords what is not first established in public opinion.
>
> Raúl Proença[1]

The period from the collapse of the New Republic to the abortive military coup of April 1925 was marked by excessive political instability and economic distress, the disappearance of the pre-1918 Republican leadership, and the rise of new parties and politicians.

By 1919 most of the more celebrated Republican leaders had been consumed, in one way or another, by the fires of political office. Arriaga and Braga, the presidents, were dead. Others retired permanently from politics, exhausted. The ultimate political man of 1910–17, Afonso Costa, had spent four months of imprisonment under the New Republic and then gone into exile in Paris. In early 1919, in a letter to the PRP Directorate, Costa announced his intention to withdraw from active participation in politics. Whatever his motives for not returning to Portugal, fear, disgust, or pragmatism, Costa remained thereafter in Paris. In March 1919 he was appointed Portugal's chief delegate to the Paris Peace Conference. Meanwhile he carried on a lucrative law practice in Paris with Portuguese clients; although he still took part in inner PRP counsels, he never returned to Portugal for any length of time. Brief visits in subsequent years, such as that of late 1923, invariably raised political hopes and speculation. As an absentee candidate in elections in 1919, 1921, and 1925, he was consistently elected by a Lisbon district, but he never took his seat. When asked by President Teixeira Gomes to become premier in 1923, he refused.

In 1919 the Unionist party disintegrated. Brito Camacho dropped out of politics and never again entered the parliamentary lists. Instead, he accepted a colonial post as high commissioner and governor-general of Mozambique, which removed him from Lisbon politics and made him a renowned colonial authority. Evolutionist A. J. Almeida, only fifty-three in 1919, also refused to participate in any more political struggles. Though deeply discouraged, the romantic Almeida, his hair now white, his health ruined, felt a debt to the republic. He became a "non-partisan" Republican. Elected by the Congress of 1919, on 5 October 1919 he became the sixth president of the republic; he was destined to be the only chief of state to serve a full four-year term.

Republic in Peril, December 1918—February 1919

As the charismatic champion of order, Sidónio Pais had enjoyed brief popularity. His murder brought mass disorder and a scramble for political power. The New Republic frightened the majority of Republicans and raised false expectations among monarchists. With the leader of the New Republic gone, the struggle for control of the administration became anarchic. Monarchists plotted for a restoration; army officers conspired to set up a military dictatorship. Survivors in Pais's cabinet met in emergency session and nominated as president their senior member, Admiral João do Canto e Castro, a passive monarchist. Shortly afterwards, the Congress elected Canto e Castro president.

A conservative Presidentialist, Minister of Finance João Tamagnini Barbosa, was named premier.

At best this government was a weak caretaker for the dying New Republic. Decisive military action was the first order of business; there were numerous plots by several groups: Monarchists, organized mainly around the juntas militares, Republicans from the old Republican parties, and some independents still sitting in the lameduck New Republic's Congress.

Even before Pais's death, committees of army officers planned for a strong government, probably a military dictatorship. The best-organized and most united military committee was the Junta Militar do Norte in Oporto. In its manifesto published at Oporto on 3 January 1919 these officers claimed that they represented the political last will and testament of the deceased Pais, "the Holy Constable of the Republic."[2] Their intention was to establish a military government in which the interests of the army officer corps were a first priority, along with order. The whiff of military authoritarianism or praetorianism in this manifesto anticipated some of the principles underlying the 1926 Military Dictatorship. The term "national" as opposed to "partisan" interests was a revealing choice of words.

Between 23 December 1918 and 20 January 1919 there were no fewer than four pronunciamentos. The first came on 23 December at Monsanto Park, near Lisbon, where a small monarchist clique led by African hero João de Almeida incited several military units to rebellion. Premier Tamagnini Barbosa did not attack but waited out the rebels, who protested the "composition" of the cabinet, demanding a new one made up of elements of the juntas militares.[3] Rebel units soon retired, but on 7 January 1919, the cabinet was reshuffled, which revealed that Almeida had influenced the premier.

The second pronunciamento came at Santarém on 10 January 1919; it was a Republican exercise. Convinced Republicans in and near Lisbon, caught up in the "conspiratorial fervor" of the hour, feared for the existence of their republic. With Pais dead, little appeared to stand in the way of a long-dreamed-of monarchist restoration.

The Republican conspiracy was born after Tamagnini Barbosa refused to allow some younger Democrats into his cabinet, in order to oppose the rising threats of the juntas militares. The conspiracy included such Republican officers as Álvaro de Castro on the Left, and Francisco Cunha Leal on the Right and affected several towns: Santarém, Abrantes, Tomar, and Caldas da Rainha. After Cunha Leal's verbal attack on the government in Congress on 8 January, the conspirators took to the field. Civil war followed.[4]

When the Republicans at Santarém aroused local military units, captured the town's municipal government, and set up a junta revolucionária, the government reacted vigorously. On 14 January the government brought up artillery to bombard the rebels in Santarém, and in desultory fighting a dozen combatants died. To the inhabitants of Santarém it must have seemed that the world war in Europe had been devilishly transferred to their unprepared town. As artillery shells crashed into the town, inhabitants took refuge in their wine cellars and basements. The Republican rebels surrendered to government forces on 15 January.[5]

National attention now turned to the north. Even in Lisbon, the danger of monarchist plots was clear; the Tamagnini Barbosa administration severely censored the daily press. The Socialist party issued a manifesto warning the country of the "imminent" dangers of a monarchist restoration and urged all Republicans to unite in order to support the new president.

Monarchists planned a coordinated rising of the garrisons of Oporto and Lisbon. Negotiations with the Lisbon administration were unsuccessful and even the refusal of numbers of Integralists to support a monarchist coup and restoration did not dissuade the hard-core plotters.[6] On 19 January, Paiva Couceiro, "Captain Phantom," struck in Oporto and proclaimed the restoration of the monarchy. A good portion of the Oporto garrison adhered to the proclamation; dissenting Republican officers were arrested and jailed. The Lisbon monarchist junta militar was divided and vacillatory and failed to coordinate with the Oporto group. Meanwhile the Republican urban masses and the government organized effective resistance. On 23 January the monarchist forces, under the command of the monarchist deputy Aires de Ornellas, who was another hero of Africa and King Manuel's chief representative in Portugal, were surrounded at Monsanto fortress. Their choice of ground, their hesitant, reluctant leadership, and small numbers spelled their doom. Lisbon's Republicans rallied in adversity and united for a fight. The government declared a national emergency and released all political prisoners. In one of the few united, energetic, mass mobilization efforts during the First Republic, thousands of students, workers, clerks, and soldiers volunteered to fight and gathered at central locations. One central point was the bullfight arena at Campo Pequeno. Late on the afternoon of 24 January, the monarchist forces at Monsanto were overwhelmed by a combination of civilian and military forces.

With the monarchist threat at Lisbon crushed, the government turned its attention to the "Monarchy of the North" at Oporto. Other towns in the north in which "the monarchy" had been grandly proclaimed were Vila Real, Braga, Regoa, Covilhã, Lamego; Republican officers held out at Chaves. In Oporto, the monarchist leaders took advantage of monarchist sentiments among the population. Crowds sang the traditional monarchist anthem, "Hino da Carta," women carried portraits of King Manuel and his Queen, and Couceiro set up a skeletal administration.[7] Stamps with King Manuel's portrait were issued; passes for police officials bore royal arms. Couceiro received some arms through the Spanish border, but he waited in vain for Spanish diplomatic recognition.[8]

On 27 January with the Monarchy of the North, only eight days old, the Tamagnini Barbosa cabinet fell. It was a victim of the premier's vacillation toward the monarchists which resulted in the monarchist takeover of Oporto and northern towns, and his refusal to allow Democrats into the cabinet. President Canto e Castro named a new premier, independent José Relvas. The Relvas government was a Republican coalition which included three independents, two Democrats, three Sidonists, two Unionists, an Evolutionist, and a Socialist, the first Socialist to hold power in a Republican cabinet: Augusto Dias da Silva, labor minister.[9] Relvas came under considerable pressure from his Congress, which remained in session throughout the brief civil war. Cunha Leal, oratorical enfant terrible, criticized the government for its slowness in defeating the monarchist rebels and for not censoring the press to his satisfaction—especially when possibly strategic military information was involved.[10]

Despite its heartening victory at Monsanto, the Republican regime was in a precarious position. Its armed forces were in a state of turmoil; the officer corps was polarized between activist monarchists and Republicans and sections of the ranks were mutinous. The Relvas regime learned to its dismay that its forces lacked the sufficient arms owing to the distribution to volunteer-civilians of large numbers of weapons for the battle of Monsanto and because the minister of war in Pais's final government, a monarchist, had hidden government arms.[11]

The anti-Republican mood in army circles was revealed in Cunha Leal's heckling speech in Congress on 11 February 1919. When he was a young cadet, he remembered, it was fashionable to be a Republican. Now when the majority of officers were at least nominally Republican, it was "chic" to be monarchist. He strongly urged the government to dismiss all monarchist officers, especially during a time of "real civil war."[12]

A study of unpublished military records suggests that in 1919 the officer corps was carrying on its own civil war. The government was aware that the forces converging on Oporto and the northern rebel towns were divided, confused, and sometimes poorly led. Professional officers in command grew angry when they confronted civilian intervention—not unlike that during the monarchist incursions of 1911–12—and they resented the presence in the north of civilian volunteers from Lisbon's city hall and the National Press, part of the Democrats' political machine. At the Ministry of War, officials were concerned lest their army near Oporto become demoralized under unreliable monarchist officers.[13] Lisbon replaced commanders with some frequency in January 1919.

On 13 February the Monarchy of the North at Oporto suddenly collapsed. The monarchist threat had brought out of his sick bed in an Oporto hospital the remarkable Republican Captain João Sarmento Pimentel. This dashing officer, probably still afflicted with influenza, rallied sections of the GNR, temporarily renamed by Couceiro Guarda Real ("Royal Guard"), and defeated the monarchist forces.[14]

The Monarchy of the North survived from 19 January to 13 February 1919. Once it fell in Oporto, other northern towns capitulated. The consequences of this brief but bitter civil war of five weeks, if one counts the Santarém episode, were serious. Paiva Couceiro fled the country, but some chief monarchist leaders, including Almeida, Aires de Ornellas, and Azevedo Coutinho were captured and tried. In August 1919 they received fairly light sentences.[15] Effects of the monarchist failure, with *opéra bouffe* overtones, were significant. The monarchist cause was once more definitively compromised. More monarchists as well as Republicans now recognized the restoration of Manuel to be a hopeless cause. The 1919 disasters further divided the monarchists. Those seen responsible for the failed coups of 1919 faced widespread ridicule, a severe political liability in a country with citizens sensitive to the opinions of others.

The Monarchy of the North alienated many conservatives who had been monarchists: Catholics and Integralists. Their leadership was dismayed. The nationalist-Catholic Jacinto Cândido da Silva wrote in his memoirs that the 1919 monarchist insurrection was "not only an error," but "a crime."[16] If fewer persons could take the monarchist cause seriously, other issues, such as Catholic rights and law and order, now took priority. The monarchist disasters of 1919 also helped provoke the 1920 split among monarchists over succession.

In retrospect, at least one die-hard monarchist claimed that if the monarchists had proclaimed the monarchy in Lisbon and Oporto on the night of Pais's death, their cause would have prevailed, yet the same monarchist disavowed any responsibility for the Monsanto disaster. Even ex-King Manuel from England had urged his partisans not to conspire for restoration until after the signing of the peace treaty, for fear of hurting Portugal's colonial claims with the Allies. The 1919 disasters so disoriented some monarchists that they wondered if a few monarchist leaders were Republican double-agents.[17]

Fears of foreign intervention multiplied during the civil war, as they had in previous civil conflicts in 1910, 1915, and 1917. Unknown to many, such a fear briefly had some reality in the thoughts and writings of the veteran American minister in Lisbon, Colonel Thomas Birch. Dismayed by the civil war and prompted in part by an inflated opinion of American influence and power in Portugal, Birch wanted to act decisively at the end of January 1919. He proposed to Washington that the Allies—with the United States as the main agent—set up a protectorate over Portugal and, if necessary, actively intervene in Portuguese affairs.[18]

How did Birch arrive at such a plan and how did he propose to carry it out? Birch believed that the 1919 civil war was "the worst revolution since 1910."[19] His contacts and major informants appear to have been chiefly important monarchists who were attempting to use American influence and possibly Allied intervention to prevent the return of the

Democrats and to restore a liberal monarchy. Perhaps for the first time in Portuguese history, the Bolshevik menace was evoked in order to arouse foreign interest in an internal political dispute.

Birch's plan of intervention was influenced by the ideas of a prominent monarchist, the duke of Palmela, who on 23 January 1919 had taken refuge in the American Legation in Lisbon. If his plan had been carried out, undoubtedly the monarchists would have taken full advantage in order to return to power. Birch believed that President Woodrow Wilson had a powerful influence in Portugal and that with a "joint note" from the Allies (i.e., the United States, France, and Britain), Portugal could somehow miraculously let bygones be bygones and have an "open and fair election" which the Allies would oversee. Birch proposed to Washington that the Allies would threaten to refuse to recognize any Portuguese government which had been brought to power by "force or military mutiny." Birch was determined to eliminate the army "as a political factor," and he based his unusual proposal on his conviction that "the chief reason why it has been impossible to maintain order in the past is that there has been no capital punishment penalty. In my opinion the Portuguese are as capable of self-Government as the Cubans. If they establish a government by legitimate methods and if that government is protected by the Allies as the United States protects that of Cuba. . . ."[20]

Birch believed that Allied intervention would only be necessary if an "open and fair election" did not work. Despite the American minister's fanciful assumptions and naiveté, he desired the establishment of effective government and "better conditions." He urged the State Department to forward his idea to the "American Commission to Negotiate Peace" which would, in turn, issue a "joint note" to Portugal. Birch admitted that he had little evidence that bolshevism was a threat to anyone, much less the Portuguese in Portugal.[21]

Birch's proposal for an Allied protectorate in Portugal, which was somewhat in the spirit of American "dollar diplomacy" in the Caribbean and Allied intervention in Russia, was not acted upon by the State Department. His assumption that Wilson's influence in the country would easily clear the way for a fundamental reform in politics failed to take into account two important facts about Portugal: (1) British influence in Portugal still retained an edge over the American; (2) the Portuguese elite were divided over the virtues of President Wilson.[22] In 1919 there would be neither an Allied nor an American intervention in Portugal.

Casualties in the brief 1919 civil war were heavier than standard accounts have previously acknowledged. At least 150 persons died and hundreds more were wounded.[23] There was property damage in Lisbon and Oporto. The republic survived, but the price was heavy.

Nadir: February 1919—October 1921

A political and economic low was reached during the two-and-a-half years following the collapse of the Monarchy of the North. Economically, the years 1919 and 1920 were perhaps the most catastrophic. The escudo was devalued 400 percent; the public debt reached the greatest sum since 1911 (£140,455), five banks failed, and the budget deficit in 1918–19 was £15,156. The trade deficit in 1920 reached £25,690,000.[24]

Government instability intensified. The legal term of Congress was three years, but few congresses survived that long. For example, the Congress elected in June 1919 was dissolved by presidential decree on 1 June 1921; a new Congress was elected thereafter in July, but its term was even shorter. President Almeida dissolved it in October 1921, again because of a military insurrection. Among the brief governments were one that lasted one day (Francisco Fernandes Costa) and one that lasted six days (Alfredo Sá Cardoso) during January 1920. Civic disorder was rampant and, as a result, public confidence in the very existence of the republic plummeted.

The period began with some hope, expressed by leading observers, for the establishment of a fairly stable and progressive political system. In the fall of 1919 it seemed possible that the next years would prove a happy contrast with the instability and confusion of the first nine years of the republic. Two episodes which encouraged this feeling were the failure of the monarchists' insurrections in early 1919 and the reasonably orderly conduct of the June 1919 elections, when the PRP was returned with a majority of seats in Congress. An era of political quiet and reformist accomplishment seemed to be in the offing.

These hopes were further encouraged by the passage in Congress of the long-discussed and awaited revision of the 1911 Constitution: the presidential power of congressional dissolution. On 13 September 1919 the new PRP-dominated Congress voted in the only significant constitutional revision with any bearing on domestic affairs. The chief of state, the president, now possessed expanded power in order to dissolve the Congress before its legal term was up, if, in the president's judgment and in the opinion of an eighteen-member Parliamentary Council, the act of dissolution was in "the high interests of the country and the Republic."[25]

The history of the public reaction to this constitutional revision and the debate over its passage in Congress nicely illustrates key problems in the political system and how the passage of laws, whatever their anticipated effectiveness, could not guarantee effective government and stable institutions in an atmosphere of conspiracy and political manipulation. As mentioned in chapter 5, the 1911 Constituent National Assembly had defeated an amendment which would have granted the president the power of congressional dissolution; despite the cogent arguments of a minority of deputies, such as Egas Moniz, a majority of deputies feared that granting such a power to the president would lead to a risky presidentialism which would undermine parliamentary dominance. By 1914, however, irresolvable deadlocks between the government and both houses of Congress prevented the system from functioning. This situation prompted a reconsideration of the question beginning in the years 1914 and 1915. By late 1917 the dissolution question was a major political issue, though the majority of Democrats in Congress were reluctant to consider such a constitutional revision, fearing that the opposition would attempt to use this power to oust the electorally dominant PRP. The groups which supported Sidónio Pais's coup d'etat of 5–8 December 1917 in effect used the dissolution question as a major program point in order to gain support. As president, however, Pais never instituted the presidential power of congressional dissolution.

While in exile and in opposition, anti-Sidonistas found their only clear basis of agreement in the idea of a constitutional revision along the lines of the presidential power to dissolve Congress, and many groups agreed that once they returned to power after the New Republic, they would work to get the revision through Congress. The revision question thus was the rallying point of the opposition, and once the New Republic was replaced by a PRP-dominated regime in 1919, public acclaim for a revision was remarkably intense in the press and among political groups.[26] Influential Lisbon daily papers considered the impending constitutional revision as nothing less than a panacea for the political troubles of the republic. O Século went so far as to state that the 1919 Congress must pass the revision since it was no less than "a question of public salvation,"[27] which was, as it added later, "indispensable for the tranquility and order of the country."[28] Much of the public opinion of the hour, indeed, seemed to echo this feeling that the passage of a law or constitutional revision alone would somehow make the difference between stability and instability amidst the increasingly tiresome confusion of government and politics. There was a penchant among even the most sophisticated political observers for credulity and gullibility when it came to the importance of laws.

Opinion among the PRP deputies, however, was divided. In the congressional debate over the revision the emerging PRP leader—Afonso Costa's successor in the managing of the party—António Maria da

Silva openly stated his doubts. Silva said that he and his PRP deputies would vote for the revision out of a sense of duty in order to honor promises made while in opposition to the New Republic, but that this revision would not bring calm to government and politics. Indeed, it might act as a "serious danger," since the ulterior motive behind the opposition's intense desire for the revision was merely to oust the Democrats from control of Congress. Since the other parties lacked electoral strength, the law could provide them with a lever to oust the PPR delegation periodically and call new elections.[29]

The desire to defeat the Democrats, however, was not the only motive of those who voted for the revision in 1919. Some believed that the revision would strengthen the executive and pressure the legislative—the Congress—to modify its largely turbulent and do-nothing behavior. The congressional committee that drafted the revision believed that the law would act as "the last and most effective form of guaranteeing the irrevocability and the independence of the executive power."[30] Others believed that presidential power to dissolve a chaotic Congress was a reasonable, peaceful alternative to a military coup. This belief had been put forward during the deadlock of January 1915 as well as by Egas Moniz in 1911.

Subsequent political events proved these hopes to be illusory. If anything the 1919 constitutional revision added a provocation—based on a much-discussed law—to opposition groups to conspire and to plan insurrections which could pressure the president to dissolve Congress and call new elections. The 1919 revision, in enhancing the powers of the president, justified conspiracies to pressure the president to dissolve as a shortcut to power and control of the national administration. Twice in 1921 the president dissolved Congress when intimidated by military insurrections.

That the revision would now serve as a political excuse for insurrection, and therefore promote more political conflict rather than less, was at last clear to Álvaro de Castro, the chairman of the committee which drafted the 1919 revision. After the shocking insurrection of May 1921 when President Almeida bowed to demands, Castro warned that now the president would henceforth be the prey of "the illegitimate force of the first adventurer that owns a rifle or can maneuver a machine gun."[31]

There was a lot to Castro's warning. Oppositionists and PRP-related groups sought to use the presidential power of dissolution as a first step in their quest for public office. There were no fewer than ten recorded coup d'etat attempts which reached the streets between 1921 and 1926 (May and October 1921; February 1922; December 1923; December

1924; 5 March, 18 April, and 19 July 1925; 1 February and 28 May 1926). And the paramount demand of rebel leaders in virtually every case was that the president immediately dissolve the current Congress. While the two coups of 1921 forced the dissolution of Congress and the fall of cabinets, that of 28 May 1926 set the stage for a major institutional change—the end of the republic.

During 1919-21 the Liberal party's attempt to win power and to replace the Democrats in office was ultimately thwarted, at heavy cost. For a brief period in 1920-21 the Democrats' political monopoly seemed to be in some jeopardy; several Liberal governments held office briefly only to be dislodged through pressures from Congress or from the street and the barracks. Democratic-dominated governments, however, were no more successful in remaining long in office. One such government (that of Colonel António Maria Baptista) remained in power for about two months (8 March–6 June 1920). But Premier Baptista, assailed by the cares of office, suddenly died. In the midst of a cabinet meeting, he succumbed to either a stroke or an attack of apoplexy.[32] Afonso Costa's successor as the working leader of the PRP, António Maria da Silva, had not yet achieved the reputation of "consummate political maneuverer," and in a short-lived ministry in June–July 1920 found himself outmaneuvered by the Liberals' rising leader António Granjo, and by the Reconstituent leader Álvaro de Castro, and he had to resign. Granjo succeeded in remaining in power from late August to late November 1920 heading a coalition of Liberals, independents, and Popular party members. But Granjo, too, was forced to resign in the face of intransigent opposition.

Meanwhile, the government built up the power of the GNR, which became the chief means of defending the government and of maintaining law and order in the streets of the capital and in Oporto. The Guard was now provided with heavier weaponry including artillery and machine guns, and a larger contingent of troops and officers (see chap. 10). It served as a counterforce to an army of questionable loyalty and ability. Like most other institutions during the First Republic, the Guard was controlled by Democratic officers. Its chief of staff was Colonel Liberato Damião Ribeiro Pinto, who headed a government as premier from 30 November 1920 to 2 March 1921.[33] For a period during 1919-21, the Guard's internal politics became those of the nation and its forces intervened in politics. Yet even the leader of the Guard could not sustain himself in power. His government confronted a printers' strike of three months' duration and severe disorder in the streets. The Bernardino Machado coalition ministry (2 March–21 May 1921) did little better in office, despite the noted conciliatory nature of its leader. As in 1914, Machado entered office in 1921 with the mandate to legislate a long overdue political amnesty for monarchists. A limited, compromise amnesty for many 1919 monarchist prisoners was, with siderable difficulty, passed by Congress in April 1921.[34] This new amnesty, nevertheless, did not include the major leaders of the Monarchy of the North, such as Paiva Couceiro.

On 21 May, after an insurrection of the Guard, Machado was brought down. The original grievance of some of the Lisbon units was Machado's dismissal of Liberato Pinto—GNR second in command and Machado's predecessor as premier—coupled with Pinto's being summoned before a military court to be tried for malfeasance while in command. The Guard units ostensibly protested an alleged conspiracy by Machado to assume, after a coup, the presidency of the republic, with Álvaro de Castro as premier. The rebels claimed that the Guard resented the planned transfer of key officers and the loss of its heavy armament. The consequences of this insurrection were important: President Almeida dissolved Congress, the first such act since Congress revised the Constitution in 1919, and called new elections (the legal term of the 1919 Congress was not up until summer 1922). Putting up no resistance, the Machado government resigned.[35] The Twenty-first of May led to further excessive instability, public violence, alarmism among the most disruptive PRP elements, and to the even more serious crisis of October 1921.

The president called to power the Liberal government of Tomé de Barros Queiros, a former Unionist. Congress was then dissolved and in the June 1921 elections the Liberals managed by electoral manipulation to hand the Democrats a marginal defeat. The Liberals won slightly less than half the seats in Congress (48 percent), while for the first and only time in a general election, the Democrats won only 33 percent and were consigned to a minority position. The Liberals' bare majority alarmed Democratic groups, who remained in firm control of the armed services and civil service. As usual, the PRP also controlled the key urban political arm, the administration of Lisbon's câmara municipal,[36] an important part of national political patronage and leverage. A second Liberal government succeeded Barros Queiros in the form of the ill-fated Granjo administration of 30 August–19 October 1921, which ended with an insurrection of the Guard and other militarized units, and the murder of the hapless premier and five others. Granjo's calls for political conciliation, calm, and compromise with the Church, met stiff resistance and hostility in Congress, the press, and the streets. Granjo's predecessor, Barros Queiros, in a letter to President Almeida, gave his analysis of why he had been unable to introduce such useful reforms as a tax increase and a reduction of expenses: "In Portugal, in the field of politics, ideas are not discussed, [instead] people discuss men in order to ruin them, as if that destructive activity would not bring about a grave evil both for the regime and for the country."[37]

A shower of abuse fell upon Granjo. He was accused of being a monarchist and monopolist. The martyred premier, who was a staunch Republican, a Mason, and Carbonário, as well as a hero in World War I, bore the brunt of the hostile atmosphere. Ultimately, he paid with his life. Several groups, all with PRP links, constructed a conspiracy to overthrow the Granjo government by means of an insurrection of the Guard and other military units. A variety of political figures both in and out of the PRP were approached to join the conspirators. Their leader was an army colonel and historic Republican, Manuel Maria Coelho; his lieutenants were GNR officers. Yet another junta revolucionária formed and after an abortive first attempt on 30 September, the movement went into the streets on 19 October. The initial insurrection scenario was familiar: the password was "Coelho-Coimbra"; the first move was in the morning, when GNR units fired from key positions in Rotunda. Three cannon shots signalled the coup's beginning; rebellious sailors occupied the arsenal and armed civilian vigilantes patrolled the city and distributed propaganda leaflets. Coup leader Coelho stated in a press interview that the honesty of his movement (whose program had only one concrete proposal—dissolution of the 1921 Congress) was proved by his "name" as a famous, historic Republican who symbolized the 1891 Oporto rebellion against monarchy. Granjo, finding himself isolated and defenseless, submitted his resignation to President Almeida, who intended to submit the resignation to Congress shortly afterward. From two o'clock in the afternoon of 19 October until evening, Portugal had no legal government, while an expectant junta awaited word from the president. Even as the news of political murders circulated in Lisbon's streets, President Almeida had named rebel leader Coelho as premier.[38]

That night Granjo and four other major political figures were murdered. There are many theories concerning the perpetrators of this sensational bloodletting, Bloody Night, but investigations and trials in subsequent years produced no satisfactory answer to the mystery. The five murdered politicians were Granjo, Machado Santos, Carlos da Maia, Commander Freitas da Silva, who was secretary of the navy minister, and Botelho de Vasconcelos, a colonel who helped initiate Sidónio Pais's New Republic. A sixth person, innocent of any political links, an obscure chauffeur, was also gunned down.

It was proved that the murderers were sailors, enlisted men of the GNR, and some radical civilian vigilantes. At least six other public figures, including ex-premiers Barros Queiros, Tamagnini Barbosa, and the industrial magnate Alfredo da Silva of Companhia União Fabril (CUF), were also marked for murder, but escaped. Who planned this scheme, gave the orders, and paid off the assassins? Contemporary politicians blamed the murders simply on "this accursed politics," or on the "mindless mob," "moral dissoluteness," or "class hatreds."[39] Others hinted darkly that Spain had a hand in financing the murderers to discredit the republic and justify Spanish intervention. It was significant that sailors took part in the killing, and that the victims were members of a Sidónio Pais cabinet. Admiral Machado Santos had had serious disputes with leftist sailors, and evidence from his son suggested that as the sailors took away his father on the "phantom truck" of death, one sailor accused Machado Santos of wanting to bombard the naval barracks during the January 1918 *Vasco da Gama* insurrection, which had been promptly crushed by Pais and his supporters, among whom was Machado Santos. Evidently the murderers were radical leftists determined to settle old scores that went back at least to 1918 and the ill-fated New Republic.[40]

The shocking crime of 19 October 1921 brought yet more national and international infamy to Portugal. The Coelho government, discredited and desperate and blamed by many for the murders, lasted but sixteen days. It was replaced by the cabinet of Carlos Maia Pinto. As British and Spanish naval vessels briefly demonstrated off the Portuguese coast and anchored at Lisbon, rumors circulated of foreign intervention. Portugal's First Republic had reached its political and moral nadir.

Brief Remission: November 1921—November 1923

The Nineteenth of October shocked the political nation. Some persons plunged into a mourning which deepened their commitment to abstain from politics. Others were outraged and sought vengeance. Some in the army officer corps responded with an increasingly common suggestion—a revolution, but one with a different goal: a military dictatorship. Despite his denials of conspiracy in a November 1921 newspaper interview, General Manuel de Oliveira Gomes da Costa was briefly involved in leading such a conspiracy. When the coup signal was given in early February 1922, just after the Silva government had taken office, few supporters appeared and the insurrection never reached the streets.[41] The government learned of the general's role in the abortive coup, which briefly caused alarm in official circles, and Silva took steps to render Gomes da Costa ineffective as a potential rebel. Often in financial straits, the impecunious general accepted a lucrative commission as "inspector" of Portuguese armed forces in the colonies. He left on a long journey which kept him in Asia and Africa until late spring of the following year (1923), thus removing him from Lisbon intrigue.[42]

Other groups responded with energetic campaigns to spread their ideas among the elite in order to reform government and politics. The period 1921–26 is a most important one in the realm of Portuguese ideas and intellectual history, for it was during this period that a number of study-action groups initiated a major debate among the elite. One question often asked was: If the Republican experience has so far been largely a failure, what can be done? The ideas and activities of at least two groups deserve attention: the Seara Nova group and the Integralists, who were members of an association called Integralismo Lusitano.

The conventional labels applied to groups in other European states are not of much value in Portuguese politics. Instead of classifying Seara Nova simply as belonging to the Left and the Integralists as members of the Right and as Fascists, in some cases, it is more accurate to place them within the context of the debate over Portuguese decline, decadence, and revival which developed between the Modernists and the Traditionalists during the First Republic (see chap. 1).

The Modernists, or the Seara Nova group, consisted largely of urban middle-class intellectuals who were historians, journalists, educators (teachers), essayists, writers, doctors, a handful of military officers, and businessmen. Some, like the essayist-educator António Sérgio, were leading members of earlier study-action groups, such as the National Crusade of Nun' Alvares Pereira, which by 1921 had become largely conservative, rightist, with many Integralist members. The more liberal and democratic members among them decided to abandon the Crusade and to form their own study-action group with national goals, one which would put forward their ideas of reform and regeneration.

The most obvious initial result of the group's efforts was embodied in their Lisbon monthly review magazine, *Seara Nova,* whose first number was published 15 October 1921, only a few days before Bloody Night. In their journal's first number the group pledged that its goal was to "renovate the mentality of the Portuguese elite, rendering it capable of a true movement of salvation; [and] To create a national public opinion which demands and supports the necessary reforms."[43]

The major beliefs of the Seara Nova group included: the defense of democratic freedoms—press, association, expression—the maintenance of a form of parliamentary democracy, despite the fact that many Seareiros fully realized the weaknesses of Portugal's parliamentary system, and a progressive educational campaign to integrate the Portuguese masses and elite into modern Western Europe. Thinkers such as António Sérgio and Raúl Proença[44] believed that the Portuguese elite had not been fully Europeanized and that a campaign to achieve this goal would be both difficult and lengthy. Above all the writers of this remarkable periodical, which during the years of the New State dictatorship acted as the liberal conscience of the opposition, looked to the future rather than to the past.

In strong contrast to these beliefs were the ideas of the Portuguese Traditionalists, the Integralists. Although the writings which make up this body of thought are scattered and disparate,[45] the ideas represented a fairly coherent, and to some, a convincing ideology. After 1914, when the Integralists' first major publication appeared, this ideology became increasingly popular among the elite youth and leaders of the middle and upper classes. While the programs and ideas of the feuding Left and Right Republicans were vague, the ideas of the Integralists had clarity and simplicity, and they were more widely disseminated. The Integralists offered an oversimplified explanation of the failures of the First Republic, and they put forth remedies. They attacked the Republican concepts of democracy and popular sovereignty and substituted their ideas: rule by one person—a monarch—rather than "electoral somersaults,"[46] the return to Portugal's oldest and—in their opinion— most cherished traditions: Church, monarchy, family, the land, and professional corporations based on medieval guilds. The Integralists wished to revive local autonomy through the strengthening of the decayed municipal and county (concelho) freedoms and to restore those Portuguese traditions which were, they claimed, "corrupted" by the foreign ideas of centralized statism, anticlericalism, Masonry, individualism, and popular democracy. Railing against what they referred to as *desnacionalização* ("denationalization") on which they blamed Portugal's decadence in recent centuries, the Integralists espoused a doctrine of looking to the past. They proposed that integralism could help Portugal, now "a vast field in ruins," and restore the country to her "past of glories."

In 1926, the debate between the Modernists and Traditionalists of the First Republic moved beyond the printed page into the public arena. The paramount fear of the Modernists was that if the parliamentary republic fell the Integralists' ideas might become the dominant doctrine of a successor dictatorial regime. Indeed, what was left unsaid in the debates but was implicit in Integralists writings and propaganda was that if they dominated a reform government of *força,* they would put its law into effect by force not by consent. Symbolic of the threat of violence and of the conflict of ideas mixed with short tempers was an

incident which occurred in Lisbon on 9 February 1926. At a meeting of
the conservative study group Cruzada Nacional D. Nun' Alvares
Pereira, Integralists openly praised Spanish dictator Primo de Rivera's
work of "resolving the internal political problem" with force; *Seara
Nova* writers in the audience, including historian Jaime Cortesão,
violently disagreed, and a fistfight ensued.[47]

In late 1923 the brief stability and political peace under the enduring
cabinet of Premier Silva ended; on 15 November, Silva's government
resigned. Manuel Teixeira Gomes had been elected president by Congress.[48] The new president called to power a cabinet composed of Nationalists, the first time that conservative party held power as a group in
parliament, even though they had a minority of seats in Congress. On
10 December 1923 there was an abortive military coup. A naval vessel
signalled the onset of a revolution, and armed men assaulted the
presidential palace but were repulsed by the guards of the residence.
Leaders of the abortive coup claimed that their goals were to "save the
country and to honor the republic,"[49] though neither of these goals was
much furthered by their activity. The Nationalist government of
Ginestral Machado sought to use the incident and unfavorable votes in
the Congress to pressure the president to dissolve the Congress and to
call new elections. The premier hoped that in new elections the Nationalists could deprive the PRP of their majority. President Teixeira
Gomes, however, refused to accede to his request for dissolution, and
the Machado cabinet resigned on 15 December. Thus Portugal entered
a new phase of its political crisis.

Crisis, 15 December 1923—18 April 1925: Vested-Interest Groups and Reform

Four governments held office during the next sixteen-and-a-half
months, each one surviving about four months, the average lifespan for
governments during the First Republic. In the realm of economics and
finance, there were distinct improvements, but the political and social
crises worsened.

As noted in chapter 9, the Álvaro de Castro government (December
1923—July 1924) dealt successfully with economics and finance. The
currency was stabilized, and although more strikes occurred in 1924
than in 1921-23, most indications were that the position of the urban
working classes was beginning to improve.

Attempts to increase revenues provoked a conflict between reformist
governments and business and industry. During 1924-26 this conflict
reflected basic issues of government and politics. In July, August, and

September 1924 the Rodrigues Gaspar coalition government passed laws which increased taxes on bottled beverages and perfume, and it attempted to enforce already existing industrial and building taxes. Opposing the new measures were the majority of urban businessmen and industrialists; on 14 October 1924, many commercial establishments closed their doors in a one-day shutdown protest, an act which provoked a counterprotest by groups of workers. From this businessmen's protest emerged an important organization: the Union of Economic Interests (UIE), which began as a group composed of urban and rural managers and landowners.[50]

The UIE, dominated by Lisbon industrialists and businessmen, became both a defender of business interests against the state, and a political party which entered the general elections of November 1925. Beneath this façade of economic self-interest and political activity, the UIE was involved in the growing conspiracy within the professional military. The influential Lisbon daily *O Século* became the UIE mouthpiece. Leading businessmen acted as liaisons between conspiring officers. The UIE was the only known group which provided financial support for the abortive coup of 18–19 April 1925 and for the successful golpe of 28 May 1926.

The failure of reformist governments to remain long in power—despite their good intentions and the need for reform—was due not only to the splintering political-party system but also to the rising opposition from such groups as the business and industrial interests represented by the UIE and by the important Commercial Association of Lisbon. On 22 November 1924, another reformist government came to power led by lawyer José Domingues dos Santos, leader of a splinter group of Democrats which called themselves Democratic Leftists. Domingues dos Santos's political style and program were distinctly Jacobin and semi-Socialist. Aside from the usual references to a balanced budget and a reduction of the size of the civil service, his program called for "social justice." The premier dared to propose real change in areas of social welfare and increased rights for consumers and tenants. On 6 February 1925 his government forcibly dissolved the Commercial Association of Lisbon, which had opposed decrees to reform banking.[51]

The conflict went into the streets on the evening of that same day and this in turn led to the intervention of the GNR, the target of bombs during the street riots. Premier Domingues dos Santos gave a public speech, thanking the crowd which came to support his government's measures. His words aroused a grave outcry against his remaining in power. The speech, some of which is quoted below, gave the conservative opposition both in Congress and at large an opportunity to topple the Democratic Leftists.

People of Lisbon! . . . The people have been exploited by high commerce and by high finance. The Government of the Republic places itself openly on the side of the exploited against the exploiters. The Government is going to carry out a grandiose work of moral *saneamento*! I deeply deplore the event which just occurred. I am going to order immediately a rigorous inquiry. I will not allow the public force to exist in order to shoot the people.[52]

A motion of lack of confidence in Congress at dawn on 11 February 1925 went against the government 65 to 45. The Domingues dos Santos government then resigned.

President Teixeira Gomes did not attempt to save the premier but instead called Democrat Vitorino Guimarães to form a cabinet composed of seven Democrats, two Republican Actionists, and two independents. The new government, while it modified some reforms of its predecessors, proclaimed its desire to identify with the spirit of the Domingues dos Santos government, that is, "on the side of the exploited against the exploiters." In the meantime, the parliamentary deadlock attained a new stage as the Nationalist deputies abandoned the halls of Congress in protest and later launched new personal attacks on the president.

The 18 April 1925 Coup Attempt

Nationalist party sympathy with professional military grievances had manifested itself before 1925. In a celebrated speech of 17 December 1923 made in the Society of Geography of Lisbon, Nationalist leader Cunha Leal appealed for the intervention of "the only force still disciplined—the Armed Force." He continued:

The Army ought not to serve private political interests. . . . The Army ought not, really, to act against the parties, but has the right to make its voice heard and to indicate to the public powers that, if the right belongs to it to neutralize the threats of dissolution in Portuguese society, it also has the right to speak up, lest everything be lost, absolutely everything, in Portugal.[53]

Support for decisive military intervention in politics grew within military ranks. Gradually all restraints were loosened. Conservative politicians openly advocated military intervention and a new role for the military.

On 18 April 1925 a military conspiracy, involving Nationalists, monarchists, and Integralists, attempted to overthrow the Guimarães government. Led by monarchist officers Colonel João Sinel de Cordes and Lieutenant Colonel Raúl Esteves, and Nationalist-Fascist Filomeno da Câmara, with Integralist backing, the rebel soldiers managed to gain the support of some hostile units and demanded that the president dismiss the government, call to power a military-backed regime with Sinel de Cordes as minister of war, and dissolve Congress. Despite their political demands, the principal point in their published program concerned military professionalism: they demanded reorganization and purging (saneamento) of the armed forces.[54] After a brief fight, the rebels surrendered when they failed to win the support of most of the Lisbon garrison or of the GNR. The casualties included at least fourteen dead.[55]

The rebels' cause was lost when many compromised units in on the conspiracy failed to support the coup and defended the government. It was significant that the rebels refused much civilian aid and openly claimed the movement was solely military. The British ambassador was later informed confidentially that the rebel leaders modelled their proposed government on the Primo de Rivera dictatorship in Spain.[56] Yet the Lisbon working classes, dominated by the anarcho-syndicalist union federation, the CGT, fearing a monarchist coup and the fall of the Republican system, opposed the military movement by declaring a general strike and pledged loyalty to the government.[57]

Despite the apparent military nature of the coup, the government arrested in addition to the rebels caught in the act, perhaps as many as five hundred civilians, who included Nationalists, Presidentialists, Sidonistas, and even syndicalists. Most were released after paying small fines, but the government wanted to punish the military rebels—four high-ranking officers, sixty-four officers of company grade, and numbers of sergeants. Among these, some thirty-five were veterans of World War I campaigns in Flanders and Africa, and twenty-two possessed high military decorations.[58] Government spokesman General Ernesto Vieira da Rocha, minister of war during the coup attempt, was inaccurate and bluffing when he stated in a press interview, "This proves that the army is on the government's side and on the side of discipline, since it obeyed rigorously all the government's orders."[59] In fact large numbers of officers, possibly as many as three hundred,[60] had promised to join the coup but had desisted when it was obvious that the rebels' cause would fail. Another factor in the regime's favor was the loyalty of the GNR.

But the Eighteenth of April movement was not just one more abortive golpe de estado. A few high-ranking officers had committed themselves to insurrection against the government and a military conspiracy had deliberately avoided recruiting civilians. The leaders of the group used their imprisonment, their public trials, and the publicity surrounding their movement, in order to discredit the Republican regime and the Democrats. A little over a year later, the government in power had few defenders left: virtually all the political parties supported the overthrow of the Democrats, the military movement was more unified, and since they had experienced repression and persecution by the government in the meantime, the militant working-class organizations, chiefly the CGT, did not oppose the coup as they had on 18 April 1925. In their defeat in 1925, the military rebels learned a valuable strategic lesson which they would later put to use: in order to overthrow the regime the conspirators had to have the loyalty of the northern garrisons and to isolate the Lisbon garrison.

For leftists who were involved with labor unions and who knew the attitudes of the poor masses, the Eighteenth of April was an ominous event, political handwriting on the wall. As an early Portuguese Marxist wrote shortly afterwards:

We are now in the phase in which the indifferent are turning hostile. We have against us all the rich and well-off, all the clericals, all the well-employed, all the bosses, great and small, all the militarists, the wives, the mothers, the daughters, the sisters, the sweethearts of all of them, and to support them, the immense legion of the exploited, without ideas, the simple, the primitive.[61]

The Eighteenth of April, despite its failure, demonstrated that the Republican regime had lost the support not only of the lower classes, but of the very class which had helped to found the republic, the lower middle class. The successful coup of 28 May 1926 was, in many respects, a "natural continuation" of the abortive movement of 18 April 1925.[62]

12 / The Politics of Despair

18 April 1925—28 May 1926

> Upon the ruins of the Republic, made gangrenous by the hatreds of its partisans, by the illegitimate ambitions of its leaders, by the rampant commercialism of its petty politicians will rise up a new political constitution, served by men of sane conscience and of honest character, who have respect for justice and morals and who do not make a lucrative profession out of politics. Only in this way will there be an avoidance of the mortification of the republic, which, spreading gangrene to all the nation, will destroy and annihilate it.
>
> Anselmo Vieira[1]

> The country is sick.
>
> General Óscar Carmona[2]

Public Opinion and Conspiracy

In the spring of 1925 Portugal's flawed parliamentary republic reached a new political crossroads. Even to circumspect Republicans the parliamentary system appeared to be symbolized by the turmoil of the daily sessions in the halls of Congress, housed in the São Bento building. "Permanent Carnival," quipped one student of Portuguese society.[3] Important reforms were proposed; there were plans but few accomplishments. As a group, politicians had become the butt of a special vocabulary of political cynicism and ridicule. The educated elite, despairing of improvement in the system, became more enamored of the authoritarian governments newly installed by dictators in Italy (1922), in their influential neighbor, Spain (1923), and in Greece (1925).

During the remaining thirteen months of the First Republic, there were four important attempts by the military to overthrow the government, the last of which, on 28 May 1926, succeeded. While the final parliamentary governments struggled to implement naval reconstruction, road building, financial and currency reform, pay increases for

various professions including the military, and other new measures, opposition to the Democrats significantly increased. In the parliament,
when the PRP's strength was increased after the November 1925 legislative elections, the opposition employed more desperate tactics. The
press generally opposed the rule of the Democrats; by spring 1926 only
one daily paper, *O Rebate,* the organ of the PRP itself, defended the
government's record. Within the political parties fragmentation and
personal bickering increased.

Splits and leadership struggles produced two new parties in 1925-26
(the Democratic Leftists, split from the PRP, and the Liberal Unionists
of Francisco Cunha Leal, from the Nationalists), neither of which had
real prospects of winning many votes in future elections. In the armed
services, the opposition—especially agents of the Nationalists and the
Radicals—were deeply involved in conspiracies with civilian conservatives, monarchists, and Integralists.

The 18 April 1925 coup attempt provoked the Guimarães government
to take countermeasures. The government banned the publication of
the hostile *O Século* from 19 April to 6 May and also suspended *A
Capital* 21-24 April. Several foreign journalists, including the London
Times correspondent in Lisbon, were arrested for spreading "false" information, and one reporter (a Spaniard) was deported.[4] Those military
units which were active against the government—the Battalion of Tele-
graphers, the First Machine Gun Group, the Mounted Artillery of
Queluz and the Railway Sappers Battalion—were disbanded by government order. Ten officers were suspended from service and many of
those implicated were transferred from Lisbon to rural posts. The
government also retired from active service those officers who had been
in on the conspiracy but who had refused to take part in the coup; at
the top of this list was the "neutral" commandant of the Lisbon garrison himself, General Adriano da Sá.[5]

Despite government countermeasures, however, the rising tide of unfavorable public opinion continued. The increasingly hostile press convinced a large portion of the urban as well as the rural public that "national salvation" required more than just one more change of
Republican cabinets. The effect of the press campaign, also echoed in
speeches in Congress and in political-party meetings, led to a widespread assumption that the First Republic had come to a dead end, that
the system required radical change, or even, to use the parlance of
Iberian politics, an "iron surgeon." Those opposing the Democrats
could not agree on the precise means to bring about lasting reform, on
the names of the persons who could engineer it, or on the role of the
military, which was increasingly considered the way out of the political

labyrinth. Many, however, came to agree that: (1) only military leadership could initiate significant change; (2) an army-backed regime would not lead to a monarchist restoration or to a significant loss of freedom; and (3) the Democrats' republic was becoming increasingly arbitrary, repressive, statist, and was thoroughly corrupt. They believed that the PRP now lacked authority and legitimacy and was out of step with new ideas which could help the country pull itself out of the worst crisis since the sixteenth-century Spanish takeover. Thus, a press campaign, as in 1908–10, was the public façade over a conspiracy to organize a decisive military coup.

Once again conspiracy became a way of life. Not just the Right sought to change governments. Many oppositionists of a variety of beliefs hoped to unseat the Democrats and unhinge their control of elections and of Congress. Especially after the Bloody Night of October 1921, plotting army officers gained more support for the idea of a military-led coup which would set up a dictatorship. Organizing protests and obstructive tactics was comparatively simple. Organizing a coup was a different matter. It required skillful and prestigious leaders who would lend the movement respectability. It required unity of forces where there was disunity and conflict.

Such a political goal was difficult to achieve until the Democrats had become irretrievably mired in corruption and ineptitude. A violent press campaign could hasten the process, but it could not guarantee success when it came to garnering enough officers to command a decisive combination of units. Until larger numbers of officers were willing to join a conspiracy and remain loyal under fire, a coup was not possible.

The movement which resulted in the 1926 coup directed its efforts toward discrediting the dominant party and its leaders and convincing the armed-forces leadership to join the burgeoning conspiracy. A strange form of struggle for the minds and hearts of army officers—a specialized sort of public-opinion exercise—was at work. At the same time a public-opinion campaign was pursued by the urban press, where increasingly the major daily *O Século*—now owned, directed, and edited by conservative forces involved in financing, encouraging, and hoping to profit from the conspiracy within the army—fostered a kind of Fascist campaign against the PRP.

One aspect of the conspiracy involved tedious negotiations between the military leaders, dominated by monarchist and Integralist officers Colonel Raúl Esteves and Colonel João Sinel de Cordes. Junior officers, the active vanguard of the Eighteenth of April, plotted with conservative, rightist elements in the parliamentary opposition—the Nationalists. At one point in late 1923 parliamentary leaders Álvaro de

Castro and Fernando Ultra Machado actually participated in the budding conspiracy, and when confronted by Cunha Leal,[6] they justified their involvement by claiming that though they could not prevent an insurrection, they could influence it in such a way so as to prevent the emergence of a monarchist movement.

By 1925, when chances for a monarchist restoration were quite slim, such arguments to support collaboration in the military conspiracy were sophistry and blatant opportunism. The rightist Nationalist party, which acted as a kind of "popular front" for groups of Integralists and monarchists, and the more centrist Radicals were involved in the conspiracy largely out of self-interest: they hankered for public office. By collaborating with a group which was going to lead a successful coup— despite the inherent dangers of gaining power by force—the leaders of these parliamentary parties believed they had a better chance of scoring politically than if they depended upon elections over which the Democrats appeared to have a guaranteed dominance. Political opportunism thus helped to shape the spreading military conspiracy.

Social and economic factors, too, played a role in the rising wave of hostility to both the Democrats' monopoly of power and to the parliamentary system as it was operating. By the mid-1920s most of big business and industry, landowners, and small and middle-sized business groups were ready to try a new system. Despite signs in 1924–26 that financial reforms were under way, despair dominated. A crisis in the African colonies complicated internal affairs. Grave problems in Angola, the most important African colony, became of increasing concern and were intimately involved with metropolitan finance and politics.

The Politicization of Colonialism:
The Norton de Matos Affair

Among an important part of the Republican—and the monarchist— leadership, Portugal's two main African colonies provided major hopes for the country's future prosperity and prestige. An upsurge in concern with colonial affairs was partly related to a financial crisis which hit Angola and Mozambique after World War I. For various reasons colonial finances worsened and reached a state of crisis in 1923–26. Each colony acquired such debts that Portugal was forced to provide large loans from metropolitan funds at a time when the country itself neared bankruptcy. By 1925 Angola's debt was more than £4,500,000,[7] an amount equal to one-fifth of the total Portuguese external debt.

A change in colonial administration instead of improving matters had led to an unprecedented crisis. A Republican nostrum for colonial development was autonomy. With the installation in 1921 of powerful high commissioners in both colonies, armed with powers far beyond those of the old governors-general, Portugal hoped to reform colonial affairs in a manner befitting the cultivated reputation of the "third colonial power" in Africa. In the process, colonial affairs, as in the days of the Anglo-Portuguese conflicts over the scramble for Africa, again became intensely politicized.

The high commissioners first appointed were both Republican politicians of note: José de Norton de Matos for Angola and Manuel Brito Camacho for Mozambique. Although these proconsuls now had the power to control the colonies' budgets and to contract loans, they did not succeed in pulling their charges out of the trough of trade deficits, debts, and financial crisis. Moreover, the elite in Portugal disagreed over the means by which they could develop their backward colonies. They confronted serious obstacles: Portugal's own economic plight which resulted in little capital being available; the reluctance of banks and capitalists to risk investment in remote regions with traditionally bad reputations; more powerful and aggressive foreign capitalists; and international developments which put pressures on Portugal as a colonial power and which undermined financial and economic progress.

In the years 1923–26 humanitarian campaigns in England, in the European press, and in the League of Nations, assailed Portugal's administration of her African colonies and brought to light reports, such as the 1925 report by the American sociologist Edward Ross, which accused officials of complicity in slavery and forced labor. The South African government, which wanted greater control of the port of Lourenço Marques, also brought pressure to bear. There was, as well, greater interest in colonial affairs in Fascist Italy and in Germany, which joined the League in 1926.[8]

With the best intentions High Commissioner Norton de Matos designed ambitious plans to develop Angola; during 1921–23 his administration attracted a lot of national attention. Since few Portuguese banks wished to risk funds in Angolan development—the subject of much speculation and dishonest dealings—Norton de Matos turned to foreign loans. By 1923, the colony was deep in debt, and the poverty-stricken metropole was obliged to bail it out with large subsidies.

The financial crisis in Angola raised the specter of loss of Portuguese control of the large colony and even aroused fears that Portugal's own financial independence might be imperiled. A wild press and parliamentary campaign led by the Nationalists and other conservatives exploited the issue. Norton de Matos's administration in Angola was easy prey. In September 1923 this campaign and ill health forced the high commissioner to return to Lisbon. After bitter debate in Congress, a vote of confidence in his work was passed,[9] but the harried officer resigned his post and was appointed Portugal's ambassador in London.

Norton de Matos was justified in complaining that his development policy was not only opposed by the important, conservative Banco Nacional Ultramarino, but was actively obstructed. That reactionary institution, already renowned for its negative impact on colonial development,[10] refused to grant Angola necessary loans and hindered currency transactions. It was no coincidence that the Nationalist party, led by the vitriolic and slanderous Cunha Leal, had close links with this and other important banks and big-business circles, which were more concerned about home finances than colonial. Ironically, Norton de Matos's final report as high commissioner invoked the argument that colonial development had to be financed entirely from colonial resources, a wily defense of his own record which was an anticipation of and a prologue to the New State colonial finance policy of the 1930s.[11]

Alarm over colonial affairs and accusations of treason in colonial and home finance were now traditional in politics. The surge of concern over colonial finance and administration in 1923-26, however, had an important role in the fall of the Democrats and in the collapse of the parliamentary system. A discredited colonial policy, however many the justifications and excuses, was tantamount to a diminished sovereignty. Despite the simplistic and alarmist character of most of the antigovernment arguments, an elite long sensitive to foreign dangers and to Portugal's traditionally weak position would not regard threats to the colonies or to national independence lightly. Just as the Ultimatum of 1890 and Republican allegations of a failed colonial policy helped to undermine the Constitutional Monarchy in its last years, so the colonial crisis of 1923-26 was an essential element in the collapse of the parliamentary system.

President Teixeira Gomes and the Ghost of Afonso Costa

Manuel Teixeira Gomes (1867-1941), businessman and writer turned diplomat, had served as Portuguese ambassador in London. In the fall of 1923, Congress elected him president of the republic. He succeeded the ailing but persistent veteran Republican, Almeida. Reluctant to sacrifice himself, Teixeira Gomes consented to be a candidate only at the urging of his close friend, the self-exiled Afonso Costa. Teixeira Gomes's difficult, traumatic, and short term as president epitomized the political standstill and the chronic instability of the parliamentary system. The Nationalist party's presidential candidate had been ex-president and ex-premier Bernardino Machado, who had turned against the Democrats. When their candidate lost out to Teixeira Gomes in the congressional balloting, the Nationalists returned "white" (blank) ballots as a gesture of contempt and lack of confidence in the sophisticated author of *Blue August* and other noted works.[12]

Teixeira Gomes had few original political ideas; he was a liberal Republican intellectual who had been a member of Brito Camacho's Unionist party. The most definitive element in his political armory was his friendship with and trust in Costa, who still retained influence—in absentia—in the PRP. Teixeira Gomes was obsessed with the notion that the only hope for Portugal's parliamentary system was for Costa to return from Paris and lead a national government. On numerous occasions he appealed to Costa to return from his lucrative posts in Paris. On several occasions during the hapless president's term, Costa did indeed return to Portugal for brief visits, but he could not be prevailed upon to form a government.

The Nationalists mounted a campaign against the president and remained permanently hostile to his person and to his office. When the suggestion of Costa forming a government coalition in which they might be included was raised, they refused to cooperate. President Teixeira Gomes later confided his despair when he wrote that Costa's refusals to return to public office in Portugal had left him "in a blind alley."[13] A legalist, Teixeira Gomes was reluctant to dissolve Congress, despite many threats and demands to do so from both the Left and the Right, and especially from the Nationalists. Since the PRP usually held a majority of seats and since the Nationalists were a minority, he felt that he could not justify handing power to an all-Nationalist cabinet. He preferred to use the power of dissolution only as an emergency measure, when all else had failed.

The Nationalists, meanwhile, were conspiring secretly with military plotters to organize a coup. They claimed that the president had cheated them of power, and that he had approved of the Democrats' permanent control of the machinery of the elections and of public office. They argued that a coup was the only way to gain power since the Democrats rigged the congressional elections. Various members of the Nationalist party were implicated in military plots and in coup attempts on 18 April 1925. It was significant that a major demand of the Eighteenth of April rebels was that the president "dissolve" the Congress immediately.[14]

Teixeira Gomes found the pressures of his office too great. During the 18 April coup attempt, he suddenly submitted his resignation to

Congress. After the deputies displayed sympathy and support for him, however, he reluctantly withdrew it.

Military insurrection continued. On 19 July 1925 a few military and naval units in the Lisbon area rebelled in an attempt to overthrow the ministry of António Maria da Silva (1 July–1 August). The rebels were led by Nationalist party member and professional naval officer, one of the heroes of the Fifth of October 1910: Commander José Mendes Cabeçadas. After a few hours of desultory firing, the rebels surrendered to the government forces and were taken to jail to join the Eighteenth of April rebels.

The Military Trials: The Government in the Dock

The military trials of the April and July 1925 rebels became public forums and political showcases used by the increasingly bold conservative opposition in order to discredit the government. These trials were among the most extraordinary political trials held under military law in modern European history. During these court-martial proceedings held in September (for the Eighteenth of April rebels) and in November (for the Nineteenth of July rebels), the government found itself on trial, with the much-maligned "Democrats' republic," as codefendant.[15]

The rebels were defended by Nationalist leader, deputy, and gadfly, Cunha Leal, and by Presidentialist-Nationalist and ex-premier, Tamagnini Barbosa. These devious lawyer-officers attempted to bypass the issue of military insubordination against the government and to concentrate on other points. They tried to establish that the "moral character" of the 160 April rebels on trial was irreproachable, that their "services to the republic," including their World War I service in some cases were outstanding. They claimed that the rebels' intentions were patriotic rather than treasonous. Observers were startled when numbers of soldiers, not on trial and not charged with rebellion, insisted on "volunteering" as defendants and going on trial with their compatriots! Indeed, the number of witnesses who appeared in support of the rebels was quite large, while few supported the government's case against them.

The chief prosecutor, General Carmona, was supposedly pursuing the government's case. Soon, however, it became evident that he supported the rebels. His public statements, published widely in the daily press in Lisbon, attacked the government, declared that some members of the government deserved to be in the defendant's box, and called for acquittal. Only two of the generals on the military court-martial jury voted to condemn the rebels, the majority voted for acquittal. The

rebels succeeded in convincing the jury that their military movement
was national, not partisan, was not monarchist but Republican, and
was inspired by noble patriotic motives. They urged the jury and the
public who attended the trials (mainly military officers, youth, and
women from the elite) to conclude that the republic could be saved only
by a military-backed regime of national force. They urged the now
familiar theme that Portugal was in imminent danger of losing both her
colonies and her independence.

The trials discredited the government and shocked liberal
Republicans. Some of the more remarkable statements came from one
"character witness" testifying on behalf of Nineteenth of July rebel
leader Cabeçadas. General Alberto da Silveira stated that he believed
Cabeçadas should be acquitted since that officer was a "poor and hard-
pressed head of a large family," and had been shoddily treated by the
republic for which he had risked his life on the Fifth of October.
Defense lawyer Tamagnini Barbosa then asked a unique leading question of the witness in order to launch an attack on the political status
quo: "Under determined circumstances is it admissable for the armed
forces to intervene in political affairs, when these affairs could be prej-
udicial to the regime and to the country itself?" The witness's answer,
published in the press, caused a sensation: "It [the armed forces]
should intervene. It is one of its duties, one recognized even by the
military codes themselves."[16]

The rebels constantly accused the government of inability to cope
with increasing "social disorder," that is, both civil and military crimes
and unrest among the working classes. The attack was extended to include the government's alleged failure to develop the African colonies
and to stave off what were described as "serious threats to our colonial
dominion."[17]

The immediate results of these bizarre trials were ominous: all the
defendants were acquitted of the charges of treason, even though they
were self-confessed rebels against the civil authority and against a
legally constituted government. The minister of war at the time of the
April movement, General Vieira da Rocha, openly praised the rebel
leaders and urged the court to absolve them of any guilt. Some
observers were impressed with the legalistic ploy of the defense: that the
government had no case of insubordination against the president,
whom the rebels pressured to dismiss the government and dissolve Congress, since Teixeira Gomes had submitted his resignation and was
therefore not legally in office at the time!

Reactions to the verdicts varied from euphoria and self-righteous
self-congratulation on the Right, to indifference on the Left. Old-line

Republican liberals such as ex-premier Colonel Sá Cardoso strongly responded to the acquittal of the rebels at the famed courtroom Sala do Risco ("Room of Risk"), dubbed Sala do Riso ("Room of Laughter") by wits. He formed the League for the Defense of the Republic (Liga da Defesa da República), a loose grouping of liberal Republican officers which never amounted to much.[18] Several moderate publications, such as *Seara Nova* and *A Capital,* criticized the outcome and urged the government to defend itself lest a dictatorship arise. The government was shocked by the verdicts and in various ways chastised the hostile military judges for acquitting the rebels, though the measures taken were much milder than those meted out by Minister of Justice Costa in 1911 against his recalcitrant court judges. General Carmona was removed as commander of the Fourth Military District, General Ilharco, who voted for acquittal, was stripped of his Order of Christ medal, and Dr. Almeida Ribeiro was dismissed as a judge for military courts.[19]

A portion of the Portuguese public remained indifferent to the "public document" of the 1925 trials. Nevertheless, the statements of the military rebels were worthy of attention, for they meant what they said. As rebel leader Colonel Sinel de Cordes testified on the first day of the trial 1 September 1925): "The Army organization of 1911 . . . did not correspond to the needs of the national defense, since with the Army we now have, if attacked, we could not even die with honor." The general went on to predict that his group, if in power, would establish a military dictatorship, would close down parliament, and would put Portugal's house in order, "during a long dictatorial period."[20]

The strange results of the 1925 military treason trials exposed the authority problem in Portugal's political system. The proceedings clearly demonstrated that the government had a largely undisciplined armed force, an increasingly rebellious officer corps, and a group of insubordinate generals. Rebel testimony, the daily press, and provocative memoirs by rebel leaders revealed that a large number of soldiers were no longer loyal and would betray the government once the Eighteenth of April movement gathered enough public support.

The government's countermeasures were ineffective. Officers could be transferred but prevailing public opinion and military pressure would not tolerate their separation from the service. Although the government retired the commandant of the Lisbon garrison for being a "crypto-rebel," the leaders of the rebellion were released and reinstated. The government had full reason now to place little trust in the army or the navy.[21]

The spirit of impunity went beyond the foreseeable consequences of the 1925 military trials. Military indiscipline in various units in and out

of Lisbon became a persistent threat to civil order as well as to the
health and longevity of cabinets. Whenever a military unit rebelled during the unstable post–World War I years, careworn cabinets, with as
many ministers as they could gather, would retire collectively to forti-
fied places which were protected by reliable units. A favorite place of
refuge during hours of military insubordination was the Lisbon headquarters of the republic's second army, the GNR's Carmo barracks.

The law was broken frequently yet juries feared the consequences of
harsh verdicts. With the crime rate soaring and military insubordination
increasing, civil authority was constantly under siege. Precedents for excessive leniency were on record well before the trials of 1925. Many
amnesties had been granted to a variety of military rebels. In a session
of the Chamber of Deputies only two months before the fall of the First
Republic, Premier Silva warned deputies of possible consequences. He
noted that since 1910 Republican governments had voted a total of
thirty-nine amnesty laws, freeing all military rebels, including those involved in the movements of 27 April 1924, 4 June 1924, 28 August
1924, 8 September 1924, 5 March 1925, 18 April 1925, and 19 July
1925.[22] Knowledge that they would be acquitted or let off with light
sentences freed military conspirators of the last vestiges of restraint.

"Order," the November 1925 General Elections, and the Banknote Case

At the end of the First Republic, the most abused word in politics
and government was "order." There was no common definition of the
provocative word. Individuals, parties, and groups tended to view
"order" as a condition enabling them but not their antagonists to do
what they wished. For labor movements "order" was when management did not abuse their rights. For management, "order," given the
atmosphere of social unrest, public violence, and militant demands,
meant government protection of management from working-class action. A major issue became: Will order be maintained by violence, by
force, or by a balance of power? By 1925–26 it was clear that force had
prevailed, because the government was beginning to use the force at its
disposal, especially the burgeoning police organizations and the GNR,
to repress extremist agitators and labor actions.

As a response to higher levels of crime, violence, and civic and
military unrest, the government developed a larger national police ap-
paratus. By 1921 Republican governments had at their disposal no
fewer than three national police forces, concentrated in the capital, in
Coimbra, and in Oporto. Two of these forces were ostensibly non-

political: PSP (Polícia de Segurança), and PIC (Polícia de Investigaçao Criminal). The third, PSE (Polícia de Segurança do Estado, or State Security Police) had an ominous title which fairly described its nature: it was the nucleus of a national political (and secret) police. In fact, the PSE was an early model—ironically created by the parliamentary system's government—for the New State's main strong-arm, political police force, eventually called PIDE (Polícia Internacional e da Defesa do Estado), which in later years effectively terrorized the population.[23] The last Republican governments were quite concerned with order and claimed that their large security establishment was purely defensive. As Premier Silva stated in a speech in the Chamber of Deputies on 22 April 1926: "The government threatens no one, but must carry out its duty, maintaining public order. And we have the certainty of being able to do this, because the armed forces have a great love of order. And the government cannot be intimidated by revolutionary blackmail."[24]

The use of repressive force against anarchists, anarcho-syndicalists and others destroyed any hope of labor-union support for the government in a future military coup. In the summer and fall of 1925 the government temporarily banned and suspended the anarcho-syndicalists paper *A Batalha,* deported to Africa hundreds of workers, some of whom were accused of being members of the Red Legion, and repressed strikes in Lisbon and Setúbal. Police employed brutality against workers and there was evidence that the police murdered workers who attempted to escape arrest. By March 1926 the weekly paper *A Batalha* angrily suggested that the political forces of the country were in "the last stages of decomposition. The republic in Portugal failed."[25] By this time much of the urban working class was hostile or indifferent to the republic. Some considered the system a scarcely veiled form of civilian dictatorship, an opinion shared by most political parties from Left to Right with the exception of the ruling PRP.

The business and industrial interests which were willing to support a military takeover to get what they wanted feared one thing as much as disorder: statism. Resentment of government intervention in their affairs in 1924-25, which included a genuine attempt to collect the industrial and income taxes, gave the Union of Economic Interests (UIE) the necessary grievances to gather monetary and political support for a coup. It was no coincidence that the literature published to win popular support for the Eighteenth of April rebels emphasized two main grievances besides professional military gripes: (1) the danger of "bolshevism," a term used to describe radical-socialist measures to benefit the lower classes, and (2) the state's interference in business by imposing "excessive" taxation.

An important measure of the distrust of and lack of confidence in the Republican regime by the entrepreneurial classes was the flight of capital out of the country. After 1910 monarchist wealth flowed to Brazil, Europe, and North America. Portuguese emigrants in one New England community, for example, complained of high Republican taxation.[26] The flight of capital increased after the war, as Portuguese capitalists, through fear of taxation, lack of confidence, and the profit motive, kept a lot of their money—just how much may never be known—in foreign banks. One historian estimates that by 1925 some £8,000,000 (in sterling) was abroad, not counting more Portuguese capital tied up in contraband business in Spain. Portuguese capital abroad represented at least six or seven times the total monetary circulation in Portugal, not including individual gold and silver hoarding in rural areas.[27] It can be argued with some validity then, that part of the blame for the economic difficulties of the First Republic could be placed on businessmen who deprived Portugal of needed capital.

Shrewd Premier Silva, head of the conservative PRP wing, nicknamed the "Bonzos" ("Buddhist priests"), was an able manipulator and was willing to compromise to keep his party in power and to stabilize the Republican regime. He attempted to mollify business and military interests by such acts as raising officers' salaries and repressing labor movements. He repeatedly invoked the word "order" to defend his administration, and he was well aware of the budding military conspiracy against him.

Silva believed, along with some remaining moderates, that the general elections of November 1925 gave his party a chance to consolidate their hold on Congress and to allow a stable cabinet to carry out reforms after a decent period in office. But political fragmentation became more common as parties split and splinter groups formed new parties. Socialist-leaning Democrats had joined José Domingues dos Santos's splinter group, Esquerda Democrática, and a new Center-Right party, which evolved from the Regionalist party, picked up strength in various rural areas, principally in the center and south.

The way in which the elections on 7 November 1925 were conducted symbolized the ambiguous role of elections as an expression of popular opinion. The rule of one party, with minimum freedom for a few rivals, was maintained. The Democrats had the only electoral organization worthy of the name. The electoral machine brought out their vote and discouraged rivals, especially monarchists, Catholics, and Nationalists. The Democrats' hold was strongest in Lisbon, where they usually won large majorities. They did less well in rural areas, especially in the north. To some extent non-PRP voters were discouraged from voting by the now familiar form of Republican populist terror, euphemistically described by partisans as "popular vigilance."[28] Violence in the 1925 election was, however, no greater than at previous Republican elections. At some polling places, nevertheless, the freedom to vote was very restricted. In the Viseu area, for example, one voter was beaten to death by toughs.[29] In other cases the caciques merely agreed ahead of time to give their rivals a negotiated portion of the vote without a contest.

The last elections of the parliamentary regime were not openly rigged upon orders of the government,[30] but local conditions did not favor non-Democrats for several reasons: Most of the conservative voters, including many Integralists and monarchists, did not bother to vote for fear of being physically assaulted or out of disdain for Republican elections. And most voters who did turn out favored the Democrats, that is, they voted "for the government," because that group controlled political patronage. In short, the Democrats' electoral organization remained intact. Thus the 1925 elections were not a democratic exercise, but the preelection campaign had important features which should be discussed.

The right-wing's major mouthpiece, the organ of the UIE, *O Século,* claimed that Portugal's problem was "fundamentally, a problem of order,"[31] echoing Mussolini's Fascist principles which were now in vogue among many elite Portuguese youths and the middle class. At a rally in Oporto, Democrat ex-premier Silva similarly stressed that his party favored "political order and financial order" in a distinctly expedient political program. The PRP program was moderate, sensible, and unassailable: reduce the size of the bureaucracy, reform the taxation system in order to make it more just, keep order to allow the republic to progress. The premier-to-be stated that his party opposed "class struggle" in favor of "cooperation."[32] In the PRP program there was something for everyone.

A contemporary newspaper survey of party programs on the eve of the election suggested that there was little differentiation on substantive issues. Although the party of Democratic Leftist José Domingues dos Santos claimed that it was opposed to "monopolies," a vague point never explained, the remainder of its program strongly resembled that of its PRP rival.[33] There were the usual references to balancing the budget, new tax laws, education for the lower classes, and a reform of public administration.

Those parties which were maneuvering to take advantage of a future military takeover made a point of emphasizing military interests in their programs. The Nationalists, the Radicals, and the Democratic Left featured demands for the reform and reorganization of the armed forces, all points mentioned in military leaders' statements. Civilian politicians jostled for the favor and approval of military leaders in order to insure places for their respective parties when the military named the cabinet. One Democratic Left candidate, Alfredo da Cruz Nordeste, obviously for the benefit of the military readers of the press, stated in an interview: "This is not an Army; this is a lie."[34] Such pro-military pandering by civilians of even the supposedly Socialist "Left" party indicated that the political struggle was shifting from the ballot box and the halls of São Bento to the garrisons and barracks.

Few observers were surprised by the results of the last parliamentary vote. For weeks *O Século* had been sarcastically repeating that the PRP had the elections sewed up and had only to "divide among itself the great electoral cake" and leave the "crumbs" to others.[35] In one town, Vila Nova de Ourem, all non-PRP parties agreed ahead of time to abstain from voting since the government gave the town no tax money for road building; the PRP, suggested the newspaper, need not worry about this *retraimento* since electoral victory was assured.

The Democrats emerged from the elections with an even stronger majority.[36]

	Chamber of Deputies	Senate
Democrats (PRP)	80	39
Nationalists (PRN)	36	8
Independents	18	8
Monarchists	6	5
Democratic Left (PRED)	6	1
Union of Economic Interests (UIE)	4	0
Catholics (CADC)	4	1
Socialists (PS)	2	0

There was a larger voter turnout than in the 1922 general election; in Lisbon the monarchists and Democratic Left made good showings and won minorities. Though it was nothing like the turnout of 1911, the number of votes cast in Lisbon in 1925 demonstrates that citizens there, in any case, continued to exercise their right to vote (see table 11).

However, the election results were overshadowed by sensational incidents within a few weeks. During the first ten days of December the republic was shaken by two developments: the exposé of the "Angola e Metropole" banknote swindle, and the final resignation and departure of the president.

Pleading ill health, but actually in despair over politics, Teixeira Gomes resigned on 10 December and took the first boat out of Lisbon harbor. He chose exile in Algeria, where he remained for the rest of his life.[37]

TABLE 11

Votes Cast in General Elections for Congress in Lisbon, 1911–25

Election Date	Number of Votes Cast
May 1911	37,386
June 1915	23,964
Apr. 1918	20,842
June 1919	11,472
June 1921	18,076
Jan. 1922	17,891
Nov. 1925	24,000 (approx.)

Sources: Election data for 1911–22 are from *O Século,* 30 Jan. 1922. Data for the Nov. 1925 election are from PRO, F.O. 371/11933, "Portugal, Annual Report, 1925," p. 13.

What became known as the Banknote Case in England, and as Angola e Metropole in Portugal, was among the largest financial swindles in the West in modern times. Despite rumors and allegations that sinister German financial plots to control Angola were involved and despite the existence of widespread corruption in high political and financial circles in Portugal, the planning and execution of the crime was the work of one man, a relatively obscure businessman. In 1924–25 Alves Reis, a twenty-eight-year-old entrepreneur with a shady past in Angolan enterprises, arranged to have the official government currency printers, Waterlow and Sons, Limited, of London, secretly print some two million pounds worth of 500-escudo notes (each worth approximately $20.00 in 1975 currency exchange). Convincing the English firm that he represented the Bank of Portugal, the state currency agency, he obtained the money for his own use.* In order to spend it conveniently he launched his own personal bank, Angola e Metropole. Ironically, Alves Reis first thought of the initial part of his scheme after reading a speech in Congress by Cunha Leal,[38] who revealed that there was a "fifth," irregular, method of issuing national currency notes, whereby the Bank of Portugal secretly had notes printed, did not record such transactions in the account books, and did not inform the government of the increase in the number of circulating notes.[39] When the Bank of Portugal discovered the swindle in December 1925, the Lisbon daily press took up the sensational case which soon struck the Silva government with a bombshell of embarrassment. Having begun a series of articles on 23 November 1925 which questioned the sources of the money deposited in Alves Reis's new bank, Angola e Metropole, and having

* The 500-escudo notes were to have the word "Angola" overprinted on them for use in Angola. This overprinting was not done, and the notes were circulated only in Portugal.

alleged there had been German intrigue and conspiracy, *O Século* on 5 December revealed the swindle. This led to Alves Reis's arrest, trial, and conviction.[40]

The Banknote Case rocked but did not topple the Silva government, which had entered office soon after the exposé began. Nor did the repercussions result in a major financial downturn for the First Republic. Despite claims by some that the extraordinary swindle sealed the fate of the republic, available evidence suggests a more complex interpretation. The financial troubles spurred by Alves Reis's swindle were eventually ironed out, and the 1926–27 budget of the last minister of finance, Armando Marques Guedes, in fact planned for a slight surplus and for measures to alleviate the country's foreign-debt problems.[41]

Rather than financial, the Banknote Case had a severe political, even moral, impact. The problems of financing Angolan colonial development, Alves Reis's unsavory record in Angolan business ventures, and fears of German and British attempts to "grab" potentially rich Angola coincided in the public mind. Fear, not reason or long-term thinking along rational lines, informed the majority of newspaper and periodical readers. Even if high officials in the Bank of Portugal, the diplomatic corps, and in several ministries and businesses were not implicated in Alves Reis's swindle,[42] it was enough for the Right now to be able to convince many readers of the conservative, pro-Fascist press, that not only was the Democrats' leadership thoroughly compromised and corrupted but that Portugal's still undeveloped colonial empire in Africa was soon to be lost to foreign powers owing to the "disorder" allowed by the Silva regime. Portugal could not, the Right asserted, allow the regime to lose Angola; even a dictatorship was preferable, and one with the officer corps playing a key role was the only way out. The most important political and moral result of the revelation of Alves Reis's bizarre swindle was further to undermine confidence in the system. The smell of corruption—whatever the real evidence—discouraged even the moderate, liberal Lisbon press.[43] Even though it was not the final blow to the First Republic, the Banknote Case contributed to the politics of despair of 1925–26.

From São Bento to the Barracks

"A vida é uma roleta," wrote the novelist-writer Raúl Brandao, "Life is a roulette wheel."[44] This seemed to be an accurate description of the social and economic ferment of the elite society of mid-1920s

Lisbon. As the First Republic collapsed, the Alves Reis swindle was only one among the more sensational events in an era of corruption, malfeasance, decadence, wild adventurousness, and vulgarity mixed with derring-do. In the same era the historian must also count as important the deeds of more lawful geniuses than Alves Reis, such as the exposés by star investigative reporter and opium addict, nicknamed Reporter X, Reinaldo Ferreira,[45] the record-breaking flights of the pioneer aviators Gago Coutinho and Sacadura Cabral,[46] and the extraordinarily ambitious plans and unfulfilled (for over a generation) schemes to begin to develop Angola by High Commissioner Norton de Matos.[47]

Ironically, it was partly because of the extraordinarily ambitious schemes for money-making, investment, and development in Lisbon and in Luanda that the public lost confidence in the ability of the Democrats' republic to provide stability and freedom for the Portuguese capital. Alves Reis's self-styled patriotic schemes to develop Angola and to extract himself from debt only further encouraged growing Portuguese fears that Angola would go under. Worse than the much exaggerated Portuguese internal and external debts were anxieties of the elite, perhaps amounting to a national superstition, that unless an authoritarian system replaced the Republican regime, not only the colony of Angola but Portugal itself and therefore national independence would perish.[48]

Despite the good intentions of the Silva government, such deep-seated despair could not be eradicated by normal measures. The conspiracy to arouse the armed forces continued. On 1–2 February 1926, several military units were attacked and—in part—enlisted to revolt against the government. Within a few hours forces loyal to the regime crushed the rebellion, which had been the work of the Center-Left Radical party under the construction magnate João Martins Júnior.[49]

São Bento was now the scene of a confusing struggle. Aged Bernardino Machado, now seventy-five, had succeeded self-exiled Teixeira Gomes in the presidential palace at Belém. The final Silva government, in office from 17 December 1925 to 30 May 1926, spent considerable effort dealing with the financial crisis and the "tobacco question." The tobacco monopoly, an arrangement whereby a company processed all tobacco under a contract with the government, was due to expire in April 1926. The minister of finance proposed a government monopoly, a *regie,* to replace the previous arrangement. The Nationalists attacked the scheme as a "monopoly" which would not benefit any group except the Democrats, whom they accused of planning to use the profits for

Do vivo ao pintado...

Impressão grafica de uma das menos peores sessões do parlamento

... Entretanto, atravez do reposteiro, uma curiosidade impertinente contempla a tragedia das carteiras feitas em cavaoos...

"From real life to the made up: a graphic impression of one of the least bad sessions of parliament . . . meanwhile, from the door curtain, an impertinent curiosity contemplates the tragedy of the desk tops broken into sticks. . . ." So reads the caption of a political cartoon which appeared in the Lisbon daily paper *A Época* on 17 May 1926, only eleven days before the May 28 coup. The cartoonist depicts an anonymous brigadier general, from behind the cloakroom curtain, ominously observing the riot in the Chamber of Deputies.

political leverage. The opposition in Congress, although in a minority in 1925–26, aroused so much excitement that the fact that their anti-regie arguments were largely specious was lost in the confusion.

As the opposition's tactics became more violent, Silva took a firm but defensive stance. Apparently he believed that the military conspiracy in progress had no real program and would not succeed in winning public support, that it lacked the expert leadership to be effective in public office. Silva hoped that the minister of war, Lieutenant Colonel José Mascarenhas, who had been carefully selected with the views of the plotting sector of the officer corps in mind, would stave off a coup. Mascarenhas was in touch with leading conspirators.

Despite some reasonably sensible plans and the ability of Silva's competent Minister of Finance Marques Guedes, the crucial struggle in the ongoing political battle for the survival of the Silva government shifted from the halls of Congress to the press, the streets, and the barracks. The "permanent carnival" was being scrutinized carefully by the plotting military leaders. The unfortunate reputation of Congress, which argued more than it acted, was a most useful pretext for armed-forces intervention in politics and for a military takeover of the state. The discrediting of Congress, which was the work of opposition parties anxious to gain power and to please the army leadership, played a crucial part of the final collapse of the First Republic. It was highly prophetic when this process was depicted in a political cartoon which appeared in the Catholic-Integralist daily, A Época, only eleven days before the military coup began at Braga.[50] The cartoon shows a scene of riot in Congress while at the side of the chamber the curtain of the cloakroom is held open by an officer (a brigadier general) whose insignia shows on the cuff of his uniformed arm. The destiny of the republic was now increasingly in the hands of those in command of the barracks. High politics was about to undergo militarization.

13 / The Twenty-eighth of May

> Portuguese! The Nation wants a national military government, surrounded by the best talents, in order to bring to the state administration, the discipline and honor lost long ago. . . . It wants a strong government which has as its mission to save the Fatherland.
>
> General Manuel Gomes da Costa[1]

The army pronunciamento which began on 28 May 1926 at Braga in northern Portugal did more than bring a change of governments. Unlike coups in 1915, 1917, and 1921, the coup of late May 1926 not only forced a government to resign—the last Democrat government of António Maria da Silva—but also established the Military Dictatorship (1926–33) which led, in turn, to the New State (1933–74). This military act set the stage for a conservative turn of thought and the entrenchment in the government of conservative political figures who attempted to disavow much of the Republican experience of the previous sixteen years.

Interpretations of the 1926 coup range between two extremes, both of them partisan and semipropagandistic. The official interpretation supported by the New State regime is often labeled the "National Revolution,"[2] a term which also refers to the general process of change during the tenure of the New State. Partisans of this interpretation thus view the coup as a nonpartisan, patriotic, altruistic act which somehow spoke for the nation.

At the other extreme, some writers hostile to the New State have suggested that the Twenty-eighth of May was a partisan, selfish act, the result of a narrow conspiracy, which undermined a democratic republic and destroyed freedoms enjoyed under the parliamentary regime.[3] Other interpretations introduce qualifications. During the zenith of Dr. Salazar's popularity, some saw the coup in 1926 as perhaps initially useful and well-meaning, but still rudderless, without a great leader or idea, which was rescued by the expertise of Dr. Salazar.[4] A recent interpretation by a young professional historian who has been a strong

234

critic of the dictatorship emphasizes that the movement was an "army rebellion," but that it reflected the general hostility of a large portion of the public and the political bankruptcy of both the system of government and its elite.[5]

It is perhaps a mistake to view the Twenty-eighth of May as a purely military phenomenon. While it was largely a movement of military officers, it functioned in the context of political rivalry and a struggle for power. The complexity of the long and well-developed conspiracy which led to the pronunciamento draws attention to two important features which distinguish the successful 1926 coup from any other similar phenomenon during the First Republic: it was bloodless—not one casualty occurred from street combat, though a suicide and some related road accidents took place—and the public knew that officers were planning a serious move weeks before the conspiracy went into the streets. The Twenty-eighth of May was not a sudden, spontaneous act; it was the result of intricate, involved, and convoluted conspiracies. The conspiratorial groups had goals similar to those of political parties: to achieve and maintain power. Although their leadership consisted of military officers, the conspiracies involved groups in various occupations and classes.

Initial public response to the fall of the Silva government was largely favorable; the impunity and despair of 1925–26 had been pervasive. In the Portuguese political arena, however, one conspiracy is invariably father to the next. There were many coup attempts before the Twenty-eighth of May and there would be many after. It is important to recognize, nevertheless, that although the 1926 coup was no panacea for Portuguese troubles, the parliamentary republic never recovered from the blow delivered on that spring day.

The Twenty-eighth of May Plot: Rival Committees and Parties Jostle for Position

The army movement that emerged on 28 May 1926 was the result of organizing by not one network of committees but several. There was an orgy of cafe conspiracies, barracks meetings, hotel encounters, and office whispering. Never in the history of the First Republic was there so much conspiring, by so many people, over so long a period; by mid-May, or perhaps earlier, some of the plot was public knowledge, acknowledged by certain daily newspapers in editorials, feature articles, and political cartoons (see p. 232).

The conspiracy network was much more complex than previous studies have acknowledged. Relying largely on the interviews and research of Óscar Paxeco, the Spanish historian Pabón[6] admitted the possibility that several revolutions were being planned simultaneously, and that there was diversity in the groups conspiring, but that the main conspiracy, or *conjura,* consisted of three nuclei: the leaders, mainly high-ranking army officers Sinel de Cordes, Alves Roçadas, Garcia Rosado, Roberto Baptista, Raúl Esteves, and Amilcar Mota; young, junior-grade officers, anxious not to postpone the coup; and civilians from the Radical Republican party, who were allied with Naval Commander José Mendes Cabeçadas. This analysis is an oversimplification which does not examine a key problem of the conspiracy: the heterogeneity of the participants and their allies.

The Twenty-eighth of May movement was primarily an officers' corps conspiracy which deliberately avoided involvement with civilian groups. Most of the decisive organization work, *ligaçoes* ("connections"), discussions, and travel were carried out by junior-grade army officers in the northern garrisons, especially in Braga and Coimbra. These young officers sought leadership from older, higher-ranking officers, but carefully selected those whom they approached or informed of the conspiracy. In the Seventh Military Division (Tomar), the commander did not inform his chief of staff of the conspiracy.[7] These officers were backed by civilians from the Integralist party, including schoolboys and university students who had been infected with the conservative teachings of their professors and with the propaganda of the pro-Integralist press.[8] In conformity with traditional preparations for pronunciamento, junior officers did the groundwork while senior officers retained a more detached wait-and-see attitude. Like the 1915 Movement of Swords, and later coups, the Twenty-eighth of May conspiracy involved the army officers in negotiating with political parties for support. Unlike previous movements in the army officer corps, in 1926 a fair number of senior officers (generals and colonels) took part in the conspiracy from an early stage. Noncommissioned officers and enlisted men were largely excluded from knowledge of or participation in the plot.

The earliest junta revolucionária to form was at Braga on 10 January 1926. Gradually juntas were organized in nearly every army regiment (approximately thirty-five) within the eight military divisions in the country. The most active and successful committees were in Braga, Coimbra, and Lisbon. Officers committed to support, or at least not oppose, the coup were asked to make verbal or written statements to authorized agents of ligação who gave the officers some idea of the program of the movement. Crucial activity came from the juntas in Braga and Coimbra in the north, which were dominated by eager Integralist young officers.

Once the conspiracy began, the major opposition parties attempted to assume leadership and hoped to benefit from an army victory. Three parties in particular made a point of wooing high-ranking army and navy officers as potential candidates for leadership in a future "non-partisan, national government." The Nationalist party, which underwent a split in March 1926, was sympathetic with the ideas of some young, Integralist officers, and had as a member one of the Eighteenth of April group of officers, Naval Commander Filomeno da Câmara, clearly a potential leader of a pronunciamento and member of a cabinet. The Radical party also wooed the army leadership. General Gomes da Costa was a member of the Radical Republican party, led by João Martins Júnior, and was, in effect, the Radicals' potential army candidate. Former Nationalist party leader, Francisco Cunha Leal, who had split from his party in March 1926 and formed the Republican Liberal Union (ULR), soon began to agitate for an army intervention in politics, and for army patronage of the ULR as its political guide and beneficiary. Cunha Leal hankered for high office and was a popular critic of the Democrats. He knew of the army conspiracy in progress and hoped to channel it in his and his party's favor. On the evening of 26 April at Braga, Cunha Leal gave a political speech to a large audience which included army officers and party members; he openly incited the army to "save" the republic by political intervention and to allow his party, the ULR, to be the army's political ally. He suggested that Sidónio Pais had been undermined politically in 1918 because the Unionist party had withdrawn its support, and that now in 1926 only his party, the ULR could save the country and clean up the government.[9] Cunha Leal hoped to use one of his party members, Commander Cabeçadas, as a springboard to either the cabinet or the premiership after 30 May; in his party's newspaper the aggressive politician later admitted that his party had been in on the conspiracy, though as a leader he had not,[10] and after 30 May, he lavishly praised the new head of government, Cabeçadas, who however did not reward him with a political payoff.[11] Even the leftist offshoot of the Democratic party, the Democratic Left, hoped to benefit politically from the military movement; its main newspaper praised the success of the movement and the fall of their rivals the Democrats; the Democratic Leftists hungered for office, too.[12]

In the course of the conspiracy, there were, broadly, two different revolutions being planned. A Republican one, with Republican armed-forces officers in the lead, which proposed to "save the country" by means of financial reforms and a cleanup of corruption and waste, with a continuation of civil liberties. The leader of this element of the conspiracy was the naval commander, hero of the Fifth of October 1910 Revolution, Cabeçadas. A second element was essentially an Integralist army and navy officers' conspiracy, which planned to reform the government using the "sword" of the armed forces. This group planned a thorough curtailment of civil liberties including the closing of parliament and the employment of censorship. The question of whether Portugal should be a republic or a monarchy, they left open for discussion. Although specific, detailed programs of these two conspiratorial elements were not made public until a few days after the revolt at Braga, little need was felt at the time for detailed programs. In view of the unpopularity of the Democrats' government, the lack of differentiation between political programs during the republic, and the fear of certain groups that the full revelation of their plans might occasion opposition, the lack of programs was natural.[13] A modified version of integralism emerged in July 1926 as a kind of program for military dictatorship, but until then the Integralists carefully remained in the background for fear of arousing Republican fears of a restoration of the monarchy. In fact, though many of the younger Integralists were monarchists, their monarchism was sentimental rather than ideological; since the monarchist failure of early 1919, the restoration of the monarchy had come to be considered less and less practicable. "Republican integralism" was growing in popularity.[14]

The military conspiracy proceeded with some unity of purpose and composition in the northern garrisons, but in Lisbon there were two rival conspiracy committees which reflected the Republican-Integralist dichotomy of opposition to the government. At first there was only one Lisbon junta revolucionária, which was controlled by the group of senior Integralist officers led by Colonel Sinel de Cordes (the Eighteenth of April group); these officers operated in considerable secrecy, their names were not publicized, and a "front" committee of lesser-known army officers headed by a Lieutenant Colonel Júlio Achemann, surfaced after the movement began. A second junta, led by Commander Cabeçadas, was known as the Junta of Public Salvation, and included Lieutenant Carlos Vilhena, Jaime Baptista, and Commander Armando da Gama Ochoa.[15] This committee had been purposely excluded from the inner Integralist conspiracy and was a rival. Cabeçadas's conspiracy committee received no monetary support.[16]

The main Lisbon junta was controlled by Integralist officers and supported by the Union of Economic Interests, now a political party made up of business and industrial interests. The UIE owned *O Século,* whose owners and backers, including the editor, Dr. Henrique Trindade Coelho (1885–1934), had prepared public opinion for the fall of the Democrats and for the establishment of a dictatorship. How much money the conspirators received from the UIE-*Século* group is not known; the UIE had previously helped to finance the abortive Eighteenth of April pronunciamento,[17] and its member companies, such as Alfredo da Silva's Companhia União Fabril (CUF), and the Tobacco Company of Portugal quite possibly helped finance the Eighteenth of April group's part of the conspiracy.[18] Also, certain wealthy individuals, such as Luís Charters de Azevedo, third viscount of São Sebastião, a monarchist and militia veteran of World War I, and others, contributed money for travel, for the purchase of automobiles, and for other necessities. Numbers of young Integralists, with varying degrees of Catholic and monarchist leanings, some of them high school and university students, contributed their services as messengers, agents of ligação, and press propagandists. These individuals included Teotónio Pereira, Manuel Múrias, Rodrigues Cavalheiro, and others who later assumed important positions in the Estado Novo regime. The program promised by the Eighteenth of April group, therefore, was evidently more attractive to the economic interest groups in on the conspiracy.[19]

If there was disagreement concerning programs and who would participate in the movement, there was remarkable unanimity on one important point: the Silva government and the Democrats had to be replaced by a "nonpartisan, national government."[20] Important questions remained: Which groups would dominate the new government? Whose program would dominate? What role might the monarchists play? And how would a new government institute necessary reforms?

That an important conspiracy against the government was in the making was the worst-kept secret of the decade. As an experienced monarchist commented a few years earlier, in Portuguese politics it is "impossible" to keep secrets.[21] The government was aware of the plots and did not remain passive. But it had little political ammunition and few friends left. The Silva government's efforts to disarm the plot by transferring disaffected officers from Lisbon to the provinces caused some problems, but they were not as serious as two internal problems: leadership and the heterogeneity of the conspirators. The Braga committee required a leader who was a general with military prestige, a good reputation as a Republican, and a nonpolitical name. They found their man in General Alves Roçadas, a conservative and African hero, but to their dismay he died suddenly of cirrhosis of the liver on 28 April. The plotters then decided to postpone the movement until June.[22] A number of high-ranking officers were approached, including the monarchist Colonel Gonçalo Pimenta de Castro.[23] Cabeçadas made an effort to be named the movement's leader by the Eighteenth of April group, but was rejected. This group preferred an officer who espoused nondemocratic or Integralist beliefs, or who at least would permit such ideas in a successor government. When Gomes da Costa consented on 25 May, after being invited to lead the movement by Lieutenant J. M. Pereira de Carvalho of the Braga committee, the Eighteenth of April group balked and promised to do nothing until they saw how Gomes da Costa's pronunciamento was received nationally. Gomes da Costa's decisions to lead the movement and to travel by car to Braga on 26 May were momentous; the movement now had the name of a senior Republican general, a famous war hero and African hero who was known for his toughness and his willingness to stand and fight. With this sensational development, the leadership problem was momentarily solved.

"Situation Obscure," 28 May–17 June: Struggle for Control

At Braga early in the morning of 28 May, General Gomes da Costa unexpectedly "pronounced" and, backed by the local army garrison, declared his intention to overthrow the Lisbon government and to win support from all army regiments. During the next few days he dispatched many telegrams to military units in all eight divisions inviting them to join him.[24] Meanwhile in Lisbon, conflicts within the conspiracy were emerging. It is not clear if Cabeçadas knew earlier that Gomes da Costa had become the leader of the movement and was on his way to Braga. On 27 May Cabeçadas wrote a letter to Bernardino Machado, president of the republic, and proposed that the Silva government be dismissed and that a national government be installed. Machado, who had long been concerned about the army conspiracy, earlier had failed to get retired Republican General Augusto Ribeiro de Carvalho to promise to head a new government.[25] In effect, Cabeçadas proposed his own candidacy. Either on 28 May or 29 May Cabeçadas, along with Commander Ochoa, was arrested by police at Santarém. Apparently Cabeçadas was on his way to Braga to join Gomes da Costa; because he was detained by the government near Lisbon, he was available as a potential leader who could be immediately useful to

President Machado. The Braga-based movement rapidly won coun-
trywide support from military units; by the evening of 29 May the
government's cause was collapsing.

Despite arrests of suspected conspirators, severe censorship of the
Lisbon press on 29 May, orders for reinforcements from provincial garrisons, and the dispatch of columns of reputedly loyal armed sailors
from Lisbon to oppose the army in the north, the military movement
spread rapidly.[26] The government's final bulwark, the GNR, refused to
oppose the rebels in the provinces. Late in the evening of 29 May, the
Silva government resigned. President Machado, disconsolate, was
preparing to resign himself.

The situation remained not only "obscure," as the American
minister in Lisbon telegraphed Washington,[27] but dangerous. To some
observers a civil war appeared possible. Would the Lisbon garrison oppose Gomes da Costa's march from the north? Would civilians be
armed, as in previous pronunciamentos, and sent to fight? Persuaded
not to resign by Lieutenant Colonel António Ribeiro de Carvalho,
former minister of war, Machado named Commander Cabeçadas as
premier, a move which caught the Braga committee by surprise.[28]
Later, angry Integralists accused Machado of trying to sabotage their
reform plans by handing power to Cabeçadas, a man caught in the toils
of political-party interests.[29] Machado's surrender of power to
Cabeçadas convinced Colonel Fernando Freiria, commander of the Sixteenth Infantry Regiment at Santarém to cease his planned resistance to
the army movement.[30] Machado's last official act reflected his concern
for constitutional legality, for avoiding a civil war, and for preventing
the restoration of the monarchy.[31] Cabeçadas was known as an honest
historic Republican officer who would oppose the restoration of the
monarchy; he had helped to prepare the conspiracy in the Lisbon fleet
and in the Algarve, where his uncle, an army colonel, aided the movement. To Machado, appointing Cabeçadas appeared to be the only way
to keep the transition between a parliamentary republic and a successor
government both constitutional and Republican.

After a period of disillusionment and hesitation,[32] during which a
priest in Braga helped to arm the vacillating leader with the necessary
timely resolve,[33] Gomes da Costa moved on Oporto on 30 May and
then by train proceeded south toward Lisbon. By 4 June over six thousand troops of the northern garrisons, with headquarters at Sacavém,
formed an armed ring around Lisbon. On 1 June, Cabeçadas, as
premier (Machado resigned the same day), formed a triumvirate with
Gomes da Costa as minister of war, colonies, and agriculture, and

Ochoa as minister of foreign affairs.[34] Gradually the "Integralist inner core," using Gomes da Costa as its front man, began to maneuver around Cabeçadas, and to place officers in key government positions. Control of the War Ministry by Gomes da Costa and by rightist officers on his staff was decisive.

On 17 June Commander Cabeçadas was ousted from power by Gomes da Costa and the Integralist officers around him. Republican stalwarts later suggested that Cabeçadas failed because he was apathetic and timid;[35] Gomes da Costa's triumph, however, cannot be explained solely by a personalist thesis, a tendency of many amateur Republican historians. Cabeçadas fell from power mainly because the Military Dictatorship was controlled by the commanders of the army forces surrounding Lisbon. Cabeçadas was a naval officer whose status was at best tenuous with army leaders. He was unwilling to shed blood in order to remain in power, and Gomes da Costa, as minister of war, had the support of the army in and near Lisbon. Despite a last-minute offer of aid from liberal General Ernesto Sá Cardoso,[36] Cabeçadas bowed out without resistance.

Gomes da Costa was in nominal control of the Military Dictatorship from 17 June until 9 July, when he was ousted by an internal coup d'etat organized by the commanders of the Lisbon garrison, the Lisbon GNR, and the Sacavém camp. Although Gomes da Costa had been crucial to ensure success in the initial phase of the movement and had met certain Integralist demands, he was not the leader that the Eighteenth of April group required to preside over the political counter-revolution. He was thought to be ill and perhaps was suffering from amnesia. He remained impetuous and mercurial, and he lacked any desire or competence to institute a complete Integralist program. Moreover, despite Gomes da Costa's earlier identification in 1918 with the New Republic and Egas Moniz's Centrist party, by 1926 he had moved Left in the parliamentary party spectrum to the Radical party and was now known to be close to Radical party leadership. He advocated an early restoration of parliamentary freedom, a position which the rightist officers found unacceptable.[37] When his plans for a cabinet shuffle, in which General Óscar Carmona was to be dropped from the Foreign Ministry, were revealed, the Eighteenth of April group demanded his resignation. At first he refused to leave Belém Palace and won the support of one Lisbon army unit.[38] He soon capitulated, however, and was sent into exile in the Azores, where he later was awarded the consolation prize of the army's highest rank and honor, marshal of the army. On 9 July, General Carmona was named premier and minister of war and the conservative phase of the Military Dictatorship began. Sinel de Cordes, a powerful conservative leader behind the scenes, was appointed minister of finance.[39]

The Twenty-eighth of May:
Counterrevolution within an Army Pronunciamento

How had the Integralist officer group, inspired and led by an inner core of Eighteenth of April officers, "palmed" the pronunciamento? First, the group was able to use General Gomes da Costa as a respectable cover, then as the eliminator of Cabeçadas, and finally as a scapegoat. Second, the leading officers of the northern garrisons, probably acting on earlier experience with Lisbon's political dominance in coup strategies, decided to isolate Lisbon and then to undermine potential army resistance in that area. The ring of armed troop camps around Lisbon remained in place until mid-July. Just as crucial, beginning in early June in Lisbon regiments, the leadership carefully replaced officers of doubtful loyalty to their revolutionary program with young Integralist officers, some from Coimbra's army regiments, who were influenced by the teachings of conservative professors such as António de Oliveira Salazar.[40] These officers, perhaps two or three hundred in strength, helped assure the success of the counterrevolution within the military movement; they participated in regimental votes for leadership and made suggestions for nominations to cabinet posts. Even before 9 July, when Gomes da Costa was deposed, the Integralist influence could be seen in the decrees establishing military press censorship and the dismissal of certain Democrats.[41]

Despite early fears of a monarchist attempt to restore King Manuel to power, the success of the movement in overthrowing the Silva government met overwhelming approval from the Lisbon political press. The opposition parties saw an opportunity to gain the political power they had so long been denied. Public approval was facilitated by the fact that the movement was bloodless; the only shot fired was that fired by a desperate young army lieutenant who committed suicide when he saw that the revolt was victorious.[42]

The race to win control of the revolution was not to the swift but to the stealthy. The parties attempted but failed to ride the coup into high office. They failed to do so not only because of the weaknesses of Cabeçadas and Gomes da Costa, but because of the outcry of many classes—including much of the syndicalist labor movement—against the politicians and parties, attitudes and actions of a substantial part of middle- and upper-class youth, and because of the predominance of an elite group of conservative and largely but not entirely Integralist officers over the *barriguista* majority of the officer corps.[43] From the political machine of the Democrats, control of the state passed to a selected group of the officer corps. By July virtually all civil-service and government posts in Lisbon and in much of the rest of the country were in the hands of the army command. At first many of these posts were filled by regimental junior officers.

The opposition party leaders, especially Cunha Leal and the Radical Martins Júnior had cried "army" perhaps once too often.[44] Their constant wooing of the army and the incitement to assume power had boomeranged on them and on the parliamentary republic. It was not only that "disorder" in the last years of the republic had helped to kill what democracy remained, as the liberal intellectuals of *Seara Nova* claimed.[45] A growing proportion of the public, especially after the sweeping Democratic victory in the 1925 elections, became convinced that there was no longer any legal way to break the electoral machine of the Silva government. Of about twenty-two political party newspapers in Lisbon in 1926, only one openly defended the Democrats against almost universal abuse. Even the traditional mouthpiece of the Democrats, *O Mundo,* now a Democratic Left paper, referred to the Silva cabinet as "nine criminals" in a "dictatorship" and urged its readers to use "violence" in order to "save the republic."[46]

Probably a majority of persons concerned with politics desired both a change of government and a reform of politics. But there was little agreement on the means to bring about such changes. Public opinion concerning a military government was probably divided, but some believed that *initial* army control was a reasonable solution. The feuding opposition Republican parties wanted the army to act only as a temporary caretaker, and they would not support a military dictatorship. By the time the nature of the leadership and the program of the conservative Military Dictatorship became apparent, when it was clear that the Twenty-eighth of May movement had in fact prepared the way for a political counterrevolution by conservatives who had "robbed the revolution," it was too late to do more than begin more conspiracies. The army controlled the state. If the opposition parties had known beforehand that the conservatives would take the high ground by means of the coup, the Twenty-eighth of May would not have been a bloodless golpe de estado.

The familiar cycle of conspiracy and counterconspiracy would soon be renewed. This cycle, which appeared to be as true to Portuguese politics as is the law of thermodynamics to physics, was, of course, nothing new. An acute observer who withdrew in dejection from politics after the fall of the New Republic had earlier summed up that fatal political formula: "Nevertheless, the Portuguese political problem cannot have a revolutionary [i.e. armed coup] solution. Intolerance always follows a revolution and the spirit of counterrevolution is immediately born."[47]

Only in Integralist and New State literature and propaganda would the Twenty-eighth of May become a true national revolution, cosmetically spruced up for later public consumption. The army was by no means "the only legitimate representative of national opinion."[48] The small group of officers who won control exploited the growing unpopularity of the Democrats and used the thirst for power by the opposition parties. Finally, they overwhelmed two Republican officers who had promised the restoration of civil liberties. Conservative officers placed high on their list of reforms the transformation of the army, a change they considered impossible without the expulsion of the PRP from power. Yet in order to do this, the army used the moral and material aid of opposition political parties and interest groups. There was an interesting irony to the position of the army after the successful coup: in order to rid the state of politicians and to work out desired reforms, the officer corps was obliged to enter politics in a way and on a scale unknown before, even in the 1917–18 New Republic.

When the order came on 31 May to close down the Congress by force, few protested or realized that the army was going to run the country for an indefinite period. Nor could they know that the congressional doors at São Bento would not be opened again for nearly nine years, and then only under very different circumstances. In the afternoon of 31 May, before soldiers locked the big doors of the hall, a few deputies filed out. There was no quorum. At 3:20 P.M. several deputies cried out, "Long live the republic!"[49] Those words signalled the last parliamentary business of the First Republic.

14 / Aftermath: From Military Dictatorship to New State

1926–33

> It is easy to begin a dictatorship, but it is always difficult to end it.
>
> Attributed to General Miguel Primo de Rivera[1]

Portugal's First Republic was a prologue to an enduring dictatorship which, at the time of its collapse in 1974, was Western Europe's longest surviving authoritarian regime. Established by an earlier generation of officers, the Dictatorship was overthrown by officers who were also mobilized to rebel by professional grievances and by the ravages of a distant, controversial war. Despite differences in style and ideology, the "Young Lieutenants" of 1926 were the historical antecedents of the "Captains" of 1974. The professional military was again crucial to the change of regimes, the move from one political age to another.

The Dictatorship established in 1926 reached maturity in the 1930s and 1940s and entered various stages of degeneration in the 1950s, 1960s, and early 1970s. Despite its origins, however, the Dictatorship was not a military regime. Except for the initial phase of 1926–28 when the military administered the state, civilians, many of them academics, formulated policies. Like other groups, the military came to be subordinated to a centralized statism run by a restricted circle of civilians.

There is space here for only a brief summary of the major features of the Dictatorship. Historians usually divide this regime's history into two eras: the Military Dictatorship (1926–33) and the New State (1933–74), although this division is more schematic than real. The earlier era will be of chief concern here and it, in turn, may be divided into three phases: the regime of the Young Lieutenants, 1926–28; the rise of Salazar and civilian authoritarianism, 1928–30 and, the birth of the New State, 1930–33.

246

The Regime of the Young Lieutenants, May 1926—April 1928

> They make 'em or break 'em quick over here. You don't get four years' trial like you-all do over home, and then we have to put up with the regardless. A Premier never unpacks his grip over here. He just engages his room by the day. Portugal, the week I was in Madrid, had three Revolutions and 4 changes of Government in one day, and they haven't got daylight saving either, or else they could have squeezed in another Revolution.
>
> Will Rogers[2]

Dominated by a group of rightist professional army officers, the early years of the Military Dictatorship were troubled by many of the same problems which had undermined the First Republic: financial and economic weaknesses, public violence, unrest in the military, political conspiracy, and factionalistm. Try as they might, the soldiers could not on their own create a new and stable system. The regime censored the press, closed down the Congress (no legislative body met again until January 1935), and jailed and deported politicians. As conspiracies continued in cafés, universities, streets, offices, and barracks, the initially good reputation of the Dictatorship began to deteriorate. Groups attempted to bring down the victorious Eighteenth of April group of officers and their allies, and the familiar cycle of coup attempts began again. Between mid-1926 and mid-1931 there were no fewer than a dozen planned insurrections; of these, eight reached the streets and resulted in violence. Yet the fragmented Left and Center were unable to break the army officers' hold on the state. As golpismo continued until late 1931, the regime carried out purges in the civil and military bureaucracies. Labor unrest continued in the towns, and in the tropical African colonies transported political exiles plotted. All of the pronunciamentos of 1927-31, nevertheless, failed.

The regime of the Young Lieutenants was discredited by proved incompetence, factionalism, and corruption among those who replaced the Republicans. For all its initially daring appeal, "barracks' parliamentarism"[3] provided no solution to Republican failures. Nor did the temporary dominance of a conservative set of officers redeem the honor of the army. Officers showed that they were as capable of unrestrained adventurism, personalism, and empregomania as were Republicans before them. Some of the more extreme officer elements, such as Integralist-Fascist "crazies" like the bizarre Lieutenant Morais Sarmento,[4] or the hapless Nationalist Filomeno da Câmara,[5] muddled into comic-opera incidents. Officers, too, once in power became involved in jobbery, their own militarist version of devorismo.

By the spring of 1928 it was clear that if the military remained the sole masters of the administration much longer, dishonor might permanently infect their collective reputation. The military lacked the expertise and the political unity required to work a counterrevolution, what later came to be known in New State propaganda as the National Revolution.

The failure of Finance Minister Sinel de Cordes to solve the nation's financial problems prompted General Carmona to seek the services of a civilian expert. On 27 April 1928 he named Coimbra Professor António de Oliveira Salazar minister of finances, a most auspicious appointment. Backed by the military command, President Carmona, and some of his former students, who were new officers in key garrisons, Salazar proceeded to balance the 1929–30 budget and to restore his version of order in economic affairs.[6] In accepting this crucial position in a country on the verge of bankruptcy, Salazar stated publicly: "I know very well what I want and where I am going." He added quietly that his financial surgery would require a term in office longer than a "few months."[7]

Salazar and Civilian Authoritarianism, April 1928—July 1930

In Salazar the "dictatorship without a dictator,"[8] found a disciplined civilian expert who worked himself into the position of dictator. From the Ministry of Finances, where he was given control of all expenditure and revenues, the professorial Salazar soon dominated all cabinets. In 1930 he was made minister of colonies, briefly, and in 1932, replacing the last military premier under Carmona, Salazar was made premier, an office he held until he was disabled by a stroke in 1968. Despite his inflated reputation as a long-awaited fiscal Sebastian, Salazar was unpopular among groups of younger rightist officers, and in his reforms he confronted jostling sets of interest groups, each with its own recipe for reform. Salazar had his own conservative doctrine and he imposed it in part upon the regime; yet until 1930 the Dictatorship had no definite structure and was committed to no clear doctrine. By mid-1930, however, the bases of a highly centralized, statist regime began to take shape.

A gradual civilianization of the administration occurred. University professors and their students replaced professional officers in important posts, and the soldiers began to return to their barracks. In the major security positions, the Ministry of Interior, which controlled the increasingly important police, and the Ministry of War, civilians began to replace the officers. In 1931 a civilian was named minister of interior, and in 1934, for the first time since before World War I in Portugal, a civilian was appointed by Salazar to be minister of war. Civilianization also proceeded in the civil service, foreign service, and in appointments at the district and municipal levels.

Fundamentals in structures and ideology were also established. The policies of the new academic-based officials were influenced by various doctrines of monarchism, Catholicism, and integralism. Would a republic be retained, or a monarchy restored? Although Salazar himself was a crypto-monarchist,[9] he did not favor the restoration of the monarchy. This sensitive issue became less important with the premature death of the exiled Manuel in 1932 and the government's ostentatious State funeral for the ex-king in Lisbon. With no obvious candidate for a restored throne and with the monarchists badly split and discredited, the Dictatorship preferred maintaining the Republican façade.

A colonial crisis in Angola in 1930 provided the occasion for the regime's commitment to a strongly centralized, nationalist colonial policy and a reversal of Republican policy. Salazar temporarily assumed the Ministry of Colonies and drafted the important Colonial Act. In an extraordinary gesture, the regime quickly accepted this act as law and published it in July 1930.[10] Adopted verbatim as a section of the 1933 Constitution, the Colonial Act suggested just how much importance—both for economic and spiritual reasons—the regime gave to colonialism and the colonies. By this act, the regime of the high commissioners was abolished, and Lisbon assumed a tightly managed new control over the colonies. The Colonial Act was an essential part of the regime's superstructure. It derived from the elite's fears of foreign economic dominance in Angola and Mozambique and from disappointing results of the Republican policies of colonial autonomy and development.[11]

On 30 July 1930, the National Union was established. It was a "movement" of regime loyalists which was intended to replace a political-party system and to attract both monarchists and Republicans. Not a real party but an officially sponsored claque of situacionistas, the National Union was intended to muffle partisan strife and support the regime. All political parties and secret societies were eventually banned. Although some opposition groups were allowed to campaign—under heavy restrictions—in elections beginning in the 1940s, the National Union remained the only legal political group.

The Birth of the New State, July 1930—April 1933

During 1930, the Dictatorship acquired a new name: people were beginning to call it the "New State," a euphemistic title which bore some relationship to the title of Sidónio Pais's regime. The ruling group, what one diplomat described as "a constitutional oligarchy,"[12] put increasingly large resources into its image, its propaganda, and police activity. Concerned with the appearances of legality, the New State built an elaborate constitutional structure on paper. In a speech as early as 1929, Salazar had called for a new constitution as the basis for a "new political order." He urged the adoption of a strongly nationalist policy which would be founded upon the "active elements" of Portuguese society: "family, moral and economic corporations, the parish, and the municipality."[13] The constitution which finally emerged, however, was a compromise among factions. A first draft was drawn up by a group of Coimbra professors and was then discussed by a national board of experts, the Conselho Político Nacional, selected in February 1932. On 28 May 1932, the sixth anniversary of Gomes da Costa's coup, a final draft of the constitution was published in the daily press in order to encourage public commentary and discussion. After a rigged national plebiscite in March 1933, the constitution was formally installed as law on 11 April 1933.

According to this document, Portugal was a "unitary, corporative, republic." It featured a bicephalic executive structure, a president, and a premier, which reflected elements of the 1826 Monarchist Charter, the 1911 Constitution, with its 1919 revision, and the 1919 Weimar Constitution. The president of the republic, as was the case under Sidónio Pais in 1918, was elected by universal suffrage,* not by the legislature, but the term of office was lengthened to seven years. While the military were not mentioned in the articles on the presidency, it became customary that only professional military officers became presidential candidates. The premier, or president of the Council, was to be named freely by the elected president, and the premier was not responsible to the legislature. In this structure, the president possessed virtually the same powers as did the king and during the Constitutional Monarchy after 1834. But with civilians managing the state, the president reigned while the premier actually ruled. The executive held the power of the purse and initiated all important legislation.

Contrary to the claim of one historian that General Carmona in 1928-29 had "ceased to play any major role in politics,"[14] the

---

* Under Sidónio Pais women were not allowed to vote, but in 1931 the Dictatorship instituted a very restricted suffrage for women, for the first time.

diminutive general remained into the 1930s and 1940s the essential high
military patron, a kind of secular monarch, the army's executive
representative and main arbiter among military factions. On several occasions in the early years of Salazar's premiership, when militant
rightist officers demanded Salazar's dismissal, Carmona protected his
premier and insisted on his retention.[15] Carmona played an essential
role in easing the difficult transition from the uncertainty of a failed
military rule to the certainty of civilian authoritarianism with a military
façade.

With the strengthening of the secret political police, known as PIDE
after 1945,[16] the New State's structure was almost complete. Although
corporatism became fashionable in the 1930s, it remained virtually a
sham operation until the 1950s, when the regime attempted to revive it.
Except for a few Fascist institutions, which were set up in 1936 in the
heat of the passion for German and Italian Fascist models (namely, the
Portuguese Youth and the Portuguese Legion), the regime which
emerged from the Constitution of 1933 was not so much Fascist or
Clerico-Fascist,[17] as it was absolutist statist. There was no dominant
ideology. Rather, there was an amalgam of conflicting factions and
their ideas on the Right: presidentialists, monarchists, Integralists, syndicalists, Catholics, and nationalists. Of the interest groups and classes
which supported the regime, one can discern sections of the middle
classes, what remained of the upper class, the Church, the military,
business and industry, and large landowners. Not one of these, however, got a free hand in the regime, nor were all or even many of their
demands fulfilled. The peasant masses, as before, remained largely indifferent to politics.

The New State imposed order by means of censorship, police terror,
and more subtle devices,[18] and gained some internal support and international credit for balancing the budget, reducing the debt, and
building up some economic prosperity in the towns. But the Dictatorship, for all its unprecedented centralized power, was unable to
eliminate the four classic political tensions. Nor was it able to seal up
totally the springs of opposition or to suppress memories of the positive
aspects of the Republican experience. Unlike the First Republic, the
New State had the time, the economic good fortune, and some of the
means to "build a modern people," to integrate the nation into the
state, and to reduce injustice. The regime survived for half a century
but failed to evolve a system which would allow the majority of Portuguese to participate meaningfully in answering the question: What
kind of government does Portugal need?

The human price for New State "order" was heavy. During the early years of the Dictatorship, 1926–31, the death toll from political disturbances was at least 400 with possibly 1,250 wounded. Thousands were arrested; many were deported to the Atlantic islands or to Africa. Many more chose voluntary exile in Europe, Brazil, or the United States. Portuguese law continued to forbid capital punishment except in time of war,[19] but this too was a sweet façade. In the jails lives were broken in various other ways by ruined health, poor medical treatment, suicides, and unexplained deaths which the government never allowed to be investigated properly.

This brief essay on what one 1930s *oposicionista* called the "Mystery Train,"[20] the New State, suggests that the origins of this regime were less mysterious than its long journey and its enigmatic collapse.

15 / Conclusions

No, violence resolves nothing. . . . The duty of the
statesman is to be far-sighted, to seek a formula for a just
way of life. . . . There is no one who detests more than
we do the serious defects of Parliamentarism in its southern form. . . . We desire a very profound reform of all
the parliamentary system, and a severe law for the work
of the Chamber; we want a remodeling of the economic
system; we want order, like the Patriot-fascist: but not
obtained artificially by the machine gun and by the police
(an unreal group which generates hatreds, which in turn
generate tomorrow's disorders), but only by means of the
unquestionable prestige of tolerance and of justice.

António Sérgio[1]

The First Portuguese Republic (1910–26) was Portugal's first sustained
attempt to establish and keep a parliamentary democracy. For all the
Republicans' generous intentions, ideals, and initial energy and enthusiasm, they failed to create a stable, fully progressive, and enduring
system. This regime was handicapped by frequent public violence,
political instability, lack of administrative continuity, and impotence.
With forty-five governments during fifteen years and eight months, the
First Republic was Western Europe's most unstable parliamentary
regime. In "the bullring of the republic," personal and ideological passions clashed, rent the fabric of both society and polity, and released
forces which set the stage for the military to establish a dictatorship. As
Portugal went from a constitutional monarchy to a democratic republic
to a military-backed dictatorship, a great deal happened, but the nation's historic problems remained.

It is not surprising that many judgments on the First Republic have
been harsh. New State writers claimed that the republic tried to do too
much, too fast, and that it was determined to destroy the foundations
of traditional Portugal. The more extreme rightist critics have suggested
that the republic was nothing more than a Masonic conspiracy, thereby
emphasizing the "Nightmare Republic" interpretation. When asked
why the First Republic failed, ex-premier Marcello Caetano answered:
"The failure of the First Republic was due, in my opinion, to the

253

religious policy initially adopted; and to the parliamentary institutions which facilitated the pulverization of the parties and the instability and weakness of the governments.''[2]

Leftist writers have accused the republic of being too weak, too slow in making reforms, and timid in carrying out its ideals. Some suggested that the republic failed because its policies were directed toward the middle class and clashed with the just demands of the working classes.[3]

During the Republican era British observers were very critical of the regime. Writer Aubrey Bell believed that Portugal's major political problem was that the Republicans were obsessed with "the imagination of evil,"[4] and that needless conflict resulted. British diplomats generally welcomed the Dictatorship and remained critical of the parliamentary regime. Patronizingly, they believed that attempting to maintain a democracy in Portugal was futile. In early 1925 the British minister in Lisbon wrote that the Portuguese parliamentary system was already dead and that such a regime was "so unsuited in many ways to the Latin nations."[5]

The criticisms of the nondemocratic Right and some democrats coincide in their emphasis upon the view that, given the political structures and conditions, the collapse of the First Republic was inevitable. Like Dr. Caetano, Dr. Oliveira Marques has stressed structural connections between the Constitutional Monarchy and the First Republic: He writes that the republic was "not the beginning of something structurally new but was rather the last phase of something which had started much before, in 1820. The Republic meant the climax of a process, the natural result of the evolution of monarchical liberalism. . . . Thus it had no future. It must die and be replaced by something totally different. That something was Fascism."[6]

Agreeing with some of the views of the Traditionalist school of Portuguese historiography, a number of writers have concluded from their study of the First Republic that the Portuguese people are not capable of establishing or maintaining a democracy. To explain why, writers have emphasized national character or temperament. The Modernists, including Oliveira Marques's school of historians, have stressed the difficult contemporary conditions and inadequate structures.

My conclusion, based upon the materials in this study, is that none of these explanations is sufficient to explain the failure of the First Republic. The burden of a complex inheritance from the past—structural as well as behavioral legacies—played a vital part in the frenzied years of 1910–26. Equally important, if not more so, were the attitudes and actions of both the friends and enemies of the First

Republic. The development of the immobilized system, the standstill polity, was due as much to political behavior as to structures, as much to friends as to enemies. Despite similarities, the First Republic was not simply a last, repetitive phase of "monarchical liberalism."

In three respects, the First Republic was a new phenomenon in Portuguese politics and government. First, in the area of civic freedoms and in political mobilization the republic attempted to do what no previous regime had tried. Intending to "build a modern people," to bring Portugal into the circle of Western European nations by creating a more open, self-sufficient society and a more representative system of government, Republican leaders espoused ideals that matched those of leaders in other parliamentary regimes. Second, Republican leaders attempted to put into practice their ideals of social justice and democratization. Especially during the years 1910–11 and 1923–25, when key PRP leaders and a few others shared a desire to bring profound reform to a poor country with great social and economic inequities, such reformist attempts were initiated in education, tax policies, fiscal order, social welfare, agrarian reform, public works, and army reforms. Finally, the First Republic released and indeed provoked an explosion of energies which, though they led to unprecedented conflicts and tensions, also produced an unexampled mobilization of society, which was part of a general process of modernization and change. Hundreds of thousands of Portuguese were uprooted in various ways for political, economic, social, and military purposes. Several waves of dislocations occurred: Provoked by disillusionment with the republic in 1910–15, massive emigration took place to Brazil and North America. Strikes rocked the country, especially during 1910–17 and 1919–21. Owing to Portugal's foreign and colonial policies, what was up to then the largest military mobilization in Portugal's history caused thousands of soldiers to be shipped to Africa, 1914–18, or to Flanders, 1916–18. Other forms of mass mobilization, on a scale unheard-of before in the country, included civilian and military insurrections; civilian mobilization in the Carbonária, the PRP, and in various other associations and civic groups on the Left and Right; the growth of Catholic and monarchist youth groups after 1917; and the launching of various elite study-action groups who were determined to find the recipe for national salvation.

In my view, the First Republic, despite some structural connections with nineteenth-century liberalism, was a complex, singular phenomenon which attempted, despite its failures, to put into practice its ideals and which like no regime before it, was forced to pay the

costs, both human and nonhuman. The republic's failure was expressed
in the form of a long-drawn-out political crisis, an interrupted civil war,
a latent state of siege, in which one party, the Democrats, usually held
an unassailable monopoly of power in Congress and civil administration. The overthrow of this standstill polity by an organization of
rightist army officers was made possible by a conjunction of factors:
the officer corps' sense of a historic role in politics, the rise of temporary rightist unity in reaction to threats of leftist Republican social
and economic reforms in 1923–25, the fragmentation of the Left and
general discrediting of the political-party system, and a decisive aban-
donment of the republic by the middle classes.

The First Republic was hobbled by a number of problems. Apart
from unusually severe economic and financial problems, of which a
large public debt inherited from the monarchy and from new military
expenses, and inflation and currency depreciation were the most prominent, the political behavior of politicians and parties and the nature and
role of the military were crucial to the failure of the regime.

The Portuguese Republican party was effective in mobilizing support
in elections and dominated all but one general election (June 1921). The
PRP regained mastery of the civil administration and entrenched itself
in the military and civil bureaucracy. The party had some leaders of
talent and integrity, including Afonso Costa, who dominated the party
up to his self-exile in Paris. After 1919, the party became increasingly
disunited, conservative, and immobile. Some of the younger leaders
who succeeded the burnt-out generation of 1910 were men of skill and
honesty, and they courageously attempted to execute long-overdue
reforms despite an awareness of the political dangers of initiating such
changes. The conservative PRP rump, however, led by António Maria
da Silva, remained too cautious to attempt such an effort. With a
courageous, united leadership and a disciplined rank and file the PRP
might have been able to lay the bases for necessary reforms in order to
bring credit to the political-party system and to discredit the extremists
on the Left and Right. But the PRP in 1926, or what remained of it,
lacked both ingredients which might have made possible an attempt to
metamorphose the standstill polity, discredit the extremists, and prevent
a military takeover. The PRP conquered the lion's share of the administration but lost public support. Despite the fact that the last
minister of finance in the First Republic offered a basically sound
financial program, his party had exhausted its political credit. By the
Twenty-eighth of May the PRP was fragmented, isolated, and abandoned. If not anti-Republican or monarchist, elite youth were indifferent to the regime and were mobilized now to join rightist groups.

If the PRP learned that power corrupted, the opposition found that powerlessness also corrupted. The opposition failed to build durable, alternative parties to the PRP. In part to blame were the traditional tensions that beset the country. Personalism and factionalism paralyzed the PRP. The opposition was dispersed among groups which reflected divergent landowning patterns, north and south of the Tagus, and was embroiled in the historic conflicts between urban and rural areas. The Republican leaders attempted but failed to balance power between the capital and the provinces and to solve the problem of land reform.

Voting restrictions and PRP manipulation during elections insured that the opposition would view elections as a sham, a source of grievance, not opportunity. Factionalized and increasingly disloyal to the regime, the opposition parties conspired more than they participated. Some of them, especially but not exclusively parties on the Right, encouraged military intervention to oust the PRP. Armed insurrection became a substitute for seeking changes of government by constitutional means.

The role of the military in politics became more important. The republic had severe authority and security problems. Public violence without precedent occurred in civic life. The costs were high in human life, property, energy, and time. Apart from the wartime casualties, at least three thousand and possibly as many as four to five thousand Portuguese died as a result of civil strife during the First Republic, and thousands more were wounded. The cost in property damage has never been accurately estimated. Thousands of persons, monarchist and Republican, were arrested and jailed. Several thousand, too, were deported to the African colonies and the Atlantic islands. Another cost of this penal mobilization, usually hidden in the political accounting, was the loss of skills from the metropole. Yet another loss caused by the withdrawal of trust among the wealthier classes was a large flight of capital. Portugal's financial loss profited foreign banks and businesses.

With such security problems, the republic required a loyal armed force. Though larger and better armed than under the monarchy, the security forces became politicized, mutinous, and, at times, brutal. Mutual distrust between political leaders and the military, union activities among various civilian groups, and political instability sorely tested the loyalty of the military. Despite the large portion of public monies devoted to the armed forces by 1926, civil authorities failed to establish a secure and stable relationship with the professional soldiers. By the end of the First Republic, virtually all parties, Left to Right, had encouraged military insurrection to further their partisan causes. Military discontent was exacerbated by the Republican army reforms and by World War I. A revival among the officer corps of a traditional belief that the armed forces were "the guardian and bulwark of national independence, conqueror and guardian of public freedoms," emerged in full force once the parliamentary system was considered to be hopelessly discredited. The Democrats' control of the state was replaced by that of a conservative but energetic section of the army officer corps.

Structural problems there were. Despite its propensity to topple governments and to obstruct legislation, on key issues the two-house Congress was usually dominated by the executive. Even with increasingly longer legislative sessions, important legislation was introduced by executive decree while Congress was adjourned. Like the Congress, the judiciary was rarely independent and during crises was manipulated by the executive.

The office of president of the republic, the chief of state, had little effective power until the 1919 constitutional revision. The public urged that the president be given greater power, but the power of dissolution was no panacea. Still, the political nation now looked to the authority and formalized prestige of the office of president to find a high guide out of the political maze.

In explaining the causes of the conflicts which afflicted the First Republic, recurring patterns of political behavior are just as essential as general conditions and structures. This study has attached particular significance to two tensions: personalism and factionalism. Idealism, hard work, and rational planning were mixed with opportunism, passions, and a strong tendency of some leaders to temporize. Despite Bell's belief that "the imagination of evil" was based largely on myth, it is more accurate to state that the spirit of conspiracy abounded, that there was ample, real evidence of plots from the Left and Right, and that moderates with good reason feared the extremists who reached for power.

Different individuals and groups held different conceptions of what a republic was or could be. There were conflicting views of the proper role of various institutions. Within the middle class there were widely differing opinions on the nature of the republic and on ideas for reform. The difficulties for the Republican regime were increased when individuals in politics were guilty of "lack of self-control and individual self-restraint," in the phrases of a member of the Seara Nova group.[7] As early as 1921 a writer in the same group claimed that political behavior was a factor, when he criticized leaders who bowed easily to pressures and who abstained or resigned because of an excessive "fear of ridicule."[8]

Analysis of the problems of the First Republic, suggests that many of the most important issues during the early years could have been accommodated within parliamentarism, since they were discussed at length and were the subject of partial compromises by 1926. After the defeat of the Monarchy of the North in 1919, the monarchist issue, for all the sound and fury surrounding it, was much less significant. The Republican regime initiated an accommodation with the monarchists, legalized them as a party in Congress in 1921, and passed a number of amnesties. The regime had begun an accommodation with the Catholic church. In 1923 the president of the republic publicly invested a new Papal Nuncio with the symbols of office. Various parties, the press, and Congress discussed aspects of restoring some pre-1910 rights and privileges to Catholics, especially in worship and education. By 1926, the religious issue was less troublesome; the Nationalists proposed that Catholic instruction be restored in private education.

Other issues were being discussed by 1926 and an elite consensus was more possible than ten years earlier. By 1926, some moderate and liberal Republicans, including members of the Seara Nova group, were willing to discuss the creation of a representative body or chamber in which economic interest groups and occupations would be represented. There was a discussion of the problem of authority, and some suggested increasing the power of the president and decreasing the power of the Congress to obstruct legislation.

Within the Republican regime there were heated discussions of how to reduce political instability. Some advanced suggestions which António Sérgio aptly referred to as mere "mechanical solutions."[9] There were such popular nostrums as: mass literacy campaigns, giving the president power to dissolve Congress, reinstating the death penalty in peacetime, depoliticizing the civil service, liability laws for cabinet officers and others.

The First Republic left behind a frustrated and ambiguous legacy of plans, proposals, small beginnings but little lasting accomplishment. In some respects, the Republicans could be proud of their work and their vision. In primary and in higher education, significant reforms were carried out. In welfare, in tax policy, where the principle of a personal, progressive, income tax was introduced, in wage policies, and in working conditions, the republic made significant initial efforts. Some Republican leaders nursed a vision of a just society in which a poor country like Portugal could work to "build a modern people" and to reduce social and economic inequality. Admiring what they knew of the more noble aspects of British democracy and France's Third Republic, Portuguese Republicans wished to bring their country into a changing

European community. They wanted to hold a free discussion of questions such as: What kind of government does Portugal want? What kind of army for a democracy? Who are the "exploiters" and the "exploited"?

When historians judge the significance of the First Republic, they must work within the perspective of what followed. For the Dictatorship not only attempted to rewrite the history of the republic to suit its myths and prejudices, but it sought to adopt various Republican policies, claim credit for them, and then adapt them to later conditions. Some credit must be given Republican planners for later programs of education, public works, road-building, and naval reconstruction (based on the work of Pereira da Silva). An important increase in the taxation of business and industry, an acceptance of the principle of a personal, progressive—if mild—income tax after World War II, deficit financing of public projects, opening up the colonies to foreign investment in the 1960s, the *indigenato* system, and economic autonomy for Angola and Mozambique also had their origins in Republican policies.

Historians should perhaps beware of drawing lessons from this complex Republican experience. "Which lessons and for whom?" one might well ask in response. It seems reasonable, however, to suggest that at least two general principles have been learned. First, reform and modernization cannot be easily achieved in a system which channels so much energy into obstructing change or into activities which perpetuate conflict and instability. Unless participation is open, sustained, and supported by key institutions, such a regime cannot accomplish much. When conspiracy replaces participation, a regime cannot remain democratic for long.

Second, as Portuguese observers pointed out at the time, democracy is a delicate flower, especially among a suggestible elite. Political freedoms are indivisible, and intolerance and the use of force are double-edged phenomena. Those who learned their political methods in pre-1910 student agitation at Coimbra University too seldom valued the concept of tolerance for the rights of others. Nor did the historical heroes of most antagonists symbolize tolerance and compromise. Jacobin Democrats adopted the autocratic Pombal as their cherished symbol. Not a few monarchists, Catholics, and Integralists fancied strong men on horseback like the medieval warrior-monk Nun' Alvares Pereira, the colonial African hero Mousinho de Albuquerque, or admired Fascists like Mussolini. Republican radicals could hardly expect fair treatment from the monarchists after the abuses practiced by the Provisional Government in 1910–11. In all fairness, conservatives who took power by force against the Democrats in 1917–18 could not complain of the pernicious role of force in politics. For all the reforms suggested by the Democratic Left party, or by the anarcho-syndicalists during 1925–26, they could not complain of the use of force while their newspapers applauded the military's ousting of their PRP enemies. After 1926 New State situacionistas, whose regime was based on a system of police terror, could not have been surprised that surviving liberal Republicans, old Democrats, or even the working-class leftists— the political orphans of the post-1926 age as were monarchists before them—plotted and used force to attempt to regain lost freedoms.

After the overthrow of the New State, when the Second Republic initiated a provisional government, the first premier, Dr. Adelino Palma Carlos, attempted to draw his own lessons from what he experienced during the First Republic. As he stated upon taking office on 15 May 1974:

Those who have never known freedom will perhaps find difficulty in understanding, except after the experience on the brink of which we are poised, that it demands from all a self-discipline to prevent our freedom from encroaching on others' [freedom]. The men of my generation, who knew liberty, then lost it and only now have fully recovered it, do not need to learn this lesson; but, just as we pass on the torch of our faith and shall not let it go out, so we also hope that this basic concept will be understood and that each individual will wait in patience and discipline for the achievement of his ambitions. . . . The new world we all desire cannot be built on hatred.[10]

As this study has suggested, the first Republican experience began as an idea, and, despite the disappearance of tangible aspects, the failures, and the crushed hopes, "the republic" remained as an idea in the minds and hearts of more than one generation. One of the republic's most astute supporters and critics wrote in 1925, that the republic for him was: "an Idea, a fact of Conscience, a moral affirmation, an aspiration of the Spirit."[11]

The first Republicans were anxious to earn the respect of civilized Europe. Moderate Republicans, who deplored the "popular terror,"[12] of the young republic, desired a just society and a humane, responsive government of which most citizens could be rightfully proud. These ideals did not die out with the Dictatorship. Some leaders lived to see a better day. As for the people, they survived both the kingdom of the pronunciamento and the silent dominion of the police state. Raúl Brandão observed that "the great inert mass adapts itself to all regimes."[13]

Against the intransigents of the far Left or the far Right, who had no use for a true democracy, and against the misguided partisans, who mistook insurrection for revolution, Portuguese moderates perhaps had little chance to maintain a regime of liberty. Later wisdom advised that the experiment's timing was bad.

But History rarely allows revolutionaries the freedom to choose their moments of power. Like the doers, the dreamers must take their opportunities when they appear. So it was in 1910 and so it was again in 1974. It was the tragedy of the first Republicans that their opportunity coincided with World War I, renewed alarm over the African colonies, the worst financial and economic crisis the country had seen, and the awakening of aspirations of various classes which the republic could not constructively satisfy or reconcile.

A wealthier nation with a more substantial democratic past might have failed in such a perilous enterprise. Portugal was Western Europe's smallest, poorest, and least-educated nation. That the Republican effort was made, and its ideals advanced, was probably more remarkable than the failure of the First Republic. Like other historic movements of national revival in 1640, 1820, 1890, 1926, and 1974, the First Republic was yet another time when even political enemies nursed a concern for ressurgimento. The ultimate meaning of this republic may long generate controversy, but its central place in modern history is secure.

Reference Matter

Appendix A
Premiers (Presidents of Ministry), 1910–33

1	Teófilo Braga	5 Oct. 1910—3 Sept. 1911
2	João Chagas	3 Sept. 1911—12 Nov. 1911
3	Augusto de Vasconcelos	12 Nov. 1911—16 June 1912
4	Duarte Leite	16 June 1912—9 Jan. 1913
5	Afonso Costa	9 June 1913—9 Feb. 1914
6	Bernardino Machado	9 Feb. 1914—23 June 1914
7	Bernardino Machado	23 June 1914—12 Dec. 1914
8	Vitor Hugo de Azevedo Coutinho	12 Dec. 1914—25 Jan. 1915
9	Joaquim Pimenta de Castro	25 Jan. 1915—14 May 1915
	Junta Revolucionária	14 May 1915—15 May 1915
	João Chagas (never took office)	15 May 1915—17 May 1915
10	José de Castro	17 May 1915—18 June 1915
11	José de Castro	18 June 1915—29 Nov. 1915
12	Afonso Costa	29 Nov. 1915—15 March 1916
13	António José de Almeida	15 March 1916—25 April 1917
14	Afonso Costa	25 Apr. 1917—8 Dec. 1917
	Junta Revolucionária	8 Dec. 1917—11 Dec. 1917
15	Sidónio Pais	11 Dec. 1917—14 Dec. 1918
16	João do Canto e Castro	14 Dec. 1918—23 Dec. 1918
17	João Tamagnini Barbosa	23 Dec. 1918—7 Jan. 1919
18	João Tamagnini Barbosa	7 Jan. 1919—27 Jan. 1919
19	José Relvas	27 Jan. 1919—30 Mar. 1919
20	Domingos Pereira	30 Mar. 1919—29 June 1919
21	Alfredo Sá Cardoso	29 June 1919—15 Jan. 1920
	Francisco Fernandes Costa (never took office)	15-16 Jan. 1920
	Alfredo Sá Cardoso (restored to office)	16-21 Jan. 1920
22	Domingos Pereira	21 Jan. 1920—8 Mar. 1920
23	António Maria Baptista	8 Mar. 1920—6 June 1920
24	José Ramos Preto	6 June 1920—26 June 1920
25	António Maria da Silva	26 June 1920—19 Aug. 1920
26	António Granjo	19 Aug. 1920—20 Nov. 1920
27	Álvaro de Castro	20 Nov. 1920—29 Nov. 1920
28	Liberato Pinto	29 Nov. 1920—2 Mar. 1921
29	Bernardino Machado	2 Mar. 1921—23 May 1921
30	Tomé de Barros Queiros	23 May 1921—30 Aug. 1921
31	António Granjo	30 Aug. 1921—19 Oct. 1921
32	Manuel Maria Coelho	19 Oct. 1921—5 Nov. 1921

33	Carlos Maia Pinto	5 Nov. 1921—16 Dec. 1921
34	Francisco Cunha Leal	16 Dec. 1921—6 Feb. 1922
35	António Maria da Silva	6 Feb. 1922—30 Nov. 1922
36	António Maria da Silva	30 Nov. 1922—7 Dec. 1922
37	António Maria da Silva	7 Dec. 1922—15 Nov. 1923
38	António Ginestral Machado	15 Nov. 1923—18 Dec. 1923
39	Álvaro de Castro	18 Dec. 1923—6 July 1924
40	Alfredo Rodrigues Gaspar	6 July 1924—22 Nov. 1924
41	José Domingues dos Santos	22 Nov. 1924—15 Feb. 1925
42	Vitorino Guimarães	15 Feb. 1925—1 July 1925
43	António Maria da Silva	1 July 1925—1 Aug. 1925
44	Domingos Pereira	1 Aug. 1925—17 Dec. 1925
45	António Maria da Silva	17 Dec. 1925—30 May 1926

Military Dictatorship, 1926-32

1	José Mendes Cabeçadas Júnior	30 May—17 June 1926
2	Manuel de Oliveira Gomes da Costa	17 June—9 July 1926
3	Antonio Óscar de Fragoso Carmona	9 July 1926—18 Apr. 1928
4	José Vicente de Freitas	18 Apr.—10 Nov. 1928
5	José Vicente de Freitas	10 Nov. 1928—8 July 1929
6	Artur Ivens Ferraz	8 July 1929—21 Jan. 1930
7	Domingos da Costa Oliveira	21 Jan. 1930—5 July 1932
8	António de Oliveira Salazar[a]	5 July 1932—

Sources: *OG,* pp. 17-71; A. H. de Oliveira Marques, *A Primeira República Portuguesa* (Lisbon, 1972), pp. 185-87.

[a] Premier Salazar served as chief of government from 5 July 1932 until officially relieved of his duties (he did not resign) because of physical incapacity on 27 Sept. 1968. Officially in this 36-year period, despite numerous cabinet changes, he presided over only three cabinets (designated as the 54th, 55th, and 56th of the republic): those of 5 July 1932—11 Apr. 1933, 11 Apr. 1933—18 Jan. 1936, and 18 Jan. 1936—27 Sept. 1968 (*OG,* pp. 71-78).

Appendix B
Presidents of the Republic (Chiefs of State), 1910–33

1	Teófilo Braga (also president of Provisional Government)	5 Oct. 1910—24 Aug. 1911
2	Manuel de Arriaga	24 Aug. 1911—29 May 1915
3	Teófilo Braga	29 May 1915—5 Oct. 1915
4	Bernardino Machado	5 Oct. 1915—11 Dec. 1917
5	Sidónio Pais (officially elected president, however, only after 9 May 1918)	
	João do Canto e Castro (acting president)	14–16 Dec. 1918
6	João do Canto e Castro	16 Dec. 1918—5 Oct. 1919
7	António José de Almeida	5 Oct. 1919—5 Oct. 1923
8	Manuel Teixeira Gomes	5 Oct. 1923—11 Nov. 1925
9	Bernardino Machado	11 Nov. 1925—31 May 1926
10	António Óscar de Fragoso Carmona (acting president)[a]	26 Nov. 1926—18 Apr. 1928
11	António Óscar de Fragoso Carmona	18 Apr. 1928—

Sources: *OG*, pp. 17-71; A. H. de Oliveira Marques, *A Primeira República Portuguesa* (Lisbon, 1972), 185-87.

[a] General Óscar Carmona was acting president beginning 26 Nov. 1926, while also remaining prime minister until his election 18 Apr. 1928 as president and the appointment of a new prime minister, Vicente de Freitas. In effect, there was no president until the decree of 26 Nov. 1926, naming Carmona the replacement of Machado, the republic's last president. In the interim, 9 July-26 Nov., there was only a prime minister, Carmona.

Appendix C
Selected List of Political Organizations

Acção Republicana (Republican Action party), 1923–26. Small group of liberal Republicans, a splinter from the PRN, led by Álvaro de Castro.

Acção Realista Portuguesa (Portuguese Royalist Action), 1923–? Conservative monarchist coalition which included Legitimists, Integralists, and apparently some Manuelist monarchists. Ca. 1924 founded a youth wing, Juventude Monárquica Conservador.

Causa Monárquica (Monarchist [Manuelist] Cause), 1914–? Major monarchist organization, mainly concerned with restoration of ex-king Manuel II (1908–10); until 1920, included Integralists. Elected deputies to Congress 1918, 1921, 1922, and 1925.

Centro Académico da Democracia Cristã (CADC) (Academic Center for Christian Democracy), 1912–? Elite intellectual group of Catholics. Won seats to Congress, in 1915, 1918, 1919, 1921, 1922, and 1925. New State Premier Salazar was member of group, which was strong in central and north Portugal.

Confederação Geral do Trabalho (CGT) (General Confederation of Labor), 1919–27? Succeeding UON in 1919, major federation of unions, with strong anarcho-syndicalist tendencies.

Cruzada Nacional D. Nun' Alvares Pereira (National Crusade of Nun' Alvares Pereira), 1918–35? Influential study-action organization of elite members of various political beliefs, successor to Liga de Ação Nacional. Emphasis on nonpartisan reform.

Federação Nacional Republicana (FNR) (National Republican Federation), 1921–26? Independent Republicans, originally led by Adm. António Machado Santo and including nucleus of old Reformist party, 1911–21.

Integralismo Lusitano (Portuguese Integralists), 1914–? Amalgam of rightists, including monarchists, Catholics, Nationalists (Nationalist party, 1901–10). Part of its ideology adopted by the Dictatorship, 1926–74.

Liga de Acção Nacional (League for National Action), 1915–18. Elite study-action group concerned with nonpartisan reforms and regeneration.

Partido Centrista (PC) (Centrist party), 1917–19. Small group of moderate intellectuals led by Dr. Egas Moniz. Advocates of revision of 1911 Constitution to include presidential power of dissolution of Congress. Supported Sidónio Pais regime, 1917–18.

Partido Comunista Português (PCP) (Portuguese Communist party), 1921–. Despite official government banning and repression during 1927–36, the PCP survived abortive insurrections including that of Jan. 1934.

Partido Legitimista (Legitimist party, Miguelist), origins in nineteenth cen-
tury-? Fought for restoration of Miguelist line of kings. In 1920 when Integralists bolted Causa Monárquica, they adhered to the Legitimists, who
were conservative, authoritarian, traditionalist.

Partido Nacional Republicano (PNR) (National Republican party, Sidonists),
1918. Official party of Sidónio Pais's presidentialist regime; consisted of
conservative Republicans; won Apr. 1918 elections (140 out of 228 seats in
Congress).

Partido Português Popular (PPP) (Popular Portuguese party), 1919–22. Group
of Republican deputies from old Evolutionist party who in 1919 refused to
be fused into new Liberal party; led by Júlio Martins, it consisted of little
more than seven deputies in Congress and it collapsed when all but one of
its number were not reelected in 1922.

Partido Presidencialista (PP) (Presidentialists), 1919?–21? Led by former
premier under Sidónio Pais, Tamagnini Barbosa, Republican grouping
which advocated strong executive. Never won seat in election.

Partido Radical (PR) (Radicals), 1922–27? First led by Júlio Martins of the
PPP, later by entrepreneur Martins Júnior, it was a small group which
never won a seat in Congress. Fomented a military insurrection which failed
in early 1926; hoped to profit from 28 May coup.

Partido Radical Republicano Outobrista (PRRO) (Octobrists, Octobrist
Radical Republicans), 1921–22. Led by Col. Manuel Maria Coelho, briefly
premier in late 1921. Party discredited by public reaction to political
murders 19 Oct. 1921.

Partido Reformista (PR) (Reformists), 1911–21? Small moderate group under
independent Machado Santos; unable to win one seat in Congress.

Partido Regionalista (Regionalist party), 1921–? Small, ephemeral organization
of politicians, based in part on idea of regional autonomy for Beira
districts; won two seats in Chamber of Deputies in July 1921.

Partido Republicano Esquerdista Democrático (PRED) (Democratic Left),
1925–27? Leftists under PRP deputy and ex-premier José Domingues dos
Santos. Splinter of leftist PRP members who bolted PRP in 1925 and won
seven seats in Nov. 1925. Popular, slang term for PRED members, the left
wing of PRP, was *canhotos* ("lefties" or "devils") as opposed to majority
PRP members, the *bonzos* ("Buddhist priests"), i.e., hypocrites,
charlatans.

Partido Republicano Evolucionista (PRE) (Evolutionists), 1912–19. Republican
moderates led by A. J. Almeida, formerly PRP member; more liberal than
Unionists. In fall 1919 merged with Unionists, and Centrists to form PRL
(Liberals).

Partido Republicano Liberal (PRL) (Liberals), 1919–23. Coalition of Evolutionists, Unionists, Centrists, independents, and Presidentialists who
hoped to form an effective second main party to oppose the PRP. In June
1921 managed to win over PRP in elections.

Partido Republicano Nacionalista (PRN) (Nationalists), 1923–35. Successor to
Liberals as main opposition party to PRP. Coalition of moderate-

conservative Republicans, increasingly conservative towards end of First Republic; made bid to gain Catholic adherents by concessions in program.

Partido Republicano Português (PRP) (Portuguese Republican party; Democratic party; Democrats), 1871–1935? Only political party during First Republic with claims to be large, mass organization. Largest membership of all parties, with an electoral machine in urban and rural areas. Fragmented after 1926–27, as major leaders went into exile; splinters of exiled group in Paris, Madrid, and elsewhere, never managed to recover its original organization.

Partido Republicano Reconstituente Nacional (PRRN) (Reconstituents), 1920–23. Led by PRP member Álvaro de Castro, who bolted Democrats in 1920.

Partido Socialista (PS) (Portuguese Socialist party), 1875–1927? Reorganized after World War I. Won Congressional seats in general elections of 1911, 1915, 1919, and 1925. Zenith of Congressional influence, 1919–21.

Seara Nova (Intellectual monthly journal and name of group of liberal intellectuals, also called Seareiros, lit.: "New Harvest"), 1921–. Reformist-study-action group which advocated nonpartisan reforms and regeneration of polity and society. Led by essayist-educator António Sérgio.

União dos Interesses Económicos (UIE) (Union of Economic Interests), 1925–? Association of conservative bankers, managers, and businessmen from main towns and cities, based in Lisbon. UIE put up candidates in Nov. 1925 general election and won four seats in Chamber of Deputies. Interest group as well as political party which supported coup of 28 May 1926.

União Liberal Republicana (ULR) (Liberal Unionists, Lealistas), 1926–30? Led by Nationalist deputy and former premier Francisco Cunha Leal, splinter group bolted PRN over issues of PRN leadership and party corruption. Like most political groups had its own newspaper which gave views of its leader, Cunha Leal. Supported 1926 coup.

União Nacional (UN) (National Union), 1930–69. Officially sanctioned loyalists of New State Dictatorship. Coalition of conservatives from Republican and monarchist groups willing to collaborate with New State. Replaced in 1969–70 by Salazar's successor, Premier Caetano, who re-named organization Acção Nacional Popular (ANP).

União Nacional Republicana (UNR) (National Republican Union), 1911–12. Formed in Nov. 1911 by Republican moderates who opposed the radicals, the UNR split into two parties of Republican moderates in 1912, the Evolutionists under Almeida and the Unionists under Manuel Brito Camacho. Camacho's Unionists (UR) formed the remainder of the UNR after Almeida's members split.

União Operária Nacional (UON) (National Workers' Union), 1914–19. Until 1919 largest federation of unions, chiefly syndicalist.

União Republicana (UR) (Unionists), 1911–19. Led by Brito Camacho, party of conservative Republicans with members in armed forces, bureaucracy, and intelligentsia. Some regional roots in Camacho's home district, Alentejo. Splinter from original PRP in 1911.

Notes

Abbreviations Used in Notes

AHM   Arquivo Histórico Militar, Lisbon, Museu Militar. Official archives of the army staff.

BAMNE   Arquivo e Biblioteca do Ministério dos Negócios Estrangeiros, Lisbon, Necessidades Palace. Official archives of the Foreign Ministry.

BHP   *História de Portugal,* ed. Damião Peres, Barcelos Edição Monumental, 7 vols. and Suplemento (Barcelos, 1935–54).

DANC   *Diário da Assembleia Nacional Constituente* (Lisbon, 1911). Record of Constituent Assembly, 1911.

DCD   *Diário da Câmara dos Deputados* (Lisbon, 1911–26). Record of Chamber of Deputies, 1911–26.

DHP   *Dicionário De História De Portugal,* ed. Joel Serrão, 4 vols. (Lisbon, 1963–71).

DS   *Diário do Senado* (Lisbon, 1911–26). Record of Senate, 1911–26.

ELBC   *Enciclopédia Luso-Brasileira da Cultura,* 18 vols. (Lisbon, 1963–).

GEPB   *Grande Enciclopédia Portuguesa e Brasileira,* 40 vols. (Lisbon and Rio de Janeiro, 1924–60).

NA   U.S. National Archives, Washington, D.C. Record Group 853, "Records of Department of State Relating to Internal Affairs of Portugal, 1910–1929"; Record Group 866, "Records of Department of State Relating to Internal Affairs in Portugal, 1906–1910."

OG   *Orgânica Governamental, Sua Evolução, E Elencos Ministeriais Constituidos Desde 5 De Outubro De 1910 A 31 De Março De 1972* (Lisbon, 1972). List of all names of personnel in all cabinets, 1910–72.

PRO   Great Britain, Public Record Office, London. Foreign Office records (F.O. 179, F.O. 371, and F.O. 425), including diplomatic and consular reports on Portugal and Portuguese Africa, 1906–38.

Chapter 1: An Introduction to Modern Portuguese History

1   António Quadros, "Portugalinho?" *Expresso* (Lisbon), 29 October 1976, p. 8. A noted writer and literary critic, Quadros refers to his country as "little Portugal."

2   A. H. de Oliveira Marques, *History of Portugal,* 2 vols. (New York, 1972), 1:1–4. This historian generally follows the interpretations of

geographer Orlando Ribeiro, *Portugal, o Mediterrâneo e o Atlántico,* 2d ed. (Lisbon, 1963).

3   See James Duffy, *Portugal in Africa* (Cambridge, Mass., 1962).

4   Oliveira Marques, *History of Portugal,* 1:322.

5   British Broadcasting Corporation, *600 Years of Anglo-Portuguese Alliance, with a Foreword by Sir Alec Douglas-Home* (London, 1973).

6   Joel Serrão, "Decadência," *DHP,* 1:786-88.

7   Cited in António Sérgio, *Ensaios* (in *Obras Completas*), 3 vols. (Lisbon, 1972), 2:74.

8   See J. P. Oliveira Martins, *Brazil e as Colónias Portuguesas* (Lisbon, 1880).

9   Artur Ribeiro Lopes, *A Convenção secreta* (Lisbon, 1933), p. 47.

10 J. P. Oliveira Martins, *Política e Economia Nacional* (Oporto, 1885), p. 103.

11 Teles's theory is discussed in Sérgio's essay "As Duas Políticas Nacionais," *Ensaios,* 2:74-76.

12 Ibid., pp. 79-91. See also chap. 3 of his *Breve Interpretação da História de Portugal* (Lisbon, 1972), pp. 95-107. This work appeared first in a Spanish edition in 1929, while Sérgio was in exile, having opposed the Military Dictatorship.

13 See V. Magalhães Godinho, "Portugal and Her Empire, 1550-1668," in *The New Cambridge Modern History,* vol. 5, *The Ascendancy of France, 1648-1668* (Cambridge, 1961), pp. 384/497.

14 C. R. Boxer, *Four Centuries of Portuguese Expansion, 1415-1825: A Succinct Survey* (Johannesburg, 1961) and *The Portuguese Seaborne Empire, 1415-1825* (London, 1969).

15 Oliveira Marques, *History of Portugal,* 1:266.

16 Gilberto Freyre, *The Masters and the Slaves,* 2d Eng. lang. ed., rev. (New York, 1966), pp. 245-47.

17 Miguel Torga, *Portugal* (Coimbra, 1957), pp. 57, 111-17. "Miguel Torga" is the *nom de plume* of Dr. Adolfo Coelho da Rocha.

18 Examples of "scare" literature published toward the end of the First Republic include: Anselmo Vieira, *A crise nacional* (Lisbon, 1926); David Magno, *A Situação Portuguesa* (Oporto, 1926); J. C. de Vasconcelos, *O Movimento Nacional do 18 de Abril* (Oporto, 1925).

19 See João Ameal, *História de Portugal* (Oporto, 1942). For a clear summary of the major ideas of Sardinha, see Hermínio Martins, "Portugal," in S. J. Woolf, ed., *European Fascism* (London and New York, 1969), pp. 302-36.

20 See Jacinto Cândido da Silva, *A Doutrina Nacionalista* (Oporto, 1909), pp. 62-63, 77.

21 See Jesús Pabón, *La Revolución Portuguesa,* 2 vols. (Madrid, 1941-45), which was translated into Portuguese as *A Revolução Portuguesa,* trans. Manuel Emídio and Ricardo Tavares (Lisbon, 1961). Pabón's work received the Camões Prize in Portugal in 1941.

22 See the study of Portuguese history since 1820 by Caetano Beirão, a Traditionalist and Legitimist thinker, in Manuel Ferrandis and Caetano Beirão, *História Contemporánea de España Y Portugal* (Barcelona, 1966), pp. 627-828.

23 Fidelino de Figueiredo, *O pensamento político do Exército* (Lisbon, 1926), p. 48.

24 António de Oliveira Salazar, *Discursos E Notas Políticas,* 5th ed., rev., 6 vols. (Coimbra, 1961), 6:237-67. This was published as "Principles and Realities of Portuguese Policies," in *International Affairs* 39, no. 2 (April 1963):169-83.

25 Salazar, *Discursos,* 6:246-47.

26 Sérgio, "A Educação Cívica, a Liberdade E O Patriotismo . . . ," *Ensaios,* 1:201-24.

27 Sérgio, ed., *Antologia dos Economistas Portugueses, Século XVII: Obras em Português* (Lisbon, 1924), pp. vi-vii, as cited and translated in Richard J. Hammond, *Portugal and Africa, 1815-1910* (Stanford, 1966), pp. 6-7.

28 Torga, *Portugal,* p. 57; see also Raúl Proença, *Páginas de política* (in *Obra política de Raúl Proença*), 2 vols. (Lisbon, 1972), 1:11-19 ff.

29 See Carlos Ferrão, *História da República* (Lisbon, 1959), *Em Defesa da República* (Lisbon, 1963), *Em Defesa de Verdade* (Lisbon, 1961), *A Obra da República* (Lisbon, 1965).

30 Oliveira Marques, *History of Portugal,* 2:162-64. See Marcello Caetano's summary of Portuguese constitutional history, *História Breve das Constituições Portuguesas,* 3d ed. (Lisbon, 1971).

31 Personal interviews with liberal Republicans in Lisbon, Oct. 1972-Apr. 1973 confirmed that this was a common explanation of political instability during the First Republic.

32 See Joel Serrão, *Do Sebastianismo ao Socialismo em Portugal* (Lisbon, 1973).

33 Oliveira Marques's first book on the First Republic was attacked in a series of review articles which appeared first in the rightist Lisbon daily *A Época,* May-July 1972; these articles were published together in a booklet under the name Fernando Jasmins Pereira, *A Primeira República: Comentários ao livro de Oliveira Marques* (Braga, 1972).

34 A leftist attack on Oliveira Marques's work on the republic came from those who viewed the history of the republic as little more than a class struggle between a reactionary middle class and the oppressed working classes. See Jofre Amaral Nogueira, *A República de Ontem Nos Livros De Hoje* (Coimbra, 1972), published originally as long review articles in the journal *Vértice* (Aug.-Nov. 1972).

35 J. B. Trend, *Portugal* (New York, 1957); H. V. Livermore, *A New History of Portugal* (Cambridge, 1966), pp. 328-31; Charles Nowell, *A History of Portugal* (Garden City, N.J., 1952), and *Portugal* (Englewood Cliffs, N.J., 1973).

36   Sarah Bradford, *Portugal* (London, 1973), p. 76.
37   See Gilberto Freyre, *The Portuguese in the Tropics* (Lisbon, 1961).
38   Richard Herr, *Spain* (Englewood Cliffs, N.J., 1971), pp. 262-63, 282-83.
39   Ibid., p. 283.
40   *Personalismo* is defined as "egoism" in *Dicionário Prático Ilustrado* (Oporto, 1961 ed.), p. 944.
41   For a discussion of early Sebastianism, see Mary Elizabeth Brooks, *A King for Portugal* (Madison, Wis., 1964).
42   Douglas L. Wheeler and René Pélissier, *Angola* (New York and London, 1971), pp. 16-19.
43   As cited in Herr, *Spain,* p. 270.
44   Torga, *Portugal,* p. 115. See Glossary for a definition of *Terreiro do Paço.*

Chapter 2: A Monarchy without Monarchists

1   Raúl Brandão, entry for Aug. 1917, *Memórias* (in *Obras Completas*), 3 vols. (Lisbon, 1969), 2:360-61.
2   Almeida Garrett, *Portugal na Balança da Europa* (Lisbon, 1830), p. 328. For various aspects of the impact on Portugal of the French campaigns during 1807-11, see Albert Silbert, *Do Portugal de Antigo Regime ao Portugal Oitocentista* (Lisbon, 1972), pp. 51-83.
3   Silbert, *Do Portugal de Antigo Regime,* pp. 78-83; see also Fernando Piteira Santos, *Geografia E Economia Da Revolução De 1820* (Lisbon, 1962), pp. 27-103.
4   Silbert, *Do Portugal de Antigo Regime,* pp. 80-81.
5   A. H. de Oliveira Marques, *History of Portugal,* 2 vols. (New York, 1972), 2:55-58; J. P. Oliveira Martins, *Portugal Contemporâneo,* 4th ed., 2 vols. (Lisbon, 1906), 1:56-68.
6   Oliveira Marques, *History of Portugal,* 2:60.
7   *BHP,* 7:243-44.
8   "Amélia," *ELBC,* 1:1678-79; Rocha Martins, *D. Carlos: História Do Seu Reinado* (Lisbon, 1926).
9   Eça de Queiroz, *The Maias,* trans. P. M. Pinheiro and Ann Stevens (London, 1965), pp. 149-50.
10   Marcello Caetano, *História Breve das Constituições Portuguesas,* 3d ed. (Lisbon, 1971), p. 35.
11   Ibid., pp. 27-92; see also Artur Ribeiro Lopes, *Histoire de la République Portugaise* (Paris, 1939), pp. 21-66.
12   On attitudes and interests of the Portuguese upper middle-class oligarchy in the nineteenth century, see Victor de Sá, *A Crise do Liberalismo e as Primeiras Manifestações das Ideias Socialistas em Portugal (1820-1852)* (Lisbon, 1969). See also Joel Serrão, *Temas Oitocentistas-II: Para a história de Portugal no século passado* (Lisbon, 1962), pp. 275-86.
13   Caetano, *História Breve,* pp. 79-92.

14 The first true party program appeared in Portugal only in 1843. Jorge
    Borges de Macedo, "O aparecimento em Portugal do conceito de pro-
    grama política," *Revista portuguesa de História* (Coimbra), 13
    (1971):396-423. Even the major Regenerador party as late as 1910 did
    not have a published program, and in 1908 when one compendium listed
    programs, the only way to discern the Regenerador program was to
    follow the 1826 Charter and its later revisions. For the text of the 1826
    Charter, see J. F. Trindade Coelho, *Manuel Político Do Cidadão Por-
    tuguez,* 2d rev. ed. (Oporto, 1908), pp. 635-36.

15 Jacques Godechot, ed., *Les Constitutions de La France Depuis 1789*
    (Paris, 1970), pp. 217-24.

16 A. H. de Oliveira Marques, "Portugal," *Ocidente* (Lisbon), 76 (June
    1969):268.

17 *DANC,* 12 July 1911, p. 14. For the texts of various Portuguese constitu-
    tions, 1822-1908, see Trindade Coelho, *Manuel Político,* p. 193.

18 See Douglas L. Wheeler, "The Portuguese Revolution of 1910," *Journal
    of Modern History* 44, no. 2 (June 1972):172-77.

19 Caetano, *História Breve,* pp. 65-89.

20 Trindade Coelho, *Manual Político,* pp. 635-41.

21 Herbert Feis, *Europe, The World's Banker 1870-1914* (New Haven,
    1930), pp. 242-46; PRO, F.O. 425/288, confidential, "Portugal, Annual
    Report, 1906," pp. 4-5.

22 Oliveira Martins, *Portugal Contemporâneo,* 2:429. "This little Turkey of
    the West," was another term the historian applied.

23 Eça de Queiroz, *The Maias,* p. 147.

24 João Medina, "O Pessimismo Nacional De Eça De Queiros (Estudo
    sobre "Os Maias"), *Seara Nova,* no. 1514 (Dec. 1971), pp. 22-30;
    reprinted in João Medina, *Eça Político* (Lisbon, 1974), pp. 49-71.

25 Miguel de Unamuno, *Por Tierras de Portugal y de Espana* (Madrid,
    1911), pp. 122-23.

26 Helder Macedo, guest ed. for Portugal, *Modern Poetry in Translation,*
    no. 13/14, Daniel Weissbort (London, 1972), pp. 3-9; Rocha Martins, *D.
    Carlos,* pp. 414-18.

27 Eça de Queiroz, *The Illustrious House of Ramires,* trans. Ann Stevens
    (London, 1968).

28 Amadeu Cunha, *Mousinho e A Sua Obra* (Lisbon, 1944), p. 24; J. P.
    Oliveira Martins, *Brazil e as Colónias Portuguesas* (Lisbon, 1880), pp.
    429 ff.

29 Armando Castro, *A Economia Portuguesa Do Século XX 1900-1925*
    (Lisbon, 1973), pp. 208-31; Miriam Halpern Pereira, *Livre Câmbio e
    Desenvolvimento Económico, Portugal na segunda metade do século XIX*
    (Lisbon, 1971), pp. 296-315.

30 For the sense of "national failure," see Jacinto Baptista, *O Cinco de
    Outubro* (Lisbon, 1965), pp. 124-32; Ramalho Ortigão, *Últimas Far-
    pas (1911-1914),* 2d ed. (Lisbon, 1946), pp. 226-27.

31 D. G. Nogueira Soares, *Considerações Sobre O Presente E O Futuro Político De Portugal* (Lisbon, 1883).

32 Eça de Queiroz, *The Maias*.

33 Ibid., pp. 149–50.

34 Nogueira Soares, *Considerações*, pp. 285–91. Duarte Gustavo Nogueira Soares (1831–1901) was a graduate in law from Coimbra who entered the civil service in 1852. Spending most of his career in the Ministry of Foreign Affairs, he rose to head the staff at the ministry in 1883 and was later named as Portuguese minister to Brazil and Switzerland.

35 Ibid., pp. 530–87.

36 Ibid., pp. 450–51.

37 Ibid., pp. 530–88.

38 Ibid., p. 588.

39 Medina, *Eça Político*, pp. 113–58.

40 "Um Perfil e Uma Obra: Rafael Bordalo Pinheiro," *Vida Mundial*, no. 1519 (19 July 1968), pp. 39–45. Pinheiro lived from 1846 to 1905.

41 Eça de Queiroz, *O Primo Basílio* (Oporto, 1878).

42 Medina, *Eça Político*, pp. 11–31. The pejorative use of such political words as *político* and *politicantes* became common in the 1880s (see Nogueira Soares, *Considerações*, p. 96).

43 "Como El-Rei D. Carlos Via O Oficial Da Armada: Páginas Do Seu Diário Íntimo (1901)," *Anais Do Clube Militar Naval* 13, nos. 1–3 (Jan.–Mar. 1973):19–24. A copy of this document, written in the hand of King Carlos, was on display in the Navy Museum, Lisbon (Museu da Marinha). Published citation courtesy of Commdr. Avelino Teixeira da Mota.

44 The famous phrase "a monarchy without monarchists" was attributed to King Carlos in a statement he made about 1900. Cited in Baptista, *O Cinco de Outubro*, p. 183.

Chapter 3: Republicanization

1 Joel Serrão, "Revolta De 31 De Janeiro De 1891," *DHP*, 2:575.

2 D. G. Nogueira Soares, *Considerações Sobre O Presente E O Futuro Político De Portugal* (Lisbon, 1883), pp. 367–85.

3 Joel Serrão, *Temas Oitocentistas-II: Para a história de Portugal no século passado* (Lisbon, 1962), pp. 252–53.

4 Two top Republican leaders with peasant backgrounds were Dr. Eusebio Leão (named civil governor of Lisbon in 1910), and Augusto M. Alves da Veiga, named minister to Brussels in 1910 (see *GEPB*, 14:789–90, and 2:22). On rich landowners José Relvas and Bernardino Machado, see *GEPB*, 25:540 and 15:755–56.

5 On Bombarda see *GEPB*, 4:871–72; on Chagas, see *GEPB*, 21:750; and see Rocha Martins, *D. Carlos: História Do Seu Reinado* (Lisbon, 1926), pp. 274–82.

6   See the biographical materials on Machado in his son's book, António
    Machado, *Bernardino Machado: Memórias* (Oporto, 1945).

7   Victor de Sá, *Perspectivas Do Século XIX* (Lisbon, 1964), p. 285; see
    also Sá's doctoral dissertation, published as *A Crise Do Liberalismo E As
    Primeiras Manifestações Das Ideias Socialistas Em Portugal
    (1820-1852)* (Lisbon, 1969), pp. 13–37, 305–74.

8   Joel Serrão, *Antologia Do Pensamento Político Português*, vol. 1,
    Liberalismo, Socialismo, Republicanismo (Oporto, 1970), pp. 38–52,
    327–44.

9   Ibid., pp. 38–49.

10 Arthur Ribeiro Lopes, *Histoire de la République Portugaise* (Paris, 1939),
    pp. 119–21.

11 Aspects of Portuguese republicanism, particularly as it influenced the
    lower class in the towns, appears to have had a personal impact on
    individuals that might be compared to that of the influence of Spanish
    anarchism in the 1930s, which George Orwell suggested was a kind of
    substitute for religion (see his *Homage to Catalonia* [London, 1938]).

12 "Carbonária," *GEPB*, 5:868.

13 On the Carbonária, see "Artur Augusto Duarte de Luz de Almeida,"
    GEPB, 15:668–69; Luís de Montalvor, ed., *História do Regimen
    Republicano em Portugal*, 2 vols. (Lisbon, 1930–32), 2:213; Jesús Pabón,
    A Revolução Portuguesa, trans. Manuel Emídio and Ricardo Tavares
    (Lisbon, 1961), p. 47; Francis Gribble, *The Royal House of Portugal*
    (London, 1915; reprint ed., New York, 1970), pp. 307–8.

14 Jacinto Baptista, *O Cinco de Outubro* (Lisbon, 1965), pp. 217–21.

15 See Lisbon daily newspapers *O Século* and *Diário de Notícias,* 5–9 Oct.
    1910.

16 PRO, F.O. 425/288, confidential, "Portugal, Annual Report, 1906," p.
    17.

17 See Lopes de Oliveira, "A Obra da Propaganda Republicana," in
    História Do Regimen Republicano, 2 (part 2):9–256.

18 This generalization is based upon a study of the provincial press,
    1895-1910, in newspapers deposited in Lisbon's Biblioteca Nacional de
    Lisboa. Papers studied for their editorial opinions on politics included a
    variety from different regions: *Independente Regoense* (Regua, Upper
    Douro district); *O Campino* (Vila Franca de Xira); *O Algarve* (Por-
    timão); *O Commercio De Barcellos* (Barcelos); *O Districto de Leiria*
    (Leiria); and *Jornal de Cabeçeiras* (Cabeçeiras).

19 Francisco Cunha Leal, *As Minhas Memórias,* 3 vols. (Lisbon, 1966–68),
    1:185.

20 Serrão, *Antologia,* 1:46. The translation of Professor Serrão's perceptive
    term *o salto em frente* as "a leap forward" is mine.

21 F. Keil do Amaral, *Histórias A Margem De Um Século De História*
    (Lisbon, 1970), "Uma Mulher-A-Dias Republicana," pp. 203–9.

22 Eça de Queiroz, *The Maias,* trans. P. M. Pinheiro and Ann Stevens
    (London, 1965), pp. 90–91.

23 Considerable evidence suggests the validity of the term "Republican Sebastianism," especially during 1909-10. The messianic language of Republican futurism is seen in the writings of such Republican patriarchs as Teófilo Braga (see Serrão, *Antologia,* 1:45-46). Among the lower classes of Lisbon after the 1910 Revolution it was reported that the "republic" had been predicted in one of the new popularized texts circulated among the masses, a version of the old texts of the Sebastianists, *Trovas de Bandarra,* some originating in the sixteenth century. See "Sebastianismo," *GEPB,* 28:11.

24 Afonso Costa, speech in Cortes, 20 Nov. 1906, reprinted in A. H. de Oliveira Marques, ed., *Obras de Afonso Costa,* vol. 1, *Discursos Parlamentares 1900-1910* (Lisbon, 1973), p. 182.

25 Ibid., pp. 20-21.

26 Guerra Junqueira, *Horas De Combate,* ed. Mayer Garção (Oporto, 1924), pp. 39-40: "The tyranny of Sr. D. Carlos derives from the most obese of beasts: from the pig. . . ."

27 *Os Ridículos* (Lisbon), 3 Nov. 1909, p. 1, lead cartoon.

28 Ramalho Ortigão, *Últimas Farpas 1911-1914,* 2d ed. (Lisbon, 1946), p. 79, cited in Baptista, *O Cinco de Outubro,* p. 129.

29 For living conditions in Portugal, 1900-1910, see Baptista, *O Cinco de Outubro,* pp. 133-69; Flausino Torres, *As Origens Da República* (Lisbon, 1965), pp. 15-21; Leon Poinsard, *Portugal Ignorado* (Oporto, 1912); Maria Angela Montenegro, "O Movimento Operário Em Portugal Na Segunda Metade Do Século XIX" (Licenciatura diss., University of Lisbon, 1940), part 1. See A. H. de Oliveira Marques, *History of Portugal,* 2 vols. (New York, 1972), 2:19-20, on population growth in the cities.

30 Raúl Brandão, *Memórias* (in *Obras Completas*), 3 vols. (Lisbon, 1969), 1:168. Cited also in Baptista, *O Cinco de Outubro,* p. 133.

31 Joel Serrão, *Emigração Portuguesa* (Lisbon, 1971), pp. 151-52.

32 *BHP,* 7:430-47.

33 *O Século,* reflected the Portuguese response to the Ultimatum in the years 1890-1910. See also César Nogueira, *Notas Para a História Do Socialismo Em Portugal,* 2 vols. (Lisbon, 1966), 2:248-49, 280-94. Nogueira noted that much of the working class by 1910 was "republicanized," despite Socialist party efforts to instill more radical ideologies.

34 César Oliveira, "Do 31 De Janeiro," & *etc.* (Lisbon), 31 Jan. 1973, p. 14; see also Jorge D'Abreu, *A revolução portugueza: O 31 de janeiro (Porto, 1891)* (Lisbon, 1912).

35 Rocha Martins, *D. Carlos,* pp. 274-82.

36 For the 1895 Republican abortive plot to arouse army units to rebellion in Oporto, see Basílio Teles, *Memórias Políticas* (in *Obras de Basílio Teles*) (Lisbon, 1969), Preface by Augusto de Costa Dias, p. lxv.

37 Armando Ribeiro, *A Revolução Portugueza,* 3 vols. (Lisbon, n.d.), 2:94-95. For some political ideas of "Mousinho," see his sensational

book published upon his return from Mozambique: *Moçambique (1896-1898)* (Lisbon, 1899).

38 Hermínio Martins, "Portugal," in S. J. Woolf, ed., *European Fascism* (London and New York, 1969), pp. 302-5.

39 Serrão, *Antologia,* 1:325-26. See Mousinho de Albuquerque's famous letter of 1900 to his pupil, Crown Prince Luís Filipe, concerning colonialism and the monarchy, excerpted in José Carlos Amado, *História de Portugal,* 2 vols. (Lisbon, 1966), 2:62.

40 Marcello Caetano, *História Breve das Constituições Portuguesas,* 3d ed. (Lisbon, 1971), pp. 64-65; see the ideas of the Nationalist party in Jacinto Cândido da Silva's pamphlet *A Doutrina Nacionalista* (Oporto, 1909). For some similar ideas of the Miguelist (Legitimist) party, see their program as recorded in J. F. Trindade Coelho, *Manual Político Do Cidadão, Portuguez,* 2d rev. ed. (Oporto, 1908), pp. 651-56.

41 Caetano, *História Breve,* p. 77.

42 PRO, F.O. 425/350, "Portugal, Annual Report, 1910," confidential, pp. 1, 4, 10-11.

43 *O Século,* 6 Feb. 1908. The major Republican moderate daily newspaper, only five days after the regicide, published the text of a private letter from King Carlos to a French duchess, dated 15 Dec. 1907, in which Carlos cited Portuguese colonial "victories" in Africa as a factor aiding his work. In the letter, he revealed that he was "morally and almost physically exhausted" and that he longed for a vacation in France. His Brazilian trip was more important, since he hoped that political support from some two million Portuguese citizens in Brazil could help to save his throne. This interesting letter was first published on 3 Feb. 1908 in *Le Figaro* (Paris).

44 *O Século,* 1-11 Feb. 1908.

45 *O Século,* 11 Feb.-June 1908.

46 Poinsard's findings were first published in the periodical *La Science Sociale,* 2d ser., 25, fascicles 67, 68 (Mar.-Apr. 1910):3-230; a revised and augmented Portuguese edition, with notes on the 1910 Revolution, appeared in 1912 as *Portugal Ignorado.*

47 As the British minister in Lisbon wrote London in 1909: ". . . notwithstanding a liberal constitution, direct responsibility devolves in this country upon the Sovereign" (PRO, F.O. 179/493, "Portugal, Annual Report, 1909," p. 1.

48 Cited in Baptista, *O Cinco de Outubro,* p. 183.

49 Ibid., pp. 180-84; António Teixeira de Sousa, *Para a História da Revolução,* 2 vols. (Lisbon, 1912) 2:54-56.

50 *New York Times,* 6, 8 Oct. 1910; José Brissa, *La revolución portuguesa* (Barcelona, 1911), pp. 170-72, 264-66. The Republican representatives were José Relvas and Magalhães Lima. The British ambassador in Madrid told the American minister that England would not intervene to save the monarchy since "a monarchy cannot long be sustained if the people are determined to overthrow it" (Collier to Root, 24 Mar. 1908,

NA, Record Group 866/42, no. 512). Plans for King Manuel II to marry an English princess, daughter of the duke of Connaught, were delayed in the spring of 1910 as King Edward VII was horrified by the Portuguese regicide and refused to consent to such a match until there was strong evidence "of the permanency of the existing institutions" (American minister to secretary of state, 15 Mar. 1910, NA, Record Group 853.00/74). The planned marriage did not occur.

51 Minister Augusto de Vasconcelos to foreign minister, 16 Apr. 1911, enclosed in 11 Apr. 1911 report, BAMNE, Portuguese Legation in Madrid, 1910–13, Queen Amélia visited Premier Canalejas in spring 1910, in Madrid, probably in March (see BAMNE, Paris Legation, 1909–10, box 187, series A, clippings from French press in letter to Lisbon, 7 Apr. 1910). Canalejas in talking in 1911 with the Portuguese minister to Madrid also suggested that similar pleas came from Queen Amélia on the occasion of the 5 Oct. 1910 Revolution.

52 *O Século* and *Diário de Notícias,* 1 Aug.–1 Oct. 1910.

53 Alberto Xavier, *História Da Greve Académica De 1907* (Coimbra, 1962).

54 Baptista, *O Cinco de Outubro,* pp. 57–85.

55 António Maria da Silva, *O Meu Depoimento,* vol. 1, *Da Monarquia a 5 de Outubro de 1910* (Lisbon, 1974), pp. 223–303.

56 David Ferreira, "Partido Republicano Português," *DHP,* 3:602.

Chapter 4: The Fifth of October

1 In "Order of the Day No 1," Rotunda General Headquarters, 5 Oct. 1910, cited in Jacinto Baptista, *O Cinco de Outubro* (Lisbon, 1965), pp. 348–49.

2 *O Século,* 22 Dec. 1910. A different, longer version of this chapter appeared as an article under my authorship, "The Portuguese Revolution of 1910," in *Journal of Modern History* 44, no. 2 (June 1972):172–94 (© 1972 by the University of Chicago).

3 Hunter to king of England, 15 Oct. 1910, PRO, F.O. 179/494.

4 Oral evidence from personal interview with Colonel Helder Ribeiro, Republican soldier-politician, Oct. 1972, Oporto. Ribeiro stated that he was surprised when the outbreak occurred.

5 *O Século,* 4, 5 Oct. 1910; *O Mundo* (Lisbon), 5 Oct. 1910.

6 *O Século,* 22 Dec. 1910; *A Palavra* (Oporto), 6 Oct. 1910.

7 *O Século,* 5, 6, 7 Oct. 1910; *O Primeiro de Janeiro* (Oporto), 6, 7, 8 Oct. 1910.

8 António Teixeira de Sousa, *Para a História da Revolução,* 2 vols. (Lisbon, 1912), 2:355–58.

9 *O Século,* 5, 6 Oct. 1910.

10 Teixeira de Sousa, *Para a História,* 2:449–50; Gomes da Costa's boast is cited in Baptista, *O Cinco de Outubro,* p. 221; see also General Manuel Gomes da Costa, *Memórias* (Lisbon, 1930), pp. 186–88.

11 British Ministry, Lisbon, "Portugal," typed hour-by-hour account of 1910 Revolution, PRO, F.O. 179/494, confidential.

12 Teixeira de Sousa, *Para a História,* 2:355-58.

13 *BHP,* 7:462-64.

14 Adelina Abranches, *Memórias* (Lisbon, 1947), pp. 252-62. The memoirs of this famous Lisbon actress who remained a monarchist during the republic are most interesting.

15 St. Anthony's Day, celebrated 13 June in Portugal, commemorates the feast day of the thirteenth-century Franciscan friar, born in Lisbon and educated at Coimbra, who died in Padua. Known as "Saint Anthony of Lisbon," he is reputedly the most popular saint in the country (*Dicionário Prático Ilustrado* [Oporto, 1961], p. 1404).

16 *O Século,* 10 Oct. 1910, cites testimony of a corporal of Third Company, Second Battalion, Fifth Infantry Regiment.

17 Ibid.; see also *O Século,* 5, 6, 7, 8 Oct.; José Brissa, *La revolución portuguesa* (Barcelona, 1911).

18 Brissa, *La revolución,* pp. 170-72, 264-66; *New York Times,* 6 Oct. 1910. Some members of the Portuguese royal family expected that Britain would intervene to save King Manuel's throne; Britain did nothing but send two warships to Lisbon by 6 Oct. in order to "watch British interests in Portugal." Among the unaccounted-for monarchist casualties was a suicide by a naval officer outside Lisbon who refused to contemplate life under the republic (Editorial Século, *História Da República* [Lisbon, 1959-60], p. 642).

19 H. V. Livermore, *A New History of Portugal* (New York, 1970), pp. 317-18; Jesús Pabón, *A Revolução Portuguesa,* trans. Manuel Emídio and Ricardo Tavares (Lisbon, 1961), pp. 115-16, also emphasizes the incident.

20 See n. 11 above.

21 The most reliable estimate is in *Diário de Notícias* (Lisbon), 11 Oct. 1910. Most accounts, however, include only bodies at the city morgue and at hospitals; some casualties did not reach hospitals or the morgue, so the estimates are low. Accounts of casualties vary; see also *O Século,* 9, 10 Oct. 1910. Felix Lorenzo (*Portugal* [*cinco años de republica*] [Madrid, 1915], p. 8) claims there were 42 dead and 707 wounded; A Vivero and A. De La Villa (*Como Cae Un Trono* [Madrid, 1910], p. 153) estimate 61 dead and 416 wounded.

22 *O Século,* 5, 6, 7 Oct. 1910; *O Mundo,* 5 Oct. 1910, as reproduced in Jacinto Baptista, *Um jornal Na revolução* (Lisbon, 1966), pp. 135-208.

23 *Diário de Notícias,* 5 Oct. 1910; *O Século,* 6 Oct. 1910.

24 *O Primeiro de Janeiro,* 7-8 Oct. 1910.

25 *O Século,* 10, 11, 12 Oct. 1910.

26 *O Primeiro de Janeiro,* 4, 5, 6 Oct. 1910.

27 Teixeira de Sousa, *Para a História,* 2:355-57.

28 António Machado Santos, *1907-1910: A revolução portugueza* (Lisbon, 1911), p. 174.

29 Ibid., p. 173. David Ferreira emphasizes that the revolution was an "intensely popular movement" ("um movimento nítidamente popular"). Out of the entire army officer corps, only two captains were committed to the conspiracy on 5 Oct., and they withdrew once they feared failure at Rotunda (see Ferreira, *História Política de Primeira República Portuguesa (1910-1915)*, 2 vols. [Lisbon, 1973], 1:264).

30 Lorenzo, *Portugal*, pp. 11-50; see also Francis McCullagh, "Some Causes of the Portuguese Revolution," *Nineteenth Century and After* 68 (Nov. 1910):934-35.

31 McCullagh, "Some Causes of the Portuguese Revolution," pp. 934-36.

32 *O Primeiro de Janeiro*, 1, 2, 3, 4, 5 Oct. 1910.

33 *O Século*, 5, 6, 7, 8 Oct. 1910.

34 *O Século*, 14 Oct. 1910; on Pombal, see José Teixeira Soares, *O Marquês de Pombal* (Rio de Janeiro, 1961).

35 Baptista, *O Cinco de Outubro*, pp. 77-81.

36 *O Século*, 6, 7 Oct. 1910; *Diário de Notícias*, 5, 6 Oct. 1910.

37 *O Primeiro de Janeiro*, 6, 7 Oct. and "Suplemento," 7 Oct. 1910.

38 *O Século*, 13 Oct. 1910; *A Palavra*, 9 Oct. 1910.

39 *O Século*, 5, 6, 7 Oct. 1910; *O Mundo*, 5 Oct. 1910; see such decrees reproduced verbatim in Raúl Brandão, *Memórias* (in *Obras Completas*) 3 vols. (Lisbon, 1969), 1:233-36.

40 Cited in Baptista, *O Cinco de Outubro*, p. 21.

41 Cited in appendix in Baptista, *O Cinco de Outubro*, pp. 348-49 and see full quote at beginning of this chapter.

42 *O Diário de Notícias*, 8 Oct. 1910.

43 Many accounts suggest that a normal daily routine and commerce had resumed by 8 or 9 Oct. (*O Século*, 10 Oct. 1910; *New York Times*, 8, 9 Oct. 1910).

44 Cited in Baptista, *O Cinco de Outubro*, p. 286.

45 *New York Times* 8 Oct. 1910.

46 *O Século*, 21 Oct. 1910; *New York Times*, 6, 7 Oct. 1910; Baptista, *Um jornal Na revolução*, p. 56. Gage to State Department, telegram, 6 Oct. 1910, notes that the Provisional Government had ordered food shops opened on 6 Oct.

47 The Provisional Government's notice to "the officers of the army and the navy," dated 5 Oct. 1910, is reprinted in Brandão, *Memoriás*, 1:230. See also Lorenzo, *Portugal*, p. 104.

48 See chap. 3, n. 23.

49 Joel Serrão, *Antologia Do Pensamento Político Português*, vol. 1, *Liberalismo, Socialismo, Republicanismo* (Oporto, 1970), p. 46.

50 Lorenzo, *Portugal*, pp. 29-30.

51 The Catholic paper *Portugal* (Lisbon), edited by a priest, welcomed the republic after it was proclaimed (see Teixeira de Sousa, *Para a História*, 1:398-99; Baptista, *Um jornal Na revolução*, p. 57). The Catholic Nationalist *A Palavra* (Oporto), however, was reluctant to welcome the republic. Its editorial of 14 Oct. 1910, hostile to the revolution, made a

number of false allegations and sensational accusations which, repeated over the years, became part of a "black legend" regarding the First Republic. For another hostile reaction, see the statements of the duke of Orleans, brother of exiled Queen Amélia, quoted in the *New York Times,* 7 Oct. 1910.

52 Baptista, *O Cinco de Outubro,* pp. 227–28.

53 *Diário de Notícias,* 22 Oct. 1910.

54 General Gomes da Costa, who was on colonial service in Mozambique during the 1910 Revolution, wrote later that the Republicans won only because the army had been inactive during "80 years of rotten peace," and that the Lisbon defenders were incompetent. See his *Memórias,* pp. 186–88.

55 In a different version of this chapter, I compare the Portuguese Revolution of 1910 with similar revolutions in Turkey (1908) and Greece (1909) (see note 2 above).

56 Francisco Cunha Leal, *As Minhas Memórias,* 3 vols. (Lisbon, 1966–68), 1:256.

57 *New York Times* 6 Oct. 1910.

Chapter 5: Young Republic

1 A. M. Alves da Veiga, *Política Nova* (Lisbon, 1911), p. 43.

2 Alfredo Pimenta, *Política Portuguesa* (Coimbra, 1913), p. 10.

3 Hoyt to Jusserand, 11 Oct. 1910, NA, Record Group 853.00/89, roll 3; Department of State to American Ambassador, Petropolis, Brazil, telegram, 13 Oct. 1910, NA, Record Group 853.00/100, roll 3.

4 J. F. Trindade Coelho, *Manuel Político Do Cidadão Portuguez,* 2d rev. ed. (Oporto, 1908), p. 161.

5 Armando Castro, *A Economia Portuguesa, 1900–1925* (Lisbon, 1973), p. 244.

6 Ibid., pp. 52–53.

7 Ibid., p. 243.

8 Ibid., pp. 52–53.

9 Ide to secretary of state, 2 Jan. 1911, NA, Record Group 853.00/161.

10 PRO, F.O. 371/1463, confidential, "Portugal; Annual Report, 1911," p. 5.

11 *GEPB,* 22:819.

12 *O Século,* Oct. 1910—Sept. 1911; José Cutileiro, *A Portuguese Rural Society* (Oxford, 1971), pp. 75–79.

13 Vasco Pulido Valente, "A República e as classes trabalhadoras (Outubro de 1910–Agosto de 1911)," in *Análise Social* (Lisbon), 2d ser., 9, no. 34, (1972):293–316; see also Cesár Oliveira, *O Operariado E A República Democrática, 1910–1914* (Oporto, 1972), pp. 34–56 and appendix; Alexandre Vieira, *Para a história do sindicalismo em Portugal* (Lisbon, 1970).

14 *O Século,* 24 Aug. 1911; this article discusses the burning by corkworkers of cork-processing factories near Lisbon.

15 Cited in J. M. Costa Júnior, *História Breve do Movimento Operário Português* (Lisbon, 1964), p. 65.

16 Costa Júnior, *História Breve,* pp. 65–75; see also material in David Ferreira, "Greves," *DHP,* 2:382.

17 Cutileiro, *Portuguese Rural Society,* pp. 88–89.

18 Ibid., p. 79; Jaçinto Cândido da Silva, nationalist leader in exile (*Memórias Íntimas* [Lisbon, 1963], 1, 126), blames "egoistic behavior" of landowners in rural areas.

19 Figures cited in A. H. de Oliveira Marques, *A Primeira República Portuguesa* (Lisbon, 1972), p. 153; on emigration see Joel Serrão, *Emigração Portuguesa* (Lisbon, 1971).

20 "Correspondência" from commanders of the Eighth Military Division (Braga Hqs.) suggests unusually high desertion rates by Sept. 1911, some 400 more than in 1910 (AHM, division 1; section 34, box 1, folder 1 [1911], no. 59P, 25 Sept. 1911); see also Gen. Luís Ferreira Martins, *História do Exército Portuguêz* (Lisbon, 1945), pp. 500–501.

21 Valente, "A Republica," p. 313.

22 *O Século,* 11 Feb. 1913.

23 Cited in Joel Serrão, "Emigração," *DHP,* 2:26.

24 Stanley G. Payne, *A History of Spain and Portugal,* 2 vols. (Madison, Wis., 1973), 2:599.

25 See A. H. de Oliveira Marques's defense of Costa's anticlerical policy in his *Afonso Costa* (Lisbon, 1972), p. 37. It is significant that the debate over the wisdom of this policy has persisted to the present day in Portugal. In a written interview I received by mail on 29 Oct. 1973 from Prof. Marcello Caetano, then premier of Portugal, Caetano attempted to explain the failure of the First Republic as in part the result of the initial religious policy. See chap. 15.

26 Opponents of the republic's divorce law claimed that such a law would encourage divorces and thus undermine the Portuguese family. There is no definitive study of divorce during the republic, but what contemporary statistics are available suggest that the law had little effect. In the first six months of its operation, the total number of divorces in Lisbon, a city of some 400,000, was only 341 (*O Século,* 28 Apr. 1911).

27 AHM, division 1, section 33, box 2, folder 1, no. 610, 24 May 1911, "Precautions to be taken in case of a counterrevolution rising due to the separation of Church from the State."

28 A. J. Almeida Coutinho and Lemos Ferreira, *António Sardinha* (Oporto, 1930), p. 17.

29 Hardinge to Grey, 16 Mar. 1912, PRO, F.O. 371/1463.1794, "Portugal, Annual Report, 1911." For disputes see pp. 5, 8–9, 13, and 15–17.

30 Ibid., p. 5. France recognized the republic on 24 Aug., upon the election of the president of the republic.

31 See documents 1910–13 in BAMNE.

32 PRO, F.O. 371/1463, confidential, "Portugal, Annual Report, 1911," pp. 7–8.

33 Ibid.

34 António Machado Santos suggests that the first government (João Chagas) fell in Nov. 1911 in part through the foreign pressures for compromise on the clerical question and the hostile reaction of the radical Republicans to such compromises (*A Ordem Pública E O 14 De Maio* [Lisbon, 1916], p. 22).

35 Rocha Martins, *História de Portugal* (Lisbon, 1930), p. 464.

36 PRO, F.O. 371/1463, "Portugal, Annual Report, 1911," p. 3; see also Mário Soares, "Constituição de 1911," *DHP,* 1:679.

37 Marcello Caetano, *História Breve das Constituições Portuguesas,* 3d ed. (Lisbon, 1971), p. 101. The remainder of the Assembly was composed of landowners (18), university professors (11), teachers (12), merchants (8), journalists (8), pharmacists (6), judges (5), solicitors (3), salesmen (2), students (2), priests (2), farm foreman (1), engineer (1), veterinarian (1), barber (1), and 1 worker.

38 Brief biographies of each of the 226 deputies are found in *As Constituentes De 1911 E Os Seus Deputados* (Lisbon, 1911).

39 See editorials in *O Século,* 4, 6 July 1911, front page.

40 *O Século,* 3 Aug. 1911 and editorial commentary 5 Aug. 1911.

41 *DANC,* 6 July 1911, pp. 19-21.

42 Ibid., 10 July 1911, pp. 9-10.

43 Ibid., 7, 12 July 1911, pp. 11, 13-14.

44 Ibid., 8 Aug. 1911, pp. 15-16.

45 See *As Constituentes De 1911* (Title 3, Article 5), p. 474 of text.

46 Information on the composition of the 1926 Chamber of Deputies was provided by Katherine Wells Wheeler, who carried out research in 1973.

47 For text of draft constitution written by a constitutional commission of five, see *As Constituentes De 1911,* pp. 443-67.

48 Editorial by Manuel Brito Camacho, in *A Lucta,* 27 Oct. 1911. Camacho defended PRP rigging in May elections as justified because of a need for "security and prestige" for the republic.

49 António Sérgio, "Da Opinião Pública E Da Competência Em Democracia," *Ensaios* (in *Obras Completas*), 3 vols. (Lisbon, 1972), 1:227.

50 *DANC,* 11 July 1911, p. 12.

51 *O Século,* 6 July 1911.

52 *DANC,* 12 July 1911, p. 14.

53 Some of the "white ants" were employed by the civil government of Lisbon. A facsimile copy of an official identification pass is found in Machado Santos, *A Ordem Pública,* p. 30.

54 Carlos Malheiro Dias, *Do Desafio A Debandada,* 2 vols. (Lisbon, 1912), 1:46.

55 *DCD,* 16 Oct. 1911, pp. 4-5.

56 PRO, F.O. 371/1463, "Portugal, Annual Report, 1911," p. 12, and F.O. 425/350, "Portugal, Annual Report, 1910," pp. 17-18.

57 Raúl Brandão, *Memórias* (in *Obras Completas*), 3 vols. (Lisbon, 1969), 2:326-30. Like so many other Republicans, Brandão believed that if the Republican party had not fragmented in 1911-12 the acts of the Provisional Government might have been more acceptable. Costa, he suggested, was less to blame than were his political opponents.

58 *A Lucta,* 24 Sept., 26-30 Oct., 4 Nov. 1911.

59 *A Lucta,* 2 Nov. 1911; Ferreira de Miro and Aquilino Ribeiro, *Brito Camacho* (Lisbon, 1942), pp. 80-82.

60 *A Lucta* 18 Nov. 1911.

61 Basílio Teles, *I - As dictaduras, II - O regimen revolucionário* (Famalição, 1911), pp. 67-86.

62 Anselmo Vieira, *A crise nacional* (Lisbon, 1926), pp. 266-67; Francisco Cunha Leal, *As Minhas Memórias,* 3 vols. (Lisbon, 1966-68), 1:267-70; Pimenta, *Política Portuguesa,* pp. 93-94.

63 Cunha Leal, *As Minhas Memórias,* 2:269.

64 Machado Santos, *A Ordem Pública,* pp. 13-20; Brandão, *Memórias,* 2:326-30.

65 *A República,* 25 Feb. 1912.

66 For critiques of political journalism in the republic, see Almeida's *A República,* 9, 10 Jan. 1912; and Sérgio's essay "Da Opinião Pública e . . . ," *Ensaios,* 1:227 ff.

67 Machado Santos's newspaper began publication Nov. 1910 and was published sporadically until 1921.

68 *DCD,* 16 Oct. 1911, p. 16.

69 *A República,* 10 Oct.-7 Nov. 1911, editorials.

70 *BHP,* 7:483-84.

71 Machado Santos, *A Ordem Pública,* p. 22.

72 Some 1100 active duty officers in the army had, by late Nov. 1910, signed sworn statements of Republican loyalty, a clear majority of the army officer corps (AHM, division 1, section 33, box 1, 30 Nov. 1910). The 1911 and 1912 incursions were partially financed by Portuguese monarchists who resided in Brazil (BAMNE, Portuguese Legation in Rio de Janeiro, 1909-11, box 230 and 1912-14, box. 231).

73 For one personal view of the incursions, see António d'Eça de Queiroz, *Na Fronteira: Incursões monarchicas de 1911 e 1912* (Oporto, 1915).

74 Included among the monarchist officers who resigned or were dismissed were 5 counts, 1 viscount, and a marquis (AHM, division 1, section 34; box 1, folder 4/19, 22 Mar. 1912).

75 Ferreira Martins, *História Do Exército Portuguêz,* pp. 500-501.

76 Ide to secretary of state, 2 Jan. 1911, NA, Record Group 853.00/161.

77 Ide to secretary of state, 2 Jan. 1911, NA, Record Group 853.00/161.

78 Vicente Pilapil, *Alfonso XIII* (New York, 1969), pp. 129-30. A Portuguese monarchist officer who knew Villalobar claims that despite the physical defects of the Spanish minister, who had an artificial leg and a withered arm, he was most brave. The marquis was also foolhardy; he is

said to have shouted publicly, in one of Lisbon's most frequented cafés (Martinho), "Just give me one shot, give me one shot, and I can restore the monarchy in Portugal!" (cited in Col. Gonçalo Pimenta de Castro, *As Minhas Memórias,* 3 vols. [Oporto, 1947–50], 1:336).

79 PRO, F.O. 371/1740, "Portugal, Annual Report, 1912," pp. 16–18. For discussion of 1913 transfer of Spanish minister from Lisbon, and King Alfonso's belief that Spain's eventual absorption of Portugal was, in the British minister's words, "a legitimate Spanish national aspiration," see PRO, F.O. 425/377, "Portugal, Annual Report, 1913," pp. 9–10.

80 *DCD,* 12 Nov. 1912, p. 7.

81 Oliveira Marques, *A Primeira República Portuguesa,* p. 185; Machado Santos, *A Ordem Pública,* p. 38.

Chapter 6: Democrats' Republic

1 João Chagas, *Diário 1914–1918,* 3 vols. (Lisbon, 1929–30), 1:4.

2 See A. H. de Oliveira Marques, *Afonso Costa* (Lisbon, 1972), p. 15. Materials for a full-scale biography of Costa are being assembled by Oliveira Marques.

3 Even the highly intelligent British writer Aubrey Bell was, to a degree, taken in by the anti-PRP propaganda of 1914–15 and could write: ". . . the Democrat party will always be known as the party, which, under cover of the World War, raised itself to power over the dead bodies of its fellow-countrymen" (*Portugal of the Portuguese* [London, 1915], p. 215).

4 António Machado Santos's most bitter personal attacks are saved for Afonso Costa in his important book, *A Ordem Pública E O 14 De Maio* (Lisbon, 1916), pp. 26–35; see also A. J. de Almeida, *Quarenta Anos de vida literária e política,* 4 vols. (Lisbon, 1933–34).

5 See the 24 Feb. 1927 editorial in *O Século,* also included in Hollis to State Department, 25 Feb. 1927; NA, Record Group 853.44/2, roll 14.

6 Jesús Pabón, *A Revolução Portuguesa,* trans. Manuel Emídio and Ricardo Tavares (Lisbon, 1961), pp. 31–32, 173–74.

7 João Ameal, *História de Portugal* (Oporto, 1942 and successive editions).

8 Jofre Amaral Nogueira, *A República De Ontem Nos Livros De Hoje* (reprint booklet from *Vértice;* Coimbra, 1972), pp. 13–29; a rejoinder to Amaral Nogueira's hypothesis that Costa was "a personal political failure" as an ideologue and pragmatist in fashioning a policy to satisfy the demands of the working classes is found in the preface to the first volume of Costa's collected parliamentary speeches, *Discursos Parlamentares de Afonso Costa, 1900–1910* (Lisbon, 1973–), 1:1–10.

9 Arthur Ribeiro Lopes, *Histoire de la République Portugaise* (Paris, 1939), pp. 179–82, 205–8.

10 Francisco Cunha Leal, *As Minhas Memórias,* 3 vols. (Lisbon, 1966–68), 1:261–63.

11 Oliveira Marques, *Afonso Costa,* pp. 338-42.

12 Ibid., p. 372; Oliveira Marques errs in his work *A Primeira República Portuguesa* (Lisbon, 1972), p. 42, where he states that the superavit was £1,000,000. The superavit of about 1,000 contos (each conto = 1,000 escudos) equalled 1,000,000 escudos. As of 1961, an escudo was worth a little less than $.04 (U.S.) and thus each conto was worth about $38. Fifty years earlier the conto was worth a good deal more, but one thousand contos was worth probably close to $100,000.

13 Text of law is found in *Diário do Governo,* no. 153, 3 Aug. 1913, pp. 2445-51. It is reprinted in part in Oliveira Marques, *Afonso Costa,* pp. 354-58.

14 Carnegie to Grey, p. 5. PRO, F.O. 425/377, confidential, "Portugal, Annual Report, 1913," p. 5.

15 AHM, division 1, section 34, box 4, folder 1 (1911-13), confidential, "Movimentos Políticos, Correspondencia." Note extensive reports from a number of Portuguese consuls in several Galician towns, including Orense, Vigo and Verin, suggesting that the government knew most of the monarchists' plans in Oct. 1913.

16 As early as Mar. 1912, however, A. J. de Almeida, leader of the newly formed Evolutionist party, had begun to call for amnesty in his party newspaper and in Congress (*A República* 3 Mar. 1912, editorials).

17 See John H. Harris, *Portuguese Slavery: Britain's Dilemma* (London, 1913). For a general study of the antislavery protests, see James Duffy, *A Question of Slavery* (Oxford, 1967), especially pp. 60-229.

18 Before 7 Jan. 1913, Evolutionist leader Almeida had tried to form a non-PRP government with amnesty as his program and had failed since the independent deputies had judged it was too early for amnesty, and since only a partial amnesty was viable (*O Século,* 8 Jan. 1913).

19 BAMNE, Rio de Janeiro Legation of Portugal, box 231 (1912-14). See, for example, Machado to foreign minister in Lisbon, 8 Apr. 1913, no. 25, series A (1913).

20 Machado to Lisbon, telegram, 22 Aug. 1913, BAMNE, box 231, no. 24.

21 PRO, F.O. 371/9480, confidential, "Portugal, Annual Reports, 1914-1918," p. 3.

22 Cited in E. M. Tenison, *Portuguese Political Prisoners,* 5th ed. (London, 1913), pp. 1-14.

23 Philip Gibbs, *The Tragedy of Portugal* (London, 1914).

24 Tenison, *Portuguese Political Prisoners,* pp. 1-14.

25 Gibbs, *The Tragedy of Portugal,* pp. 12-14; Adeline, duchess of Bedford, "Republican Tyranny in Portugal," *Twentieth Century,* May 1913, pp. 1055-59.

26 Aubrey Bell, *In Portugal* (London, 1912); Sir Arthur Hardinge, *A Diplomatist in Europe* (London, 1927). On p. 248, where Hardinge states, ". . . the manner in which political prisoners were dealt with continued to remain a deep blot upon the administration of the Portuguese Government," he is discussing the period 1911-13 in general, not specifically Costa's administration.

27 See McCullagh's article in *Nineteenth Century,* Jan. 1914, and another article unfavorable to the Portuguese government by Rev. C. Torrend, S.J., "Anti-Clerical Policy in Portugal," in *Dublin Review,* Jan. 1912. During 1911–14 many writers attacked the Portuguese government in such well-known periodicals as *National Review, Saturday Review, The Spectator, Outlook, Contemporary Review.* The list of writers, who often tended to be hostile to the Democrats, and specifically to Afonso Costa, included Aubrey Bell and Vicente de Bragança-Cunha, whose fairly sympathetic view of the overthrow of the Portuguese monarchy in his book *Eight Centuries of Portuguese Monarchy* (New York, 1911) was followed by disillusionment with the politics of the First Republic. José Soares da Cunha e Costa (1868–1928) was a historic Republican until 1911, when he quit the party and became a monarchist. A famous lawyer, he later defended Alves Reis in the Banknote Case (*GEPB,* 8:276).

28 See Duffy, *A Question of Slavery,* pp. 219–223.

29 Egas Moniz quit in April 1912 (*Um ano de política* [Lisbon, 1919]). The 1911 Congress was still meeting in late May 1915.

30 *OG,* p. 21.

31 *As Constituentes De 1911 E Os Seus Deputados* (Lisbon, 1911), p. 483.

32 Oliveira Marques, *A Primeira República,* p. 179.

33 Machado Santos, *A Ordem Pública,* pp. 33–35.

34 Ibid., pp. 34–35.

35 See *O Século,* 2 Jan.–25 Apr. 1914.

36 By Article 25 of the Constitution, all nominations of colonial governors had to be passed by secret vote of the Senate (*As Constituentes De 1911,* p. 477).

37 For the Senate dispute, see *O Século,* 15–25 Jan. 1914; *DS* for Jan. 1914, especially 19–21 Jan. 1914; and Machado Santos, *A Ordem Pública,* p. 36.

38 *BHP,* Suplemento, p. 24.

39 *O Século,* 26 Jan.–10 Feb. 1914.

40 PRO, F.O. 371/9480, confidential, "Portugal, Annual Reports, 1914–1918," pp. 3–4.

41 *GEPB,* 15:755–57.

42 J. Leite de Vasconcellos, *Etnografia Portuguesa: Tentame de sistematização,* 4 vols. (Lisbon, 1933–58), 1:73.

43 Anselmo Vieira, *A crise nacional* (Lisbon, 1926), p. 343.

44 PRO, F.O. 371/9480, "Portugal, Annual Reports, 1914–1918," pp. 4–5.

45 Ibid., p. 5; for the text of the Amnesty Law, see *Diário do Governo,* no. 27, 21 Feb. 1914, Suplemento, pp. 1–2.

46 *O Século,* 9 Feb. 1914, front page story with photo.

47 *DCD,* for 1914; *DS,* 19 Jan. 1914, pp. 8–10, complaints of Senator Abílio Barreto.

48 *O Século,* 17, 18 Mar. and 21 July 1914.

49 Sebastião de Magalhães Lima, *Episódios da Minha Vida,* 2 vols. (Lisbon, 1927), 1:293: Magalhães Lima suggests that the Portuguese Carbonária was disbanded after 1913, after the last monarchist incursions.

50 For complaints of vigilante intervention in Oporto and Lisbon police affairs, see *DS,* 10 Feb. 1914, p. 24.
51 *O Século,* 8 Aug. 1914; *BHP,* Suplemento, pp. 52–54.
52 *O Século,* 9 Aug. 1914).
53 See *A Lucta,* 6 Aug.–Dec. 1914.
54 Douglas L. Wheeler and René Pélissier, *Angola* (London and New York, 1971), pp. 73–76; Augusto Casimiro, *Naulila* (Lisbon, 1922).
55 Opposition political punsters could not resist referring to the Azevedo Coutinho government as "The Miserable ones of Vitor Hugo," a takeoff on the title of Victor Hugo's famous novel *Les Misérables* (Pabón, *A Revolução Portuguesa,* p. 182).
56 *O Século,* 10–15 Jan. 1913.
57 Pabón, *A Revolução Portuguesa,* p. 182; *DS,* 10 Feb. 1914, p. 24.
58 Bell, *Portugal of the Portuguese,* pp. 211–12.
59 *DCD,* 11 Jan. 1915, pp. 16–18.
60 *A Lucta,* 5 Jan. 1915, lead editorial by Brito Camacho. Arriaga's statement issued on 24 Feb. 1914 was evidently not published in the *Diário do Governo* (*O Século,* 30 May 1915).
61 *A Lucta,* 5 Jan. 1914); PRO, F.O. 371/9480, "Portugal, Annual Reports, 1914–1918," pp. 8–13.
62 PRO, F.O. 371/9480," Portugal, Annual Reports, 1914–1918," p. 13.
63 *O Século,* 18 Jan. 1915, lead editorial, "Elections."

Chapter 7: Wars and Revolutions

1 David Magno, *Livro da Guerra de Portugal na Flandres* (Porto, 1920), p. 20.
2 António Machado Santos, *1907–1910, A Revolução Portugueza* (Lisbon, 1911), p. 173.
3 For material on the junior officers known as the "Young Turks," see Francisco Cunha Leal, *As Minhas Memórias,* 3 vols. (Lisbon, 1966–68), 1:226–86.
4 Raúl Brandão, *Memórias* (in *Obras Completas*), 3 vols. (Lisbon, 1969), 2:306–7; Col. Gonçalo Pimenta De Castro, *As Minhas Memórias,* 3 vols. (Oporto, 1947–50), 1:400–424.
5 Anselmo Vieira, *A crise nacional* (Lisbon, 1926), pp. 548–50; Pedro Fazenda, *A Crise Política* (Lisbon, 1926), pp. 80–83.
6 António Machado Santos, *A Ordem Pública E O 14 De Maio* (Lisbon, 1916), pp. 35–58; see also this author's newspaper, *O Intransigente,* 1911–14.
7 Felix Lorenzo, *Portugal (cinco años de republica)* (Madrid, 1915), pp. 104–5.
8 Ibid.
9 On the navy in the early Republican period, see Maurício de Oliveira, *Armada Glosiosa* (Lisbon, 1936), pp. 140–61; for acid commentary on

naval indiscipline, 1911-13, see the PRO, F.O. 371 series, "Portugal," annual reports for 1910, 1911, 1912, and 1913.

10 David Ferreira, *História Política da Primeira República Portuguesa (1910-1915)*, 2 vols. (Lisbon, 1973), 1:165-66, 210-16, 203-16.

11 Ibid., pp. 203-16.

12 *A Lucta* 18 Nov. 1914.

13 Gen. António Gomes de Sousa, *Meio Século de vida militar, 1888-1938* (Coimbra, 1939), pp. 131-32.

14 Ibid., p. 131; on discipline problems in the army, see also (Gen.) Alberto Ilharco, *Memórias: Alguns Apontamentos Sobre A Influência Da Política No Exército* (Oporto, 1926), pp. 30-47.

15 For a general discussion of the 1911 army reforms see Gen. Luís Ferreira Martins, *História do Exército Portuguez* (Lisbon, 1945).

16 For critical works by military authorities late in the monarchy, see Lt. Col. Mesquita de Carvalho, *A Verdadeira Situação Militar De Portugal* (Oporto, 1888), pp. 150-52; Lt. Raúl Esteves, *A Função do Exército* (Lisbon, 1907), pp. 5, 113-29.

17 Capt. Cristovão Ayres, *A Evolução Orgânica Do Exército: Memória* (Lisbon, 1894), pp. 111-17.

18 "Os Principaes exércitos em 1911," *Revista Militar* (Lisbon), 63, no. 6 (June 1911):534-35.

19 See complaints and criticisms by officers voiced in such newspaper articles as that of Lt. Col. M. Garcia in *O Século*, 8 Feb. 1913. There were other complaints about low morale among officers, poor equipment and armament, and a lack of trained instructors at the repetition schools ("A Situação do Exército," series, in *O Século*, 24, 27 Apr. 1914).

20 See Garcia article, *O Século*, 8 Feb. 1913.

21 "O Sr. General Morais Sarmento e a 'Revista Militar,' 1886-1926," *Revista Militar* 78, nos. 5-6 (May-June, 1926):249-57.

22 AHM, division 1, section 34, box 1, folder 4/19 (1912), letter, 19 Mar. 1912, "Tribunal da Relação," on anti-Republican conspirators.

23 *O Século*, 14 Oct. 1910; one general noted, however, that a good number of high-ranking officers with monarchist sentiments went into reserve status immediately after the 1910 Revolution. See Gen. Gomes de Sousa, *Meio Século*, p. 110. The heavy retirement of generals after 1910 appears to be confirmed by official statistics (*Almanaque do Exército: 1915* [Lisbon, 1916], 1:10, 248, 263). Here it is noted that of twenty-two generals on active duty only one had not been promoted to general under the republic, as of Dec. 1915, and all but five of the twenty-two had been promoted to general between June 1912 and Dec. 1915.

24 Gonçalo Pimenta de Castro, *As Minhas Memórias*, 1:400-407.

25 *A Lucta*, 18 Nov. 1914; *BHP*, Suplemento, p. 78.

26 *O Século*, 20-29 Jan. 1915.

27 In his *As Minhas Memórias* (1:400-402), Gonçalo Pimenta de Castro, who was apparently no relation to Gen. Pimenta de Castro, gives a brief discus-

sion of the original monarchist conspiracy, in which he participated as an officer of the Seventh Infantry Regiment stationed at Leiria.

28 For news reports and documents on the crisis of January 1915, see *O Século,* 15-28 Jan. 1915.

29 *BHP,* Suplemento, p. 79. Pabón suggests that Machado Santos handed in the "sword of the Rotunda," on 23 Jan. (Jesús Pabón, *A Revolução Portuguesa,* trans. Manuel Emídio and Ricardo Tavares [Lisbon, 1961], p. 183).

30 *A Lucta,* 21 Jan.-27 Jan. 1915. Significantly, the Azevedo Coutinho government, with little basis in law, responded to Camacho's attacks on it first by harassment and then by banning publication of his partisan newspaper from 22 Jan. to 25 Jan.

31 Ferreira, *A História Política,* 1:212-16.

32 João Chagas, *Diário 1914-1918,* 3 vols. (Lisbon, 1929-30), 1:262-83, 2:4-49.

33 For the text of Arriaga's famous letter to Pimenta de Castro see his memoir, *Na primeira presidência da República Portugueza: Um rápido relatório* (Lisbon, 1916), pp. 138 ff.

34 Capt. José A. Correia Dos Santos, *Subsídios Para a História Política e Militar Da Revolução de 14 de Maio de 1915* (Lisbon, 1915), pp. 11-12.

35 *O Século,* 26 Jan. 1915. Costa's words were: "uma saldanhada de via reduzida."

36 See the program of the Democrats' Junta Revolucionária of May 1915, *O Século,* 16 May 1915; and Afonso Costa's later address when appointed premier in Dec. 1915, in A. H. de Oliveira Marques, *Afonso Costa* (Lisbon, 1972), pp. 380-81.

37 *GEPB,* 21:660-61; *ELBC,* 4:1443.

38 Arriaga, *Na primeira presidência,* p. 138; Machado Santos, *A Ordem Pública,* pp. 54-58.

39 *BHP,* Suplemento, p. 84, cites press commentary of 24-28 Feb. 1915.

40 *O Século,* 27, 28 Jan. 1915; *A Lucta,* 27 Jan. 1915; *BHP,* Suplemento, p. 89.

41 A group of young Integralists held a conference in Lisbon in Apr. 1915; the conference was broken up by Republicans, but conference lectures were published in 1916 in António Sardinha et al., *A Questão Ibérica* (Lisbon, 1916).

42 Vieira, *A crise nacional,* pp. 356-59; see *O Século* and *A Lucta* for 5-6 May 1915.

43 *O Século,* 16 May 1915.

44 Correia Dos Santos, *Subsídios,* preface.

45 Ibid., pp. 37-39.

46 *A Lucta,* 6 May 1915.

47 *GEPB,* 5:547-48.

48 Correia Dos Santos, *Subsídios,* pp. 175-76; AHM, division 1, section 36, box 13, folder 2, "Movimentos Monarquicas," 26 July 1915.

49 I have revised the standard and erroneous casualty estimate (*BHP,* Suplemento, p. 101) after locating new, larger casualty records. See *O Século,* 17, 19 May 1915, which suggests at least 121 died in Lisbon alone

by 16 May 1915 and that there were dead also in Oporto, Santarém, Peniche, Braga, and Guimarães. This does not take into account those wounded seriously who died after 16 May in homes and hospitals. One British estimate based on "hospital returns" suggested that 170 were killed and 300 wounded by 19 May (Carnegie to Grey, 19 May 1915, PRO, F.O. 371/2442/2581). The estimate of 102 dead might have been an erroneous transcription of the figure of 120 given on 17 May 1915 in *O Século*. If one counts wounded in towns outside Lisbon, the figure of 1,000 may be an underestimate (see Correia Dos Santos, *Subsídios*, pp. 238-39).

50   *O Século* 17-22 May 1915; Correia Dos Santos, *Subsídios*, p. 172.
51   *BHP*, 7:489-90.
52   Chagas, *Diário*, 1:80; 2:52, 66-67.
53   The text of Arriaga's resignation speech was printed in *O Século*, 30 May 1915. It bore the date of 26 May, but it was read on 29 May before a joint session of Congress. See also Arriaga's memoir on his presidency, *Na primeira presidência*, pp. 188-90, where he blames parties and "professional politicians."
54   The text of the Junta's manifesto, dated 18 May 1915 was published in *O Século*, 20 May 1915.
55   *O Século*, 22 June 1915. See also *O Século*'s lead editorial of 24 June, which attacked what it referred to as "the intransigence of the parties," as an obstacle to the formation of a "national" government of acalmação.
56   Chagas, *Diário*, 1:82, entry for 6 June 1914.
57   Joel Serrão, *Emigração Portuguesa* (Lisbon, 1970), p. 152.
58   For British comments on Portugal's wartime aid, see Lord Hardinge of Penshurst, *Old Diplomacy* (London, 1947), p. 202, in which Hardinge suggests that British officials viewed Portugal's apparent anxiety to send troops to France as "not welcome at all." See also John Vincent-Smith, "Britain and Portugal, 1910-16" (Ph.D. diss., University of London, 1971), pp. 315 ff; and Gen. Luís Ferreira Martins, ed., *Portugal na Grande Guerra*, 2 vols. (Lisbon, 1945).
59   A. H. de Oliveira Marques, *A Primeira República Portuguesa* (Lisbon, 1972), pp. 20-22.
60   Birch to State Department on May 1917 food riots, telegram, 21 May 1917, NA, Record Group 853.00/325. The American minister suggested that at least 20 people were killed in food riots and that these riots delayed embarkation of Portuguese troops to France.
61   PRO, F.O. 371/9480/1923, "Portugal, Annual Reports, 1914-1918," p. 28. There had been food riots (mainly concerning bread) in Lisbon on 30 Jan. 1916 as workers attacked food shops; food riots spread to some rural districts as hungry mobs, sometimes led by town officials, found hidden grain supplies and freely distributed them to the people. See Alexandre Vieira (syndicalist leader), *Para a história do sindicalismo em Portugal* (Lisbon, 1970), pp. 81-82.
62   PRO, F.O. 371/9480/1923, "Portugal, Annual Reports, 1914-1918," p. 28.

63 Vincent-Smith, "Britain and Portugal," pp. 311–13.

64 Marcello Caetano, "The Tower and the Sword Military Order," officially printed speech (Secretária De Estado Da Informação E Turismo, 1971), p. 6. In a speech made in Oct. 1919 to Congress, President of the Republic A. J. Almeida had suggested that Portugal entered the world war actively to "assure, with the integrity of her territory, the prosperity and benefits of an honorable independence" (Almeida, *Quarenta Anos de vida literária e política*, 4 vols. [Lisbon, 1933–34], 4:56).

65 Vincent-Smith, "Britain and Portugal," pp. 311–13.

66 See *O Século*, 24 Feb.–10 Mar. 1916.

67 Vincent-Smith's useful dissertation on the Anglo-Portuguese alliance during the first six years of the First Republic ("Britain and Portugal") has used a few published German sources, including the memoirs of the German minister in Lisbon, Baron Rosen, but no systematic study of German sources has been made. On the Lisbon warehouse fire which may have been caused by German sabotage, see *O Século*, 14 Jan. 1916.

68 Chagas, *Diário*, 1:382.

69 Bell, *Portugal of the Portuguese* (London, 1915), p. 220.

70 Sabastião de Magalhães Lima, *Episódios da Minha Vida*, 2 vols. (Lisbon, 1927), 2:130.

71 For Unionist opposition see *A Lucta*, 1914–17, and Camacho's collected editorials in *Rescaldo da Guerra* (Lisbon, 1936) and *Portugal na Guerra* (Lisbon, 1936).

72 Oporto, 1916. This 29-page pamphlet was signed by Cortesão with the patriotic name Pela Pátria ("For the Fatherland"). There is a copy in the Biblioteca Nacional de Lisboa. *Cartilha* means, literally, "a little book with which one learns to read." A famous precedent for use of this colloquial word was in the title of a popular booklet using a new method for teaching reading, *Cartilha Maternal*, by the nineteenth-century poet-educator, João de Deus Ramos (1830–95).

73 On Cortesão's complaint, made in a speech of 20 May 1916, see Cunha Leal, *As Minhas Memórias*, 2:30.

74 Cortesão, *Cartilha*, pp. 9–13, 17.

75 Ibid., pp. 28–29.

76 V. de Bragança-Cunha, *Revolutionary Portugal, 1910–1936* (London, 1937), p. 203.

77 Egas Moniz, *Um ano de política* (Lisbon, 1919), pp. 247–48; David Ferreira, "Grande Guerra," *DHP*, 2:273–74; Ferreira Martins, *Portugal na Grande Guerra*, 2:55.

78 Casualty figures are from *O Século* 13 Mar. 1918 and 4 Aug. 1919; *BHP*, 7:521–22; Oliveira, *Armada Gloriosa*, p. 135; Magno, *Livro da Guerra*, pp. 255–56. Moniz (*Um ano de política*, p. 380) estimated that a total of 8,500 Portuguese soldiers died in all campaigns.

79 PRO, F.O. 371/4125, report of Mr. Seeds, first secretary to British Legation in Portugal, "War Expenditures of Portugal," p. 6, enclosed in Carnegie to Curzon, 30 June 1919.

80 Information given as result of question asked in parliament, 29 June 1925; PRO, F.O. 371/11091/2625.
81 In late 1918 Portuguese losses in colonies were claimed officially to be £26,038,500 (PRO, F.O. 371/3376, enclosed in "Notes on the Portuguese Colonies," 18 Dec. 1918).
82 Portugal's Unknown Soldiers were buried in the Battle Abbey (Mosteiro da Batalha), erected in the early fifteenth century under King João I to commemorate Portugal's victory at Aljubarrota in 1383. The magnificent abbey is located in the town of Alcobaça.
83 See *O Século,* 1 July-31 Aug. 1917.
84 *Anuário Estatística de Portugal: 1927* (Lisbon, 1928), p. 220.
85 Theophilo Duarte, *Sidónio Pais e o seu Consulado* (Lisbon, 1941), pp. 72-75; Urbano Rodrigues, *A Vida Romanesca de Teixeira Gomes* (Lisbon, 1946), pp. 136-37.
86 See series of articles by Campos Lima in *Portugal* (Lisbon), July-Aug. 1917. An article of 9 Aug. 1917 called for "an alliance of revolutionaries" to bring unity among diverse working-men's groups.
87 Vieira, *Para a história do sindicalismo,* pp. 71-93; J. M. Costa Júnior, *História Breve do Movimento Operário Português* (Lisbon, 1964). Written for the Editorial Verbo "short history" series (no. 17), Costa Júnior's book was banned by the government after its publication and remained difficult to find as late as 1973.
88 *O Século,* 1 Oct.-20 Nov. 1917; Duarte, *Sidónio Pais,* pp. 76-80.
89 See Machado Santos, *A Ordem Pública,* pp. 104-16, for text of "national statute."
90 AHM, division 1, section 36, box 12, folder 4, "Relatório" on 13-14 Dec. 1916 revolt of units at Alcobaça, Tomar, and Leiria.
91 In *O Século,* 18 Jan. 1915, a lead editorial urges an early constitutional revision to give the president power of congressional dissolution. See also *O Século,* 17-18 Oct. 1917. As early as Apr. 1915 in their annual party congress, the Evolutionists put the dissolution power in their program (*BHP,* Suplemento, p. 91).
92 Moniz, *Um ano de política,* pp. 50-62; *O Século* 18 Oct. 1917.
93 *A Lucta,* 1 Sept. 1917, 1 Feb. 1918,21 Feb. 1918.
94 Cunha Leal, *As Minhas Memórias,* 2:65-69; see also Duarte, *Sidónio Pais,* p. 158.
95 It was well known that Machado Santos had close links with syndicalist workers. See, for example, Editorial Século, *Cinquenta anos de História do Mundo: 1900-1950,* 2 vols. (Lisbon, 1959), 2:995-97; see also Gomes de Sousa, *Meio Século de vida militar,* pp. 126-27.
96 Complaints by officers of very low pay and favoritism shown toward civil servants appeared in the daily press (*Portugal,* 11 Aug. 1917). That anti-Democrat movements might find support among junior officers in the army and that the army might intervene in politics was prophesied even by some Democrats. One with considerable perspective, at the time governor-general of Mozambique, PRP younger leader Álvaro de Castro

wrote in a prophetic letter from South Africa in Nov. 1917, not long before the December coup, that the PRP was unfortunately "divorced" from the working classes and that it was determined to stay in power "indefinitely." Castro added that if the parties were discredited, the army might consider itself the "possessor of the destinies of the Nation" and act (Caetano Gonçalves, *Álvaro de Castro* [Lisbon, 1933], pp. 31-33). See also Duarte, *Sidónio Pais,* pp. 41-66.

97 Duarte, *Sidónio Pais,* p. 178; "António Miguel de Sousa Fernandes, Agricultor e político," [1870-1937], *GEPB,* 11:99; José Cutileiro, *A Portuguese Rural Society* (Oxford, 1971), pp. 217-18 n; Rocha Martins, *Memórias sobre Sidónio Pais* (Lisbon, 1921), p. 8.

98 *O Século,* 9 Mar. 1918.

99 Duarte, *Sidónio Pais,* pp. 158-65. Interestingly, one of Sidónio Pais's young officer-cadets and disciples was Lt. Henrique Galvão, who was given an administrative post in 1918 (see *ELBC,* 9:107; *GEBP,* 12:101). Numbers of Pais's young "lieutenants" became early supporters of the authoritarian New State (see the book of one of them, Jorge Botelho Moniz, *O 18 de Abril* [Lisbon, 1925], pp. 9-12).

100 *O Século,* 8-16 Dec. 1917; PRO, F.O. 371/9480/1923, "Portugal, Annual Reports, 1914-1918," p. 32. British official estimates were "about 250" killed. A lead editorial of *O Século* on the day fighting ceased (8 Dec. 1917) summed up the feelings of many when it decried the horrors and costs of the brief but "true civil war."

101 Duarte, *Sidónio Pais,* pp. 175-76; *O Século,* 7-9 Dec. 1917; Rocha Martins, *Memórias,* pp. 12-13.

102 Rocha Martins, *Memórias,* p. 65, and also pp. 50-65.

103 Ibid., pp. 68-70.

104 Pabón, *A Revolução Portuguesa,* p. 288.

105 *O Século,* 9 Dec. 1917.

Chapter 8: President Sidónio Pais and the New Republic

1 T. E. Lawrence, *Seven Pillars of Wisdom,* Penguin ed. (London, 1969), p. 24.

2 Colonel Birch, the American minister in Lisbon, is cited in Rocha Martins, *Memórias Sobre Sidónio Pais* (Lisbon, 1921), p. 316, as having made this statement at the funeral of the slain President Pais, 18 Dec., Jerónimos Monastery.

3 *Anais Da Assembleia Nacional E Da Câmara Corporativa: 1935* (Lisbon, 1936), pp. 115-36.

4 Ibid., pp. 204-26.

5 Rocha Martins, *Memórias,* p. 56.

6 Among the students in an honor guard standing by the slain president's casket was twelve-year-old Humberto Delgado—later a "young lieutenant" of the 28 May coup (Delgado, *The Memoirs of General Delgado*

[London, 1964]); Henrique Galvão, *Santa Maria: My Crusade for Portugal* (New York, 1962), pp. 48-51.

7 João Chagas, *Diário 1914-1918*, 3 vols. (Lisbon, 1929-30), 3:26.

8 *OG*, pp. 25, 31-32; Rocha Martins, *Memórias*, p. 200.

9 Maurício de Oliveira, *O Drama de Canto E Castro* (Lisbon, 1944), pp. 72-73.

10 Jorge Botelho Moniz, *O 18 de Abril* (Lisbon, 1925), pp. 9-11, 331-35.

11 The government "proclamation" of the Junta Revolucionária was published in the official *Diário do Governo* on 16 Dec. 1917 (see *O Século*, 16 Dec. 1917).

12 Damião de Peres, ed., *História de Portugal*, 7 vols. and Suplemento (Barcelos, 1928-35), Suplemento, p. 170.

13 Francisco Cunha Leal, *As Minhas Memórias*, 3 vols. (Lisbon, 1966-68), 2:72-81; Peres, *História de Portugal*, Suplemento, pp. 170-74; *O Século*, 9 Jan.-10 Feb. 1918.

14 Theophilo Duarte, *Sidónio Pais e o seu Consulado* (Lisbon, 1941), pp. 162-63.

15 Personal interview with David Ferreira, Lisbon, May 1973.

16 Chagas, *Diário*, 2:222-23.

17 Raúl Brandão, *Memórias* (in *Obras Completas*), 3 vols. (Lisbon, 1969), 3:443.

18 Cunha Leal, *As Minhas Memórias*, 2:67, employs the term "mimetismo."

19 On Pais's presidentialism see the text of Machado Santos's proposed draft constitution, in his *A Ordem Pública E O 14 De Maio* (Lisbon, 1916), pp. 104-16; Duarte, *Sidónio Pais*, pp. 190-96; Cunha Leal, *As Minhas Memórias*, 2:71-81.

20 Richard A. H. Robinson, "The Religious Question and the Catholic Revival in Portugal, 1900-1930," in *Journal of Contemporary History* 12 (1977):345-62.

21 Chagas, *Diário*, 2:336-37.

22 See *A Lucta* (Lisbon), 1 Feb.-2 May 1918.

23 Bento Carqueja, *Política Portuguesa* (Oporto, 1925), p. 471.

24 José Cutileiro, *A Portuguese Rural Society* (Oxford, 1971), pp. 217-18 and p. 218 n.; Arthur Ribeiro Lopes, *Histoire de la République Portugaise* (Paris, 1939), pp. 194-95; personal interviews with Sr. António Cavalheiro, Lisbon, Dec. 1972; Mar., May 1973. The latifundista in the Évora region of Alentejo district referred to by anthropologist Cutileiro in his 1971 work was in fact Sr. António Miguel de Sousa Fernandes (1870-1937), previously a Unionist deputy for Estremoz, financier of the 5 Dec. 1917 coup, and friend of Sidónio Pais. Fernandes has been credited with saving at personal risk from an angry lynch mob Republican leaders António Maria da Silva and Sebastião de Magalhães Lima, accused of responsibility for the murder of Pais (see *O Século*, 9 Mar. 1918; *GEPB*, 11:99; Rocha Martins, *Memórias*, p. 8).

25   See lead editorials by Camacho and José Barbosa in *A Lucta*, 1, 15, 18 Feb., 9, 10, 28 Mar. 1918.
26   *A Lucta*, 14 Feb. 1918.
27   *O Século*, 7 Feb. 1918.
28   Jacinto Cândido da Silva, *A Doutrina Nacionalista* (Oporto, 1909); Machado Santos, *A Ordem Pública*, appendix.
29   A. H. de Oliveira Marques, *A Primeira República Portuguesa* (Lisbon, 1972), p. 180.
30   *O Século*, 10 May 1918.
31   Carlos Ernesto Sá Cardoso, *Memórias Duma Época E Apontamentos Políticos* (Lisbon, 1973), pp. 20-25; David Ferreira, "Grande Guerra," *DHP*, 2:370-77.
32   Duarte, *Sidónio Pais*, pp. 57-64; Rocha Martins, *Memórias*, pp. 5-64.
33   PRO, F.O. 371/9480/1923, "Portugal, Annual Reports, 1914-1918," p. 34. After the suppression of the sailors' mutiny, Pais promised his government would send more troops to the European front.
34   Birch to State Department, 4 Feb. 1919, NA, Record Group 853.00/363, no. 467, enclosure copy of *Illustração Portuguesa*, 20 Jan. 1919; Page to Balfour, 2 Apr. 1918, PRO, F.O. 371/3373/59693.
35   Pais's PNR leader, Egas Moniz, in late 1918 evidently opposed the presidential power of dissolution of Congress in a presidentialist system. He was quoted as stating: "[whereas] parliamentarism without dissolution was a dictatorship of the many, presidentialism with dissolution was personal [and dominant] power" (*O Século*, 6 Aug. 1918). See also Egas Moniz, *Um ano de política* (Lisbon, 1919), pp. 143-45; Rocha Martins, *História de Portugal* (Lisbon, 1930), pp. 504-5.
36   *BHP*, Suplemento, pp. 178-84.
37   Jacinto Cândido da Silva, *Memórias Íntimas* (Lisbon, 1963), pp. 277-87. Although Cândido da Silva had retired from public life, his private correspondence concerning politics is both revealing and significant.
38   Moniz, *Um ano de política*, p. 155.
39   *O Século*, 6 Dec. 1918.
40   See *Diário do Governo* for the period of the New Republic. A lead editorial in *O Século*, 7 Aug. 1918, attacked the "decretomania" of the Pais government which, according to the newspaper report, had published in the *Diário do Governo*, 1,042 decrees and 111 amendments since 5 Dec. 1917.
41   Vasco Pulido Valente, "Estudos Sobre Sidónio Pais: Agricultura e Proletariado Agricola; Indústria e Sindicatos; Comércio Externo," *O Tempo e o Modo* (Lisbon), nos. 62-63 (July-Aug. 1968), pp. 705-6.
42   Moniz, *Um ano de política*, p. 166.
43   *O Século*, 10 Mar. 1918.
44   Cunha Leal, *As Minhas Memórias*, 2:114.
45   *O Século*, 14-19 Oct. 1918.
46   Rocha Martins, *Memórias*, pp. 243-46; Cunha Leal, *As Minhas Memórias*, 2:114.

47 *O Século,* 17 Oct. 1918. An editorial in this same number, entitled "Blood! Blood!," was a plea for calm and an end to brutality in public affairs. See also Rocha Martins, *Memórias,* pp. 242-46.

48 Cunha Leal, *As Minhas Memórias,* 26.

49 Ribeiro Lopes, *Histoire,* p. 192.

50 *O Século,* 12 Nov. and 2d ed. "Free Supplement" for 11 Nov. 1918.

51 "Aspetos Da Miséria Em Lisboa," *O Século,* 12 Mar. 1918. See also *O Século,* 12 Oct. 1918.

52 *O Século,* 12 Oct. 1918.

53 *O Século,* 8 Mar. 1918.

54 João Ameal, *História de Portugal* (Oporto, 1942), pp. 701-2; *BHP, Suplemento,* pp. 173-84; Cunha Leal, *As Minhas Memórias,* 2:70-71; Chagas, *Diário,* 3:106-29.

55 Anselmo Vieira, *A crise nacional* (Lisbon, 1926), pp. 405-6; Cândido da Silva, *Memórias Íntimas,* pp. 198-260, 277-90, especially private letters of 30 Apr. and 6 Dec. 1918, and 24 Feb. 1919.

56 Sá Cardoso, *Memórias Duma Época,* p. 26.

57 Cunha Leal, *As Minhas Memórias,* 2:123; personal interview with former colleague of Cunha Leal, Pedro Pita, 5 Mar. 1973, Lisbon.

58 Rocha Martins, *Memórias,* pp. 294-307. Rocha Martins was a monarchist who believed the allegations that Magalhães Lima and Masons were implicated in the assassination. See also Pedro Teotónio Pereira, *Memórias,* 3 vols. (Lisbon, 1972), 1:29.

59 Rocha Martins, *Memórias,* p. 302.

60 Ibid., p. 310. A British official account suggests two others assisted Costa in the assassination (PRO, F.O. 371/9480/1923, "Portugal, Annual Reports, 1914-1918," p. 42). From other evidence (Rocha Martins, *Memórias,* p. 304) these two possibly were sailors who were recruited at the last moment by Costa on the way to the Rossio Station.

61 Duarte, *Sidónio Pais,* p. 369.

62 For figures on 1918 developments, see Oliveira Marques, *A Primeira República Portuguesa,* pp. 153-61. For laudatory judgments of Pais, see Duarte, *Sidónio Pais,* especially pp. 369-72; João Sarmento Pimentel, *Memórias Do Capitão* (Oporto, 1974), pp. 189-92. For mixed and negative judgments, see Moniz, *Um ano de política,* pp. 50-155; Ameal, *História de Portugal,* p. 173; Brandão, *Memórias,* 3:443; Vieira, *A crise nacional,* pp. 395-407; Pedro Fazenda, *A Crise Política* (Lisbon, 1926), pp. 87-90; Jesús Pabón, *A Revolução Portuguesa,* trans. Manuel Emídio and Ricardo Tavares (Lisbon, 1961), pp. 342-57; António Cabral, *Em Plena República,* 4 vols. (Lisbon, 1932), 4:383.

63 Cunha Leal, *As Minhas Memórias,* 2:67-68.

64 Brandão, *Memórias,* 3:442-43.

65 For material on the Sidónio Pais cult of the early 1920s, see José Soares da Cunha e Costa, *A Egreja Catholica e Sidónio Pais* (Coimbra, 1921), p. 5. According to this monarchist source, numbers of women still prayed for Pais's soul in 1921. Later evidence of a Sebastianist cult of

Sidónio Pais includes mention of the president in a romantic tale by a French writer, Pierre Benoit, with the scene set in Alfama, the oldest quarter of Lisbon (in Jacques Chardonne, Paul Morand, Michel Deon, *The Portugal I Love,* trans. from the French by Ruth W. Fermaud [New York, 1968], pp. 11–12).

66 From Pessoa's poem *A Memória do Presidente-Rei Sidónio Paes,* first published in the journal *Acção,* no. 4 (27 Feb. 1920), cited in António Machado Pires, *D. Sebastião E O Encoberto* (Lisbon, 1971), pp. 105–5.

67 Teotónio Pereira, *Memórias,* 1:30.

Chapter 9: Republic Immobile

1 Raúl Proença, ed., *Guia de Portugal,* 3 vols. (Lisbon, 1924), 1:61–62.

2 *A República,* 1 Oct. 1919; *O Mundo,* 27 Apr. 1926.

3 António Sérgio, *Ensaios* (In *Obras Completas),* 3 vols. (Lisbon, 1972), 1:75.

4 Aquilino Ribeiro, "Crónica Da Quinzena," *Ilustração Portuguesa,* 16 July 1926.

5 Theophilo Duarte, *Sidónio Pais e o seu Consulado* (Lisbon, 1941), p. 366.

6 Armando Marques Guedes, *Cinco meses no govêrno* (Oporto, 1926), p. 354.

7 Jorge Botelho Moniz, *O 18 De Abril* (Lisbon, 1925), p. 35.

8 *A Época,* 8 Apr. 1926.

9 Ibid.

10 In a newspaper interview after he lost an election for Congress in 1921, Machado Santos said, "From the moment in which the government shut the door of Parliament to the founder of the Republic in order to open it to the monarchists, there remains for me only one path: revolution" (*O Século,* 12 July 1921).

11 Rodrigues Cavalheiro, "Um Inédito De António Sardinha Sobre A Monarquia Do Norte," *Sulco,* nos. 15–16 (1968), pp. 37–38.

12 A. H. de Oliveira Marques, *History of Portugal,* 2 vols. (New York, 1972), 2:137.

13 Ibid., pp. 137–39. See also data on the "Salaries of Public Functionaries, 1914–1925," in A. H. de Oliveira Marques, ed., *História Da 1ª República Portuguesa* (Lisbon, 1973–), pp. 403–7.

14 Oliveira Marques, *History of Portugal,* 2:174.

15 Martin Kilson, "The Emergent Elites of Black Africa, 1900–1960," in L. H. Gann and Peter Duignan, eds., *Colonialism in Africa,* 5 vols. (Cambridge, 1970–), 2:351–74, 392–93.

16 *GEPB,* 28:770–71.

17 William Leon Smyser, "General Carmona: Dictatorship without a Dictator in Portugal," *Contemporary Review,* 138 (Sept. 1930):330.

18 Jesús Pabón, *A Revolução Portuguesa,* trans. Manuel Emídio and Ricardo Tavares (Lisbon, 1961), p. 407. See also Rocha Martins, *A Monarquia do Norte,* 2 vols. (Lisbon, 1922–23), 2:171; Marques Guedes, *Cinco meses,* p. 354.

19   Fidelino de Figueiredo, *O pensamento político do Exército* (Lisbon, 1926), p. 21.
20   "Devorismo," *Dicionário Prático Ilustrado* (Oporto, 1961), p. 378. For pressures by office seekers on politicians in the early Republican years, see Tomas da Fonseca, *Memórias dum Chefe De Gabinete* (Lisbon, 1949).
21   Anselmo Vieira, *A crise nacional* (Lisbon, 1926).
22   John Martin Vincent, "Causes of Portugal's Twenty-one Revolutions," *Current History* 26, no. 1 (Apr. 1927):122–24.
23   Smyser, "General Carmona," p. 330; Francisco Cunha Leal, *As Minhas Memórias*, 3 vols. (Lisbon, 1966–68), 1:181–91.
24   There is abundant evidence of the PRP power of patronage not only in distributing civil service and military posts, but in influencing promotion decisions in the military, and in co-opting persons to accede to party wishes. See interview of Lisbon University student and his comments on how party membership influenced job opportunities in *A Capital* (Lisbon), 4 Apr. 1920; Carnegie to Curzon, PRO, F.O. 371/8366/W/1870/11/36, confidential, p. 2.
25   Proença, *Guia de Portugal*, 1:60.
26   Raúl Brandão, *Memórias* (in *Obras Completas*), 3 vols. (Lisbon, 1969), 3:494–95.
27   Oliveira Marques, *History of Portugal*, 2:128.
28   *BHP*, Suplemento, pp. 381–83.
29   Caetano Gonçalves, *Álvaro de Castro* (Lisbon, 1933), p. 33.
30   Oliveira Marques, *Afonso Costa* (Lisbon, 1972), pp. 42, 58.
31   For example, the 1919 Constitutional Revision Committee, see its draft law, "Parecer no. 8," *DCD*, 30 July–13 Sept. 1919.
32   See numbers of *O Século*, 19 Apr.–6 May 1925; 28 May–1 June 1926.
33   Cunha Leal, *As Minhas Memórias*, 1:269.
34   *O Século*, 9, 10 Sept. 1919.
35   *A República*, 1 Oct. 1919.
36   *O Século*, 17 Feb. 1923.
37   *O Século*, 1 Nov. 1925.

Chapter 10: The Honor of the Army

1   Fernando Freiria, *Os Portugueses na Flandres* (Lisbon, 1918), p. 235.
2   António Sardinha, "Exército E Tradição . . ." (ca. 1924), *A Prol do Comum* (Lisbon, 1934), p. 106.
3   *Anuário Estatística de Portugal: 1926* (Lisbon, 1927), pp. 362–63; Gen. Luís Ferreira Martins, *História do Exército Português* (Lisbon, 1945), p. 504.
4   On the navy during the republic see Maurício de Oliveira, *Pereira da Silva* (Lisbon, 1968) and *Armada Gloriosa* (Lisbon, 1936), pp. 140–61.
5   Oliveira, *Armada Gloriosa*, p. 161.
6   As a 1912 report stated: "The Portuguese navy was unfortunate in losing last year the gunboat 'Faro' which was run down and sunk in Lagos Bay,

with the loss of her captain and several officers and men, whilst the 'Almirante Reis,' on her way up with reinforcements in July to the seat of civil war . . . went ashore and was slightly damaged" (PRO, F.O. 371/1740, "Portugal, Annual Report, 1912," p. 24).

7 For a good biography of Pereira da Silva, see Oliveira, *Pereira da Silva.*

8 Oliveira, *Armada Gloriosa,* pp. 148–49.

9 Oliveira, *Pereira da Silva,* p. 68.

10 Rear Admiral Mariano da Silva, "Assuntos Navais," *Revista Militar* 78, nos. 1–2 (Jan.–Feb. 1926):10–11.

11 The text of the declaration of 2 Dec. 1915 is reproduced in A. H. de Oliveira Marques, *Afonso Costa* (Lisbon, 1972), pp. 379–84, as taken from *DCD.*

12 Personal interview with Col. Helder Ribeiro, Oporto, Oct. 1972. The most comprehensive account of Portugal's participation in World War I may be found in Gen. Luís Ferreira Martins, ed., *Portugal na Grande Guerra,* 2 vols. (Lisbon, 1945); on the Flanders campaign, see David Magno, *Livro da Guerra de Portugal na Flandres* (Oporto, 1920); see also David Ferreira, "Grande Guerra," *DHP,* 2:370–77; and *BHP,* 7:491–522.

13 See statements by Afonso Costa, 1916–Apr. 1917, on the war, in Oliveira Marques, *Afonso Costa,* pp. 403–10. For other war literature, see Maj. J. Bras de Oliveira, *O Exército Portuguez na Grande Guerra* (Lisbon, 1924); R. Coelho, *Horas de Guerra: Memórias de um miliciano* (Lisbon, 1924).

14 Carlos Vieira da Rocha, *João Teixeira Pinto* (Lisbon, 1971), pp. 206–8. This book represents an extension of the "Mousinho school" of militarism-colonialism into the present. The army officer–colonial hero Teixeira Pinto of Guiné is presented as an early inspiration for post-1961 "African heroes"; thus the book is dedicated to "General António de Spínola, worthy *continuador* of the work of João Teixeira Pinto."

15 Lisbon, 1919. This work is reviewed in *Revista Militar* of June–July 1919.

16 Cortesão, *Memórias da Grande Guerra* (Lisbon, 1919), pp. 230–33, reprinted in *Obras Completas de Jaime Cortesão,* Portugália ed. (Lisbon, 1969).

17 Quote, allegedly from some British officers, cited in Frank Jellinek, *The Civil War in Spain,* 2d ed. (London, 1969), p. 361.

18 S. L. A. Marshall, *World War I,* American Heritage Press ed. (New York, 1971), p. 359. For a more detailed account of Lys by another great military historian, see Winston Churchill, *The World Crisis, 1916–1918,* 6 vols. (London, 1927), 2:429–35.

19 Cortesão, *Memórias da Grande Guerra,* p. 224.

20 Ibid., p. 252.

21 Ibid., p. 253.

22 Ibid., p. 252.

23 Ferreira Martins, *História do Exército Portuguêz,* p. 563.

24 See the complaints of Jorge Botelho Moniz, *O 18 de Abril* (Lisbon, 1925), pp. 35-54; Ferreira Martins, *História do Exército Portuguêz,* p. 563.

25 David Magno, *A Situação Portuguesa* (Oporto, 1926), pp. 102-3; António Gomes de Sousa, *Meio Século de vida militar, 1888-1938* (Coimbra, 1939), pp. 11-20.

26 AHM, division 1, section 35, box 1264, folder 2, "Reorganização do Exército" (1919), telegrams, letters. See especially doc. no. 2, 13 Dec. 1918, chief of staff of army to chief of department in office of minister of war; also, chief of staff to minister of war, 21 Mar. 1919.

27 See *Revista Militar* 81, nos. 1-2 (Jan.-Feb. 1929):87-90.

28 *BHP,* Suplemento, pp. 205-6.

29 Stanley G. Payne, *A History of Spain and Portugal,* 2 vols. (Madison, Wis., 1973), 2:608-9; Richard Herr, *Spain* (Englewood Cliffs, N.J., 1970), pp. 135-36. The Spanish officers' organizations were called Juntas Militares de Defensa.

30 Rocha Martins, *Memórias sobre Sidónio Pais* (Lisbon, 1921), pp. 287-90; Theophilo Duarte, *Sidónio Pais e o seu Consulado* (Lisbon, 1941), pp. 331-36.

31 Duarte, *Sidónio Pais,* pp. 337-68.

32 *O Século,* 13 Sept. 1919; Birch to State Department, NA, Record Group 853.000/477.

33 Francisco Cunha Leal, *As Minhas Memórias,* 3 vols. (Lisbon, 1966-68), 2:363-65, 380.

34 *O Século,* 4 May 1911; *A Noite* 17 Apr. 1926; *Anuário Estatística de Portugal: 1927, 1928, 1929* (Lisbon, 1928-30).

35 PRO, F.O. 371/14159, "Portugal, Annual Report, 1928," p. 31.

36 Botelho Moniz, *O 18 DE Abril,* p. 33.

37 Ibid., pp. 33-34.

38 A. H. de Oliveira Marques, *History of Portugal,* 2 vols. (New York, 1972), 2:172.

39 Magno, *A Situação Portuguesa,* pp. 133-233; Raphael Ribeiro, *O Exército e A Política* (Lisbon, 1924), pp. 50-52; Gen. José Morais Sarmento, "Portugal na Guerra Mundial," *Revista Militar* 71, nos. 6-7 (June-July 1919): 322-23; *A Época,* 17, 18, 19 May 1926; *Diário de Notícias,* 23 July 1925.

40 Ferreira Martins, *História do Exército Portuguêz,* p. 7.

41 For a series of articles on the colonies, see *O Século,* 1 Jan. 1922-20 May 1926. See also *Diário de Notícias* and *A Época* during the same period.

42 For a brief survey of colonialism and the First Republic, particularly with regard to the Portuguese in Angola, see Douglas L. Wheeler and René Pélissier, *Angola* (London and New York, 1971), pp. 81-83, 109-28; see also the classic work of Democrat J. M. Norton de Matos, *A Província de Angola* (Oporto, 1926).

43 The proceedings of the Second National Colonial Congress are discussed in *Revista Militar* 76 (1924):165-66.

44 Norton de Matos, *A Província de Angola,* pp. 214, 234.

45 *O Século,* 29 Apr. 1911.

46 *O Libertador* (Lisbon), 20 July 1924, 19 Apr. 1925.

47 *A Época,* 17, 19 May 1926; Óscar Paxeco, *Os Que Arrancaram Em 28 De Maio* (Lisbon, 1937), p. 153.

48 Oliveira Marques, *History of Portugal,* 2:174.

49 A. H. de Oliveira Marques, ed., *História Da 1ª República Portuguesa* (Lisbon, 1973–), pp. 401–7.

50 Ibid., pp. 402–6.

51 Ibid., p. 401.

52 A. H. de Oliveira Marques, *A Primeira República Portuguesa* (Lisbon, 1972), p. 160.

53 *Ordem do Exército* (Lisbon, 1926), no. 8, 1st series, pp. 321–90; *Anuário Estatística de Portugal: 1929* (Lisbon, 1930), p. 379.

54 Capt. Cristovão Ayres, *Evolução Orgânica do Exército; Memória* (Lisbon, 1894), p. 128.

55 J. C. Vasconcelos, *O Movimento Nacional de 18 de Abril* (Oporto, 1925), pp. 37–38; "Lutuosa," *Revista Militar* 71, no. 1 (Jan. 1919):5.

56 Ayres, *Evolução Orgânica do Exército,* pp. 125–28.

57 The complete text of the famous letter Mousinho de Albuquerque wrote to the crown prince, which includes the sentence, "This kingdom is the work of soldiers," may be found in Mouzinho de Albuquerque, *Carta De Mouzinho De Albuquerque A Sua Alteza O Principe Real D. Luís De Bragança* (Lisbon, 1940). Sections of this letter were frequently quoted during the New State; a fragment of it was printed in a popular, juvenile history reader, José Carlos Amado, *História De Portugal,* 2 vols. (Lisbon, 1966), 2:62.

Chapter 11: In the Kingdom of the Pronunciamento

1 Raúl Proença, "A Salvação nacional e os movimentos revolucionarios," *Seara Nova,* no. 20 (Jan. 1923), cited in *Páginas de política* (in *Obra Política de Raúl Proença*), 2 vols. (Lisbon, 1972), 2:194–95.

2 "Ao País: A Junta Militar do Norte e a sua razão de ser," as cited in facsimile of proclamation published in A. H. de Oliveira Marques, *História de Portugal,* 2 vols. (Lisbon, 1972–73).

3 *O Século,* 15–19 Jan. 1919.

4 *O Século,* 1 Jan. 1919. Beginning 4 Jan. and going into Feb. 1919 the Lisbon government extensively censored *O Século.*

5 Francisco Cunha Leal, *As Minhas Memórias,* 3 vols. (Lisbon, 1966–68), 2:143–44.

6 Ibid., pp. 146–55.

7 Ibid., p. 154, citing text of surrender document, dated 15 Jan. 1919, Santarém. See section by Caetano Beirão in Beirão and Manuel Ferandis, *História Contemporânea De España y Portugal* (Madrid, 1966), pp. 812–14; Theophilo Duarte, *Sidónio Pais e o seu Consulado* (Lisbon, 1941), pp. 347–48 ff.

8 *BHP,* Suplemento, pp. 215-16.
9 *OG,* p. 35.
10 Cunha Leal, *As Minhas Memórias,* 2:160-69.
11 Gen. Alberto Ilharco, *Memórias* (Oporto, 1926), p. 79.
12 Cunha Leal, *As Minhas Memórias,* 2:165.
13 See Chefe de Gabinete to Secretariat of War, 6 Feb. 1919, and Comm. Gen. to Ministry of War, 3 Mar. 1919, AHM, division 1, section 37, nos. 8 and 34.
14 *BHP,* Suplemento, p. 216; João Sarmento Pimentel, *Memórias Do Capitão* (Oporto, 1974), pp. 193-97.
15 *O Século,* 16-19 Aug. 1919.
16 Jacinto Cândido da Silva, *Memórias Íntimas* (Lisbon, 1963), pp. 290-91, 304.
17 António Cabral, *Em Plena República* (Lisbon, 1932), p. 395.
18 Birch to State Department, telegrams, 23 Jan. 1919, and 25 Jan. 1919, NA, Record Group 853.00/404.
19 Ibid.
20 Birch to State Department, 4 Feb. 1919, NA, Record Group 853.00/430.
21 U.S. minister to Italy to State Department, telegram, 25 Jan. 1919, NA, Record Group 853.00/408, no. 2566, wherein new Portuguese minister to Italy claimed that "monarchy" was "the only solution to save Portugal from bolshevism."
22 Gen. José Morais Sarmento, "Portugal na Guerra Mundial," *Revista Militar* 71 (June-July 1919): 322-23. This influential general in the leading professional military journal railed against "pacifist" Woodrow Wilson and praised recently deceased Teddy Roosevelt for his love of "power" and his "Teutonic blood."
23 *O Século,* 23 Jan.-23 Feb. 1919. After the Monsanto battle at least 25 persons died of wounds in Lisbon hospitals (AHM, division 1, section 37, box 61, folder 5, no. 623, 11 Mar. 1919).
24 A. H. de Oliveira Marques, *A Primeira República Portuguesa* (Lisbon, 1972), pp. 155-61.
25 PRO, F.O. 371/7112, "Constitution of the Republic of Portugal-Lisbon."
26 *DCD,* 30 July 1919, pp. 11-16.
27 *O Século,* 11 Sept. 1919.
28 *O Século,* 13 Sept. 1919.
29 See *DCD,* 30 July-13 Sept. 1919.
30 *DCD,* 22 July 1919, p. 18.
31 *O Século,* article by Álvaro de Castro, 26 May 1921.
32 *BHP,* Suplemento, pp. 278-79.
33 Jesús Pabón, *A Revolução Portuguesa,* trans. Manuel Emídio and Ricardo Tavares (Lisbon, 1961), p. 472; *OG,* p. 45.
34 Pabón, *A Revolução Portuguesa,* p. 476; Carnegie to Curzon, 2 May 1921, PRO, F.O. 371/7100, confidential, p. 1.
35 *O Século,* 1, 2 June 1921.

36 Cunha Leal, *As Minhas Memórias,* 2:273, 319–20.

37 Pabón, *A Revolução Portuguesa,* p. 479.

38 *O Século,* 19–21 Oct. 1921; *Diário de Notícias,* 19–22 Oct. 1921.

39 *O Século,* 22 Oct., 6 Nov. 1921.

40 Carnegie to Curzon, 13 Nov. 1922, PRO, F.O. 371/8370/1911, secret.

41 Gen. Manuel Gomes da Costa, *Memórias* (Lisbon, 1930), pp. 229–34; Salgueiro Rego, *Memórias dum Chefe da Polícia* (Lisbon, 1955), pp. 11–12; Ezequiel de Campos, *Política,* 2d ed. (Lisbon, 1954), pp. 24–25; *O Século,* 19 Feb. 1922.

42 Gomes da Costa, *Memórias,* pp. 235–38.

43 *Seara Nova,* 15 Oct. 1921, p. 1, cited in Sottomayor Cardia, ed., *Seara Nova Antologia,* 2 vols. (Lisbon, 1971), 1:89.

44 For the collected writings of essayist Proença see *Obra Política de Raúl Proença.*

45 See António Sardinha's preface to an edition of Visconde de Santarém, *Memórias do Visconde de Santarém* (Lisbon, 1924); see Hermínio Martins, "Portugal," in S. J. Woolf, ed., *European Fascism* (London and New York, 1969), pp. 302–36. For a contemporary summary of Integralist doctrine in pamphlet form, see Fernão da Vide, *O Pensamento Integralista* (Lisbon, 1923), especially pp. 26–85.

46 Vide, *O Pensamento Integralista,* p. 28.

47 *Diário de Notícias,* 10 Feb. 1926.

48 *BHP,* Suplemento, p. 360.

49 Ibid., pp. 269–70.

50 Ibid., p. 385; *GEPB,* 33:389.

51 *BHP,* Suplemento, p. 391.

52 Ibid., pp. 391–92, citing quote from Oporto newspaper *A Tribuna,* 8 Feb. 1925.

53 Quote from Francisco Cunha Leal's book *Eu, os políticos e a nação* (Lisbon, 1930), cited in *BHP,* Suplemento, p. 394.

54 Leopoldo Nunes, *Carmona* (Lisbon, 1942), p. 86.

55 *O Século,* 18 Apr. 1925; *Diário de Notícias,* 19–20 Apr. 1925; *A Capital,* 20 Apr. 1925; Jorge Botelho Moniz, *O 18 de Abril* (Lisbon, 1925), pp. 330–35.

56 PRO, F.O. 371/11933, confidential, "Portugal, Annual Report, 1925," p. 7.

57 *Almanaque de "A Batalha"* (Lisbon, 1926), p. 132.

58 Nunes, *Carmona,* p. 86.

59 *A Capital,* 20 Apr. 1925.

60 Botelho Moniz, *O 18 de Abril,* p. 217.

61 Emílio Costa, "O Bloco Das Esquerdas" (from periodical *A Internacional* 2 [1 May 1925]:2), as cited in "Emílio Costa 34 Anos Depois," *Seara Nova,* no. 1570 (Aug. 1976), p. 17.

62 Óscar Paxeco, *Os Que Arrancaram Em 28 De Maio* (Lisbon, 1937), p. 71.

Chapter 12: The Politics of Despair

1 Anselmo Vieira, *A crise nacional* (Lisbon, 1926), p. 560.
2 Chief prosecutor, military tribunal trying Eighteenth of April rebels, 25 Sept. 1925, as cited in Leopoldo Nunes, *Carmona* (Lisbon, 1942), p. 96.
3 Bento Carqueja, *Política Portuguesa* (Oporto, 1925), p. 89.
4 Carnegie to Chamberlain, 23 Feb. 1926, PRO, F.O. 371.11933, "Portugal, Annual Report, 1925," p. 7.
5 Personal interview with Sr. Rodrigues Cavalheiro, 4 May 1973, Lisbon.
6 Francisco Cunha Leal, *As Minhas Memórias,* 3 vols. (Lisbon, 1966-68), 2:367-68.
7 PRO, F.O. 371/11933, "Portugal, Annual Report, 1925," p. 24.
8 Douglas L. Wheeler and René Pélissier, *Angola* (London and New York, 1971), pp. 81-83, 124-28; J. M. Norton de Matos, *A Província de Angola* (Oporto, 1926), p. 19.
9 Renato Mascarenhas, "Norton de Matos: Alto Comissário E Governador-Geral de Angola" (M.A. diss., Technical University of Lisbon, 1970), see especially pp. 165-80.
10 Douglas L. Wheeler, "The Portuguese in Angola, 1836-1891: A Study in Expansion and Administration" (Ph.D. diss., Boston University, 1963), p. 349.
11 Norton de Matos's confidential report on Angola to the minister of colonies is found in the Arquivo Histórico Ultramarino, Lisbon. room 5, bundle 1, folder 604, process no. 442c, "Relatório sobre a Situação Política . . . de Angola," 10 Feb. 1924, 132 pp.
12 *BHP,* Suplemento, p. 360.
13 Urbano Rodrigues, *A Vida Romanesca de Teixeira Gomes* (Lisbon, 1946), p. 278.
14 Ibid., pp. 275-78; see also Cunha Leal, *As Minhas Memórias,* 2:412.
15 See *O Século,* 1-25 Sept. and 1-10 Nov. 1925; *A Capital* during same period.
16 *Diário de Notícias,* 13 Nov. 1925.
17 *A Capital,* 9 Sept. 1925.
18 Carlos Sá Cardoso, *Memórias Duma Época E Apontamentos Políticos* (Lisbon, 1973), p. 66.
19 Nunes, *Carmona,* pp. 97-98.
20 *O Século,* 2 Sept. 1925.
21 Jorge Botelho Moniz, *O 18 de Abril* (Lisbon, 1925); J. C. Vasconcelos, *O Movimento Nacional do 18 de Abril* (Oporto, 1925).
22 *DCD,* 17 Mar. 1926, discussion of Draft Law no. 13 (Amnesty); see also AHM, division 1, section 36, box 7, folder 3, "Revolução de 27 de Abril" (1924); Lisbon to State Department, 12 June 1924, NA, Record Group 853.00/623, roll 6.
23 *Anuário Estatística de Portugal: 1921* (Lisbon, 1925), pp. 493-94. The evolution of the political police of the dictatorship involved name changes: Polícia Secreta in Dec. 1926, PIP (Polícia Internacional Por-

tuguesa) in July 1931, PVDE (Polícia de Vigilância e de Defesa do Estado) in Aug. 1933, PIDE (Polícia Internacional e da Defesa do Estado) in Oct. 1945, and DGS (Direcção-Geral de Segurança) in Nov. 1969 (see Fernando Luso Soares, *PIDE/DGS: Um Estado Dentro Do Estado* [Lisbon, 1974]).

24 *DCD,* 22 Apr. 1926, p. 13.

25 *Almanaque de "A Batalha"* (Lisbon, 1926), p. 132.

26 John Skeehan, "The Portuguese Community in Gloucester, Massachusetts, 1800-1920" (M.A. diss., University of New Hampshire, Durham, 1975), pp. 153 ff.

27 A. H. de Oliveira Marques, *A Primeira República Portuguesa* (Lisbon, 1972), pp. 48-49. Raúl Brandão, *Memórias* (in *Obras Completas*), 3 vols. (Lisbon, 1969), 3:491, refers to Lisbon businessmen keeping money abroad. *O Século,* 19 Feb. 1922, estimated that as much as one-third of available Portuguese capital had fled abroad by 1922.

28 *A Batalha,* 9 Mar. 1926.

29 NA, Record Group 853.00/681, enclosure report to State Department by Oporto U.S. Consul S. H. Wiley, 24 Nov. 1925. Wiley said of the election activity in the Oporto area: "Only the more ardent and hardy voters of the opposition parties appeared at the voting places, as others lacked the temerity to face a possible physical encounter with the Democratico poll workers."

30 Ibid. See also newspaper reports of violent incidents at polling places in *O Século* and *Diário de Notícias,* 9-11 Nov. 1925.

31 *O Século,* 13 Oct. 1925.

32 Ibid., 19 Oct. 1925, reporting Silva speech, 18 Oct.

33 *Diário de Notícias,* 8 Nov. 1925.

34 Ibid.

35 *O Século,* 8, 30 Oct. 1925.

36 Oliveira Marques, *A Primeira República Portuguesa,* p. 181.

37 Norberto Lopes, *O Exilado de Bougie* (Lisbon, 1944), pp. 144-60; Rodrigues, *A Vida Romanesca de Teixeira Gomes,* pp. 278 ff.

38 Alves Reis, *O segredo da minha confissão,* 2 vols. (Lisbon, 1931-32), 1:136.

39 For further discussion of the Banknote Case see Murray Teigh Bloom, *The Man Who Stole Portugal* (New York, 1966) and Alves Reis's earlier, briefer study of the case, *O "Angola E Metropole": Dossier Secreto* (Lisbon, 1927). Alves Reis confessed that his own "vanity" was to blame for his shady dealings in Angola (*O segredo,* 1:99), but that his dream in 1923-25 was to acquire capital to help build up for Portugal "a great and prosperous Angola" (ibid., 1:110, 135, 141).

40 *O Século,* 23 Nov.-10 Dec. 1925.

41 Armando Marques Guedes, *Cinco meses no govêrno* (Oporto, 1926).

42 One of Alves Reis's purposes in publishing his long, rambling account of the case was to exonerate all others of any blame for the swindle; a major purpose of the Military Dictatorship in allowing the publication of Alves

Reis's tract, which was sprinkled with Protestant, evangelical doctrine, was to discredit further the Republican politicians, whom the military had overthrown in 1926.

43 *Diário de Lisboa,* 2 Jan. 1926, lead editorial on the crisis of confidence.

44 Brandão, *Memórias,* 3:452.

45 For biographical data on journalist Reinaldo Ferreira, see new edition of his police novel under the name Reporter X, *O Taxi No. 9297,* 2d ed. (Lisbon, 1974).

46 Francis M. Rogers, *Precision Astrolabe: Portuguese Navigators and Transoceanic Aviation* (Lisbon, 1971), pp. 1-11, 79-86.

47 Mascarenhas, "Norton de Matos," pp. 165 ff.

48 One of the most popular works in the spate of disaster literature, 1925-26, was a work by Captain David Magno, *A Situação Portuguesa* (Oporto, 1926), which painted a somber picture of the country, again raising the Spanish menace.

49 *Diário de Notícias,* 2-3 Feb. 1926. Martins Júnior authored during his brief Azorean exile a polemic against the premier who had him deported: *O Presidente Landrú na república da Calabria* (Lisbon, 1926). Beginning with the work's suggestive title, the Radical leader compared Premier Silva with the infamous French strangler, Henri Landrú.

50 *A Época,* 17 May 1926.

Chapter 13: The Twenty-eighth of May

1 Gen. Gomes da Costa, proclamation, Braga, 28 May 1926, beginning the military coup d'etat which overthrew the parliamentary republic.

2 Official or semiofficial interpretations are found in Leopoldo Nunes, *A Ditadura Militar* (Lisbon, 1928), pp. 25-26; João Ameal, ed., *Anais da Revolução Nacional,* 5 vols. (Lisbon, 1948-50); Jesús Pabón, *A Revolução Portuguesa,* trans. Manuel Emídio and Ricardo Tavares (Lisbon, 1961), p. 574; Arthur Ribeiro Lopes, *Histoire de la République Portugaise* (Paris, 1939), p. 223.

3 See books by Republican writer Carlos Ferrão such as *Em Defesa Da República* (Lisbon, 1964?), *História da República* (Lisbon, 1959), and his articles "28 de maio" in the weekly *Expresso,* starting 2 June 1973.

4 Praise for Dr. Salazar as the true "savior" of the 1926 Revolution was clearly one of the motives behind publishing Óscar Paxeco's officially approved collection of interviews with the coup participants, *Os Que Arrancaram Em 28 De Maio* (Lisbon, 1937) (see preface, and dedication).

5 A. H. de Oliveira Marques, *History of Portugal,* 2 vols. (New York, 1972), 2:179; see also an interview of Oliveira Marques, "Proposta para o estudo de uma revolução," *Expresso,* 2 June 1973. However, in an earlier article this historian suggested that the Twenty-eighth of May was "probably supported by the majority of the nation" ("Portugal no Século XX: Problemas de história portuguesa, 1900-1930," *Ocidente* [Lisbon], 76 [1969]:253-72).

6   Pabón, *A Revolução Portuguesa,* p. 577.

7   Col. G. Pimenta de Castro, *As Minhas Memórias,* 3 vols. (Oporto, 1947-50), 2:186.

8   Information from interview in May 1973, Lisbon, with Monarchist-Integralist Dr. Rodrigues Cavalheiro.

9   Francisco Cunha Leal, *As Minhas Memórias,* 3 vols. (Lisbon, 1966-68) 2:459-66.

10 *A Noite* (Lisbon), 31 May 1926.

11 When Cabeçadas fell, Cunha Leal changed his tune and disowned the leader he had praised days before (*A Noite,* 17 June 1926).

12 See *O Mundo,* 30 May-2 June 1926.

13 Carlos Ferrão rightly points out the lack of a "program" in the conspiracy, "28 de Maio," *Expresso,* 2 June 1973.

14 Fidelino de Figueiredo, *O pensamento político do Exército* (Lisbon, 1926), p. 25.

15 *Diário de Notícias,* 31 May 1926.

16 Interview with Capt. Carlos Vilhena, survivor of Cabeçadas's committee, April 1973, Lisbon. He stated that the committee received no money in 1926.

17 Information on UIE's financing the Twenty-eighth of May plot, from personal interview with Dr. Rodrigues Cavalheiro, Lisbon, May 1973. See also Ferrão, "28 de Maio," *Expresso,* 9 June 1973.

18 Paxeco, *Os Que Arrancaram,* pp. 8-10; *GEPB,* 27:628.

19 Cunha Leal, *As Minhas Memórias,* 2:454-58.

20 *Diário de Notícias,* 30 May 1926.

21 Rocha Martins, *Memórias sobre Sidónio Pais* (Lisbon, 1921), p. 185.

22 Pimenta de Castro, *As Minhas Memórias,* 2:192-93.

23 Arquivo Histórico Militar, Lisbon, division 1, section 38, folders C, D, registry booklet II. The text of one of the general's famous public statements is quoted in João Ameal, *História de Portugal,* 2d rev. ed. (Oporto, 1942), p. 784.

24 A. Ribeiro de Carvalho, *Prelúdios Duma Ditadura* (Lisbon, 1957), pp. 20-22.

25 *Diário de Notícias,* 31 May 1926. On 30 May Filomeno da Câmara, one of the Eighteenth of April group, reached Braga and was told by Gomes da Costa that for the time being his services were not required.

26 *Diário de Notícias,* 30 May-4 June 1926. Most of the railway, telegraph, and post-office workers opposed the Silva government and some had been organized into revolutionary committees by the Radical party and by syndicalist groups. They refused to transmit government orders by telephone and telegram; railway workers refused, in some cases, to transport government troops to and from Lisbon.

27 Dearing to State Department, telegram, 28 May 1926, NA, Record Group 853.00/692, microfilm roll 6. As early as 1 June, the American minister urged Washington to recognize the Cabeçadas government, (Dearing to State Department, telegram, 1 June 1926, NA Record Gro· 853.00/696).

28 Ribeiro de Carvalho, *Prelúdios*, pp. 23-25.
29 Ameal, *História de Portugal*, pp. 716-18; Figueiredo, *O pensamento político*, pp. 8-9.
30 *GEPB*, 2:840-41; Cunha Leal, *As Minhas Memórias*, 2:26-27.
31 During May 29, Gomes da Costa had telegraphed Lisbon from Braga that he was about to surrender (Ribeiro de Carvalho, *Prelúdios*, p. 23).
32 Souza Peres, *Memórias Do "28 De Maio"* (Lisbon, 1968), p. 55.
33 *OG*, p. 63.
34 Cunha Leal, *As Minhas Memórias*, 3:18-33; Carlos Sá Cardoso, *Memórias Duma Época E Apontamentos Políticos* (Lisbon, 1973), pp. 68-75.
35 Ribeiro de Carvalho, *Prelúdios*, pp. 53-55.
36 Sá Cardoso (son), *Memórias Duma Época*, pp. 69-71.
37 *O Século*, 7 Feb. 1918.
38 AHM, division 1, section 38.
39 I was unable to examine the Sinel de Cordes memoirs—referred to by Ferrão, "28 de Maio," *Expresso*, 9 June 1973, p. 13. Included in Carmona's cabinet was Lt. Col. Abílio Passos e Sousa, who was the sympathetic governor of the military prison which incarcerated the Eighteenth of April group before their trial. In Nov. 1926 Passos e Sousa was made minister of war, a key position of trust (Paxeco, *Os Que Arrancaram*, pp. 84-86).
40 Assis Gonçalves, *Intimidades De Salazar*, 2d rev. ed. (Lisbon, 1972), pp. 15-26.
41 *Diário de Notícias*, 31 May 1926—20 June 1926.
42 *Diário de Notícias*, 2, 4 June 1926; other military casualties were three deaths in road accidents.
43 Cunha Leal, *As Minhas Memórias*, 2:365.
44 João Martins Júnior, *O Presidente Landrú na República da Calabria* (Lisbon, 1927).
45 *Seara Nova*, no. 89 (27 May 1926), p. 338.
46 *Anuário Estatística de Portugal: 1926* (Lisbon, 1927), p. 121; *DCD*, 23 Apr. 1926, pp. 12-13.
47 Egas Moniz, *Um ano de política* (Lisbon, 1919), p. 82.
48 Ameal, *História de Portugal*, pp. 712-14.
49 *DCD*, 31 May 1926, p. 3.

Chapter 14: Aftermath

1 In talk with Júlio Dantas at a Galician spa, Aug. 1929, cited in Dantas, *Páginas de Memórias* (Lisbon, 1968), p. 193.
2 Will Rogers, from letter supposedly addressed to President Calvin Coolidge, Madrid, 29 June 1926, in *Letters of a Self-Made Diplomat to His President* (New York, 1935), p. 201.
3 Goerge Guyomard, *La Dictature Militaire Au Portugal* (Paris, 1927), pp. 107-9.

4   For material on the emotional nephew of Chief of Staff Colonel Morais
    Sarmento, see Leopoldo Nunes, *Carmona* (Lisbon, 1942), p. 137; and
    Assis Gonçalves, *Intimidades de Salazar* (Lisbon, 1972), pp. 71-75.
5   On the action of Filomeno da Câmara in Angola in 1930, see PRO, F.O.
    371/5758, "Portugal, Annual Report, 1930," pp. 6-7.
6   Jesús Pabón, *A Revolução Portuguesa,* trans. Manuel Emídio and Ri-
    cardo Tavares (Lisbon, 1961), p. 610; New State supporter Óscar Paxeco
    suggested that the regime was "a will without a way," before Salazar
    came into the government (Paxeco, *Os Que Arrancaram Em 28 De Maio*
    [Lisbon, 1937], preface).
7   Salazar, *Discursos E Notas Políticas,* 5th ed., rev., 6 vols. (Coimbra,
    1961), 1:6.
8   The phrase "dictatorship without a dictator," is by William Leon
    Smyser, "General Carmona: Dictatorship without a Dictator in Por-
    tugal," *Contemporary Review* 138 (Sept. 1930):328. For an interesting
    analysis of the first two years of the Dictatorship, see Luís Araquistain,
    "Dictatorship in Portugal," *Foreign Affairs* 7 (Oct. 1928):45-50.
9   That Salazar was a crypto-monarchist was revealed to me by another
    crypto-monarchist, the late Dr. Teotónio Pereira, in an interview in
    Lisbon, Oct. 1972.
10 British colonial interests and Portugal's Colonial Act of 1930 are shown
    in an interesting light in the British protest to Portugal following the
    publication of the act. See Lindley to London, 15 July 1930, PRO, F.O.
    371/15030/775.
11 For an analysis of the act's text, see Armando Gonçalves Pereira, *As
    Novas Tendências da Administração Colonial* (Lisbon, 1931); for the text
    itself, see "Legislação Colonial" (decree no. 18,570), *Boletim Da Agên-
    cia Geral Das Colónias* 6, nos. 62-63 (Aug.-Sept. 1930).
12 The term "constitutional oligarchy" is that of the British ambassador to
    Portugal. See Wingfield to Eden, 17 Mar. 1936, PRO, F.O. 371/20516,
    confidential, "Portugal, Annual Report, 1935," p. 2.
13 Salazar, *Discursos E Notas Políticas,* 1:35-37.
14 A. H. de Oliveira Marques, *History of Portugal,* 2 vols. (New York,
    1972), 2:210.
15 Assis Gonçalves, *Intimidades De Salazar,* pp. 189-97; Russell to Simon,
    1 Mar. 1935, PRO, F.O. 371/19729, confidential, "Portugal, Annual
    Report, 1934," p. 3.
16 Oliveira Marques, *History of Portugal,* 2:188-90.
17 Ibid., p. 177; the term "Clerico-Fascist" is that of Professor Charles F.
    Delzell, ed., *Mediterranean Fascism, 1919-1945* (New York, 1970), pp.
    331-32.
18 For the regime's control of who owned, directed, and published
    newspapers and journals, according to law, and the regime's encourage-
    ment of colonial activity as a patriotic diversion, see Raúl Neves Dias, *A
    Imprensa Periódica Em Moçambique, 1854-1954* (Lourenço Marques,
    1954), pp. 5-9 ff.; Alberto A. de Carvalho and A. Monteiro Cardoso, *Da*

Liberdade De Imprensa (Lisbon, 1971), pp. 213-35 ff.; Douglas L. Wheeler and René Pélissier, *Angola* (London and New York, 1971), pp. 10-19.

19 Secretariado Nacional da Informação, *Political Constitution of the Portuguese Republic* (Lisbon, 1957), p. 6 (chap. 2, art. 8, clause 11 of the Constitution).

20 This striking phrase was coined by the oppositionist lawyer, Mozambique resident, and writer, Eduardo Saldanha, *A Obra da Ditadura Militar* (Lisbon, 1932), p. 33. For the story of how this strong critic of the regime's maladministration in Mozambique managed to get his pamphlet published in Lisbon, despite censorship and the refusal of Oporto and Lisbon publishers to print it for fear of reprisals, see the pamphlet's appendixes.

Chapter 15: Conclusions

1 António Sérgio, "Democracia e Ditadura," *Ensaios* (in *Obras Completas*), 3 vols. (Lisbon, 1972), 3:158.

2 Written interview mailed to me from Office of President of Council of Ministers, Lisbon, 29 Oct. 1973.

3 See César Oliveira, *MFA E Revolução Socialista* (Lisbon, 1975), pp. 51-63.

4 Bell, *Portugal of the Portuguese* (London, 1915), p. 220.

5 Carnegie to Chamberlain, 18 Feb. 1925, PRO, F.O. 371/11090, confidential, "Portugal, Annual Report, 1924," p. 2.

6 A. H. de Oliveira Marques, *History of Portugal,* 2 vols. (New York, 1972) 2:174-75.

7 *Seara Nova,* 15 Oct. 1921, editorial, "O Que Nos É Necessário," as cited in Sottomayor Cardia, ed., *Seara Nova Antologia,* 2 vols. (Lisbon, 1971), 1:99.

8 António Sérgio, *Democracia,* 2d. ed. (Lisbon, 1974), p. 28.

9 Ibid., p. 27.

10 Ministry of Mass Communication, *Provisional Government: The Men and the Programme* (Lisbon, 1974), p. 19.

11 Raúl Proença, "A Decisão Da Sala Do Risco," *Seara Nova,* no. 57 (24 Oct. 1925), as cited in João Agostinho, "Política E Ideologia Do Grupo Seara Nova," *Seara Nova,* no. 1572 (Oct. 1976), p. 42.

12 The "popular terror" thesis has been discussed by the Portuguese historian Vasco Pulido Valente. His term describes what I have referred to in the early chapters of this study as Republican "vigilantism." See Vasco Pulido Valente (Correia Guedes), "Power and the People: The Portuguese Revolution of 1910" (Ph.D. diss., Oxford University, 1975), pp. 446-47. A revised version in Portuguese was published in Lisbon in 1976.

13 Raúl Brandão, *Memórias* (in *Obras Completas*), 3 vols. (Lisbon, 1969), 3:413.

Bibliography

This bibliography is intended as a reference tool which can introduce readers to some of the sources available for the study of modern Portuguese history. It is a selective and by no means exhaustive list. The sources include archives, interviews, official Portuguese government publications, newspapers, journals, dissertations, books and articles, and reference works.

Archives

Great Britain

Public Record Office, London. Diplomatic records, primarily Foreign Office series (F.O. 179, F.O. 371, and F.O. 425), which include consular and ministers' reports from Portugal, 1906-35, annual reports of ministers, and other documents.

Portugal

Arquivo e Biblioteca do Ministério dos Negócios Estrangeiros (Ministry of Foreign Affairs), Necessidades Palace, Lisbon. Correspondence of legations (Madrid, London, Paris, Berlin, Rio de Janeiro, Washington, D.C.), 1909-14. Various *caixas* ("boxes").
Arquivo Histórico Militar, Museu Militar, Lisbon. Correspondence, 1910-13, 1924-26.
Arquivo Histórico Ultramarino (former Overseas Ministry depository for historical documents), Lisbon. Correspondence, between high commissioners and Ministry of Colonies, 1923-24.

United States

National Archives, Washington, D.C. Record Group 853.00. "Records of the Department of State Relating to Internal Affairs of Portugal, 1910-1929," 8 microfilm rolls, 1910-27, which include reports from U.S. Ministers in Lisbon, consul in Oporto. Record Group 866.00. "Records of the Department of State Relating to Internal Affairs of Portugal, 1906-1910."

Personal Interviews, Oral and Written

Dr. João Ameal. Lisbon, May 1973.
Dr. Marcello Caetano. Lisbon, 29 Oct. 1973. (Written interview in which the former premier of Portugal wrote answers to set of written questions I submitted.)

Dr. António Rodrigues Cavalheiro. Lisbon, May 1973.
Sr. David Ferreira. Lisbon, Mar., May 1973 and letters sent to me in 1974.
Dr. José Magalhães Godinho. Lisbon, Mar. 1973. (Son-in-law of Dr. A. Maria
da Silva, First Republic's last premier; writer for *A República;* chairman,
Electoral Law Committee, 1974-75, for Second Republic's 1976 Constitu-
tion.)
Pedro Teotónio Pereira. Lisbon, Oct. 1972. (Late ambassador to U.S., Spain;
died Nov. 1972.)
Dr. Pedro Pita. Lisbon, Mar. 1973. (Last secretary of Nationalist party.)
Colonel Helder Ribeiro. Oporto, Oct. 1972. (Noted oppositionist Democrat;
minister of war in several cabinets, First Republic; died 1973.)
Captain Carlos Vilhena. Lisbon, Mar. 1973. (Member of May 1926 Junta of
National Salvation, headed by Commander José Mendes Cabeçadas.)

Official Portuguese Government Publications

Almanaque do Exército. Lisbon, 1912-30.
Anais Da Assembleia Nacional E Da Câmara Corporativa. Vol. for 1935.
Lisbon, 1936.
Anuário Estatística de Portugal (1910-30). Lisbon, 1911-31.
Censo da População de Portugal. Taken 1 Dec. 1911. Part 5. Lisbon, 1916.
Diário da Assembleia Nacional Constituente. Lisbon, 1911.
Diário da Câmara de Deputados. Lisbon, 199-26.
Diário do Governo. Lisbon, 1910-33.
Diário do Senado. Lisbon, 1911-26.
Ordem Do Exército. Lisbon, 1926-28.
*Orgânica Governamental, Sua Evolução, E Elencos Ministeriais Constituidos
Desde 5 De Outubro De 1910 A 31 De Março De 1972.* Lisbon, 1972.
Political Constitution of the Portuguese Republic. Lisbon, 1957.
Provisional Government: The Men and the Programme. Lisbon, 1974.
Revisão Constitucional: 1971: Textos e Documentos. Lisbon, 1971.

Newspapers

A Batalha, 1919-26. Lisbon daily.
A Capital, 1919-26. Lisbon daily.
A Época, 1924-26. Lisbon daily.
A Liberatador, 1924-26. Lisbon daily.
A Lucta (A Luta), 1906 418. Lisbon daily.
A Noite, 1926. Lisbon daily.
A Palavra, 1909-10. Oporto daily.
A República, 1911-26. Lisbon daily.
Diário de Lisboa, 1924-26. Lisbon daily.
Diário de Notícias, 1906-27, 1930-31. Lisbon daily.
Expresso, Jan. 1973-. Lisbon weekly.
New York Times, 1910-26.

O Mundo, 1910–12, 1925–26. Lisbon daily.
O Primeiro de Janeiro, 1910–12. Oporto daily.
O Século, 1906–27. Lisbon daily.
Portugal, 1909–10. Lisbon Catholic daily.
Portugal, 1917. Lisbon Left Republican daily with same name.
Times (London), 1890–91; 1903, 1910, 1913–14, 1926.

Journals

Anais Do Clube Militar Naval, 1973.
Análise Social, 1970–73.
Foreign Affairs, 1928, 1970.
Illustração Portuguesa, 1911–26.
Nineteenth Century and After, 1910–11.
Os Ridículos, 1908–26.
O Tempo e o Modo, 1968–73.
Revista Militar, 1890–1930.
Seara Nova, 1921–27, 1962–76.
Spectator, The, 1910–14.
Via Mundial, 1965–74.

Dissertations

Mascarenhas, Renato. "Norton de Matos: Alto Comissário E Governador-Geral de Angola." Licenciatura dissertation, Technical University of Lisbon (ISCSPU), Lisbon, 1970.
Montenegro, Maria Angela. "O Movimento Operário Em Portugal Na Segunda Metade Do Século XIX." Licenciatura dissertation, University of Lisbon, Faculty of Letters, Lisbon, 1940. Code no. D.L. 1940-H-2.
Riegelhaupt, Joyce C. "In the Shadow of the City." Ph.D. dissertation, Columbia University, Department of Anthropology, New York, 1964.
Skeehan, John. "The Portuguese Community in Gloucester, Massachusetts, 1800–1920." M.A. thesis, University of New Hampshire, Department of History, Durham, 1975.
Valente, Vasco Pulido (Correia Guedes). "Power and the People: The Portuguese Revolution of 1910." Ph.D. dissertation, Oxford University, Department of Modern History, 1975.
Vincent-Smith, John. "Britain and Portugal, 1910–1916." Ph.D. dissertation, University of London, 1971.

Books and Articles

Albuquerque, Joaquim Mousinho de. *Moçambique 1896–1898.* Lisbon, 1899.
Almeida, A. J. de. *Quarenta Anos de vida literária e política.* 4 vols. Lisbon, 1933–34.

Ameal, João, ed. *Anais da Revolução Nacional.* 5 vols. Lisbon, 1948–50.

Araquistain, Luís. "Dictatorship in Portugal." *Foreign Affairs* 7 (Oct. 1928):41–53.

Arriaga, Manuel de. *Na primeira presidência da República portugueza: Um rápido relatório.* Lisbon, 1916.

As Constituentes De 1911 E Os Seus Deputados. Lisbon, 1911.

Atkinson, William. *A History of Portugal and Spain.* London, 1960.

Baptista, Jacinto. *O Cinco de Outubro.* Lisbon, 1965.

Bell, Aubrey. *In Portugal.* London, 1912.

Botelho Moniz, Jorge. *O 18 de Abril.* Lisbon, 1925.

Bragança-Cunha, V. de. *Eight Centuries of Portuguese Monarchy: A Political Study.* New York, 1911.

Bragança-Cunha, V. de. *Revolutionary Portugal, 1910–1936.* London, 1937.

Brandão, Raúl. *Memórias.* 3 vols. In *Obras Completas.* Lisbon, 1969.

Burity, Braz (Joaquim Madureira). *A Forja da Lei.* Coimbra, 1915.

Campinos, Jorge. *A Ditadura Militar 1926–1933.* Lisbon, 1975.

Campos, Ezequiel de. *Política.* Oporto, 1924; 2d ed., Lisbon, 1954.

Cândido da Silva, Jacinto. *A Doutrina Nacionalista.* Oporto, 1909.

Cândido da Silva, Jacinto. *Memorias Íntimas: Para O Meu Filho (1898–1925).* Lisbon, 1963.

Cardia, Sottomayor, ed. *Seara Nova Antologia: Pela Reforma da República (1, 2) 1921–1926.* 2 vols. Lisbon, 1971–72.

Carqueja, Bento. *O Futuro de Portugal: Portugal Após A Guerra.* 2d. ed. Oporto, 1920.

Carqueja, Bento. *Política Portuguesa.* Oporto, 1925.

Chagas, João. *Diário 1914–1918.* 3 vols. Lisbon, 1929–30.

Cortesão, Jaime. *Cartilha do Povo. 1º encontro: Portugal e a Guerra.* Oporto, 1916.

Cortesão, Jaime. *Memórias da Grande Guerra.* In *Obras Completas de Jaime Cortesão.* Portugália ed. Lisbon, 1969.

Costa Júnior, José Maria. *História Breve do Movimento Operário Português.* Lisbon, 1964.

Cunha Leal, Francisco. *As Minhas Memórias.* 3 vols. Lisbon, 1966–68.

Cutileiro, José. *A Portuguese Rural Society.* Oxford, 1971.

Dantas, Júlio. *Páginas de Memórias.* Lisbon, 1968.

Delgado, Humberto. *Memoirs of General Delgado.* London, 1964.

Duarte, Theophilo. *Sidónio Pais e o seu Consulado.* Lisbon, 1941.

Eça de Queiroz, António. *Na Fronteira: Incursões monarchicas de 1911 e 1912.* Oporto, 1915.

Eça de Queiroz, J. M. *The Maias.* Translated by P. M. Pinheiro and Ann Stevens. London, 1965.

Esteves, Raúl. *A Função do Exército.* Lisbon, 1907.

Fazenda, Pedro. *A Crise Política.* Lisbon, 1926.

Ferrão, Carlos. *Em Defesa de Verdade.* Lisbon, 1961.

Ferreira, David. "5 De Outubro De 1910." In *Dicionário De História De Portugal,* edited by Joel Serrão, 3:264–67. 4 vols. Lisbon, 1964–71.

Ferreira, David. *História Política da Primeira República Portuguesa (1910-1915).* 2 vols. Lisbon, 1973.

Ferreira Martins, Luís. *História do Exército Portuguêz.* Lisbon, 1945.

Ferreira Martins, Luís, ed. *Portugal na Grande Guerra.* 2 vols. Lisbon, 1945.

Figueiredo, Fidelino de. *O pensamento político do Exército. Lisbon, 1926.*

Fonseca, Tómas da. *Memórias dum Chefe de Gabinete.* Lisbon, 1949.

Galvão, Henrique. *Santa Maria: My Crusade for Portugal.* New York, 1962.

Gomes da Costa, Manuel. *Memórias.* Lisbon, 1930.

Gomes de Sousa, António (General). *Meio Século de vida militar, 1888-1938.* Coimbra, 1939.

Gonçalves, Assis. *Intimidades De Salazar: O Homem E a Sua Época.* 2d rev. ed. Lisbon, 1972.

Gonçalves, Caetano. *Álvaro de Castro.* Lisbon, 1933.

Grey, Lord Edward (Viscount Grey of Falloden). *Twenty-Five Years: 1892-1916.* 2 vols. London, 1925.

Gribble, Francis. *The Royal House of Portugal.* London, 1915.

Guerra, Miller. "Egas Moniz, prémio Nobel." *Expresso,* 9 Feb. 1974.

Guyomard, George. *La Dictature Militaire Au Portugal.* Paris, 1927.

Ilharco, Alberto. *Memórias: Alguns Apontamentos Sobre A Influência Da Política No Exército.* Oporto, 1926.

Kay, Hugh. *Salazar and Modern Portugal.* New York, 1970.

Livermore, H. V. *A New History of Portugal.* Cambridge, 1966.

Livermore, H. V., ed. *Portugal and Brazil: An Introduction.* Oxford, 1953.

Lorenzo, Felix. *Portugal (cinco años de republica).* Madrid, 1915.

Machado, Bernardino. *A Irresonsibilidade Governativa e as duas reacções: monárquica e republicana.* Lisbon, 1924.

Machado, Bernardino. *Depois de 21 de Maio.* Lisbon, 1922.

Machado Santos, António. *A Ordem Pública E O 14 De Maio.* Lisbon, 1916.

Machado Santos, António. *1907-1910, A revolução Portugueza: Relatório De Machado Santos.* Lisbon, 1911.

Magno, David. *A Situação Portuguesa.* Oporto, 1926.

Magno, David. *Livro da Guerra de Portugal na Flandres.* Oporto, 1920.

Marden, Philip S. *A Wayfarer in Portugal.* London, 1927.

Marques Guedes, Armando. *Cinco meses no governo.* Oporto, 1926.

Marques Guedes, Armando. *Páginas Do Meu Diário.* Lisbon, 1957.

Martins, Hermínio. "Portugal." In *European Fascism,* edited by S. J. Woolf, pp. 302-36. London and New York, 1969.

Martins, Rocha. *História de Portugal.* Lisbon, 1930.

Martins, Rocha. *Memórias sobre Sidónio Pais.* Lisbon, 1921.

Martins Júnior, João. *O Presidente Landrú na República da Calabria.* Lisbon, 1926.

Medina, João. *Eça Político.* Lisbon, 1919.

Montalvor, Luis de, ed. *História do Regimen Republicano em Portugal.* 2 vols. Lisbon, 1930-32.

Morais Sarmento, José Estevão. *A Expansão Alemã—Causas determinantes da Guerra de 1914-1918: Suas tentativas e perigos na África Portuguesa.* Lisbon, 1919.

Moser, Gerald M. "The Campaign of Seara Nova and Its Impact on Portuguese Literature, 1921-61." *Luso-Brazilian Review* 2 (1965):15-42.

Nogueira, Jofre Amaral. *A República de Ontem Nos Livros De Hoje.* Coimbra, 1972.

Nogueira Soares, D. G. *O Presente E O Futuro Político De Portugal.* Lisbon, 1883.

Norton de Matos, J. M. *A Província de Angola.* Oporto, 1926.

Nunes, Leopoldo. *A Ditadura Militar.* Lisbon, 1928.

Nunes, Leopoldo. *Carmona (Estudo Biográfico).* Lisbon, 1942.

Oliveira, César. *O Operariado E A República Democrática, 1910-1914.* Oporto, 1972.

Oliveira, Maurício de. *Armada Gloriosa: A Marinha De Guerra Portuguesa No Século XX 1900-1936.* Lisbon, 1936.

Oliveira, Maurício de. *Diário De Um Jornalista 1926-1930.* Lisbon, 1973.

Oliveira, Maurício de. *O Drama De Canto E Castro.* Lisbon, 1944.

Oliveira, Maurício de. *Pereira da Silva: Oficial-ministro-Doutrinador.* Lisbon, 1968.

Oliveira Marques, António H. de. *Afonso Costa.* Lisbon, 1972.

Oliveira Marques, António H. de. *A Primeira República Portuguesa: Para Uma Visão Estrutural.* Lisbon, 1972.

Oliveira Marques, António H. de. "Estudos Sobre Portugal No Século XX. I-Aspectos do poder executivo, 1900-1932." *O Tempo E O Modo,* nos. 47-48 (Mar.-Apr. 1967), pp. 270-95.

Oliveira Marques, António H. de. *História de Portugal.* 2 vols. Lisbon, 1972-73.

Oliveira Marques, António H. de. *History of Portugal.* 2 vols. New York, 1972.

Oliveira Marques, António H. de. "The Portuguese 1920's: a general survey." *Iberian Studies* 2 (Spring 1973):32-40.

Oliveira Marques, António H. de, ed. *A Unidade Da Oposição A Ditadura 1928-1931.* Lisbon, 1973-.

Oliveira Marques, António H. de, ed. *Discursos Parlamentares 1900-1910.* Vol. 1 in *Obras de Afonso Costa.* Lisbon, 1973.

Oliveira Marques, António H. de, ed. *Historia Da 1ª República Portuguesa: As Estruturas De Base.* Lisbon, 1973-. Published in fascicles.

Oliveira Martins, J. P. *Portugal Contemporâneo.* 2 vols. Lisbon, 1881.

Ortigão, Ramalho. *Últimas Farpas, 1911-1914.* 2d ed. Lisbon, 1946.

Pabón, Jesús. *A Revolução Portuguesa.* Translated by Manuel Emídio and Ricardo Tavares. Lisbon, 1961.

Paxeco, Óscar. *Os Que Arrancaram Em 28 De Maio.* Lisbon, 1937.

Payne, Stanley G. *A History of Spain and Portugal.* 2 vols. Madison, Wis., 1973.

Peres, Souza. *Memórias Do "28 De Maio."* Lisbon, 1968.

Pessoa, Fernando. *A Memória do Presidente-Rei Sidónio Pais.* Lisbon, 1940.

Pimenta, Alfredo. *Política Portuguesa.* Coimbra, 1913.

Pimenta de Castro, G. *As Minhas Memórias.* 3 vols. Oporto, 1947–50.

Poinsard, Leon. *Portugal Ignorado.* Oporto, 1912.

Ribeiro, Raphael. *O Exército e A Política.* Lisbon, 1924.

Ribeiro de Carvalho, António G. G. *Prelúdios Duma Ditadura.* Lisbon, 1957.

Ribeiro Lopes, Arthur. *Histoire de la République Portugaise.* Paris, 1939.

Rodrigues, Urbano. *A Vida Romanesca de Teixeira Gomes.* Lisbon, 1946.

Sá Cardoso, Carlos Ernesto. *Memórias Duma Época E Apontamentos Políticos.* Lisbon, 1973.

Salazar, António de Oliveira. *Discursos E Notas Políticas.* 5th ed., rev. 6 vols. Coimbra, 1961.

Saldanha, Eduardo. *A Obra da Ditadura Militar.* Lisbon, 1932.

Sardinha, António, et al. *A Questão Ibérica.* Lisbon, 1916.

Sérgio, António. *Breve Interpretação Da História De Portugal.* Rev. ed. Lisbon, 1972.

Sérgio, António. *Ensaios.* 3 vols. In *Obras Completas.* Lisbon, 1972.

Serrão, Joel. *Do Sebastianismo ao Socialismo em Portugal.* 3rd ed. Lisbon, 1973.

Serrão, Joel. *Emigração Portuguesa: Sondagem Histórica.* Lisbon, 1971.

Silbert, Albert. *Do Portugal de Antigo Regime ao Portugal Oitocentista.* Lisbon, 1972.

Silva, António Maria da. *Da Monarquia a 5 de Outubro de 1910.* Vol. 1 in *O Meu Depoimento.* Lisbon, 1974.

Smyser, William Leon. "General Carmona: Dictatorship without a Dictator in Portugal." *Contemporary Review* 138, no. 777 (Sept. 1930):328–33.

Teles, Basílio. *I–As dictaduras, II–0 regimen revolucionario.* Famalição, 1911.

Teles, Basílio. *Do Ultimatum ao 31 de Janeiro.* In *Obras De Basílio Teles.* 2d ed. Lisbon, 1968.

Teles, Basílio. *Memórias Politicas.* In *Obras De Basílio Teles,* 2d ed. Lisbon, 1969.

Tenison, E. M. *Portuguese Political Prisoners: A British National Protest.* 5th ed. London, 1913.

Trend, J. B. *Portugal.* New York, 1957.

Trindade Coelho, J. F. *Manual Político Do Cidadão Portuguez.* 2d rev. ed. Oporto, 1908.

Unamuno, Miguel de. *Por Tierras de Portugal y de España.* Madrid, 1911.

Valente, Vasco Pulido (Correia Guedes). "A República e as classes Trabalhadores (Outubro de 1910–Agosto de 1911)." *Análise Social,* 2d ser., 9, no. 34 (1972):293–316.

Vasconcelos, Joaquim C. de. *O Movimento Nacional de 18 de Abril.* Oporto, 1925.

Veiga, A. M. Alves da. *Política Nova: Ideias para a reorganisação da nacionalidade.* Lisbon, 1911.

Vide, Fernão da. *O Pensamento Integralista.* Lisbon, 1923.

Vieira, Alexandre. *Para a história do sindicalismo em Portugal.* Lisbon, 1970.

Vieira, Anselmo. *A crise nacional.* Lisbon, 1926.

Vivero, Augusto, and Villa, António De La. *Como Cae Un Trono: La Revolución En Portugal.* Madrid, 1910.

Wheeler, Douglas L. "The Portuguese Revolution of 1910." *Journal of Modern History* 44 (June 1972): 172-94.

Young, George. *Portugal Old and Young.* Oxford, 1917.

Reference Works

Dicionário De História De Portugal. Edited by Joel Serrão. 4 vols. Lisbon, 1963-71.

Enciclopédia Luso-Brasileira da Cultura. 18 vols. to date. Lisbon, 1963-.

Grande Enciclopédia Portuguesa e Brasileira. 40 vols. Lisbon and Rio de Janeiro, 1924-60.

História de Portugal. Edited by Dr. Damião Peres. Barcelos Edição Monumental. 7 vols. and Suplemento. Barcelos, 1935-54. The Suplemento (1954) is especially valuable.

Glossary of Portuguese Political Words

The majority of these words were in common use in Portugal during the years 1880–1930. Some, though now obsolete in parts of Portugal, are still used in others. Spelling follows modern spelling initiated in 1911 and later. Many of these words have several meanings, and these meanings have altered through time. Where possible, I have given the literal, dictionary definition first (from Manuel J. Martins, *Dicionário De Português-Inglês,* ed. Manuel Barreira [Oporto, n.d.]), followed by political meanings.

Aliciamento.   Luring, enticing into a conspiracy, enticement into a *pronunciamento,* q.v.

Arcada.   Arcade(s); government offices in Lisbon's *Terreiro do Paço* area, q.v.

Arrancada; Arranque.   Start, dash, sudden move, "take-off"; beginning of a military movement or *pronunciamento.*

Bacharel.   Holder of university degree; prattler, idle talker.

Bacharelismo.   Babbling, empty rhetoric; practice or activity of foolish talk by petty political people.

Baralhar.   To shuffle; to shuffle papers in an office; purposeless bureaucratic activity.

Barriguista.   Haughty, self-satisfied person; two-timer; corrupt person, swindler.

Cacique.   Local or regional political boss; man of political influence during monarchy and republic.

Caciquismo.   System of local and regional political influence involving *caciques* and their clients.

Chapelada.   Hatful; greeting with a hat; sweep vote in rigged election.

Compadre.   Godfather; local patron or boss.

Compromisso.   Promise, compromise; promise or commitment to join a *pronunciamento* against government in power.

Concelho.   Subdivision of a district; administrative unit; main municipality county.

Conselheiro Acácio.   Character in Eça de Queiroz's novel *O Primo Basílio* (1878); person who embodies the traits of that character in politics in late monarchy and, by extension, during later regimes: egotism, incompetence, pompous and vacuous rhetoric.

De chapa.   All at once, at one stroke; illegal electoral sweep.

Devorismo.   Devourism; excessive, unjustified expense; use of public treasury for personal gain or in favor of someone else.

Distrito.   District, region, area.

Ditadura. Dictatorship; political regime, under monarchy and republic, in which parliament did not meet or have any control over political affairs; rule by clique.

Empregomania. Love of office-holding; tendency for people to seek positions in government bureaucracy.

Estar político com. To be political with; at loggerheads with.

Exaltado. Excited, hot-brained, hot-headed; radical person, extremist.

Fornada. Batch, ovenful; practice during Constitutional Monarchy of filling House of Peers with partisan peers from majority party to enable that party to remain in office.

Freguesia. Parish; administrative unit smaller than *Concelho,* q.v.

Golpe. Blow; coup d'etat; *golpe de estado.*

Golpismo. The tendency of groups, parties, or military units to advocate and conspire to organize coup d'etats against governments; insurrectionism on part of the police, military, or party.

Jornal de combate. Violently critical periodical or newspaper, usually political, which advocates views of one person or party.

Junta. Council, board, committee; military conspiracy group.

Ligações. Connections, bond, friendship; links between people or groups in organizing a military conspiracy.

Meter uma lança em África (lit. "to throw a lance into Africa"). To set the Thames on fire, set the world on fire, do marvelous deeds.

Município. Township, municipality; administrative unit.

Oposição. Opposition, antagonism.

Oposicionista. Oppositionist; member of the opposition.

Paços do concelho. Town hall; Lisbon's town hall.

Padrinho. Godfather; patron, boss, sponsor; political protector.

Paivantes. Monarchist followers of monarchist soldier, colonialist, and leader, Henrique Mitchell de Paiva Couceiro (1861-1944), leader of 1911, 1912, and 1919 monarchist incursions.

Parlamentarismo (from *parlamentar:* to parley, to discuss terms). Parlamentarism; parlamentary activity.

Pedintismo. Practice of begging, beggary; seeking public office.

Personalismo. Personalism; egotistical activity, individualism; allegiance to, awe and respect for, individual leaders as "great men."

Política. Politics; policy; sagacity.

Politicagem. Petty and party politics.

Politicão. Petty politician.

Politicar. To politicize.

Político. Politician.

Politiqueiro. Petty, party politician, boss.

Politiquice. Petty, party politics.

Pronunciamento (from *pronunciar:* to declare, to announce solemnly and publicly). Military insurrection, coup, uprising. (Spanish: *pronunciamiento.*)

Propaganda. Propaganda; spreading of doctrines and ideas; historical era of Republican propaganda attacks on the monarchy.

Província. Province, large administrative division, one of the eleven provinces (as of 1971 revision of Constitution) of Portugal; the countryside, or any part of Portugal outside Lisbon.

Regeneração. Regeneration, revival; the program and activity of politician-statesman Fontes Pereira de Melo (1819-1887), leader of the monarchy's Regenerator party.

Ressurgimento. Resurgence; national revival.

Reviralho. Revolt, revolution, turnabout of political situation; opposition; movement of opposition to a policy of despotism, change of regime. (*Vira* refers to traditional peasant dance of the Minho district in northern Portugal, danced by a *viradeira.*)

Rotativismo. System whereby under the Constitutional Monarchy two major parties (Regenerators and Progressists) rotated in office by arrangement; system of peaceful change of power, especially 1870-90.

Saneamento (from *sanear:* to make healthy, to correct). Sanitation, cleansing, drainage, disposal of sewage. Beginning in 1920s: to clean out politically undesirable persons from any organization, especially government; after 25 April 1974: purging or firing from various posts of persons associated with Dictatorship (1926-74), or suspected of so being.

Sebastianismo. Belief that King Sebastian (1554-78), killed in battle in Morocco in 1578, would return from Africa to "save" Portugal; messianic belief in hero who would appear to solve major problems.

Situação. Situation; present political situation; regime in office.

Situacionista. Person who supports regime in power.

Tacho. Frying pan; job or activity; political post. (One with many *tachos* in the fire holds several jobs.)

Talassa. During years 1900-1930, monarchist or royalist, and eventually any reactionary person. (Refers to Greek word *thalassa:* "sea," from Xenophon's history of the march of the ten thousand to the sea.)

Terreiro do Paço (lit. "Square of the [old] Palace"). The central government offices in Lisbon, located in a square rebuilt under direction of marquis of Pombal after the 1755 earthquake.

Tesura. Stiffness, rigidity, pride, haughtiness; someone who acts proud but has no money.

Tripeça. Meeting or gathering of three conspirators; triumverate.

Tubaronismo (from *tubarão:* shark). Rapacious, corrupt person; swindler; holder of one or more profitable posts.

Velho do Restelo. Old man in Camões' *Os Lusíadas* who opposes Portugal's imperial expansion into Asia; spoilsport, doubting Thomas; anti-imperialist.

Zé Povinho (lit. "Joe Little People"). Any person, everyman, Mr. So-and-So. (A variation is *Zé-dos anzois,* lit. "Joe of the fish-hooks.") Cartoon character created in 1875 by artist Rafael Bordalo Pinheiro; representative of the common people, whose character traits usually include simplicity or candor, patience (of the long-suffering variety), and credulity. Character depicted as a short, bearded, swarthy figure, his heavy features wreathed in smiles, dressed in white open shirt, dark trousers, hat.

Index

DESIGNED BY GARY GORE

COMPOSED BY FOX VALLEY TYPESETTING, MENASHA, WISCONSIN

MANUFACTURED BY MALLOY LITHOGRAPHING, ANN ARBOR, MICHIGAN

TEXT AND DISPLAY LINES ARE SET IN ENGLISH NO. 49

Library of Congress Cataloging in Publication Data
Wheeler, Douglas L
Republican Portugal.
Bibliography: p.
Includes index.
1. Portugal—Politics and government—1910–1974.
I. Title.
DP695.W47   946.9′04   77-15059
ISBN 0-299-07450-1